WOMEN MAKING MEANING

New Feminist Directions in Communication

Edited by

Lana F. Rakow

ROUTLEDGE • NEW YORK & LONDON

Published in 1992 by

Routledge
An imprint of Routledge, Chapman and Hall, Inc.
29 West 35 Street
New York, NY 10011

Published in Great Britain by

Routledge
11 New Fetter Lane
London EC4P 4EE

Library of Congress Cataloging-in-Publication Data

Women making meaning : new Feminist directions in communication / [compiled by] Lana F. Rakow.
    p. cm.
    Includes bibliographical references and index.
    ISBN 0-415-90629-6 (HB) ISBN 0-415-90630-X (PB)
    1. Women in communication. 2. Women—Communication.
    3. Communication—Sex differences. 4. Feminist theory. I. Rakow,
Lana, 1952–
P94.5.W65W68 1992
302.2′082—dc20   92-7187
                                           CIP

British Library Cataloguing in Publication Data
Women Making Meaning : New Feminist Directions in Communication
    I. Rakow, Lana
    305.42

    ISBN 0-415-90629-6
    ISBN 0-415-90630-X

Contents

iii

Contents

Part 2. Beyond the Field's Boundaries

Part 3. Case Studies in Making Meaning

iv

Contents

For my sisters, Linda and Liane

Preface

The title of this book, *Women Making Meaning: New Feminist Directions in Communication,* bears explanation, for I used the assumptions found in the title to help me choose and shape the direction of the book's contents. While much has been published *on* communication by feminist scholars in many disciplines, this book highlights feminist work *in* the field of communication, a viable and important enterprise in its own right. Feminist scholarship in the field of communication has been developing since the early 1970s; in the second half of the 1980s it seemed to enter a significant new phase. This collection is an attempt to take stock of what has happened, to assess some of the major issues and themes raised by feminist scholarship in the field, and to provide for those unfamiliar with the vast and growing body of literature a way to engage it. One book cannot, however, give justice to the many strands of theory and research; current work can be interpreted in a variety of ways. My objective was not to create the definitive map of feminist scholarship but rather to point in the direction of what appears to me to be interesting and fruitful lines of inquiry.

The words "women making meaning" speak to two significant developments in the field of communication. First, through the hard work of feminists, the field is awakening to what many women have known all along—that women are active participants in naming the world and making sense of it, even if their contributions and challenges more often than not have been disdained or rendered invisible. Second, feminist scholars are themselves active meaning-makers, engaging in research, talk, and writing that uncovers and validates the experiences and meanings of other women. Thus, in this book, women are making meaning about women making meaning.

I am fully aware of the theoretical pitfalls that accompany these assumptions. The terms "women" and "feminist" cannot be taken for granted; indeed, as several authors discuss in their chapters, the terms are themselves the site for significant epistemological, cultural, and political disagreements among those of us engaged in work on gender and race. I invoke the terms in order to allow the ensuing discussions of them to take place. I also recognize that concepts such as "making meaning" and "experience" are fraught with complexities. No one is simply free to generate novel and uncontaminated meanings; experience itself is not innocent, occurring somewhere outside existing meaning systems to autonomous acultural and pregendered individuals. All humans live in cultural worlds inherited from their predecessors. Fortunately for those born into cultural worlds with oppressive category systems, making reality is a messy and uncertain business, allowing the possibility for change. Meanings contradict; disjunctures occur between what people experience and what they are told they should experience. Reality, as language or like language (depending upon one's definition of language), is generative. While inheriting the meanings of the past, individuals and groups have the capacity for making novel combinations and thus generating new meanings. Women, despite their usual status as the object of men's meaning-making and despite the impact of men's meanings on their own identity formation, manage to generate novel and even resistant meanings.

The book is divided into three parts, though contributions echo back and forth across the three parts. In Part I, contributors explicitly take up some of the most significant political questions that feminist scholars in the field of communication face. In my chapter, I discuss the recent history of political challenges that feminist scholars have made to the structure of the field, particularily in its professional associations and its conceptualizations of its subject matter. Kathryn Cirksena and Lisa Cuklanz, in the second chapter, provide a history of major feminist theoretical positions that have influenced the development of feminist scholarship in the field of communication, organizing the theoretical positions around central dualisms of Western culture that feminists have worked with and against. Marsha Houston and Keya Ganguly, in their respective chapters, remind us of the theoretical pitfalls of taking notions of gender and of representation for granted. Houston establishes the deficiency of theory and research that assumes white women's experiences can be universalized to all women's experiences. Citing examples of how colonialist discourse is reproduced, Ganguly demonstrates that accounts of the world are inherently incomplete interpretations: Feminists must retain a political notion of representations rather than give in to a sanguine interpretation that the consumption of cultural texts is harmless or necessarily resistive.

Part II suggests ways that feminist scholarship takes us beyond the ways in which the discipline of communication has conceptualized its own field of study, excluding or rendering invisible much of what is important to women. Elspeth Probyn's opening chapter of this section focuses our attention on the body, a subject almost absent from the study of communication (except for those interested in kinesics), until feminist scholars made their contemporary appearance. While women's bodies have served as the locus of many cultural discourses, Probyn argues that feminists must reclaim the body and override Western dualisms. In Chapter Six, Cheris Kramarae illustrates that talk, far from being the happy binding cement of human relationships that might be supposed from some work in communication, can be a powerful means for men to enact their power over women. While sexual harassment has not yet been considered a significant topic for communication research, Kramarae demonstrates that some of men's communicative behaviors toward women—such as verbal intimidation, sexual jokes, requests for dates, compliments, demeaning references, notes and letters, and teasing—are recognized by women recipients as harassing, sexist, and racist. Linda Steiner reconstructs a history of women's alternative media, which, while ignored by most mass communication historians and scholars, represent an astonishing accomplishment for those excluded or marginalized from participation in media industries.

Ann Russo takes us beyond the usual debates about pornography to help readers understand the theoretical position of feminists who oppose poronography. While many in the field of communication and many feminists consider antipornography feminists to be naive in their analysis of gender and representations, Russo demonstrates that pornography should be seen as action rather than image, a more sophisticated and compelling argument than detractors of antipornography feminists have realized. Angharad Valdivia takes a more global look at contests over the meaning of gender. Her research on the role of Third World women, especially Latin American women, in revolutionary movements suggests that women are active participants in the movements, even if their demands for women are not always met. Valdivia notes that even conservative women cannot be considered the dupes of ideologies opposed to their best interests; they too are actively protecting their interests.

Part III brings together several examples of feminist research, representing methodologies that range from textual analysis to historical research to in-depth interviewing to discourse analysis to ethnography. Each chapter focuses our attention on a case study. Jackie Byars and Chad Dell analyze the meanings of gender and race as they were contested and played out in the television series "Frank's Place." African American women journalists have been made invisible by most journalism historians, Jane Rhodes points out. Her research project, gathering historical material on such women as Mary Ann Shadd Cary, is leading the way toward the construction of a history of African American women journalists. Victoria

Chen and Lourdes Torres have done research on Chinese American and Puerto Rican women's talk, respectively, illustrating that women from different cultural groups have unique identity problems. Through the use of one woman's story, Victoria Chen illustrates the intergenerational conflicts faced by Chinese American women whose parents expect them to be faithful Chinese daughters while living in a larger society that presents alternatives to them. Lourdes Torres uses a framework of discourse analysis to investigate how three Puerto Rican women have internalized—if ambivalently—the dominant discourse of racism. In the final chapter, Nina Gregg presents the meanings given by women clerical and technical workers in response to the organizing campaign against Yale University in 1984. Their understanding of the strike resonate with their meanings for their gender, race, and class positions, meanings conspicuously absent from official accounts of the strike.

This book was made possible by the many feminists in the field whose work preceded mine. I am grateful to the many women whose shoulders I stand on, many of whom I have had the great pleasure of getting to know. Cheris Kramarae, Marsha Houston, Kathy Cirksena, and Linda Steiner were valuable in giving me help with the initial proposal and with my chapter. The contributors of this volume deserve my heartfelt thanks for believing in the importance of this project and for their willingness to be part of it. They should not be held accountable for any shortcomings of the volume as a whole.

Lana F. Rakow
University of Wisconsin-Parkside

Part 1

The Politics of Making Meaning

*Making meaning is a political act by feminist scholars with
intentional and sometimes unintentional consequences. These
authors take up key political issues surrounding the introduction of feminist work into the field of communication, the
development of Western feminist theory, the exclusion of issues of women of color from feminist communication work,
and the inherent dangers of representing "the Other."*

1

The Field Reconsidered

Lana F. Rakow

In the second half of the 1980s the rest of the field of communication studies could no longer ignore feminist scholarship or the growing number of women calling themselves feminist scholars. Though the recognition of feminist scholarship by the rest of the field represented a new and significant phase for feminism in communication, the field's late recognition of feminist theory illustrated a great irony. Understanding communication has been central to feminist theory in many disciplines in the past several decades. In fact, feminists outside the field have made significant contributions to communication theory without most of those in communication being aware of it (Treichler and Wartella 1986, 2). We feminist scholars in communication are, in turn, making a substantial contribution to feminist theory, even while we undertake two major challenges. One is to insist that scholars in our own field not only recognize the existence of feminist work but that they also be held accountable for it, preventing feminist scholarship from being marginalized into simply another approach to studying communication. A second challenge is to complete our own internal revolution, accounting for and theorizing our own political, epistemological, and cultural differences as women and as feminists.

A History of Feminist Activism

I should make it clear that feminists and research on gender were hardly absent from the field until the 1980s. On the contrary, activist women have been challenging the field's male power structure and research agenda for almost two decades. In addition, foment from other quarters—from those in international communication, intercultural communication, racial and ethnic minority communication, critical theory, and gay and lesbian

3

communication—helped open up space in professional organizations and journals for feminist scholars to make a public presence in the field. Women of color and white women, heterosexual and lesbian, with varying political and epistemological agendas, have come to feminist scholarship from varying streams of activism and research. By and large, however, feminist scholarship as a collective and public endeavor in the field has been by and about white women.

My own reading of this history is, of course, partial.[1] Feminist theory has helped us understand that our individual standpoints provide us the framework for seeing and participating in the world around us. Those women who were at work making change in the field in the 1970s and early 1980s, those who are women of color, and those who hold a different political or epistemological approach than I will no doubt have different interpretations of the history and current state of feminist scholarship in communication. My account of feminist scholarship in the field of communication stems from my own position as a white radical feminist graduate student in the U.S. in the 1980s. Let me provide some detail about the developments that led to the feminist turning point in communication as they appear to me. I realize that I name names and choose particular events at my own peril, since I will leave out the names of many women who have been instrumental in setting the course of feminist scholarship through their hard physical and intellectual work. However, the benefits of beginning to record and document our history so that it is not lost (see Spender 1982 on the importance of women preserving their past) and so that others in the field must begin to account for our role in shaping the direction of the discipline seem to outway the risks.

An academic field or discipline exists in and through the networks of individual faculty and programs held together and made visible by professional associations and journals. In communication's associations and journals we can see how and when feminist scholarship became a viable enterprise. In U.S.-based organizations such as the International Communication Association (ICA), Speech Communication Association (SCA), and the Association for Education in Journalism and Mass Communication (AEJMC), women created committees and caucuses as early as 1972 to monitor and change the status of women in these organizations and the field and to support research on women's issues. Scholars from around the world have been affiliated with the currently named "Gender and Communication" group of the International Association for Mass Communication Research since its founding in 1981 by Madeleine Kleberg and Ulla B. Abrahamson in Stockholm, Sweden.

Research on gender conducted in the 1970s was often done within the dominant theoretical and methodological frameworks of the field at the time. To do otherwise was risky business indeed, and unlikely to get much of a hearing. Though often responding to questions they had not posed (Thorne, Kramarae, and Henley 1983, 8), feminists did manage in the 1970s to publish works that reverberated with the feminist activism of the day, drawing attention to stereotypes and discrimination in communication contexts such as conversations and television programming (see Rakow 1986). Conference panels on such topics as women and language were held in related organizations, such as at the Linguistic Society of America conference in 1975 and the American Sociological Association in 1976, with such presenters as Cheris Kramarae, Barrie Thorne, Candace West, and Julia Penelope. Some feminists were able to challenge the focus and philosophy of the communication programs they worked in, such as the 1970s challenge by feminists at the Birmingham Centre for Contemporary Cultural Studies (Long 1989, 127).

New organizations and journals were started in the 1970s as well, such as the Women's Institute for Freedom of the Press founded by Donna Allen in Washington D.C. in 1972. Allen published *Media Report to Women* until its transfer to the editorship of Sheila Gibbons and publication by Communication Research Associates in Silver Spring, Maryland in 1988. The Organization for the Study of Communication, Language, and Gender (OSCLG) formed in 1981 as the result of conferences held on communication, language, and gender that began in 1978. The official publication of the Organization for Research on Women and Communication (ORWAC) of the Western States Communication Association, *Women's Studies in Communication*, began publication in 1977 under the editorship of Sandra A. Purnell. Sonja K. Foss and Karen A. Foss were editors from 1981 to 1988, Sandra L. Ragan was editor from 1988 to 1991, and Roseann Mandziuk from 1991 on. It remains the only refereed feminist journal published in the field, but it was only included in Speech Communication Association's *Index to Journals in Communication Studies* beginning in 1990. *Women and Language* was begun by Patricia Nichols, Pam Tiedt, and Sharon Veach at Stanford University in 1976, changing hands in 1982 when Cheris Kramarae and Paula Treichler at the University of Illinois, Champaign-Urbana took over its publication (Treichler and Kramarae 1982, 1). The periodical was transferred to Anita Taylor at George Mason University in 1988.

With this kind of groundwork laid by feminists in the 1970s and early 1980s, with a period of confusion and disarray in the field as it faced a number of challenges, and with exciting developments in feminist theory and research in other academic disciplines, conditions were ripe for the launching of the distinct and visible enterprise of feminist scholarship in communication. White feminist scholarship crystalized in the field around

1986, when the Committee on the Status of Women of AEJMC, the Feminist Scholarship Interest Group of ICA, and the Women's Caucus of SCA were all sponsoring significant programming on feminist theory and research (though all three organizations had in the past sponsored programming on gender research and women's issues and some feminist papers). In the next few years, the possibilities for a diverse and multicultural feminist scholarship were introduced, along with the difficulties that confront feminists in all disciplines grappling with the issue of differences among women and among feminists.

The development and appearance of feminist scholarship in and through SCA was perhaps the most gradual of the three organizations. With a strong Women's Caucus sponsoring programs since its inception in 1972 (chaired that first year by Bonnie R. Patton who was joined by other charter members such as Anita Taylor, Karlyn Kohrs Campbell, and Sally Gearhart), the introduction of topics on feminist theory and research using feminist methodologies was less sudden. In the 1986 program of SCA's annual convention, panels ranged from some sponsored by the Women's Caucus that represented traditional research approaches to gender (for example, how women can succeed in business and the affect of gender on how managers are perceived) to some that were explicitly feminist, including one panel called "Contemporary Radical Feminist Theory: The Challenge of Finding New Rhetorical Tools," with Cheris Kramarae (see her chapter in this volume), Patricia Cramer, Cindy Jenefsky, Ann Russo (see her chapter in this volume), and Karlyn Kohrs Campbell.

With a few exceptions, paper topics on panels sponsored by the Women's Caucus of SCA dealt with research on and issues concerning white women, without their explicit reference to it. The Black Caucus, on the other hand, had a history of programming papers—if not separate panels— about women, such as Melbourne S. Cummings' 1986 paper, "Socio-Historical Continuities of Afro-American Comedy: The Case of the Black Female Comic." In the next few years, and at the prodding of women such as Marsha Houston (see her chapter in this volume), more discussion has taken place about the need to remove white middle-class women from the center of feminist scholarship and more attention has been paid to the communication issues of women of color, particularly black women. For example, beginning with the 1988 convention, the Women's Caucus has sponsored each year an open forum on issues of diversity in race and ethnicity, sexuality, religion, age, and class. The 1988 forum was facilitated by Marsha Houston and Fern Johnson; the second forum had Houston, Barbara Bate, Sally Gearhart, and Lynne Webb as speakers; Marsha Houston [Stanback], Karen A. Foss, Dorothy L. Pennington, Olga Arenivar, and Nancy L. Roth were participants in 1990.

At its annual convention in 1990, the SCA Women's Caucus became two entities, through the work of such women as Anita Taylor, Judith Trent, Rebecca Swanson-Kroll, and Cynthia Lont: the Women's Caucus remains as the group that will deal with women's professional concerns and development. The newly created Feminist and Women Studies Division [sic] will now be the research and programming group, the compromise name for the group suggesting that more traditional political and methodological approaches to gender will be included as well as feminist scholarship. By 1990 in SCA, La Raza Caucus had been formed, the Women's Caucus and Black Caucus were jointly sponsoring programs, and panels such as "Storytelling and Black Women Preachers in the traditional Black Church" were sponsored by the Black Caucus, signaling that more attention was being paid to ethnic minority groups, to women of color, and to the relationship between race and gender.

White feminist scholarship arrived more suddenly and noticeably in the International Communication Association and the Association For Education in Journalism and Mass Communication because the roles of their respective Committees on the Status of Women were less viable than SCA's Women's Caucus. While the Committee on the Status of Women of AEJMC had had periods of strong activism since its founding in 1972 (see Sharp, et. al. 1985, 1), in the mid 1980s, it was lagging. Some women members of the organization expressed the opinion at the Committee's 1985 and 1986 business meeting that the Committee had outlived its function—women no longer seemed to need the Committee to succeed in the field and no interesting research questions remained to be examined. Fortunately, women with an interest in feminist scholarship had other ideas. At the 1986 annual convention, a panel called "Taking Gender Seriously: An Introduction to Feminist Theory and Methodology" was sponsored by the Committee. On the panel were Kathryn Cirksena (see her chapter, with Lisa Cuklanz, in this volume), Georgia Anne NeSmith, Linda Steiner (see her chapter in this volume), and myself. Feminist programming continues to be a strong component of the Committee's programming although more traditional research topics and methodologies are also included.

In 1988, the Committee on the Status of Women of AEJMC began addressing the need to move beyond white feminist scholarship. A panel was sponsored with the Minorities and Communication Division and Qualitative Studies Division on "New Approaches to Gender, Race and Class: A Dialogue" and another panel was cosponsored with the Minorities and Communication Division on "Strategies for Research on Black Women and the Media." The startling degree to which feminist scholarship had made inroads into the organization (an organization characterized by its professional ties to media industries) in such a short time was reflected at its 1989 convention, where the organization's general plenary session was entitled "Freedom and Equity: A Mandate for Feminist Studies in Communication," with an address given by Brenda Dervin and remarks by Carolyn Stewart Dyer, Leslie Steeves, and myself. In 1990, after several years of threats to reduce or eliminate the Committee on the Status of Women's right to sponsor programming, the organization approved a change in the constitution and by-laws that makes the Committee a Commission on the Status of Women with full programming rights as well as a vote on the organization's executive committee. For the first time the Committee, now a Commission, is chaired by a woman of color, Jane Rhodes (see her chapter in this volume).

In 1984 and 1985 the groundwork was laid for the formal entrance of feminist scholarship into the International Communication Association in 1986. In 1984 a meeting was convened by Rita Atwood at the association's annual conference to reorganize the moribund Committee on the Status of Women. In 1985, when ICA's conference had the theme, "Paradigm Dialogues," a preconference session called "Feminist Scholarship as Paradigm" was conducted by Paula Treichler, Margaret Gallagher, and Catherine Hall. Another panel, sponsored by the Committee on the Status of Women (CSW) on "Communication at the Crossroads: The Gender Gap Connection," served as another vehicle for bringing feminist scholars together. When CSW met at the end of the conference for its business meeting, it was decided to circulate a petition to form an interest group devoted to feminist scholarship, supplementing the work of the Committee on professional issues.

At ICA's 1986 conference, the newly formed Feminist Scholarship Interest Group (FSIG) sponsored a series of panels with papers ranging from topics on mother-daughter communication to the politics of methodology to media and women-headed households in black Costa Rica. Unlike its counterparts in SCA and AEJMC, FSIG did not attempt to provide a place for both feminist scholarship and traditional gender research. FSIG recognized that feminist scholarship that needed the opportunity to be heard and not the more traditional research by or about women programmed by other divisions. Also at the 1986 conference, ICA's first woman president, Brenda Dervin, gave her presidential address on the potential of feminist scholarship. Though FSIG has been more international in its outlook, perhaps, than the other two organizations, it seems to have further to go in confronting the "whiteness" of its scholarship. In 1989, however, it did sponsor a session on "Studying Black Women and the Mass Media" with Marilyn Diana Fife, Jane Rhodes, Regina Sherard, Sharon Bramlett-Solomon, Jacqueline Bobo, and myself.

8

The annual Conference on Research in Gender and Communication (started at the University of Pennsylvania in 1982 and nurtured by women such as Karen Foss, Sonja Foss, Nancy Wyatt, and Julia Wood) took the challenge of addressing diversity among women head-on by devoting its 1990 conference to the theme, "Difficult Dialogues: Gateways and Barriers to Women's Communication Across Cultures." Among the women on the program were feminist scholars bell hooks, Elizabeth Spelman, and Maria Lugones.

While feminist scholarship was gaining ground in the professional associations, special issues of communication journals were devoted to feminist communication scholarship, such as volume 9, number 1 (1986) of *Communication* on the theme "Feminist Critiques of Popular Culture"; volume 11, number 1 (1987) of *Journal of Communication Inquiry;* volume 7, number 3 (1990) of *Critical Studies in Mass Communication* on "Gender and Empowerment"; the Winter 1992 issue of *The Southern Communication Journal* on feminist criticism; and the Winter 1992 issue of *Discourse and Society* on the silencing of women. *Howard Journal of Communication* has been a leader in carrying articles on issues of women's cultural diversity (such as Johnson 1988 and Houston Stanbeck 1989). The remarkable intellectual history and characteristics of this phase of research and writing are already being recorded as feminist scholars attempt to make sense of a field that now looks vastly different after only a few years. These attempts include essays in *Critical Studies in Mass Communication* (Press 1989, Schwichtenberg 1989, Rakow 1989, and Long 1989) and *Women's Studies in Communication* (such as Foss 1989), as well as book chapters (Gallagher 1989 and Foss and Foss 1989). Edited volumes bring feminist research and thought into one place (such as Rush and Allen 1989, Bate and Taylor 1988, Kramarae 1988, Creedon 1989, Carter and Spitzack 1989), and book length examinations of specific areas of communication are being published and commanding attention (such as Radway 1984, Lewis 1990, Brown 1990, and Houston Forthcoming).[2]

A Challenge to the Field

The introduction of a body of feminist scholarship into communication studies poses a revolutionary challenge to the field, but as feminist scholars in other disciplines have noted about their disciplines (such as Stacey and Thorne 1985 about sociology), the revolution is yet to be realized. One of the most basic challenges feminist thinking makes to the field is to the very manner in which the study of communication has been divided and conceptualized. Take the U.S. as an example: Traditionally, the field is divided into at least two major units, speech communication and mass communication, each with its distinct path of development and subset of inquiry. Scholars specialize in such areas as linguistics, public address, interpersonal communication, small group communication, marital communication, organizational communication, health communication, public relations, advertising, film studies, journalism, popular culture, technology, and mass media. By organizing inquiry as these categories do, from the starting point of the contexts, content, means, or practices of communication, rather than from the starting point of humans in their particular historical and cultural locations, much of what is most interesting and crucial to human existence and experience is made invisible; the contexts, content, means, and practices of communication are usually taken as givens; the connections between them often do not get made. The topics that arise from the field's traditional categories are not conducive to analyzing gender and race or the experiences of white women and people of color, even while the starting points and categories are passed off as gender and race-neutral. If, however, we enter the study of communication with the purpose of feminist scholarship that Sonja Foss sets forth—"The discovery of how gender is constructed through communication and how gender informs communication" (Foss 1989, 1)—we need a different concept of what and where we are to study. Indeed, feminist scholars who take gender *and race* as a starting point produce far different and more interesting and useful questions and research topics, crossing boundaries within and without the discipline, than can be produced within the confines of these traditional areas. Let me give some examples of how traditional categories of inquiry in the field of communication are challenged by feminist scholarship.

Feminist critiques of linguistics and interpersonal communication were some of the earliest in the field. As Cheris Kramarae (1990) summarizes the approaches taken in the past few decades on gender, it is apparent that feminist scholars in this area have led the way in challenging notions of what gender is—a fundamental contribution to feminist theory and a fundamental challenge to the taken-for-granted assumptions of others in communication studies. While early research by feminists sometimes assumed, as did the rest of the field, that gender was a pre-given biological fact that produced differences in language use and interaction, feminist researchers have come to theorize the differences between women and men as the *product* of language and interaction. And the differences are not innocuous; they stem from and perpetuate hierarchies of dominance and subordination by gender and, in turn, augment other hierarchical orderings by race, age, class, and sexuality. (See Kramarae's chapter on sexual harassment in this volume, which illustrates how this occurs.)

Karen Foss suggests some of the ways that feminist scholarship has the potential to transform rhetorical criticism:

> The study of public address, for example, would incorporate the talk of those other than great dead white males. Why is the discourse of Presidents necessarily more important than the leaflets distributed by social reformers on street corners or than the advice parents offer to their children? Why are formal speeches more important than radio dramas, impromptu speeches, diaries, and even art as powerful ways we create and recreate our culture through talk? To the majority of Americans, everyday talk is as or more important to their lives than formal speeches—talk in organizations, with friends after work, while dropping children off at day-care centers, in letters to the editor, and in every other way we go about taking care of and making sense of our daily lives. Why not study these texts as part of the history of American discourse? (1989, 3)

As Foss suggests, the very subject matter taken as important by those studying public address and rhetoric has limited and excluded the attention paid to the talk of those not in positions of power. Shifting attention away from powerful white men is the first step in redefining what is useful and important to study. *Women Speak: The Eloquence of Women's Lives,* edited by Karen Foss and Sonja K. Foss (1991), begins that work by examining examples of women's informal talk in such areas as children's parties, gardening, letter-writing, and newsletters.

Small group communication research, Nancy Wyatt and Sheryl Bowen point out, has perpetuated the same problems as rhetorical analysis, enforcing existing gender, social class, and racial and ethnic power relations by "attending primarily to male contexts and purposes, focusing narrowly on power and influence, and seeking ways to impel compliance and reproduce hierarchical power relationships" (Wyatt and Bowen 1989, 14). They suggest that incorporating feminist concerns into the study of small group communication would mean 1) conducting participatory research, in lieu of traditional methods of defining and studying groups from the outside; 2) redefining the concept "small group" to include the perceptions of members of the group, so that "groupness" is determined by participants, not by researchers; 3) studying groups of white women and racial and ethnic minority women and men in their own contexts; 4) accounting for lived experience; 5) judging research by the criterion "who benefits" in order to empower all people rather than to predict and control human behavior; and 6) identifying the influence of the researcher's goals and assumptions on her research.

Wyatt and Bowen's critique of small group communication is similar to critiques by feminist scholars in organizational communication. Wyatt and Bowen assert that the very concept "group" cannot be taken as a given as it has in the past. Marlene Fine makes the same observation about organizations.

In advocating the need for multicultural organizations developed out of the vision possible in "feminist revolutionary pragmatism," Fine argues that a feminist commitment means the rejection of "theory and research which denies people's capacity for creating experience, denies people their right to participate freely in shaping the organizations in which they work, and furthers the economic interests of the organization without regard to the well-being of the people who constitute the organization" (Fine forthcoming). Critical perspectives on organizations, which have constituted a challenge to traditional functionalist approaches, have generally regarded organizational power in economic terms, disguising issues of gender and race, and have not seen organizations as gendered, as some feminist researchers have come to see them. Some feminist researchers have also begun to look at women's alternative organizations that challenge traditional conceptions of organizations.

In media studies, feminist scholars have moved past initial work on women's images in content and women's employment in industries to more complex questions that make it impossible to separate study of the media from all other communication contexts. An interesting example is provided by Rosalind Coward's book, *Female Desires* (Coward 1985). Coward starts with how [white] women feel about themselves—their guilt, their pleasures, their obsessions, their contradictions—and connects these feelings to media content about fashion, beauty, the body, and the ideal home. Her work, while deficient because of its inattention to race, does show the way to understanding the interconnections of our personal lives and the ideology of media content. Cheris Kramarae's collection on technology and women's talk (Kramarae 1988) shows other interconnections previously invisible to those in the field. The organization of household, domestic, and office work involving technologies such as the washing machine, sewing machine, typewriter, and telephone have affected women's interactions with other women and their confinement to the private sphere or low-paying jobs.

The willingness of feminist scholars around the world to cross boundaries, to start from a topic significant to women or the understanding of gender and work their way out from there, has led to such interesting projects as these. Other topics—such as beauty, work, consumerism, the body, sexual and racial harassment, motherhood, transportation, soap operas, isolation, cultural continuity and change, bicultural identity, and the home have become possible subjects for study.

This general disregard of feminist scholars for the sanctity of the field's boundaries and categories flies in the face of the efforts of many in the field who feel they must continually retrace the lines that have been, however faintly, marked off as the territory of communication scholars. Given the "discipline envy" that seems particularly rampant in communication studies (Bernard 1987, 197 discusses a similar, what she calls "identity crisis" for sociology), it is no wonder that many traditionalists in the field view feminist scholarship as a messy intruder. Just when U.S. researchers such as Charles Berger and Steven Chaffee (1987, 16) could proudly make the claim that communication was becoming a discipline, in part by its lessened reliance on other fields, along came feminist scholarship.

Of course, many scholars and areas of inquiry remain untouched by the feminist invasion. Feminist scholars simply have not had time to turn their attention to all areas of the discipline, splintered as it is; also some special areas of inquiry are so entrenched in assumptions antithetical to feminist work that feminist challenges can make little headway. For example, one area deeply in need of transformation is the study of marital communication. Feminist scholars and activists have long critiqued the naturalness, inevitability, and presumed benefits of marriage. Feminists in anthropology and sociology have argued that 20th century Western notions of monogamous, heterosexual marriage are peculiar to this time and place (see Coward 1983 and Thorne 1982). Lesbian feminists know that the presumption of heterosexuality as the natural unit of humans is the means by which an oppressive binary gender system is maintained. Women who are victims of their husband's emotional and physical violence know that marriage is not the safe haven for women that patriarchal ideology espouses. African American women know that white definitions of a normal marriage and family are used to classify their own strategies for survival as deviant and unfeminine.

Yet scholars of marital communication start from the assumption that heterosexual marriage is the natural unit of human society. A review essay by Mary Anne Fitzpatrick (1987) makes a frightening socio-biological argument for the assumption of marriage as natural. "Gender differentiation is grounded in a sex dimorphism that serves the fundamental purpose of reproducing the species," she argues (p. 577). In fact, citing other authors, she observes that marriage appears to have been pivotal in the evolution of humans and that division of labor between the sexes and paternal investment patterns are crucial characteristics of human societies. Those who do research on marital communication share a commitment to the

13

strengthening and protection of the American family, she observes. Those feminists and Marxists who argue that marriage is destructive are rarely given serious hearing in the public arena, and therefore, she seems to conclude, need not be considered. Fitzpatrick's work shares a characteristic with other work in communication that has been so detrimental to understanding the lives of white women and people of color, and that is the assumption that "because it has been, it should be," mistaking history for biology. Those concerned about power are interested in changing the status quo, not shoring it up. Fortunately, feminist communication scholars are pointing the way to a redefinition of the problems and issues that ought to be of concern to those interested in marital communication. Pamela M. Fishman's work (Fishman 1983), for example, on communication between white middle-class heterosexual couples illustrates the power that men can exert over talk in the relationship. Victoria Leto DeFrancisco (1991) further explores how men silence women in marital relationships.

If the intransigence of some assumptions in communication has limited the impact of feminist scholarship in some areas, a second reason that the field has not yet felt the full impact of feminist scholarship is that feminist scholars have yet to be admitted into the ranks of senior leadership in the field. Although a handful of women sympathetic to feminist research have held leadership positions in the professional organizations and on journals (and the numbers of women reaching these positions is growing), a network of white males still generally defines the major issues and approaches of the field. These individuals are by and large unfamiliar with feminist scholarship, and their thinking remains untransformed by its potential. Thus it is still possible, after the significant impact feminist scholarship made in the field in the 1980s, to have an important volume published about the field without any women as major contributors, let alone feminist scholars. As an example, a recent volume published in conjunction with the International Communication Association featured five essays, all by men, on the state of communication scholarship (Dervin et al. 1989). While a few women were among the 25 authors who contributed short responses to the five essays, only one of the 25 essays was feminist and little explicit attention was given by any authors to issues of race. The volume's editors (which included three women) apparently recognized some of their omissions, including a feminist perspective among the major essays, yet their choices reflect what are still considered the most general and pressing issues of the field. Caren Deming's contribution posed the question in its title, "Must Gender Paradigms Shift for Themselves?" She points out, "The failure of all five position papers in the volume to acknowledge explicitly the significance of gender paradigms in itself may be evidence of gender's profound influence" (Deming 1989, 164). While essayists argued about whether positivism is or is not and should or should not be the dominant paradigm of communication studies, the suggestion remained unmade that the dominant paradigm is racist patriarchy (or patriarchal racism).

A Challenge to Feminist Scholars

Despite the challenge that feminist scholarship makes to the study of communication, then, the revolution is yet to be completed. While feminists continue to theorize our own differences as women, we must work to make the field accountable for what we have learned. We must make it impossible to discuss the history or current state of affairs of the field in terms that make us invisible. We can start by remembering our own history, as I have tried to do here. The politics of meaning-making in the field must continue to concern us as much as the politics of meaning-making in all arenas of women's lives.

Notes

1.   While my perspective is limited, it was enriched by the help of Cheris Kramarae, Marsha Houston, Karen Foss, and Sonja Foss, who read this chapter and supplied me with additional information.

2.   I do not want to ignore or discount the many books and articles by feminist communication scholars before this time period. I am pointing out the flurry of activity in the latter half of the 1980s to illustrate what seems to be a convergence of feminist work into a substantial body of literature of which even the field has had to take note.

References

Bate, Barbara and Anita Taylor, eds. 1988. *Women Communicating: Studies of Women's Talk.* Norwood, N.J.: Ablex.

Berger, Charles R. and Steven H. Chaffee, eds. 1987. *Handbook of Communication Science.* Newbury Park: Sage.

Bernard, Jessie. 1987. "Re-Viewing the Impact of Women's Studies on Sociology." In *The Impact of Feminist Research in the Academy,* ed. Christie Farnham. Bloomington: Indiana Unviersity Press, pp. 193–216.

Brown, Mary Ellen, ed. 1990. *Television and Women's Culture: The Politics of the Popular.* London: Sage.

Carter, Kathryn and Carole Spitzack, eds. 1989. *Doing Research on Women's Communication: Perspectives on Theory and Method.* Norwood, N.J.: Ablex.

Coward, Rosalind. 1983. *Patriarchal Precedents: Sexuality and Social Relations.* London: Routledge & Kegan Paul.

———. 1985. *Female Desires: How They Are Sought, Bought and Packaged.* New York: Grove Press.

Creedon, Pamela J., ed. 1989. *Women in Mass Communication: Challenging Gender Values.* Newbury Park: Sage.

DeFrancisco, Victoria Leto. 1991. "The Sounds of Silence: How Men Silence Women in Marital Relations." *Discourse and Society.* Vol. 2: 413–423.

Deming, Caren J. 1989. "Must Gender Paradigms Shift for Themselves?" In *Rethinking Communication: Vol. 1. Paradigm Issues.* Newbury Park: Sage, pp. 162–165.

Dervin, Brenda, Lawrence Grossberg, Barbara J. O'Keefe, and Ellen Wartella, eds. 1989. *Rethinking Communication: Volume 1. Paradigm Issues.* Newbury Park: Sage.

Fine, Marlene G. Forthcoming. "New Voices in Organizational Communication: A Feminist Commentary and Critique." In *Transforming Visions: Feminist Critiques in Communication Studies,* eds. Nancy Wyatt and Sheryl Perlmutter Bowen. Cresskill, N.J.: Hampton Press.

Fishman, Pamela M. 1983. "Interaction: The Work Women Do." In *Language, Gender and Society,* eds. Barie Thorne, Cheris Kramarae, and Nancy Henley. Rowley: Newbury House, pp. 89–101.

Fitzpatrick, Mary Anne. 1987. "Marital Interaction." In *Handbook of Communication Science,* eds. Charles R. Berger and Steven H. Chaffee. Newbury Park: Sage, pp. 564–618.

Foss, Karen A. 1989. "Feminist Scholarship in Speech Communication: Contributions and Obstacles." *Women's Studies in Communication* 12 (1): 1–10.

Foss, Karen A. and Sonja K. Foss. 1989. "Incorporating the Feminist Perspective in Communication Scholarship: A Research Commentary." In *Doing Research on Women's Communication,* eds. Kathryn Carter and Carole Spitzack. Norwood, N.J.: Ablex, pp. 65–91.

Foss, Karen A. and Sonja K. Foss, eds. 1991. *Women Speak: The Eloquence of Women's Lives.* Prospect Heights, Il; Waveland Press.

Foss, Sonja K. 1989. "Feminist Conceptions of *Ethos.*" Paper presented at the Speech Communication Association convention, San Francisco, November.

Gallagher, Margaret. 1989. "A Feminist Paradigm for Communication Research." In *Rethinking Communication: Vol. 2. Paradigm Exemplars,* eds. Brenda Dervin, Lawrence Grossberg, Barbara J. O'Keefe, and Ellen Wartella. Newbury Park: Sage, pp. 75–87.

Houston, Marsha. Forthcoming. *Black Middle Class Women's Culture and Communication.* Norwood, N.J.: Ablex.

16

Houston Stanbeck, Marsha. 1989. "Feminist Theory and Black Women's Talk." *Howard Journal of Communication* 1(4): 187–194.

Johnson, Fern. 1988. "Feminist Theory, Cultural Diversity and Women's Communication." *Howard Journal of Communication* 1(2): 33–41.

Kramarae, Cheris, ed. 1988. *Technology and Women's Voices: Keeping in Touch.* New York: Routledge & Kegan Paul.

Kramarae, Cheris. 1990. "Changing the Complexion of Gender in Language Research." In *Handbook of Language and Social Psychology,* eds. Howard Giles and Peter Robinson. Chichester: John Wiley, pp. 345–361.

Lewis, Lisa A. 1990. *Gender Politics and MTV: Voicing the Difference.* Philadelphia: Temple University Press.

Long, Elizabeth. 1989. "Feminism and Cultural Studies." *Critical Studies in Mass Communication* 6(4): 427–435.

Press, Andrea. 1989. "The Ongoing Feminist Revolution." *Critical Studies in Mass Communication* 6(2): 196–202.

Radway, Janice A. *Reading the Romance: Women, Patriachy, and Popular Literature.* Chapel Hill: University of North Carolina Press.

Rakow, Lana F. 1986. "Rethinking Gender Research in Communication." *Journal of Communication* 36 (4): 11–26.

———. 1989. "Feminist Studies: The Next Stage." *Critical Studies in Mass Communication* 6(2): 209–215.

Rush, Ramona R. and Donna Allen, eds. 1989. *Communications at the Crossroads: The Gender Gap Connection.* Norwood, N.J.: Ablex.

Schwichtenberg, Cathy. 1989. "Feminist Cultural Studies." *Critical Studies in Mass Communication* 6(2): 202–208.

Sharp, Nancy W., Judy Van Slyke Turk, Edna F. Einsiedel, Linda Schamber, and Sharon Hollenback. 1985. *Faculty Women in Journalism and Mass Communications: Problems and Progress.* Syracuse: Gannett Foundation.

Spender, Dale. 1982. *Women of Ideas (And What Men Have Done to Them).* London: ARK Paperbacks.

Stacey, Judith and Barrie Thorne. 1985. "The Missing Feminist Revolution in Sociology." *Social Problems* 32(4): 301–315.

Thorne, Barrie, Cheris Kramarae, and Nancy Henley, eds. 1983. *Language, Gender and Society.* Rowley: Newbury House.

Thorne, Barrie, ed., with Marilynn Yalom. 1982. *Rethinking the Family: Some Feminist Questions.* New York: Longman.

Treichler, Paula A. and Cheris Kramarae. 1982. "Editorial." *Women and Language News* 6(1): 1–2.

Treichler, Paula A. and Ellen Wartella. 1986. "Interventions: Feminist Theory and Communication Studies." *Communication* 9(1): 2–18.

Wyatt, Nancy and Sheryl P. Bowen. 1989. "Small Group Communication Through a Feminist Lens." Paper presented to the Speech Communication Association, San Francisco, November.

2

Male Is to Female As ___ Is to ___: A Guided Tour of Five Feminist Frameworks for Communication Studies

Kathryn Cirksena and Lisa Cuklanz

A glance at recent publications in the area indicates that feminist theories have much to offer the study of communication (Allen and Rush 1989, Brown 1990, Carter and Spitzack 1989, Daly 1984, Gamman and Marshmount 1989, Pribram 1988). In this chapter we describe some major trends in feminist critique that seem especially relevant to communication. In particular, we focus on how feminists have criticized fundamental assumptions in Western philosophical, political, and social thought.

Instead of a unified perspective that can be called "feminist theory," many feminist theories share common elements. Each emphasizes different aspects of social relations between women and men, attention to the status of women in society, and the nature of gender. Nearly all feminist theory, no matter how abstract, is grounded in a concern about, and desire to effect change in, the subjugated status of women. Nearly all forms of feminist analysis also attempt to explain, explicitly or implicitly, the sources of women's oppression. Finally, most feminist analysis makes assumptions about the sources of differences between women and men.

Some overviews of feminist theories seek to demonstrate that one version or perspective is the most viable. Others show how specific forms of feminist theory derive from more "general" theories. Because we find all major feminist perspectives insightful in some way, and because we believe feminist theories are more critical than derivative of other intellectual perspectives, our framework groups feminist theories according to major cognitive categories of Western thought. We present each of five basic dualisms in Western thought and discuss its feminist critiques. Such critiques have illuminated the effects of wide acceptance of each dualism on the status and roles of women in Western culture. We discuss the major points of each critique and their proponents, and examine whether or how these criticisms are generally linked to the central goals or project of this perspective in feminist thinking, as shaped by the historical context in which the ideas were developed. We then identify unsolved problems and limitations, as well as the contributions and strengths of that perspective. Finally, for each perspective, its implications for the study of communication are suggested.

We recognize that this framework for understanding important trends in feminist theorizing has limitations. However, the general project of feminist theory, so far as one can be identified, has been concerned with explicating areas of oppression arising from the Western philosophical focus on dualistic thought (Elshtain 1981, Jaggar 1983, Nye 1988, Okin 1979, Wilshire 1986). The limitations of this approach are that nearly all feminist writers have discussed more than one pair of dualisms, that there is no easy or ultimately correct way to draw boundaries among them, and that the assumptions themselves are intimately intertwined so that criticisms of one often imply, or rest on, criticisms of the others. But by focusing on these dualistic assumptions, we hope to depict the breadth of feminist critique and to enlarge the range of questions in communication studies that may be perceived as having feminist dimensions.

One characteristic feature of feminist thinking is its reflexivity. Recently, feminists have turned to criticizing feminist studies of the past twenty years for their emphasis on responding to, and thereby being limited by, the ideas of white, male North American and European scholarship. In a sense, this chapter perpetuates some of those limitations because it summarizes major intellectual trends since the eighteenth century. The most notable limitation is that the dominant ideas in Western culture, and their critiques, are limited to persons of a particular class background, with little consideration of the experiences or world view of working-class persons or people of color. Recent work in feminist theory takes issue with this tendency (Davis 1981, hooks 1989, Ramazanoglu 1989, Spelman 1988). In our system, we point out gaps created by the constraints imposed by the feminist tendency to take up and reformulate standard white, male philosophical *topoi*, and suggest alternative views (where these are appropriate and have been articulated).

In the final section of this chapter, we describe the implications of feminist criticisms for how the study of communication is conducted. The range of methods used to study communication is both frustrating and exhilarating. Feminists have given detailed critiques of the ways in which fundamental assumptions of Western thought play themselves out in the practice of our intellectual work, particularly in the conduct of social science. Similar concerns have also been raised over rhetorical and literary criticism. In this section, we summarize these discussions in order to actively and specifically discourage newcomers to the study of communication from adopting wholesale the methods of investigation currently being taught in graduate programs in communication. Although fully formed alternatives to traditional methods of study have not been clearly articulated, the critiques themselves point out significant limitations in traditional work and should therefore constitute part of mainstream discourse in communication studies. Also, evolving alternative approaches deserve a central place in discussions of methods of communication scholarship if the field is to participate in important contemporary intellectual discussions.

Our organization of this chapter is primarily heuristic: to give the reader a means of making sense of this diverse and complex body of scholarship. We hope that this chapter will stimulate further discussion and consideration of how these critiques of basic philosophical questions are integrally related to the main issues currently facing students of communication.

Feminist scholarship of the 1960s through mid-1970s was activist. In general, it sought to provide information and knowledge that would improve the lives of women. More recent theoretical work develops extended critiques that engage fundamental philosophical questions in Western thought. Such philosophically grounded critiques can also be found in 18th and early 19th century feminist work that attempted to redefine the fundamental nature of women.

The central organizing principle for much of Western thought is the nature of a set of oppositional dualisms (Arendt 1978, Elshtain 1981, Wilshire 1986). Critics have observed that this assumption of dualism generally includes a hierarchical relationship between the terms, valuing one and devaluing the other. For example, the phrases "black and white" and "light and dark" are frequently used in ways that valorize the light and the white and that impugn dark or black as wrong, dangerous, or mysterious. Such assumptions, built into language and unspoken cultural agreements about "the good" or "the real," have the result of naturalizing social inequities to make them appear unchangeable or inevitable (Donovan 1985, Hoagland 1981, Ortner 1974). Feminists further observe that women as a class or group have been, throughout Western history, associated with the devalued characteristics in such pairs. The primary dualisms of Western thought that feminists have identified as particularly instrumental in legitimizing women's subordination are those between reason and emotion, public and private, nature and culture, subject and object, and mind and body. Each of these pairs of concepts has served to conceptually relegate women to peripheral, secondary, or inferior status.

20

Liberal Feminism: Reason and Emotion

Some feminist critics have taken issue with the division between the public and the private in liberal-democratic thought and have, by extension, argued that liberal feminism is inherently radical in its challenging of this dichotomy (Eisenstein 1981). We take a more historical perspective to discuss a different dualism fundamental to Western liberal-democratic theory, one with which liberal feminist thinkers have themselves engaged extensively. This dualism, between reason and emotion, is central to assumptions about how human beings are able to participate in liberal-democratic forms of political organization.

Liberal-democratic theory is based in part on the assumption of free and equal individuals participating in politics. It rests on the principle of reasoned self-interest as the motivating force in individuals' choices in the political realm. Feminists responding within this framework found that their first task necessarily had to be the justification of political participation for women. Before women gained recognition as legitimate public participants, their arguments on any subject could gain no audience and thus no acceptance. Liberal theorists assumed that, as a class, women had a natural character that excluded them from the category of rational individuals. This assumption was so embedded in the underpinnings of liberal-democratic theory that theorists did not even feel obligated to address it explicitly in their political theory. While men were presumed to be rational individuals, women were seen as primarily emotional with a concomitant lack of ability to reason. These assumptions were reflected in arguments about the futility of education for women. Women were simply not capable of the intellectual effort required to become educated. Since women were by their nature not rational animals, they were not capable of handling the responsibilities of citizenship (Elshtain 1981, Okin 1979).

During and after the Enlightenment, male philosophers and writers continued to treat women as a separate subject from men. Thus, although Enlightenment ideas provided for self-government of rational individuals coming together to invest power in certain systems and persons, women were not included in the new ideal. And, although Enlightenment thinkers focused much attention on theorizing the best possible education for politically active citizens, these thoughts did not extend to the education of women. In fact, Rousseau went so far as to directly recommend that women's education be completely different from men's, focusing on traditionally feminine subjects such as sewing and music and the art of being pleasing companions for men. Women were not considered citizens in the same social or legal sense as men. In fact, coverture, whereby husband

21

and wife were represented politically by one person, the husband, pre-scribed the absence of legal and political participation for women.

In this social and political context the first feminist theorists began to argue for a "fully human" status for women, including legally sanctioned political rights. As a contemporary of Rousseau, Mary Wollstonecraft took on the ideas about women's education expressed in *Emile* directly in her *Vindication of the Rights of Women*. There she argued that women and men, as equally rational beings, should receive the same education and be afforded the same political rights, based on the same definition of citizenship. Wollstonecraft argued that socialization, expectations, and the narrow range of social roles open to women were responsible for the overly emotional, seemingly irrational behavior of many upper-class women. Since women were not expected to use their minds, she argued, they did not practice or display the rational behavior of which they were capable. Although her explanations of social conditioning had potentially far-reaching implications, which were later explored by others, her primary focus was on trying to fit women into the public world of politics and education at the time. At its core, Wollstonecraft's argument was based on a critique of the association of women with the emotional and men with the rational. She sought to eradicate this dichotomy in social and political thought about the respective roles of women and men.

Wollstonecraft's ideas did not gain much support during her lifetime or for many years after. In the United States, not until the mid-1800s were women allowed to attend college with men, and not until the end of that century were women admitted to graduate school. Women did not gain the right to vote until 1920, and other political rights were not achieved until much later. For much of this time, women who voiced political opinions of any sort were considered immodest and unfeminine, and it was not until the struggle for abolition in the United States that a few women were accepted as public advocates for their own political views.

Maria Stewart and the Grimké sisters enjoyed brief (one-or-two-year) speaking careers before being pressured to retire to less public occupations. All three women argued that women needed to be accepted as public speakers in order to fulfill God's ordained role for women, that of moral guardian of society. They argued that women's guardianship of social morality meant nothing if they could make no public statement in favor of what was good and right. They did not challenge the separation of social and political life into public and private spheres, or the conception that the public sphere should be mainly run by men while women were primarily responsible for family (and thus more private) concerns. The abolitionist speakers rhetorically extended the Enlightenment definition of man as a rational moral agent to women as well, emphasizing the need for public expression of women's moral ideas. Their arguments were based on the notion that women could fulfill God's ordained role only by acting as rational, publicly responsible moral beings (Campbell 1989).

The line of argument begun by Mary Wollstonecraft and elaborated by Maria Stewart and Sara and Angelina Grimké can be found today in the work of feminist advocates such as Betty Friedan and Gloria Steinem, activists such as Molly Yard of the National Organization for Women and Faye Wattleton of Planned Parenthood, journalists such as Ellen Goodman, and politicians such as Barbara Jordan and Patricia Schroeder. They base their arguments for women's rights on the idea of equal rationality: Since women and men have equal standing as rational moral agents, both are qualified to fulfill social and political roles at any level. This analysis leaves many problems unresolved, including the inadequacy of the concept of equality to solve complicated problems of women under systems of patriarchy and capitalism. For example, the persistence of vast salary differentials between men and women remains both unexplained and unsolved by liberal-feminist theorists. Traditionally, women's jobs, such as teaching, day care work, nursing, and secretarial work, pay considerably less than comparable men's occupations such as trucking, construction work, and engineering. Because many jobs do not provide for paid pregnancy leave (or any pregnancy leave at all), women often bear the entire economic burden of bearing children, losing status, seniority, or even their jobs in order to have children. In this case the focus on equality has proven problematic for women, as there is no comparable situation for men. Also, liberal-feminist theory offers no analysis of pervasive objectification of and violence toward women.

In a way, the current state of affairs in the job market reflects an enactment of liberal-feminist arguments: Women are considered potentially competent in almost all jobs, and are legally permitted to pursue them. In fact, however, factors other than law and abstract equality prevent women from achieving adequate representation in jobs with various indices of power and status. (For instance, there are currently only two women U.S. Senators). The argument and demonstration that women are autonomous rational moral agents equal to men in an abstract sense has gained popular acceptance. However, a continued push to enact this equality in economic, political, cultural, and family life has failed to eradicate (or even suggest solutions for) many important aspects of social and economic disadvantage faced by women.

In communication studies, liberal feminist ideas have influenced at least three easily distinguishable lines of inquiry. First, rhetorical studies scholars focusing on public address have been reclaiming the history of women public speakers such as Sojourner Truth, the Grimké sisters, Maria Stewart, and Ida B. Wells-Barnett. There are now several compilations of speeches by women (Anderson 1984, Campbell 1989, Manning 1988, Schneir 1972). A few biographies focusing on rhetorical strategies and careers, such as Martha Solomon's study of Emma Goldman (1983) have also recently appeared. However, the problematic relationship of women to the traditional study of public address has just begun to be explored (Campbell 1989, Foss and Foss 1991). The history of women public speakers through the mid-twentieth century is largely a history of radical movements and ideas, because women who spoke publicly were by definition radicals (only women who in large part were willing to give up their reputations as good, virtuous, feminine women could pursue careers in public speaking). Thus, the idea of public address as the study of great speeches by great thinkers and leaders more directly suggests male rhetors as legitimate subjects of study. Implicit in traditional approaches to public address is the assumption that the formulation of complex arguments was the province of the rational male.

A second area of application of liberal-feminist principles to communication studies is gender difference research, which attempts to discover areas of similarity and difference in communication habits and styles of women and men. This research has been widely criticized for being atheoretical; once differences are discovered, it is unclear what significance can be drawn from the discovery. Are women and men fundamentally different? Are they simply socialized to employ different communication strategies? Is one set of styles or strategies more effective in our cultural context? If so, should we encourage one gender to be more like the other? Traditionally, researchers have concluded that women's socialization is in some way deficient because, for example, it may not serve them as well as men's socialization in business or political contexts. In addition, gender difference research has been criticized for its assumption that the individual is the best unit of analysis. In spite of these theoretical shortcomings, gender difference research continues to be a popular application of liberal feminist ideas to communication studies. Gender difference research continues to provide evidence as to whether or not women are rational enough to justify their inclusion in the polity.

A third area of application of liberal-feminist principles to communication studies is content analysis. Here, researchers view cultural artifacts such as television programs or advertisements, in order to ascertain the numeric representation of women and men within that artifact or structure. Suggestions are usually then made for the improved equality of representation in that structure or artifact. This approach has obvious shortcomings in its narrow focus and lack of theoretical framework for interpretation of results, and has been criticized for failing to provide an adequate explanation of the continuing underrepresentation of women and other non-dominant groups in texts produced for mass consumption (Tuchman 1979).

Socialist-Feminism: Public and Private

Since the Enlightenment, developments in male political and social thought have seldom been applied to women as well as men by those who originated them. Just as it was left to Mary Wollstonecraft and Angelina Grimké to argue for the inclusion of women in the Enlightenment conception of "human," so it was left to feminist theorists to explore the implications and limitations of Marxist thought for women. Although Marx predicted the downfall of capitalism followed by the demise of patriarchy, a major flaw in his analysis was a failure to consider the work performed by women for the capitalist state: childbearing, child care, and maintenance of the household. Marx and his immediate followers focused instead on the dynamics of the public sphere of the paid labor force. As a result, the division between public and private spheres so central to the functioning of capitalism and so instrumental in the devaluation of women under this system, was neglected by traditional Marxist theorists. Eventually, the maintenance of this division of "proper" spheres for men and women came under the scrutiny of Marxist feminists, who developed three central critiques from their studies. First, the division between public and private provided a constant supply of surplus labor for capitalists. Since they could not earn a reasonable living outside the home, women provided the reproductive functions for the state free of charge. Second, women working at home provided a ready and able-bodied source of emergency labor, which could be called into the paid labor force in times of need such as during war. Whenever and in whatever capacity women did enter the paid labor force, their wages were kept low under this public/private division since the "family wage" was supposed to provide adequate support for an entire family; women's work was thus defined as "extra" rather than necessary. Third, by keeping women at home, this conceptual division between spheres defined their role as that of consumers, providing a supply of people to select and purchase products produced by capitalists. Marxist feminists and, later, socialist feminists developed detailed analyses of these benefits provided to capitalism by the maintenance of a division between public and private spheres accompanied by the ideologies of motherhood, family wages, and feminine fragility (among others). Black women consistently pointed out that their experience proved this division a myth, since black men were seldom included in fights for the "family wage," and black women had never been thought frail and worthy of special protection. Black women, they noted, were consistently a significant part of the labor force, performing physically taxing jobs which often required their virtual absence from their own homes.

In *Origin of the Family, Private Property, and the State,* Friedrich Engels did explore the relationship between Marxist ideas and women's position under capitalism, but he focused primarily on the origin of patriarchy in relation to the development of private property. His analysis was largely speculative and did not address the more contemporary questions of the functions performed by women under capitalist systems. Generally, Marxist feminists have argued that class oppression is primary, and that its eradication will inevitably lead to the eradication of gender oppression. However, women excluded from labor unions and relegated to subordinate positions within socialist hierarchies have not been convinced that their secondary status would magically disappear after a socialist revolution[1] (Hansen and Philipson 1990, Sargent 1981, Buhle 1983). Marxist feminists devoted their energies to attempting to add an analysis of gender oppression to Marxist theory, while allowing that class oppression was still the primary problem facing modern Western societies. However, the socialist-feminist strategy of providing a two-part analysis examining the problems of both capitalism and patriarchy has gained much greater popularity and attention in recent years. Socialists focus their analysis on the three main issues introduced above, all of which relate centrally to the public/private dichotomy perpetuated by capitalism and patriarchy. Socialist-feminist thought focuses on issues pertaining to the public/private dichotomy in Western culture, because this dichotomy serves to divide societies into two spheres, one traditionally female and one traditionally male. And, in Marxist and Socialist thought, as in most other political theory, the public sphere has remained the primary analytical focus, while the private sphere has tended to remain tangential, peripheral, or secondary to the public and to "politics." Socialist-feminist theorists are concerned with theorizing the private domain and thus legitimizing it as a topic for political and social analysis.

Socialist-feminism first gained momentum during the so-called first wave of the feminist movement, which coincided roughly with the Progressive Era (1890–1920), when socialist and anarchist principles were advocated and put into practice by various groups attempting to gain rights and improve the quality of life for working-class people through various means. During this time feminists such as Charlotte Perkins Gilman and Margaret Sanger attempted (in very different ways) to analyze and compensate for problems created for women by the maintenance of a public/private dichotomy in social and economic life. Gilman, in her treatise *Women and Economics*, provided a thorough critique of women's position under capitalism. She suggested a model society including communal housework and child care with paid specialists in all areas of community life, including these traditionally feminine ones. Gilman's idea was that under this new model, no one would perform tasks that they did not want to perform. This would effectively dissolve both the gendered nature of work and the public/private dichotomy, providing monetary compensation for all tasks and bestowing the status of "specialist" on all workers in all fields.

Sanger chose a very different approach, but also focused her analysis on the public/private division of social and political life. Sanger devoted her life to publicizing a subject (human sexuality and reproduction) that had previously been considered so private that it was labelled obscene and considered an extremely inappropriate subject for political discussion. Sanger argued that birth control was a valid and essential political and social issue, even though it seemed relevant primarily to women. Also, Sanger provided a class-based analysis, noting that working-class women were kept ignorant of birth control methods so that they would continue to provide "cannon food" for the capitalist war machine *(Woman Rebel)*. Sanger continually reported that working-class women sought the "secret" of birth control that more wealthy women had already obtained and practiced regularly, emphasizing capitalism's need for a continued supply of workers and soldiers. Like many socialists and feminists of her time, Sanger held and expressed racist beliefs about the potential uses of birth control in minimizing "undesirable" populations.

Current socialist-feminist theorists include Alison Jaggar in philosophy, Zillah Eisenstein in political science, and Linda Gordon in history. Their arguments are similar to those of Gilman and Sanger because they focus on issues of public/private division and combine analysis of class with analysis of gender oppression.

Most contemporary feminists include some analysis of capitalism and some analysis of patriarchy in their study of women's oppression. However, socialist feminists have been criticized by radical feminists for their failure to include an analysis of heterosexuality as a key to the operation and perpetuation of systems of gender and class oppression. Socialist feminists have also been criticized for their focus on the political rather than the cultural aspects of society. Socialist feminists spend relatively little time analyzing and discussing cultural products such as art, literature, and film. They tend to cluster in fields such as anthropology, political science, and history rather than in fields such as English, communication, or psychology.

Current socialist-feminist work in communication examines the depiction of gender and work in popular cultural texts, suggests potential uses of feminist theory in communication studies, and examines the gendered nature of systems of production of popular culture artifacts. Socialist-feminist work in communication will probably eventually explore the problematic nature of divisions between public and private communication, reviving a history of women's speech and feminist periodicals that recognizes the semipublic nature of much influential female communication. Socialist-feminist work in television will probably continue to delineate the ways in which work is represented, valued and devalued in television programming, focusing on representations of reproduction, housework, and the ways in which women balance or attempt to resolve their public and private commitments and responsibilities within television texts.

Radical Feminism: Nature and Culture

For several reasons, Radical feminist thought, and the central focus of radical feminist criticism, is more difficult to define than the other strands of feminist theory discussed in this chapter. First, radical-feminist perspectives have been sharply criticized by feminists of other persuasions, who have often misrepresented radical feminism in various ways: as uncritically essentialist in its understanding of differences between women and men or as "anti-male." Also, radical feminism is less easily summarized by reference to a few well-recognized theorists. Much radical-feminist thought is quite diverse and is often found in small alternative publications, rather than in books and academic journals. Finally, radical-feminist critiques resist affiliation with "malestream" social theories by attempting to elucidate the nature of women's oppression in very general terms; thus they do not lend themselves to understanding through comparisons with major intellectual trends in Western scholarship. Radical feminism has been described as "anti-intellectual" (Elshtain 1981) in part because it tends to assume that the academy, like all institutions in Western culture, is so thoroughly patriarchal in its structure and practices that very little produced there could be in women's best interests.

We have chosen to examine the dualism of culture and nature through the radical feminist lens. Throughout the history of Western civilization, the defining characteristic of culture has been "not nature." One of the hallmarks of "progress" or "civilization," particularly since the Industrial Revolution, has been the ability to control, predict, or transform nature. Radical feminists criticize the whole sweep of culture as male-dominated.

28

They also point out that men have traditionally viewed women as closer to nature and intrinsically uncivilized, and that, in contrast, men see themselves as apart from and superior to nature (Griffin 1978). Historically, men have used force to maintain their superiority over women and the natural world.

In feminist discourse, the label "essentialist" usually means that differences between women and men are best explained through natural biological causes. Although radical feminists are generally considered essentialist in their view of the differences between women and men, they actually hold a wide variety of views on biological difference. For example, Mary Daly, usually a prime believer in essentialism, has acknowledged that patriarchy "attacks the core consciousness in females as well as males" (Daly 1984, p. 351). Others have suggested, using information from sociobiological research that men are biologically predisposed to aggression (Holliday 1978). Although radical feminists are entirely comfortable with tracing the widespread abuse of women to male-control of society, most would be satisfied to leave the question of the ultimate or first cause of male violence unanswered. They would likely point out that such explanations are exercises that don't do very much to solve the problem of women's current situation.

Radical feminists do, however seek evidence of men's treatment of women and nature cross-culturally and historically in a wide range of institutions and social relations in order to substantiate a central thesis: that men's treatment of women and nature is violent (Daly 1984, Dworkin 1974, Griffin 1978, MacKinnon 1987). These accounts of the pervasiveness of misogyny and violence against women have been one of the most powerful contributions of radical feminism to the domain of feminist theory. The linkages to a similar treatment of the natural world have not been difficult to establish (Griffin 1978). Because of these insights into patriarchy, radical feminists ask whether women might not be better served by a repudiation of culture as we know it and the creation of completely new forms of social existence.

One such form, which produced a great deal of vitriolic reaction from anti-feminists and other feminists, was the perception by radical feminists of a need to create a separate women's culture. Many radical feminists are lesbians who believe that by living one's life as much as possible in the company of women, and particularly other lesbians, women might be able to escape from some aspects of male dominance. Thus an important strategic component of radical feminism is lesbian separatism, in which the formation of women's communities attempting to operate by a different set of values from the dominant patriarchy is a viable political activity.

One of the strengths of radical-feminist ideas is that, in dismissing "male-stream" activity, these writers have been free to emphasize different aspects of existence. By rejecting logic and reason as masculinist and oppressive, women can search for ways to revalue and invent alternative modes of knowledge. Mary Daly and others have used strategies of reclaiming words by supplying new woman-affirming definitions and highlighting how language (English) is structurally and phonetically patriarchal by breaking apart and reassembling words to remind readers of the politics of language. One oft-quoted example is Daly's word "methodolatry," a comment on the reification of method in patriarchal scholarship.

A recent direction with close links to radical-feminist ideas is eco-feminism, where ideas about the relationship of the treatment of women to the treatment of the environment have been used as the basis for political strategy in actions at nuclear power plants and nuclear test sites in the United States and Europe. This strand of political and theoretical activity also has close connections with the women's spirituality movement, which seeks to develop and to reclaim the feminine principle in political, personal, and spiritual endeavors (Starhawk 1982).

Criticism of radical feminism stems from its purported lack of feasibility: that it is extremely difficult, if not impossible, for most women to avoid or curtail their dealings with men. Another issue has been the view of radical feminism as universalist-essentialist: that radical feminism has seen women as universally bonded in their oppression by men, especially in their shared vulnerability to male violence. The essentialist impulse of radical feminism, the political practice of separatism (whose advocates are primarily white, upper-middle-class lesbians), and its critique of the institution of higher education, have all probably contributed to radical feminism's marginality in academic-feminist discourse. More recently, radical-feminist work has been consistently moving toward more complex understandings that integrate racism, heterosexism, and classism (Douglas 1990), while also taking on environmental and animal-rights issues.

Critiques of the English language are one way that radical feminism has developed ideas with a potential for contributing to understanding communication phenomena. These critiques, part of the larger project of radical feminism to show the interconnectedness of patriarchy, reveal much about the ways in which language is controlled and actively shaped to perpetuate a particular ideology (Spender 1985). Less work has been done in examining nonverbal codes in a similar vein, but one early book provides an overview of social scientific nonverbal research from a radical feminist perspective (Henley 1977).

Andrea Dworkin and Catherine MacKinnon do closely allied political and scholarly work on pornography, its effects on men, and the implications for women. They have used mass communication research on the effects of pornography to support their claims. Dworkin and MacKinnon believe that heterosexuality is intrinsically oppressive to women; they hold that, while violent pornography represents the extreme in objectification and brutalization of women, it lies along a continuum that includes most popular representations of women. They conclude that women's civil rights to freedom of movement and association are abrogated when violent pornography is protected as free speech (see Russo in this volume).

Radical-feminist ideas, particularly the more contemporary discussions that highlight the issue of racism in relation to women's oppression, serve as a potential site of exchange between theory and practice, between academic and activist. Although radical-feminist proposals may seem extreme to some, they may serve as the most consistent challenge to feminists of other perspectives to broaden and intensify their lines of inquiry, especially within the institutions of the academy.

Psychoanalytic Feminism: Subject and Object

The central questions of psychoanalytic theory concern the development of individual identity during infancy and childhood, the establishing of a sense of self apart from others. Psychoanalysis posits, as one of its central assumptions, the existence of an unconscious, where feelings and impulses repressed during the process of identity formation reside, forming a set of relatively inaccessible influences on the emotional, sexual, and symbolic life of the individual. Closely related to traditional psychoanalytic theory is "object relations" theory, which has a slightly different emphasis: the formation of relations with other people as "objects" in the environment during infancy. In general, the focus is on describing development of relations between the dualism of the "self" and the "other," the "subject" and the "object."

The two major psychoanalytic theorists of the 20th century, Freud and Lacan, each specified a series of stages through which individuals pass in the process of acquiring a sense of self separate from objects in the environment. In both Freudian and Lacanian accounts, the individual experiences certain significant events that create the repressed, unconscious dimension of the psyche while facilitating the individual's acquisition of identity. Predominant in both theories is the problem of the male child's separation from the mother as the quintessential challenge of identity formation. Identity, for both Freud and Lacan, is indistinguishable from gender identity. The acquisition of identity, and, for Lacan, the ability to participate in the symbolic realm through language acquisition, centers on

31

the presence or absence of a penis and the infant's growing awareness of this difference from his mother. In both accounts, male developmental processes are the central concern. Freud was especially contradictory and unclear in theorizing the development of women's subjectivity and sexuality. Most aspects of male development did not fit when applied, in the converse, to women. In general, truncated development was women's lot; the glorification of women's reproductive capacity was at best redemptive.

Feminist psychoanalytic theorists have pointed out that the emphasis on the gendered nature of identity acquisition processes offers a useful point of departure for feminist theory in a variety of domains, but especially psychology and philosophy. Feminist criticisms of traditional Freudian and Lacanian approaches take issue with the assumptions of the primacy of male developmental processes in these theories; of the presumption that mothers are always universally the primary caretakers of infants; and of the consequence that women's developmental processes are ineluctably partial and inconsequential compared to men's. In his original theorizing, Freud assumed that these early childhood processes were preordained by the biological sex of the child. Although early women psychoanalysts such as Horney and Klein attempted to expand Freud's theories on the development of feminine identity, feminist scholars of the late 1960s and 1970s such as Millett, Friedan, and Weisstein were highly critical of Freud (Chodorow 1989). More recent work, such as that of Chodorow, Rose, Dinnerstein and French feminist theorists, has moved to adapt and transform psychoanalytic theory for feminist purposes. Both feminists within, and those critical of, psychoanalytic approaches agree in viewing as problematic that Freudian and Lacanian approaches have structurally incorporated standard patriarchal understandings of the appropriateness of women's and men's relationships into the processes of early childhood development.

Psychoanalytic feminist theory has been criticized for two primary reasons. First, it accepts the universalist assumptions of traditional psychoanalytic theory, positing that identity formation and the subconscious are essentially human rather than specific to Western culture. There is little evidence that these phenomena are universal elements of the human experience. Thus, the underlying mechanisms explaining them remain unknown. A second important critique of psychoanalytic feminism is the assertion that traditional psychoanalytic theory is thoroughly based in masculine experience and identity formation and that, once transformed to "include" or account for female experience, the original notions lose their most important foundations. In short, critics making this argument assert that psychoanalytic theory simply cannot be adapted adequately to account for female identity formation and the feminine unconscious.

32

The clearest utilization of psychoanalytic-feminist perspectives has been in the area of feminist film theory. Positing that the "gaze is male," feminist theorists such as Mulvey (1989), Kaplan (1983), and Kuhn (1982) have articulated how films structure viewing as masculine through depiction of the female form as a prototypically masculine-subject/feminine-object relationship (Berger 1972).

Cultural Feminism: Mind and Body

In much traditional Western philosophy, the faculties of the mind were valued above the physical body. While the mind was seen as what set humans apart from animals, as essentially "human," the body was viewed as a connection to the animal and natural world and as a hindrance to free thought. Conceived in this way, the mind enabled humans to conquer and overcome physical limitations of environmental and physical barriers to human progress and cognitive development. The physical body thus received relatively little philosophical attention.

The conceptual dichotomy between mind and body was problematic for women in two primary ways. First, because of their role in childbirth (which was thought to make them unfit for intellectual pursuits), women were believed to be closer to nature than men. Women's childbearing role was thought to both proscribe and define what was importantly female. In many ways the important attributes of women were thought to be physical rather than mental. Since women were thought less mentally capable than men, and were normally associated with nature and thus with the animal and physical world, they were devalued as less human than men. In addition, theories that asserted the more "animal" nature of certain racial groups further entrenched the conceptual devaluation of the physical as opposed to the intellectual. Much energy was spent in attempts to prove that certain groups with, for example, smaller skull capacity were less evolved than others (Gould 1981).

In short, the conceptual dichotomy between mind and body underwrote the belief that white men were the most highly evolved and most purely human persons, while women and non-Caucasian racial groups were thought both less intellectually capable and more closely tied to the animal and natural world. These notions were in turn used to legitimate "natural" gender roles for men and women so that women were restricted to work related in some way to childbirth and caregiving. The conceptual division between mind and body served to naturalize the notion that nearly all roles outside of childrearing and caretaking were outside the realm of female capability. The female role was narrowly defined by these two

33

activities while the male world encompassed all activities thought to constitute culture, including art, architecture, music, finance, skilled and unskilled trades, industry, and politics. Even when women did work outside the home, this work was usually an extension of the physically defined female role, in jobs such as nursing, teaching young children, and doing other peoples' housework.

The second difficulty created for women through the conceptual bifurcation of mind and body was that this split was reinforced in the symbolic realm. Since artistic and creative endeavors were thought to be male activities, discourse about the body that did exist was usually by men and about women. As a result, the female body was often described or depicted in sexual terms. The link between women and the physical, sexual side of human existence was perpetuated in art, literature, film, and mythology. Male artists working in painting, film, literature, advertising, and other creative pursuits were able to define the ideal feminine body through their artistic work, to the extent that Western culture was (and still is) saturated with unattainable ideals of feminine beauty (see Berger 1972 and Suleiman 1986).

Feminist theorists concerned with this problem of devaluation of women through a conceptual link between the natural, animal world and feminine nature argue that the body cannot be separated so easily from the mind. In fact, they argue, there is no reason to think that women's role in childbearing necessarily means that they are incapable of creative and intellectual mental pursuits or that they are in some way better suited to perform household tasks or nurturing roles outside mothering. These theorists point out the ways in which women have come to be defined by their biology whereas men are more often defined by their intellectual potential. Furthermore, they argue, the body should not be seen as a physical limitation to thought, but as the means through which information is gathered.

These theorists also assert that different people undergo different experiences and thus gain widely varying understandings of what constitutes reality or truth. This results in the "inescapable contextuality of knowledge" (Cirksena 1987). This insight has been called "standpoint epistemology" because of its focus on the impossibility of one objective truth upon which all would agree. Standpoint epistemology can be understood in several ways. First, it can serve to highlight the notion that different cultural traditions have different epistemological premises (Harding and Hintikka 1983). Second, standpoint epistemology can serve to underscore the idea that persons from different subgroups and positions with relation to power within a particular society may have very different insights and understandings about that same culture. Finally, standpoint epistemology can

34

be used simply to refer to the ways in which much important knowledge is gathered through personal experience and cannot be quantified or adequately described. As Balsamo has observed, "the critique of the totalizing vision of the male perspective is a familiar theme within feminism" (66).

Standpoint epistemology is a central notion of modern feminist theory since it emphasizes the nonabsolute nature of knowledge, highlighting relationships between social positioning, experience and understanding of the world. Works such as Jaggar and Bordo's *Gender/Body/Knowledge* examine the complex relationships among gendered experience and understanding. Others, such as Frye's *Politics of Reality* discuss the knowledge obtained through physical experience. In addition, lesbian scholars such as Lorde (1984) and Douglas have argued and explored the importance of erotic experience as "the nurturer or nursemaid of all our deepest knowledge" (1990, p. 56). Although the relationship between feminism and what is now called "postmodernism" is complex, Balsamo (1987) suggests that this critique of "universal vision" represents an important point of similarity between the two. Postmodern feminists describe the body as a "site" at which important identity-forming yet contradictory experiences occur.

In order to counteract the negative effects of the symbolic depictions of the female body as somehow more essentially physical and sexual than the male body, feminist theorists have expanded work on their understandings of the importance of the body in philosophical theorizing (see de Lauretis 1986, introduction). This move began with the insight that images of the ideal female body reproduced in advertising, film, television, and other texts served to create a conception of the female body against which real people measured themselves and others. Since thoughts about what bodies should look like came from language and images, some theorists argued the body was actually linguistically or symbolically constructed, and thus that peoples' understandings of their own and others' bodies were actually constrained and defined by linguistic and imagistic repetition of ideals and non-ideals. Thus, what seems to us to be physical reality is actually at least partly the product of symbolic representation of human bodies. At the very least, our culture starts with certain ideals of physical beauty for each gender and then creates both symbolic representations of and activities related to these ideas.

This move toward an understanding of the body as socially constructed has most recently resulted in a movement to "theorize the body" (see Probyn in this volume). Scholars working in this area often focus on the ways in which language about and imagery of bodies serves to reinforce particular notions of what is desirable, natural, normal, and useful, particularly in relation to the female body. Scholars such as de Lauretis (1984) and Suleiman have worked within the fields of semiotics and critical theory to reveal the ways in which notions about the body have been naturalized and made "real" where they might more usefully be understood as culturally created.

Cultural feminist work which attempts to "theorize the body" has been criticized for its tendency toward abstraction and inaccessibility: Indeed, much of this work concerns the abstract cultural construction of the body while ignoring both individual experiences and connections to feminist political strategy. Just as the emphasis on the body as a social construction can lead away from an awareness of physically painful experiences (such as rape), the cultural feminist focus on the social construction and hegemony of language tend to point away from the importance of gender as an analytic category which has formed the basis of structured power relationships which affect individuals at many levels of experience.

Communication scholars working against the mind/body dichotomy and those working within semiotics and critical theory include those attempting to understand the ways in which language itself provides categories of perception that have long been naturalized in Western thought. Scholars in this area have focused on the gendered nature of our language system and the damage done to our understandings of the female through this system. For example, they note the ways in which the English language perpetuates a view of the female as importantly sexual. One need only consider the number of synonyms for "woman" with explicitly sexual connotations. In addition, language theorists note the process of pejoration through which terms used to refer to women gradually acquire negative connotations. This process can be seen at work with paired terms such as "sir" and "madame" or "master" and "mistress" (Lakoff 1975, Cameron 1990). In each case the feminine of the pair has acquired sexual and negative connotations, indicating and also further entrenching our understandings of women as essentially physical, sexual beings.

Feminist language theorists are particularly interested in elaborating the ways in which we experience the world through previously existing linguistic categories and relationships. In the above example, one can easily see how a nonsexual understanding of what is essentially female could be difficult to obtain within a language system where nearly all terms for "woman" bear sexual connotations. Although most theorists in this area do not argue that language is the original source of gender oppression, most do assert that language has been and is instrumental in constructing an understanding of gender that appears natural or unalterably real, but is actually the result of the ways in which language defines and prescribes gender and gender roles.

Cultural feminist work in communication studies will most likely continue to elaborate the processes through which the symbolic realm has constructed and made real certain ways of understanding and thinking about gender. Clearly, this area has the most direct implications for communication study because its emphasis is on the ways in which symbols of all types create and influence categories of thought.

Are Dualisms Necessary?

Dualisms—either/or, you/me, good/bad, high/low—are so deeply embedded in Western knowledge structures that they often seem like natural categories.[2] In addition to pointing out the problems in accepting such dichotomies uncritically, feminists have proposed alternatives. These fall into three general areas: integration; valorizing the female; and rejecting binarisms for more multifaceted ways of thinking about the world. Both nineteenth century and contemporary feminists have advocated integration: wholism by which each pole of a dualism is seen as necessary to constitute a whole entity—institution or individual. In this formulation no one aspect can be complete unto itself. Both the feminine and masculine components must be accepted and valued in order to be complete. The characteristics and properties commonly associated with male and female, feminine and masculine are not questioned. A catch-phrase among radical feminists of the mid-seventies was "matriarchy is the answer." Some feminists have argued that, because the dominance of masculine values and concepts has resulted in cultures founded on violence and oppression, perhaps those attributes associated with the feminine should take preeminence. Again, the terms of the dichotomies are not contested, but the evaluative weighting of them is reversed.

The most compelling current analyses are theories that account for other dimensions of difference besides that of gender; for the most part these have been articulated by women of color and Third World women scholars, and by some white North American and Western European feminists critically engaging with their race and class privilege (see Houston in this volume). Spelman, for example, reviews the history of white feminists' discussions of gender difference and dichotomies and found them to be lacking in historical perspective (1988). She argues that there has never been a time when the "pure case" of gender bifurcation was paramount in social or intellectual organization. Human identity and understanding have always been multiply determined. The variety of sources of difference as explored by black, Jewish, Asian, and Chicana/Latina feminists in the United States speaks to the many facets of identity that constitute individuals and social formations. These insights have not been applied in any systematic way to the study of communication, although some efforts to address issues from these perspectives have begun appearing in conference papers in the past few years (Nakayama 1990, Rhodes 1990).

Feminist Critiques of Methods of Communication Studies

As a field of study, communication has an identity crisis reflected in the wide array of methods used to understand communication. Classical experimental paradigms are accepted practice among communication scientists, while hermeneutic, literary, rhetorical, and ethnographic methods are also used by scholars within the discipline of communication. Despite its methodological eclecticism, communication seems to have been resistant (more so than, for example, anthropology or literary criticism) to feminist criticisms of its most commonly used methodologies. Both on the quantitative and on the interpretive fronts, feminist insights have had little impact.

Feminists have elucidated sophisticated critiques of the epistemological assumptions of logical positivist social science, especially the assumption that there is an objectively knowable reality that can be described in a set of general propositions. Feminists point out that social scientific knowledge until recently was based on limited and distorted information, was tied to norms based on men's experiences of the world, and, most significantly, any consideration of the unique aspects of women's experiences was notably absent. Numerous examples of sexism in social scientific studies have been documented that undermined any pretense of scientific validity or reliability. Social scientific aspirations to value-free methods and measures disguise the masculine bias of these methods. Testing general propositions that transcend time and space by means of quantitative measures limits the extent to which those measures provide meaningful information about people, especially women, because they ignore the social contexts in which the research occurs. When men's experiences and outlooks are taken as the norm in theorizing human behavior, women's secondary status and inferiority is tautologically reestablished.

Feminists have begun developing alternatives to standard social science practices. Instead of keeping a distance from the research questions, the relationship of the researcher to the questions posed and to the people being studied are problematized (Rakow 1986). Reducing the innate power imbalance between the supposedly "neutral" researcher and her subjects, the researcher engages them in the research process, including the formulation of research questions. Feminist social science is decidedly not disinterested or detached. Of central importance is the purpose of the research. Feminists want knowledge to serve the primary purpose of improving women's lives and counteracting women's oppressive circumstances, however these might manifest themselves. Most recent analyses of social research within a feminist framework recognize the severe limits to researchers' ability to transcend the particular space, time, and subjectivity that circumscribe their research. Feminists link their own interests, goals, and backgrounds to particular standpoints that they bring to their research.

By focusing on women as significant agents in history, literature, and communication, feminist scholars in the humanities have discovered that such work entails a reformulation of traditional notions of knowledge, truth, value, and significance. What began as an "add women and stir" approach rapidly developed into something much more complex and threatening to traditional practices of scholarship. In order to focus on women, feminist scholars have noted, it is necessary to redefine "legitimate" texts, "significant" events, and "important" ideas. Because women have been excluded either formally (legally) or informally (ideologically) from areas such as politics, public speaking, military participation, and even higher education and scholarship, scholars interested in studying women have had to search elsewhere for evidence of women's experiences of life.

Feminist scholarship thus has redefined the notion of a valid text for scholarly study. Rather than looking primarily at public speeches, published philosophical treatises, or state documents—the records of heads of state or "great thinkers"—they have turned to less public forms of communication such as the diaries, letters, and gossip of ordinary women. If women are to be studied, then these texts must become the objects of analysis, because they constitute the record of women's lives throughout most of recorded history. Of course, the information in these private documents is quantitatively different than that found in public debate or discussion—much of the knowledge gained about women's lives cannot be defined as a knowledge of "great" ideas or "significant" historical events. Thus, feminist scholarship examines nontraditional texts and gains knowledge about the ordinary, lived experience of women rather than focusing primarily on the ideas of a few elite leaders. If accepted as valid, the notion of "great thinkers" who shaped the intellectual and political climate of their times defines women as peripheral to history and as relatively insignificant as communicators and actors in most historical periods and in many cultures.

As we have discussed above, much feminist theory has worked to explicate the ways in which women's oppression has been legitimized and perpetuated. Feminist work also seeks to eliminate or reverse these patterns of oppression. By redefining what can constitute a legitimate object of analysis, what counts as knowledge, and whose experiences are significant, feminist work seriously challenges the traditions of scholarship in the humanities. Of course, these ideas have not developed in a vacuum, but neither are they derivative of other intellectual trends with similar impulses.

In general, feminist approaches to history, literature, and communication focus on or emphasize three primary elements. First, they elucidate the constructed nature of knowledge, seeking to elaborate the ways in which knowledge depends on factors such as habit, language use, perspective, and personal experience. Second, feminist work argues that what has traditionally been considered the personal or private constitute valid areas for scholarship. Third, they point out and discuss perspective, both within texts and audiences, and among scholars themselves. Feminist work in the humanities has most recently focused on the contingent nature of knowledge. The phrase "standpoint epistemology" has become a central notion in feminist work in these fields, because it refers to both the importance of perspective and experience to conceptions of truth and to the existence of differing concepts of knowledge for people of differing experiences.

In summary, feminist scholarship has developed extensive critiques of the basic dualistic assumptions that underlie Western intellectual trends. Although many of these critiques have been in existence since the eighteenth century, the greatest proliferation has occurred in the past two decades. Different feminist perspectives have evolved and provide sites for criticizing particular dualisms in ways that render them problematic, if not completely meaningless, as ways of organizing human existence and understanding. Because these dualistic assumptions inform most communication studies, feminist criticisms should be central in developing alternative modes of structuring knowledge and practice in communication. These criticisms run through *how* the study of communication is accomplished as much as they do the theorizing itself. As examples of women making meaning, they illustrate the potential contributions of feminist scholarship to understanding communication.

Notes

1. Agnes Smedley's *Daughter of Earth* provides a poignant discussion of the disillusionment and betrayal felt by many socialist activists in the early 1900s.

2. Some recent studies of brain function have been cited as evidence that binarism is 'hardwired' into the human brain: based on physiological or anatomical prop-

erties of the brain. This evidence, however, could as well be used to argue the opposite: that brain function evolves organically as a product of the kinds of socially constructed categories presented to it.

References

Allen, Donna, and Ramona R. Rush, eds. 1989. *Communication at the Crossroads: The Gender Gap Connection.* Norwood, N.J.: Ablex.

Anderson, Judith. 1984. *Outspoken Women: Speeches by American Women Reformers 1635–1935.* Dubuque, Iowa: Kendall-Hunt.

Arendt, Hannah. 1978. *The Life of the Mind.* New York: Harcourt Brace Jovanovich.

Balsamo, Anne. 1987. "Un-wrapping the Postmodern: A Feminist Glance." *Journal of Communication Inquiry* 11(1): 64–72.

Berger, John, 1972. *Ways of Seeing.* London: BBC and Penguin Books.

Brown, Mary Ellen, ed. 1990. *Television and Women's Culture: The Politics of the Popular.* Newbury Park, California: Sage.

Buhle, Mari Jo. 1983. *Women and American Socialism.* Chicago: University of Illinois Press.

Cameron, Deborah, ed. 1990. *The Feminist Critique of Language.* New York: Routledge.

Campbell, Karlyn Kohrs. 1989. *Man Cannot Speak for Her: A Critical Study of Early Feminist Rhetoric.* New York: Greenwood Press.

Carter, Kathryn and Carole Spitzack, eds. 1989. *Doing Research on Women's Communication: Perspectives on Theory and Method.* Norwood, N.J.: Ablex.

Chodorow, Nancy J. 1989. *Feminism and Psychoanalytic Theory.* New Haven, Ct: Yale University Press.

Cirksena, Kathryn. 1987. "Politics and Difference: Radical Feminist Epistemological Premises for Communication Studies." *Journal of Communication Inquiry* 11(1): 19–28.

Daly, Mary. 1984. *Pure Lust: Elemental Feminist Philosophy.* Boston: Beacon Press.

Davis, Angela Y. 1981. *Women, Race, and Class.* New York: Vintage Books.

de Lauretis, Teresa. 1984. *Alice Doesn't: Feminism, Semiotics, Cinema.* Bloomington: Indiana University Press.

de Lauretis, Teresa, ed. 1986. *Feminist Studies/Critical Studies.* Bloomington: Indiana University Press.

Donovan, Josephine. 1985. *Feminist Theory: The Intellectual Traditions of American Feminism.* New York: Frederick Ungar.

Douglas, Carol Anne. 1990. *Love and Politics: Radical Feminist and Lesbian Theories.* San Francisco: ism Press.

Dworkin, Andrea. 1974. *Woman Hating.* New York: Dutton.

Eisenstein, Zillah. 1981. *The Radical Future of Liberal Feminism.* New York: Longman.

Elshtain, Jean Bethke. 1981. *Public Man, Private Woman.* New Haven Ct: Yale University Press.

Engels, Friedrich. 1985. *The Origin of the Family, Private Property, and the State.* New York: Penguin Viking.

Foss, Karen A. and Sonja K. Foss. 1991. *Women Speak: The Eloquence of Women's Lives,* Prospect Heights: Waveland.

Frye, Marilyn. 1983. *The Politics of Reality: Essays in Feminist Theory.* Trumansburg, N.Y.: Crossing Press.

Gamman, Lorraine, and Margaret Marshmount. 1989. *The Female Gaze.* Seattle: Comet Press.

Gilman, Charlotte Perkins. 1966. *Women and Economics.* New York: Harper & Row.

Gould, Stephen J. 1981. *The Mismeasure of Man.* New York: W.W. Norton.

Gordon, Linda. 1976. *Woman's Body, Woman's Right: A Social History of Birth Control in America.* New York: Grossman.

Griffin, Susan. 1978. *Woman and Nature: The Roaring Inside Her.* New York: Harper and Row.

Hansen, Karen V., and Ilene J. Philipson, eds. 1990. *Women, Class, and the Feminist Imagination: A Socialist-Feminist Reader.* Philadelphia: Temple University Press.

Henley, Nancy. 1977. *Body Politics: Power, Sex, and Nonverbal Communication.* Englewood Cliffs, N.J.: Prentice-Hall.

Hoagland, Sarah. 1981. "Sociobiology." In *The Voices and Words of Women and Men,* ed. C. Kramarae.

Holliday, Laural. 1978. *The Violent Sex: Male Psychobiology and the Evolution of Consciousness.* Santa Cruz, Calif.: Bluestocking Press.

hooks, bell. 1989. *talking back: thinking feminist, thinking black.* Boston: South End Press.

Jaggar, Alison. 1983. *Feminist Politics and Human Nature.* Totowa, N.J.: Rowman and Allanheld.

Jaggar, Alyson and S. Bordo, eds. 1989. *Gender/Body/Knowledge: Feminist Reconstructions of Being and Knowing.* New Brunswick, N.J.: Rutgers University Press.

Kaplan, E. Ann. 1983. *Women and Film: Both Sides of the Camera.* New York: Methuer.

Kuhn, Annette. 1982. *Women's Pictures: Feminism and Cinema*. Boston: Routledge & Kegan Paul.

Lakoff, Robin. 1975. *Language and Woman's Place*. New York: Harper & Row.

Lorde, Audre. 1984. *Sister Outsider*. Trumansburg, N.Y.: Crossing Press.

MacKinnon, Catharine. 1987. *Feminism Unmodified: Discourses on Life and Law*. Cambridge: Harvard University Press.

Manning, Beverly. 1988. *We Shall Be Heard: An Index to Speeches by American Women, 1978 to 1985*. Metuchen, N.J.: Scarecrow Press.

Mulvey, Laura. 1989. *Visual and Other Pleasures*. Bloomington: Indiana U.P.

Nakayama, Thomas. 1990. *From Racial Difference to Diversity in Critical Communication Studies*. Paper presented to the International Communication Association, Dublin, Ireland, June.

Nye, Andrea. 1988. *Feminist Theory and the Philosophies of Man*. New York: Routledge.

Okin, Susan Moller. 1979. *Women in Western Political Thought*. Princeton, N.J.: Princeton University Press.

Ortner, Sherry. 1974. "Is Female to Male as Nature is to Culture." In *Women, Culture, and Society*. Eds. M. Rosaldo and L. Lamphere. Stanford, Calif.: Stanford University Press.

Pribram, Deidre, ed. 1988. *Female Spectators: Looking at Film and Television*. New York: Verso.

Rakow, Lana. 1986. "Feminist Approaches to Popular Culture: Giving Patriarchy Its Due." *Communication* 9(1): 19–42.

Ramazanoglu, Caroline. 1989. *Feminism and the Contradictions of Oppression*. New York: Routledge.

Rhodes, Jane. 1990. *"Integrating Race and Gender into Historical Analysis of the Mass Media."* Paper presented to the International Communication Association Dublin, Ireland, June.

Sanger, Margaret. 1931. *My Fight for Birth Control*. New York: Maxwell Reprint Co, 1969.

Sanger, Margaret. 1914. *The Woman Rebel*.

Sargent, Lydia. 1981. *Women and Revolution: A Discussion of the Unhappy Marriage of Marxism and Feminism*. Boston: South End Press.

Schneir, Miriam, ed. 1972. *Feminism: The Essential Historical Writings*. New York: Vintage.

Solomon, Martha. 1987. *Emma Goldman*. Boston: Twayne.

Spelman, Elizabeth. 1988. *Inessential Woman: Problems of Exclusion in Feminist Thought*. Boston: Beacon Press.

Spender, Dale. 1985. *Man Made Language*. 2nd ed. London: Routledge and Kegan Paul.

Starhawk. 1982. *Dreaming the Dark: Magic, Sex, and Politics.* Boston: Beacon Press.

Suleiman, S.R., ed. 1986. *The Female Body in Western Culture: Contemporary Perspectives.* Cambridge: Harvard University Press.

Tuchman, Gaye 1979. "Women's Depiction by the Mass Media: Review Essay." *Signs* 4(3): 528–542.

Wilshire, Donna. 1986. "The Uses of Myth, Image, and the Female Body in Re-visioning Knowledge." In *Gender/Body/Knowledge,* ed. A. M. a. S. B. Jaggar. New Brunswick: Rutgers University Press.

Wollstonecraft, Mary. 1971. *A Vindication of the Rights of Woman.* New York: Source Book Press.

3

The Politics of Difference:
Race, Class, and Women's Communication

Marsha Houston

> . . . the more universal the claim one might hope to make about
> women . . . the more likely it is to be false
>
> (Spelman, 1988, 8 9).

Ever since Sojourner Truth asked her famous question, "Ain't I a woman?"
during a speech at an 1851 women's rights meeting, feminist women from
nondominant social groups (Folb 1985) have openly challenged the exclusion of their experiences from the public discourse about women (see
examples in Davis 1981; hooks 1981; Giddings 1984; Sterling 1984). African American, Asian American, Hispanic, Native American, poor, and
working-class women continue to criticize the failure of contemporary
feminism to deal productively with women's race and class diversity, that
is, their differences based on ethnic culture and socio-economic status (for
examples see Collins 1990, and essays in Abel and Pearson 1989; AWUC
1989; Joseph and Lewis 1981; and Moraga and Anzaldua 1983). Audre
Lorde gives a rationale for their challenges:

> As women, we have been taught to either ignore our differences or
> to view them as causes for separation and suspicion, rather than as
> forces for change. Without community, there is no liberation, only
> the most vulnerable and temporary armistice between an individual
> and her oppression. But community must not mean a shedding of our
> differences, nor the pathetic pretense that these differences do not
> exist (1983a, 99).

The prevailing voices in feminist theory in the United States have been
those of white middle-class women, economically privileged members of
the dominant culture. Thus, while the intention of feminist theory is to

45

articulate the common condition of women, its frequent outcome has been to conflate the condition of white middle-class women with the condition of all women (Spelman 1988; Houston Stanback 1988). Feminist theory, particularly feminist communication theory, has not yet adequately accounted for the different worldviews, different life-chances, and differential treatment of women from nondominant U.S. social groups.

The substance of the challenges to feminist theory by nondominant women and the relevance of those challenges to feminist research on race, class, gender, and women's communication are the subjects of this chapter. At the heart of the challenges is a desire for theories and modes of analysis that not only accommodate but also celebrate women's diversity, theories and methods capable of demonstrating how difference itself can form the common ground for collaborative action.

In the sections below, I suggest some preliminary questions that we should ask, as feminist communication scholars, *before* we begin to speak and write about women who are different from us in culture or class; then I examine the ways in which feminist women from nondominant social groups (lower socio-economic women and women of color) define themselves as different from white middle-class women, and I assess the state of communication scholarship related to that definition; finally, I suggest some productive avenues for future research.

Why Difference is Political

I once asked some very vocal white, women students in a gender and communication class why they were so silent during a discussion of ethnic cultural differences among women. Their collective response was, "We're afraid we'll say the wrong thing, that we might come across to you as racist." Their fears were not unfounded; in a society where racism, like sexism, remains pervasive, speaking in nonracist ways is difficult, especially when the topic is racial differences (Hewitt 1986; Kochman 1981; vanDijk 1987).

The students' fears indicate why, as the title of this chapter indicates, "difference" is political. Race and class differences among women are not simply variations in "surface" features, such as skin color or hair texture; they are not merely interesting, but innocuous, variations in ethnic cultural practices, or economic "survival skills." These things are no more the primary social differences between white women and women of color or middle-class and working-class women than female genitalia, high-pitched voices, and "nurturing skills" are the primary social differences between women and men. The primary race and class difference among women,

46

like the primary gender difference, is power; more specifically, it is the unequal distribution of and access to social and economic power and privilege. This difference pervades all aspects of our lives in the United States, including our thinking and speaking (Kramarae et al. 1984; Spelman 1988; vanDijk 1987; Smitherman and vanDijk 1988).

Feminist theory illumines more than the differences between women and men, it illumines the inequities of power and privilege based on gender that are ingrained in the social system—the institutionalized sexism that informs and creates instances of personal sexist action. The *same* basic Western cultural value that creates sexism, the belief that a superior must control and dominate an inferior, also creates racism and classism (Davis 1981; hooks, 1984). Racism and classism are institutionalized inequities of power, based on race and socio-economic status, that confer dominance on people who are white and upper- or middle-class and disadvantage people who are not. In a racist, classist society, race and class privilege benefit white middle-class women in the same rather automatic way that male privilege benefits men in a sexist society (McIntosh 1988). As Spelman explains, "Those of us who are white may not think of ourselves as racists because we do not own slaves or hate blacks, but that does not mean that much of what props up our sense of self is not based on the racism that unfairly distributes burdens and benefits to whites and blacks" (1988, 121).

Communication theorists, researchers, and teachers exercise considerable social power through the public discourse of our discipline. But we teach, create theory, and conduct research in the same racist, sexist, classist social context experienced by all other communicators. In this context, as Spelman suggests, communicators may produce race-, sex-, or class-biased text without even the dimmest recognition that they are doing so, that is, by doing what to them seems "normal" or "natural" (Spender 1984; vanDijk 1987), "scientific" or "objective" (Daly 1978; Johnson 1984). Because scholars are no less vulnerable than other communicators to such unintentional participation in oppression, discussions of theory and research about race and class differences among women are necessarily discussions of our power to construct those differences in what we say and write—to obscure and distort, or to illumine and clarify the ways in which diverse groups of women make meaning.

Like the students in my class, we can choose to keep silent, not to engage in conversations about difference, or we can choose to approach such conversations, in our personal lives and in our research and writing, sensitively, thoughtfully, and respectfully. Before we speak and write we can seek the answers to such questions as: What must we know in order to examine and interpret the communicative lives of women who are different from us? Is it sufficient to know that others are biological females who engage in the same forms of communication as the women of our own group—that they speak in public, hold conversations, encounter the mass media? Can we assume that those who have historically controlled the definition of womanhood in the United States—white, middle- and upper-class men—have defined all American women in the same manner, for example, that they have equally valued, equally privileged, or equally constrained both white and black women? Should we assume that gender, unlike other aspects of social life, is *not* shaped by ethnic culture, that the meanings of manhood and womanhood are somehow separable from being Asian American or Native American? Should we theorize and conduct research as if the parts of a woman's identity are separable and interchangeable, for example, as if there is an essential "woman part" in each female speaker that we can examine and analyze without reference to her middle-class or Hispanic "part"? In summary, "what are the things we need to know about others, and about ourselves, in order to speak *intelligibly, intelligently, sensitively, and helpfully* about their lives, . . . [in order to] theorize in a *respectful* way (Lugones and Spelman, 1983, 579, my emphasis)?

These questions and the conception of difference as the unequal distribution of social power and privilege inform the following exploration of the ways feminist women from nondominant groups have defined themselves as different from white middle-class women.

"Multiple Jeopardy": The Different Gender Experience of Nondominant Women

In her essay in Cade's *The Black Woman* (1970), Frances Beale created the metaphor "double jeopardy" to describe the African American woman's simultaneous black and female identity as well as her simultaneous racial and sexual oppression. This metaphor is one of the most powerful and frequently used descriptions of the different gender experiences of women of color. Subsequent writers have pointed out that most African American women and other women of color in the world are poor, and thus experience the "triple jeopardy" of sexual, racial, and class oppression (Davis 1981; Brittan and Maynard 1984; Dill 1979). If they are also elderly, handicapped, non-Christian, or lesbian women, their burdens are multiple (Bulkin, Pratt, and Smith 1988; Moraga and Anzaldua, 1983; Lont and Friedley, 1989).

We should keep in mind that the "multiple jeopardy" metaphor evokes two related concepts. The first is the concept of multiple, *interlocking identities*, that one's gender, race, and class identities are interrelated and inseparable (Allen 1986; Cohambee River Collective 1983; hooks 1984; Moraga 1986; King 1988; Rich 1979). Although feminist scholars willingly acknowledge that nondominant women's identities are multifaceted, in their theories and research they often fail to account for the interdependent nature of those facets, implying instead that they are added together, summative (hooks 1984; Houston Stanback 1989). Spelman labels the perception of identity as summative, "pop-bead metaphysics," conceiving gender identity to be related to race and class identity "as the parts of pop-bead necklaces are related, separable, and insertable in other 'strands' with different racial and class 'parts', . . . each part . . . unaffected by the other parts" (1988, 11; 136). When "pop-bead metaphysics" informs theory and research, nondominant women are treated as if facets of their identity can be "subtracted," for example, as if African American women can be studied "as women" without reference to their blackness, or "as blacks" without reference to their womanhood.

The second concept evoked by the "multiple jeopardy" metaphor is that of multiple, *interlocking oppressions,* simultaneous victimization by sexism, racism, and classism (Davis 1981; Brittan and Maynard 1984; Bulkin, Pratt, and Smith 1988). Like the parts of nondominant women's identities, their experiences of oppression cannot accurately be conceived as separable, summative, or "piled on." For example, women of color do not experience sexism *in addition to* racism, but sexism *in the context of* racism; thus, they cannot be said to bear an *additional* burden that white women do not bear, but to bear an altogether *different* burden from that borne by white women (King 1988; Spelman, 1988). This different burden is illustrated by contrasts in historical or traditional definitions of white and African American women in the United States. While white women historically have been valued as sexual objects, invested with all that a patriarchal culture defines as positive femininity (for example, physical beauty, passivity, and sexual purity), African American women historically have been despised as "sexual laborers" (Lindsey 1970, 88), invested with all that a patriarchal culture defines as negative femininity, including physical unattractiveness, domineeringness, and sexual promiscuity (Davis 1981; hooks, 1981).

Sometimes white feminists are so struck by the concept of multiple oppression, and the burden it implies, that they ignore the positive aspects of multiple identities. In her "Open letter to Mary Daly," Lorde (1983a) criticizes Daly for writing in *Gyn/Ecology* (1978) about those aspects of African history and culture in which women are victimized (for example, genital mutilation), but not those in which women are celebrated and honored (for example as goddesses, queens, and women warriors). As Spelman notes, it may not occur to feminists who are white "that celebrating being white has anything to do with celebrating being woman. But that may be because celebrating being white is already taken care of by the predominantly white culture in which we live in North America" (1988, 125). Women of color view their ethnic cultures as sources of joy and pride, not simply as sites of sorrow and agony; for us, celebrating womanhood includes celebrating being Mexican American, African American, Chinese American, and so forth.

Communication Research on Nondominant Women

One result of the challenges to feminist theory by women of color during the past two decades is that scholars from a wide variety of disciplines have endeavored to give voice to the experiences of diverse groups of women (Abel and Pearson 1989; Austin 1990; Cade 1970; Hull, Scott, and Smith 1982; Newton and Rosenfelt 1985; Wade-Gayles 1984; Case 1990). Communication scholars, however, have published very few articles or books that specifically examine nondominant women's communication (exceptions are Booth-Butterfield and Jordan, 1989; Campbell, 1986; Goodwin, 1980; Houston Stanback, 1985; Williamson-Ige, 1988). Most published research on gender and communication omits, erases, or distorts the experiences of nondominant women.

For example, there are no undergraduate gender and communication textbooks that deal directly, specifically, and cogently with race or class differences and inequities in the communication of women and men. Instead, textbooks in this area give the impression that women's communication and gender differences in communication are defined by the behavior of white middle-class women and men. Pearson's *Gender and Communication* (1985), for instance, contains five photographs of women of color (four of blacks and one of an Asian American), but only *one* mention in the written text of nondominant women and men (a reference to physical attractiveness research on African American, Mexican American, and Anglo-American children on page 223).

Research in the field also suffers from the same problem. Two recent studies of African American women's communication, one quantitative and one qualitative, illustrate the state of published research on race, class, gender and women's communication. Examining the two studies from the perspective of feminist conceptions of difference helps us understand how the assumptions and processes of traditional research can erase and distort the specific communication experiences of nondominant women.

In a 1986 article, Karlyn Kohrs Campbell applies a theory that she developed in studying white women rhetors to the rhetoric of three nineteenth-century black women. She begins with an assertion that seems designed to erase the blackness from the black women whose rhetoric she studies: "Afro-American women, *in addition to* the *special problems* arising out of slavery, historically faced the *same* problems as *all other women*" (435, my emphasis). Her assertion is a clear case of "pop-bead metaphysics"; she envisions black women as the sum of their "black part" (the entire experience of slavery is encapsulated, and trivialized, in the phrase "special problems") and their "woman part" (which is assumed to be the "same" for them as for "*all* other women"). In other words, Campbell's theory cannot accommodate the ethnic cultural facet of black women's identity, so she endeavors to "subtract" it before beginning her analysis.

An even deeper problem with Campbell's essay is her purpose, to delineate "convergences and divergences" (435) from white women's rhetoric. The rhetorical style of white women becomes the standard by which that of African American women must be judged. Any uniquely black/woman features of black women's rhetoric are marked as deviant. The only important aspects of what black women do as communicators are considered to be those that are somehow related to what white women do.

The manner in which Booth-Butterfield and Jordan interpret the data from their "empirical" examination of "the differences in the verbal and nonverbal patterns of black and white women" (1989, 265) may also obscure communication patterns that are specific to black women. These researchers observed discussions among all black, all white, and mixed-race groups of women and report that black women were more "expressive" and "emotional" than white women in their same-race groups, and that they "appeared to tone down" their communication in the cross-race discussions (265). Both their definition of black women's style and their implied rationale for black women's style-switches raise questions for me.

First, have the researchers failed to account for the interconnections of race, class, and gender in defining the communication of the black women whom they observe? They unquestioningly accept previous research on "black communication style." But almost all of what has been written about black language and communication is based upon observations of working-class, black men (for example the body of research summarized in Hall and Freedle, 1975) or of black women communicating in the context of black men and/or white women and men (for example, Kochman, 1981, on whose description of "black style" Booth-Butterfield and Jordan heavily rely). It seems possible that the researchers have conflated the style of their black college women participants (at least some of whom were middle-class) with that of working-class black men. They may also

51

have misconstrued as black women's style a way of communicating that was already adapted to mixed-sex and mixed-race situations (for a contrasting approach to a similar research problem see Houston Stanback 1983).

The second question that this study raises for me is, have the researchers respected black women's meanings for the communication event? In their literature review Booth-Butterfield and Jordan cite studies based on honoring speaker's meanings for communication (Houston Stanback and Pearce 1981; Houston Stanback 1983), but their study presents only the researchers' meanings. Would the black women participants agree that they "toned down" their "black style" in order to conform to the style of white women conversational partners? Black feminist scholar Beverly Smith (Smith and Smith 1983) offers a relevant alternative interpretation of black women's communication with white women:

> Now, I don't think this is about acting white in a white context. It's about, one, a lack of inspiration. Because the way you act with black people is because they inspire the behavior. And I *do* mean inspire. And the other thing is that when you are in a white context, you think 'Well, why bother? Why waste your time?' if what you're trying to do is get things across and communicate and what-have-you, *you talk in your second language* (her emphasis, 119).

There are subtle and substantial differences between Booth-Butterfield and Jordan's, and Smith's interpretations of black women's style-shifts. Booth-Butterfield and Jordan present black women as capitulating to the style of white conversational partners, while Smith describes black women as actively redefining the conversation in their own terms and purposely switching to another level or variety of their own style. One explanation constructs black women as controlled by white women's meanings for communication, the other constructs black women as active meaning-makers.

My point is not that Campbell's and Booth-Butterfield and Jordan's studies are not valuable, but that their theoretical and methodological approaches preclude their deepening our understanding of black women's communication in truly helpful or respectful ways.

Maria Lugones and Elizabeth Spelman point out that theories and methods developed to explain the experiences of one group of women are more likely to obscure than illumine the experiences of women from other groups:

> It is one thing for both me and you to observe you and come up with our different accounts of what you are doing; it is quite another for

52

me to observe myself and others much like me culturally and in other ways and to develop an account of myself and then use that account to give an account of you (1983, 577).

Centering Ethnic Culture: Directions for Research on the Communication of Nondominant Women

So far, I have summarized the ways in which women from nondominant social groups have defined their differences from white middle-class women and assessed the state of published research on race, class, gender and women's communication. Now I want to suggest some productive directions for research in this area.

In several recent works communication theorists have emphasized the advantages of making culture the central organizing concept for the study of human communication (Pearce 1989; Shuter 1990). Feminist communication theorists, examining the issue of diversity and women's communication, have also delineated the advantages of placing women's ethnic cultures at the center of the analysis of communication by and about women (Johnson 1988, 1989; Kramarae 1989). Making women's ethnic culture the central organizing concept for feminist theory and research means thinking of women as enculturated to a gendered communication ideal *within* specific ethnic groups, that is, as learning how they should communicate as women in the context of a particular ethnic cultural experience.

The approach has at least two advantages. First, it allows us to examine "mutual (non-dominant) differences" among women (Lorde, 1983b, 99), that is, to view every ethnic cultural group of women as different from every other, and no group's experiences as more essential to defining the common condition of women, or to defining women's communication, than any other's.

For example, one of the most hopeful developments in contemporary feminist theory is that white middle-class women have begun to perceive themselves as "different," in the sense that they belong to only *one* of the many diverse groups of women in the United States, and to examine how their own "whiteness" and middle-class economic status accord them unearned social privileges and power (Spelman, 1988). In one study, Peggy McIntosh lists 46 advantages automatically accorded her as a white middle-class woman academic that either do not accrue to her nonwhite colleagues or for which they must struggle; she explains:

> . . . a man's sex provides advantages for him whether or not he approves of the ways in which dominance has been conferred on his

53

group. A 'white' skin in the United States opens many doors for whites whether or not we approve of the way dominance has been conferred on us. (1988, 18)

In several recent communication research studies scholars have taken a cultural approach to the study of women's communication. McCullough (1987) described black and white women's contrasting perceptions of their same-race and cross-race friendships. Fitch (1989) explored the disjuncture between U.S. feminist theory and the worldview of Colombian women. White and Dobris (1989) analyzed "identity discourse" of women from diverse social groups.

A second advantage of placing women's ethnic cultures at the center of our analysis of women's communication is that we can uncover the diversity of experiences *within* cultural groups. Thus, the approach can help us to understand the complex relationships between oppression and privilege that define many women's lives, for instance, poor white women who are burdened by sexism and classism but privileged by their race; or middle-class black women who are burdened by racism and sexism yet privileged by their economic status. I want to examine more closely how placing women's ethnic cultures at the center of our analysis enables us to recognize heterogeneity within nondominant cultures.

Scholars tend to reduce complex social phenomena to their simplest terms in order to study them. This includes treating social groups that are internally diverse as if they are homogenous. Differences among subgroups of women *within* ethnic cultural groups, for example between first- and second-generation Vietnamese Americans, or between middle-class and working-class Mexican Americans, create different communicative lives for each subgroup. Studying the subgroups of women within ethnic cultures will eliminate the misperception that the women of a nondominant group are an undifferentiated mass, with the same life-styles and life-chances, and identical communication values, styles, patterns, and skills.

In conducting studies of women's intra-ethnic heterogeneity, we might ask such questions as: What historic and socio-cultural features have shaped the communication of subgroups of women within cultures? How do *they* define themselves and their communication? To what extent do they identify with their ethnic culture as opposed to their socio-economic class? What specific features, skills, styles, or patterns do they consider salient to their definitions of themselves as communicators? How are these features manifest in the various contexts of their communicative lives? How is their communication perceived, constrained, enabled, or otherwise influenced by others outside their subgroup, for example, by the men of their ethnic culture, by women from other classes within their culture, or by the men or women of other ethnic cultures?

Conclusion

All scholars, regardless of social class origin, race, or sex, have the benefit of "educational privilege" (Smith and Smith, 1983, 120). Through our theorizing and research, we are empowered to speak about, and sometimes to speak for, groups of women who have no direct access to the public forums of our conferences, journals, and books, many of whom are not only different but also less socially powerful than us because of their race or socio-economic class. As feminist communication scholars, we want to develop theories, research questions, and methods of inquiry that allow the perspectives of women from nondominant groups to guide our interpretations of their communication. Earlier, I listed the sorts of questions that we should seek to answer before we begin research.

But how do we arrive at the answers we need to speak and write with intelligence and respect? Of course we must do the usual things. For example, we must review the relevant literature; in the case of women of color, that means we must read mostly outside the discipline of communication, for example, in history, literature, literary theory and feminist theory. But we must also do something *unusual* by placing women's ethnic cultures, rather than theory-testing or the communication experiences of dominant groups, at the center of our research.

Maria Lugones (Lugones and Spelman, 1983) argues that such centering should not be merely an intellectual process. She advises feminists who want to speak intelligently about women who are different from them to "follow" those women into *their* world, not just through reading and detached observation, but physically and emotionally. Feminist research on women's communication differences must be grounded in direct, not vicarious, relationships with women who are different from us; we must *earn* the right to speak about them, by learning who they are as they communicate in their own ethnic cultural contexts, their world, not simply in ours. As feminist communication scholars, we must allow the experiences of women different from us—our mutual experiences of one another—to reshape our theories and redirect our research.

References

Abel, Emily K. and Marjorie Pearson, eds. 1989. *Across Cultures: The Spectrum of Women's Lives.* New York: Gordon and Breach.

Allen, Paula Gunn. 1986. *The Sacred Hoop: Recovering the Feminine in American Indian Traditions.* Boston: Beacon Press.

Asian Women United of California (AWUC), eds. 1989. *Making Waves.* Boston: Beacon Press.

Austin, Gayle. 1990. *Feminist Theories for Dramatic Criticism.* Ann Arbor: University of Michigan Press.

Beale, Frances. 1970. "Double Jeopardy: To Be Black and Female." In *The Black Woman,* ed. Toni Cade. New York: Signet.

Booth-Butterfield, Melanie and Felicia Jordan. 1989. "Communication and Adaptation Among Racially Heterogenous and Homogenous Groups." *Southern Communication Journal.* 54 (Spring): 253–72.

Brittan, A. and M. Maynard. 1984. *Sexism, Racism, and Oppression.* New York: Basil Blackwell.

Bulkin, Elly, Minnie Bruce Pratt, and Barbara Smith. 1988. *Yours in Struggle: Three Feminist Perspectives on Anti-Semitism and Racism.* Ithaca, New York: Firebrand Books.

Cade, Toni, ed. 1970. *The Black Woman.* New York: Signet.

Campbell, Karlyn Kohrs. 1986. "Style and Content in the Rhetoric of Early Afro-American Feminists." *Quarterly Journal of Speech* 72: 434–445.

Case, Sue-Ellen, ed. 1990. *Performing Feminisms: Feminist Critical Theory and Theatre.* Baltimore: Johns Hopkins University Press.

Cohambee River Collective. 1983. "A Black Feminist Statement." In *This Bridge Called My Back: Writings by Radical Women of Color,* eds. Cherrie Moraga and Gloria Anzaldua. New York: Kitchen Table Women of Color Press.

Collins, Patricia Hill. 1990. *Black Feminist Thought: Knowledge, Consciousness, and the Politics of Empowerment.* New York: Harper Collins.

Daly, Mary. 1978. *Gyn/ecology, The Metaethics of Radical Feminism.* Boston: Beacon Press.

Davis, Angela Y. 1981. *Women, Race, and Class.* New York: Random House.

Dill, Bonnie Thornton. 1979. "The Dialectics of Black Womanhood." *Signs* 4: 543–557.

Fitch, Kristine L. 1989. "Colombianas y Gringas: A Cultural Perspective on Feminist Criticism." Paper presented to Speech Communication Association, San Francisco.

Folb, Edith 1985. "Who's got room at the top? Issues of Dominance and Nondominance in Intercultural Communication." In *Intercultural Communication: A Reader* (4th ed.), eds. L. A. Samovar and R. E. Porter. Belmont, Calif.: Wadsworth.

Giddings, Paula. 1984. *When and Where I Enter: The Impact of Black Women on Race and Sex in America.* New York: Bantam.

Goodwin, Marjorie Harness. 1980. "Directive-response Speech Sequences in Girls' and Boys' Task Activities." In *Women and Language in Literature and Society,* eds. Sally McConnell-Ginet, Ruth Borker, and Nancy Forman. New York: Praeger.

Hall, W. and J. Freedle (1975). *Culture and Language: The Black American Experience.* New York: John Wiley & Sons.

Hewitt, Roger. 1986. *White Talk Black Talk: Inter-racial Friendship and Communication Amongst Adolescents.* Cambridge: Cambridge University Press.

hooks, bell. 1981. *Ain't I a Woman?: Black Women and Feminism.* Boston: South End Press.

hooks, bell. 1984. *Feminist Theory: From Margin to Center.* Boston: South End Press.

Houston Stanback, Marsha. 1983. *Code-switching in Black Women's Speech.* Ph.D. diss., University of Massachusetts.

Houston Stanback, Marsha. 1985. "Language and Black Woman's Place: Evidence From the Black Middle Class." In *For Alma Mater: Theory and Practice in Feminist Scholarship,* eds. P. A. Treichler, C. Kramarae, and B. Stafford. Urbana: University of Illinois Press.

Houston Stanback, Marsha. 1988. "What Makes Scholarship About Black Women and Communication Feminist Scholarship?" *Women's Studies in Communication.* 11: 28–31.

Houston Stanback, Marsha. 1989. "Feminist Theory and Black Women's Talk." *Howard Journal of Communication.* 1(4): 187–194.

Houston Stanback, Marsha and W. Barnett Pearce. 1981. "Talking to 'The Man': Some Communication Strategies used by Members of 'Subordinate' Social Groups." *Quarterly Journal of Speech..* 67: 21–30.

Hull, Gloria T., Patricia Bell Scott, and Barbara Smith, eds. 1982. *All the women are white, all the blacks are men, but some of us are brave.* Old Westbury: The Feminist Press.

Johnson, Fern L. 1984. "Positions for Knowing About Gender Differences in Social Relationships." *Women's Studies in Communication.* 7(2): 77–82.

Johnson, Fern L. 1988. "Feminist Theory, Cultural Diversity, and Women's Communication." *Howard Journal of Communication.* 1(2): 33–41.

Johnson, Fern L. 1989. "Women's Culture and Communication: An Analytical Perspective." In *Beyond Boundaries: Sex and Gender Diversity in Communication,* eds. Cynthia M. Lont and Sheryl Friedley. Fairfax, Va.: George Mason University Press.

Joseph, Gloria I. and Jill Lewis, eds. 1981. *Common Differences: Conflicts in Black and White Feminist Perspectives.* New York: Anchor Books.

King, Deborah K. 1988. "Multiple Jeopardy, Multiple Consciousness: The Context of a Black Feminist Ideology." *Signs* 14(Autumn): 42–72.

Kochman, Thomas. 1981. *Black and White: Styles in Conflict.* Chicago: University of Chicago Press.

Kramarae, Cheris. (1989). "Redefining Gender, Class and Race." In *Beyond Boundaries: Sex and Gender Diversity in Communication,* eds. Cynthia M. Lont and Sheryl Friedley. Fairfax, Va.: George Mason University Press.

Kramarae, Cheris, Muriel Schulz, and William M. O'Barr, eds. 1984. *Language and Power.* Beverly Hills: Sage.

Lindsey, Kay. 1970. "The Black Woman as Woman." In *The Black Woman,* ed. Toni Cade. New York: Signet.

Lont, Cynthia M. and Sheryl Friedley, eds. 1989. *Beyond Boundaries: Sex and Gender Diversity in Communication.* Fairfax, Va.: George Mason University Press.

Lorde, Audre. 1983a. "An Open Letter to Mary Daly." In *This Bridge Called My Back: Writings by Radical Women of Color,* eds. Cherrie Moraga and Gloria Anzaldua. New York: Kitchen Table-Women of Color Press.

Lorde, Audre. 1983b. "The Master's Tools Will Never Dismantle the Master's House." In *This Bridge Called My Back: Writings by Radical Women of Color,* eds. Cherrie Moraga and Gloria Anzaldua. New York: Kitchen Table-Women of Color Press.

Lugones, Maria and Elizabeth Spelman. 1983. "Have we got a theory for you! Feminist Theory, Cultural Imperialism and the Demand for 'The Woman's Voice.'" *Women's Studies International Forum* 6(6): 573–581.

McCullough, Mary. 1987. "Women's Friendships Across Cultures: Black and White Friends Speaking." Presented to Speech Communication Association, Boston.

McIntosh, Peggy. 1988. "White Privilege and Male Privilege: A Personal Account of Coming to See Correspondences Through Work in Women's Studies." Working Paper No. 189. Wellesley College Center for Research on Women, Wellesley, Massachusetts.

Moraga, Cherrie. 1986. "From a Long Line of Venidas: Chicanas and Feminism." In *Feminist Studies/Critical Studies,* ed. Teresa de Lauretis. Bloomington: Indiana University Press.

Moraga, Cherrie and Gloria Anzaldua, eds. 1983. *This Bridge Called My Back: Writings by Radical Women of Color.* New York: Kitchen Table/Women of Color Press.

Newton, Judith and Deborah Rosenfelt, eds. 1985. *Feminist Criticism and Social Change: Sex, Class and Race in Literature and Culture.* New York: Methuen.

Pearce, W. Barnett. 1989. *Communication and the Human Condition.* Carbondale, Ill.: Southern Illinois University Press.

Pearson, Judy Cornelia. 1985. *Gender and Communication.* Dubuque, Iowa: William C. Brown.

Rich, Adrienne. 1979. "Disloyal to Civilization: Feminism, Racism, Gynephobia." In *On Lies, Secrets, and Silence.* New York: W.W. Norton.

Shuter, Robert. 1990. "The Centrality of Culture." *Southern Communication Journal.* 55: 237–49.

Smith, Barbara. 1983. *Home Girls: A Black Feminist Anthology.* New York: Kitchen Table/Women of Color Press.

Smith, Barbara and Beverly Smith. 1983. "Across the Kitchen Table: A Sister to Sister Conversation." In *This Bridge Called My Back: Writings by Radical Women of Color,* eds. Cherrie Moraga and Gloria Anzaldua. New York: Kitchen Table/Women of Color Press.

Smitherman-Donaldson, Geneva and Tuen vanDijk. 1988. "Words That Hurt." In their *Discourse and Discrimination.* Detroit: Wayne State University Press.

Spelman, Elizabeth. 1988. *Inessential Woman: Problems of Exclusion in Feminist Thought.* Boston: Beacon Press.

Spender, Dale. 1984. "Defining Reality: A Powerful Tool." In *Language and Power,* eds. Cheris Kramarae, Muriel Schulz, and William M. O'Barr. Beverly Hills: Sage.

Sterling, Dorothy, ed. 1984. *We Are Your Sisters: Black Women in the 19th Century.* New York: W.W. Norton.

Truth, Sojourner (Isabella Van Wagener). 1851. "Ain't I A Woman." In *We Shall Be Heard: Women Speakers in America,* eds. Patricia Scileppi Kennedy and Gloria Hartman O'Sheilds, 1983. Dubuque, Iowa: Kendall-Hunt.

vanDijk, Tuen. 1987. *Communicating Racism: Ethnic Prejudice in Thought and Talk.* Beverly Hills: Sage.

Wade-Gayles, Gloria. 1984. *No Crystal Stair: Visions of Race and Sex in Black Women's Fiction.* New York: Pilgrim.

White, Cindy L. and Catherine Dobris. 1989. "Rhetorical Constructions of Self and Identity: Toward a Genre View of Feminist Identity Discourse." Paper presented to Speech Communication Association, San Francisco.

Williamson-Ige, Dorothy. 1988. "Shirley Chisolm with Black and White Women's Audiences." In *Women Communicating,* eds. Anita Taylor and Barbara Bate. Norwood, N.J.: Ablex.

4

Accounting for Others:
Feminism and Representation

Keya Ganguly

Questions of representation have come to occupy central positions in contemporary cultural analysis. In this essay, I want to address the politics of representation as they pertain to feminist possibilities within communications scholarship. My discussion comprises four parts. The introduction outlines my basic premises: the need to interrogate representation is placed in the context of the increasing difficulty of localizing feminism or pinning down the constitution of feminist knowledge. In the second part, I attempt to clarify some of the issues involved in problematizing representation by drawing on the arguments of two exemplary feminist theorists, Gayatri Spivak and Angela McRobbie. Here, philosophical and ethico-political considerations surrounding the question of representability are squared in theoretical terms. The third section takes up the concept of the audience and argues for the need to move away from sociological categories to a more humanistic and interpretive construction of audiences as "constituencies." At the same time, feminist cultural analysis must resist the uncritical celebration of audience activities as "resistance"—that is, if the goal is to move beyond existing possibilities in the realm of culture. The last part of my discussion discusses some post-structuralist and feminist theories of colonial discourse and touches on the ways in which these emergent critiques have engaged representational problematics.[1]

Neither my line of reasoning nor the critics whose work I have chosen to highlight are somehow representative "mother figures."[2] I do not have the time or space to provide an overview of the entire range of scholarship on representation and the audience; moreover, to aspire to completeness would contradict the feminist impulse to be self-consciously appropriative and selective. Feminist knowledges are most productively regarded as "situated" (but not merely impressionistic), because the quest for objectivity ends up reinscribing humanist and masculinist myths of power and certitude (Haraway 1988). This should not, however, imply that my discussion is based on a purely arbitrary choice of authors and arguments. On the contrary, I think the theoretical and practical contributions of the work considered here are particularly helpful in understanding issues of representation; they illuminate the potential for carrying on a philosophically and politically informed feminist criticism.[3] But the partiality of this account should signal the most immediate problem of representation—that our accounts of the world (as well as of ourselves) are inherently incomplete *interpretations*, rather than unmediated descriptions of the "really" real.[4] In short, one begins (and ends) with, as Donna Haraway put it, the stutter—the fractured representation of fractured identities. As she says in her "germinal" manifesto of the possibilities of a socialist-feminism for the 1990s,

> It has become difficult to name one's feminism by a single adjective— or even to insist in every circumstance upon the noun. Consciousness of exclusion through naming is acute. Identities seem contradictory, partial, and strategic. With the hard-won recognition of their social and historical constitution, gender, race, and class cannot provide the basis for belief in "essential" unity. There is nothing about being "female" that naturally binds women. There is not even such a state as "being" female, itself a highly complex category constructed in contested sexual scientific discourses and other social practices. Gender, race, or class consciousness is an achievement forced on us by the terrible historical experience of the contradictory social realities of patriarchy, colonialism, and capitalism. And who counts as "us" in my own rhetoric? Which identities are available to ground such a potent political myth called "us," and what could motivate enlistment in this collectivity? Painful fragmentation among feminists (not to mention among women) along every possible fault line has made the concept of *woman* elusive, an excuse for the matrix of women's dominations of each other (Haraway 1985, 179).

One of our tasks as feminist critics, it seems to me, is to untangle "the matrix of women's dominations of each other." We must be vigilant in our representations of ourselves but, more importantly, of our subjects— those *others* whose experience, subjectivity and/or oppression we seek to address. We need to question representation both as a political and as an epistemological problem. This means that we have to scrutinize the ways in which the very attempt to represent something (or someone) can end up, paradoxically, in a totalization or *mis*representation of that subject. Obviously, there are no easy answers and our "strategies of vigilance"

61

(Spivak 1985, 8) against reproducing either masculine forms of patronization, or simplistic, ethnocentric portrayals, reside in complicating the claims to truth of representation itself.

Representation/Re-presentation

Gayatri Spivak has provided some of the most insightful retheorizations of the problematic of representation (Spivak, 1986; 1988; 1989). She returns to Marx as a first step towards unpacking the density of the term *representation*. In *The Eighteenth Brumaire of Louis Bonaparte,* Marx (1962) specified two senses of representation: *Vertretung,* or "speaking for" (as in politics), and *Darstellung,* or "making present" (as in art or philosophy). Spivak argues that for Marx, the stakes in representation are far more complicated and obtuse than they might appear in the idea of speaking for or representing the consciousness and actions of an other. This is because at one level, the level of *Vertretung,* to represent (*vertreten*) is to intervene as the bearer of another's interests. The level of *Darstellung,* however, indicates a different site of representation—that of rhetorical (and ideological) transformation in which to represent is to designate, and even predicate, the subject. Representation becomes a vexed issue given the slippage between these related but discontinuous senses of the term and the consequences of their complicitous closure around positivistic notions of presenting the "real." The import of rethinking representation in this specific sense is that it gets away from *mimetic* or "correspondence" notions of representation in aesthetics and philosophy, which have been uncritically adopted in cultural or literary criticism as well. Spivak's argument is that as a result of this hegemony of "representational realism," critics have tended to assume, naively, that representation involves the straightforward reflection or revelation of previously marginalized groups (such as women). In mimetic or realist conceptions, representation is merely theorized as "speaking of (or about)" the previously unheard subject; this leaves untouched the more troubling issue of whether that subject can—or wants—to be recovered through such an epistemic of assimilation. In other words, reality cannot be assimilated, unproblematically, into a representation that is merely descriptive, because representation also entails delegation and constitutive figuration.

In order to avoid the discursive violence implicit in such "correspondence" views of representation, Spivak recommends that feminist theory should retain an awareness of the shifting distinctions between *Vertretung/representation* and *Darstellung/re-presentation*—which work like the contrast between a proxy and a portrait. The distinction underscores the impossibility of reproducing reality totally, and this is not just because of the practical constraints on "objectivity," (although such limits also operate in our interactions with the world). Rather, this distinction constitutes an epistemological critique, which proposes a need to disavow the myths of authenticity and "real" experience that underlie accounts aspiring to present women's experience in direct, "pure" forms.

Spivak's contention is that it is not fruitful to undertake projects of representation with the hope that we will be able to let our subjects' voices or experience speak their own truth, because the description-delegation dynamic always works to complicate representation. She recommends that feminists proliferate no more accounts of the sort entitled "_____ Women Speak," where the *other* is simply a name that provides the alibi for erasing the investigator's intervention into the construction and representation of the narrative (Spivak 1986, 229). Using Marx's distinction between *Vertretung* and *Darstellung*, if feminists want to avoid being ventriloquists, they should aim to engage the latter and disavow the former. For Spivak, the problem of representation occurs in the ideological slippage between representation and re-presentation:

> [We] must note how the staging of the world of representation—its scene of writing, its *Darstellung*—dissimulates the choice of and need for "heroes," paternal proxies, agents of power—*Vertretung* (Spivak 1988, 279).

The point here is not that reality (marginal, oppressed, or otherwise) does not exist; instead, it is that we do not have access to reality outside of the effects of linguistic processes or our institutional interests (which determine our scholarly interventions). To some extent, then, the limits of representation also indicate constraints on intersubjectivity—the degree to which we can claim solidarity with the consciousness of others. Not only is it incorrect to assume that just because our intentions are good, we can occupy the same discursive space as our subjects; we would also be guilty of political irresponsibility if we elided proper consideration of the differences between our privileged positions and the circumstances of our subjects of representation. We cannot wish away the differences between ourselves (as feminist scholars and/or activists) and our audiences. Indeed sometimes these differences and gaps are insurmountable because of the barriers that language and discontinuous life experiences impose on us. As feminists, we are called upon to highlight the ways in which our interests, privilege, and circumstances determine what we represent.

These and other issues in the politics of representation are also explored by Angela McRobbie (1982). McRobbie sets out to address the most basic question guiding the commitment to feminist practice: "for whom do we do feminist research?" At one level, the answer is simply "for women"; yet, this formula effaces the care and reflexivity needed to negotiate between "talk, text and action." Again, the problem of representation takes center stage in McRobbie's scrutiny of feminist research within sociology. She traces the beginnings of feminist ethnographic work in sociology to traditions of "naturalistic" research in social anthropology, symbolic interactionism, and the variety of social history (associated with the work of E.P. Thompson, among others) concerned with writing "history from below," which attempted to bring to life the experiences of ordinary people and everyday existence, rather than adopting the focus of mainstream history on great men and great events.

McRobbie's arguments are particularly helpful to feminists with ethnographic interests, because she illustrates the theoretical concerns of representation with examples from empirical work. She points out that while it is important to articulate links between feminist research and non-academic activist work, the former is as necessary as the latter. McRobbie thus challenges critics who trivialize theoretical work as ivory-tower speculation; theory can have material impact on the lives of women (both inside and outside the academy) and is fundamental to our understanding of the mutual constitution of the world (of our subjects) and our ways of representing that world.

Of course McRobbie is also careful to underscore that intellectual politics must never be confused with the politics of feminist activism, but she says that it would be a mistake to jettison *all* disciplinary feminist work as "masculinist" or "elitist," because we cannot afford to conceive of feminist practice in such narrow or essentialist ways. The question of priorities—what is important, what needs to be done—has to be contextualized and specified with regard to the historical moment and location we inhabit.

In other words, the multiplicity of feminist practices is one of feminism's greatest strengths. The heterogeneity of women's experience and identity can only be approximated by an equivalent diversity in approach. What is crucial, according to McRobbie, is to be able to have productive exchanges among ourselves, as opposed to disputes and recriminations. It is important to communicate our differences and disagreements and regard dissent as an index of the vitality of the feminist project; the unacceptable alternatives would be either to pretend that feminism's world was seamless and untroubled, or to believe that every contending position should be equally and universally affirmed. It is worth keeping one issue straight: feminisms are not likely to be viable intellectual or political forces if they fall into academicism *or* into rampant pluralism (Rooney 1989). There is a danger, especially given the liberal-pluralist foundations of Western and, especially, U.S. culture, of simply giving in to the "anything goes" mentality, which embraces diversity for its own sake. One lesson we ought to learn from contemporary critical theory is that cultural or historical relativism is not a good basis for intellectually rigorous practice (see Mohanty 1989, for an elaboration of the varieties and flaws of relativistic thinking; and Hall 1990, on the need for arbitrary closure).

Political considerations have ethical implications. The politics of representation and of feminist practice are inextricably linked with issues of ethics. Nobody can occupy the high ground forever or shore up their position in some essential way. This would be as exclusivist and provincial as the tyranny of male privilege that feminism seeks to displace. Therefore, feminists (as much as anyone else) are required to examine the assumptions, categories, and effects of their pronouncements—both in disciplinary and epistemological terms, and also in the light of the consequences our work may (or may not) have in the lives of others. This is especially true in the case of ethnographic work *on* or *with* living subjects, namely women (see Patai 1990).

To take up the question of ethics is, perhaps, to single out "the most sensitive issue at stake [in representation]—that is, the nature of the relationship between the researcher and the researched, a relationship paralleling in its unequal power that of social worker and client, or teacher and pupil" (McRobbie 1982, 51). In highlighting the exploitive potential of the act of investigating people's lives, McRobbie echoes the sentiments of Spivak. However, Spivak's disciplinary commitments as a literary critic prompt her to overlook the special opportunities empirical work provides in dispensing with the false sense of "oneness" with all women purely on the grounds of gender, and the purely speculative cast of some theories. McRobbie, on the other hand, refers to the positive possibility of ethnographic research to represent the "surprises" of everyday life. She borrows the idea of "surprises" from Willis (1980); it refers to the capacity of living subjects to "hijack" the research and enforce a perspective that could not have been anticipated beforehand. In McRobbie's words, "[t]hese moments force the researcher into a fresh humility, into an awareness of the limitations of one form of intellectual activity and ... its absolute dependence on these 'others.' " (55)[5]

Trust is paramount in undertaking ethical representations of our subjects. The need for trust is not "mystical"; nor can it be taken as a given. In fact, as McRobbie points out, trust itself has many dimensions, and they have to be specified in order for us to be able to attend to them. As she puts it,

To begin with there is the awkwardness and even humiliation of forging a relationship with those women, girls (or men) who will provide the source material of the project. Without them and without their trust the research simply cannot proceed. More precisely there are the ways in which we censor the asking of questions which may seem important for the research, but which feel unacceptably intrusive and nosy . . . Being female undoubtedly sensitizes us to the discomforts and small humiliations which doing research can provoke. Sometimes indeed it does feel like 'holidaying on other people's misery' (McRobbie 1982, 55).

The ethico-political difficulties underlying the problem of representation are underscored if we think about the intractable power differences between us and those whom we represent in and through our practices as feminists. Here again, Spivak is instructive. She suggests that we have to "unlearn our privilege," and deconstruct our own authority as intellectuals. In this sense, feminist research (like other forms of reflexive practice) must always undertake a *deconstruction*—of its claims and accounts. I do not employ the term "deconstruction" casually, and in this usage it bears little resemblance to the grossly reductive ways in which it has been caricatured by its detractors. As I understand it, deconstruction is a form of epistemological and political accountability, and not simply the marker of a negativity—that is, a simple dismantling of something or other. Deconstruction is a means of subjecting representations to their own critique. Spivak (1989, 214) makes a powerful distinction between deconstruction and demythologizing, which are *not* synonymous. Deconstruction should be understood as persistent self-critique, not in a disabling or paralyzing mode but, rather, as a way of marking the contingency of one's subject position as well as the truth of one's claims. Spivak puts it most succinctly:

Deconstruction is not an exposure of error. Deconstruction notices how we produce "truths." Deconstruction is the move that notices that we must produce truths, that we as communicating subjects must produce meaning, that in fact there *is* always something *like* reference. Deconstruction, as we turn into a negative metaphysics, does not say that there is no meaning, there is no truth, there is no subject (1989, 214, original emphases)

Feminist representation, it seems to me, is profoundly enabled by this vision of deconstructive critique. It offers us a rigorous strategy for coming to terms with women's (or anyone else's) practices, oppression, or resistance without having to brandish experience as its own guarantee, and biology or identity as an essence. Students of communication may benefit from these ways of rethinking representation, because we too have learned to privilege discursive theories of reality that presuppose the primacy of signification, of the *active* process of making meaning, which deconstruction attempts to specify. In other words, our theories of communication have increasingly moved away from sender-receiver, "objectivist" models to "subjectivist" theories, which start from the premise that reality is socially constructed. Deconstruction provides ways of realizing the more radical imperatives of these theories by emphasizing how all representations bear "traces" of other, hidden meanings, which have their own narratives as well as their own systems of production, and so on.

Representing the Audience

So far, I have focused on interpretive difficulties. But of course we also recognize that representations are undertaken and produced with others in mind; just as cultural texts are articulated in relation to certain audiences, so our scholarly accounts are addressed to particular audiences. In the products of mass culture, audiences are by and large categorized as consumers of representations, while our own feminist practices are directed to peers within the academy and, ultimately, to the subjects of our representations—the women and men whom we wish to empower by our interventions in material and discursive struggles (see Grossberg 1988 and Smith 1988). Conceived in this way, the "audience" does not refer to the restricted category (as in "transmission" models of communication; see Carey 1975) of "receivers" to whom we are the "senders"; instead, the concept of "audience" is a philosophically and politically motivated evocation of the real human beings in our inquiries.

In this respect I depart from conventional understandings of the audience within communication and social science scholarship. In mainstream analysis, the audience is conceptualized in fairly static ways—in demographic terms and numbers (housewives who watch soaps, the "mass" audience for television, and so on). In contrast, I am concerned with examining the possibilities of a more post-structuralist rendering of the audience as the implied *other* of representation, those absent presences who both inhabit our discourses and are remade by them. Consequently, I shall not concern myself with the growing body of literature interested in examining audiences as demographic aggregates positioned by various forms of the media; although such discussions are undoubtedly important, they are not at issue here. There is also a significant amount of feminist criticism on the specificities of female audiences, readers, and spectators (see, for example, Ang 1985; Mulvey 1975; and Radway 1984).

I want to consider the term "audience" as a superordinate category. It subsumes questions of female "readership," and takes account of the constituencies of real women who have not yet entered the bourgeois discourses that authorize and constitute the very possibility of *becoming* an audience. I want, then, to appropriate the term "audience" to speak of feminism's constituency in the broadest sense—of its simultaneous *affiliations* in the worlds of criticism, readership, and representation (see Said 1983). My principal contention here is that the category "audience" must be reformulated to reflect the three categories of subjects who comprise feminism's constituents: female audiences of cultural texts, female (and male) cultural critics with feminist interests, and women who may not be feminists *or* audiences, but whose lives are also caught up in the webs of signification and representation. Recasting the concept of the audience to include the broader spectrum of women (and men) who are invoked as feminism's constituency, makes it possible to take into consideration the complex and often obscured affiliations between our scholarly productions and their links to the world.

Feminist writing with the most direct implications for communication scholars seeks to problematize the relationships between (academic) feminists and consumers of cultural forms. This has led to a fairly conservative intellectual atmosphere in which feminists (along with other nominally progressive intellectuals) have leapt to conclusions about the radical potential of mass cultural texts. The critical edge of feminism has been dulled in this spate of "recuperative" populism—in which the unreflexive assumption has been that if we, as feminists, can enjoy the pleasures of commodification and still remain feminists, then there can be no real harm for the vast majority of women who partake in popular cultural practices. In fact, so the thinking seems to go, the products of popular culture contain their own subversive potential—which merely have to be mobilized for the purposes of an oppositional politics.

Judith Williamson has criticized this tendency of contemporary leftist/feminist scholars to jump on the bandwagon of pop culture:

> It used to be an act of daring on the left to claim enjoyment of Dallas, disco-dancing, or any other piece of mass popular culture. Now it seems to require equal daring to suggest that such activities, while certainly enjoyable, are not radical ... Instead, left-wing academics are busy picking out strands of "subversion" in every piece of pop culture from Street Style to Soap Opera (Williamson 1986, 14).

Williamson is discussing the context of Thatcherite Britain, but her comments are equally relevant to circumstances in the United States. One can find many varieties of reception theory that, in the name of "interpretive communities," have sought to trace the continuities between critics and "ordinary" readers (such as Ang 1985 and Radway 1984). While feminists may have the same interests in matters of popular taste as their subjects, shared participation in particular activities does not necessarily signal the existence of a "community" or underwrite a common consciousness about feminism's goals.

Tania Modleski (1989) has also discussed problems in feminist criticism and its theorization of women audiences. In her overview of feminist analyses of romance readers, Modleski contends that the "scandal" of contemporary criticism is that it often fails to take account of contradictions in women's lives that forestall their awareness of their own subjection. These include:

> contradictions at an intrapsychic level; contradictions between conscious or unconscious fantasies and the discourses that conflict with or discredit these fantasies; and contradictions between competing ideologies and discourses as they are reflected both in popular texts and in the audience's relations to these texts. A recognition that romance readers may be self-contradictory in their attitudes and behavior does not necessarily open up the analyst to the charge of elitism . . . *especially* if we are willing to acknowledge how much we ourselves are implicated within those very structures we set out to analyze, how much our own feelings, desires, anxieties, etc., are caught up in contradiction. . . . (1989, 12).

Modleski suggests that feminist criticism must attempt to untangle the relationship between reality and representation; to understand "how performative and referential aspects of texts are interrelated" (1989, 17). That is, we need to scrutinize cultural representations to question the pleasures of the text, and also to expose how representations (even though they are not "reality") can mute women's subjectivity. To an extent, then, the enterprise of feminist criticism must be to *re-present* to our audiences the strategies by which representations (in popular culture, for example) are effective in reproducing patriarchy. Not to do so would, in Modleski's view, be to lose sight of feminism's "performative" and utopian or reconstructive dimensions.

While Modleski is right to argue that feminist criticism need not preoccupy itself with contemporary critical fashions—with practicing the most up-to-date forms of reception theory, ethnographic criticism, subcultural analysis, and so on—some of these critical developments still have a lot to offer. To be sure, some people take up the latest critical practice as they do clothing fashions, and a feminist commitment is no inoculation against such a failing. But there is also genuine concern and commitment and, above all, intellectual rigor underlying emergent interpretive work and it would be misguided to suggest that everything "new" is undertaken in bad faith. Refinements in ethnography or interpretive theory have much to teach feminists about representations and their audiences, especially if we keep in mind that knowledge is not a zero-sum game. The same insight can be put to the use of an oppositional cultural politics or it can become another trend in academic discourse and another way of enforcing disciplinary divisions.

Constructing new modes of analysis is one ingredient in being able to transcend received traditions; retaining a political vision is another. Of course, the project of formulating an oppositional academic culture is very difficult, given both the reactionary temper of our times and our own institutional positioning. We need to keep in mind that, as Western academics, our representational politics do not *guarantee* anything, because the locations from which we speak are crucially implicated in all sorts of systems of domination and subordination around the world—as part of the military-industrial-academic complex (see, for instance, Said 1983, for more on this subject).

Certainly, feminists have not always paid enough attention to issues of institutional context, their own orthodoxies, or the effects of their practices on particular audiences. Recent discussions by feminists have attempted to correct these absences. For one, they have tried to revise overly narrow conceptions of feminist practice (Rooney, 1989), as well as to recognize that we have often overlooked the ways in which mainstream, Western feminisms can become complicit with the institutional imperatives of masculism and imperialism (Mohanty 1984, Lugones and Spelman 1983, Spivak 1989).

These questions are of overwhelming importance, and deserve scrupulous consideration on their own. We cannot, in the name of "Third World" feminism, or "minority" issues, or some other label, continue to allow them to be tokenized or marginalized within our own practices. That is, minoritarian concerns must not be reduced to "special interest" issues, *outside* the central interests of feminist inquiry. Just as feminism has criticized the operations of patriarchy in marginalizing the interests and voices of half the population, so too must mainstream Western feminists come to grips with their own exclusionary practices—and not be satisfied with a token flourish in the direction of the majority of the world's women. In this, as in most other matters, the vexing question of interests must be raised: representations *for* whom? *by* whom? for what *purpose?*

I would argue that, in fact, the projects of scholars engaged in theorizing issues of race, class, and resistance to imperialism, represent the most

70

sophisticated and rigorous discussions in contemporary feminist and critical work. Because it would take rather more time than I have here to summarize all the theoretical and epistemological insights developed in the wide-ranging focus of these projects, I shall simply point to a few of the debates on representation as they have been taken up within post-colonial scholarship[6]—that is, intellectual inquiry geared to investigating the discursive and material sites of previously colonized territories.

Colonial Representations and Post-Colonial Subjects

> Colonialism is, among other things, *the perfect expression of the violence of the gaze,* and not only in the metaphorical sense of the term. Colonialism imposes upon the colonized society the everpresence and omnipotence of a gaze to which everything must be transparent. *The exercise of power, especially when the latter is arbitrary, cannot permit the maintenance of shadowy zones; it considers them equivalent to resistance.* (Malek Alloula 1986, 131; original emphases)

This section of the discussion centers on the theoretical challenges to mimetic theories of representation proposed by post-structuralist and post-colonial critics. Among the most important arguments offered from these quarters is the insistence on the need to shift debates on representation from the terrain of truth or transparency to a consideration of "regimes" of representation; that is, to a specification of the machineries and discourses that constitute both the possibility of representing an "other" and the criteria by which such representations function in the field of knowledge.

For the sake of convenience (and while sacrificing many of its complexities), let me define colonial discourse as the tropes and strategies by means of which the material and discursive agenda of colonialism is instituted and maintained. It is important to remember that this agenda did not become defunct with the official decolonization of subject countries and peoples; consequently, part of the enterprise of post-colonial scholars is to understand how history has marked the present.

Such a preoccupation with epistemological and ontological issues stems in part from the recognition that all forms of knowledge are shot through and through with operations of power (Foucault 1980). Colonial representations provide examples, *par excellence,* of the power-knowledge nexus, because they are predicated on a transparent and mimetic ideology of representation, or what Alloula refers to as "the perfect expression of the violence of the gaze." For colonial discourse functions, among other things, by eliminating any ambiguity; any instability in its attempt to fix

71

representation in a system of binary logic (us/them, black/white, colonizer/colonized) amounts to a "resistance" against the logic of domination. Post-colonial critiques of representation, then, are increasingly concerned about the paradoxical ways in which this system of oppositions risks being reproduced in the very attempt to dismantle its oppressive logic. Consequently, these critiques argue that the stakes in representation are far more complex and contradictory than is permitted by the simple strategy of inverting dichotomies (good/bad, male/female, black/white). Instead, the question of representation is posited as a radically problematic one, where the enterprise of reconstructing images is theorized in terms of taking account of the ambivalence and doubleness marking all forms of talking about reality.

Nancy Hartsock (1987, 191) has written about the continuities between colonized people and women in patriarchy. For the present purposes, I want to maintain a distinction between the two because it seems to me that while there are obvious parallels, continuities and, indeed, collusions between colonization and patriarchy, critics of colonial discourse need to make analytic separations between, on the one hand, the project of patriarchy (and its ramifications); and, on the other, the enterprises of colonialism. Conflating the two categories makes it difficult to retain the specificity of colonial discourses as historical and political constructions with their own machineries of material and figurative oppression. The need for maintaining a separation between the experience of women and the experience of being colonized is made all the more necessary if one considers the historical particulars of gender and race hierarchies. The condition of colonized women, for instance, was radically discontinuous from that of colonial (white) women and, in fact, the subordination of colonized women *and men* was enforced not only by colonial "masters" but also, and unfortunately, by the "mistresses" (see Alloula 1986 and Ganguly 1988). In colonial discourses, then, the complicity of colonial men and women makes questions of racial subordination quite distinct from, and unassimilable to, an analysis of patriarchy (see also Parmar 1983, on the need to distinguish between the institutions of patriarchy-in-general and colonialism).

It is, however, possible to make strategic connections between the experiences of the "subjects" of colonialism and those of racism in the First World; that is, to forge intellectual and political alliances between subjects who have been positioned variously within the matrix of racial and cultural difference.[7] In practice, the negotiation of such an alliance is a difficult proposition, because even though critics want to conceptualize shared forms of subjection, they also have to avoid positing essentialized conceptions of identity, experience, and/or victimhood. In this regard, the critical work of Said (1979; 1983) has been tremendously energizing to post-colonial scholars of every persuasion.

Said's *Orientalism* remains the authoritative text here. In that work, Said was concerned with providing an intellectual and cultural history of the relationships between Europe and Asia, and with tracing the overlapping and mutually constitutive discourses of representation, power, and knowledge. Orientalism, in this usage, refers to the discursive apparatus by means of which the Orient is actively produced, fixed, and objectified in Western imagery and imaginations. The problem is not simply of *theoretical* violence, because the authority of Orientalism depends on, and is reinforced by the ideologies and practices of imperialism and colonialism. Nor is Orientalism only of interest as a historical anomaly, operative during the heyday of colonialism and left behind since. Rather, Said's most powerful achievement was to demonstrate how Orientalist modes of thinking continue in contemporary intellectual and political practice.

The critique of Orientalism has been very influential in opening up a whole series of discussions and reconsiderations of the ways in which disciplines and institutions produce knowledge. The scale of this essay permits only brief references to a few feminist interpretations of colonial discourse offered by post-structuralist and post-colonial critics.

Broadly speaking, the revisionist project of post-colonial criticism has a dual purpose: to deconstruct the epistemic and ideological hegemony of colonial representations; and to represent the submerged refusals and resistances of the subjects of colonialism against their oppressors, the "shadowy zones" of Alloula's (1986) description. These two dimensions of critique, taken either singly or jointly, are not merely *reactive* in their approach and politics but, rather, signal entirely new ways of understanding and interpreting forms of representation and their discursive effects. In this context, again, deconstruction is not to be taken either as nihilistic finger-pointing *or* as the "authentic" representation of the subjectivity of the colonized. It is the much more positive (Derridean) problematic of *grammatology*—which specifies the traces and silences, in any discourse, of the presence of an Other.

Alloula's task in *The Colonial Harem*, (from which the quote at the beginning of this section is taken) is precisely to undertake such a transformation. He conducts a reading of colonial picture postcards of Algerian women under French rule, which circulated between 1900 and 1930. He challenges the constitutive power of colonial discourses by exposing the exoticization and trivialization of "native" women in imperialist representations. His study lays bare the colonizers' obsessive preoccupation with the body of the veiled Eastern woman and, in so confronting the gaze of the oppressor, he attempts "to return this immense postcard to its sender" (5). Alloula's reading of the colonial postcards is successful not only because of his exposure of the voyeuristic and fetishistic nature of the colonial gaze (a theme discussed by other, psychoanalytic, critics as well), but also because it is an intervention into contemporary global politics in which photography and spectatorship continue to be complicit technologies and machineries of domination and subordination. Alloula's book is of special value to feminist communications scholars interested in approaching issues of representation through visual media.

The post-colonial critique has mainly developed in literary criticism and in the writing of new forms of fiction (Salman Rushdie, Nuruddin Farah, Tayib Salih, and so on). While literary critics are obviously preoccupied by textual considerations, their theoretical and methodological strategies have a lot to offer those of us who want to engage in reconstructive feminist work that examines the post-colonial predicament from the perspective of material realities and cultural practices (including mass-media texts, performative rituals, and communication patterns).

In fact, of course, feminisms have been vigorous in refusing disciplinary divisions and boundaries, because the practices of feminism seek to refigure disciplines and their objects, as well as to make boundaries permeable. It should not come as a surprise, then, to find feminist theorists in the forefront in theorizing the post-colonial predicament, its connections to the past, and its goals for the future of its subjects.

The most provocative and instructive directions in this area have come, again, from Spivak. In her essay entitled, "Can the Subaltern speak?" Spivak raises the subject of the "subaltern" woman in history, whose "voice-consciousness" has been lost—to the ravages of historical processes and to the ideological suppression of her subjectivity. The term "subaltern" refers to the dominated in history, and is taken from Gramsci's discussion of the great mass of people who are ruled by "elites." The specific subaltern in Spivak's discussion is the *sati*, the Hindu widow burned at the funeral pyre of her dead husband. To deconstruct that voice for the purposes of a counter-hegemonic epistemology, the post-colonial scholar needs to avoid the absolute textualization or literalization of the subject—a tendency that may result from reading the *sati*'s voice in the gross transmutations of her name or descriptions of her burning in colonial accounts. In addition, we must refuse to interpret the *sati* by fetishizing either concrete experience or complete victimization, because the former leads to an essentialism and the latter to a benevolent recuperation of the colonialist agenda: "white men saving brown women from brown men." Instead, the deconstructively motivated project must engage the complex production of the *narrative* of *sati,* in which the subaltern woman is an integral, but not isolated, figure in resisting the discourses of patriarchy and colonial authority.[8]

74

Finally, let me mention the psychoanalytic criticism of Homi Bhabha (1984; 1986). Bhabha proposes a syncretic theory of language and subjectivity in which power and knowledge are seen to be operating ambivalently—through the colonizer as well as the colonized—resulting in a dispersed and potentially subversive set of "hybrid" psychic and social relations. On this reading as well, representation is an inherently unstable issue, because from the moment of its "enunciation"—that is, its evocation in the signifying process—the subject is displaced and fails to be fixed by the gaze of the colonizer or in textual discourses. To some extent, Bhabha's reliance on Lacanian categories of the Symbolic and the Imaginary makes it difficult to appropriate his work in a materialist analysis of cultural forms, but it does point to possibilities for taking account of the contradictory operations of power, which allow subalterns to manipulate and subvert institutions of domination to their own ends.

The openings provided by current developments in theories of representation, within literary criticism, anthropology, and sociology, are full of promise and possibility for feminist students of communication. However, we must proceed with the caution, for the promise is not one of indiscriminate eclecticism; nor is the issue merely that of channelling the languages of other disciplines and approaches into the vessel of our own pristine, and unsullied field. If communication is untroubled by the conflicts and debates that have marked other arenas of cultural representation, this is because of the field's reification of "objective" knowledge, rather than the sophistication or rigor of its theories and practices. It is time to rethink representation in the light of a politics of accountability, and through situated forms of theory and practice. The problem of representation is also a problem of vision, so I close with a series of questions from Haraway (1988, 587), of special significance to feminist communications scholars:

> How to see? Where to see from? What limits to vision? What to see for? Whom to see with? Who gets to have more than one point of view? Who gets blinded? Who wears blinders? Who interprets the visual field? What other sensory powers do we wish to cultivate besides vision?

There are no easy resolutions of these conundrums, but taking off our "blinders" is the first step towards formulating the questions for ourselves.

Notes

I should like to thank Julian Halliday for his comments and suggestions. I am immensely indebted to Carol Stabile, without whose assistance this paper would not have come into being.

1.   The term "problematic" is much overused in contemporary critical discourse. Here I am using it quite specifically, in the sense that Richard Johnson (1979) uses it, to indicate a definite theoretical structure. A "problematic" can be thought of as a "field of concepts, which organizes a particular science or individual text by making it possible to ask some kinds of questions and by suppressing others" (Johnson 1979, 201).

2.   From my perspective, it is not very productive to think of feminist practice either in exclusive terms, as the domain of women, or in paradigmatic ways, as a canon of a few feminists. For an alternative view on the former position, see Lorde (1981).

3.   It should be noted that the arguments under consideration here derive their inspiration from the work of such (male) figures as Jacques Derrida (1976), Michel Foucault (1979; 1980), Antonio Gramsci (1971), and Karl Marx (1852).

4.   To undertake a theoretical elaboration of representational politics is already to take sides in the debates concerning questions of representation and the status of theory. In some varieties of feminist thinking, the politics of representation are taken for granted as unproblematic, or dismissed as tendentious theoreticism. My own propositions are based on a refusal of the theory-practice binarism on the grounds that theory is itself a material intervention.

5.   Feminists with ethnographic interests will undoubtedly find it useful to refer to recent debates in anthropological theory. See, for instance, Clifford (1988); Moore (1988); Strathern (1987); and Trinh (1989).

6.   Readers interested in pursuing the general topic of "minority" discourse, may find it useful to look at JanMohamed and Lloyd (1987).

7.   The writings of Afro-American feminists and other "women of color" have been very influential in rethinking feminist theory and practice. *See* bell hooks (1981); and Cherrie Moraga and Gloria Anzaldua (1981).

8.   For a different reading of *sati* see Lata Mani (1987).

References

Alloula, Malek. 1986. *The Colonial Harem.* trans. Myrna Godzich and Wlad Godzich. Minneapolis: University of Minnesota Press.

Ang, Ien. 1985. *Watching Dallas: Soap Opera and the Melodramatic Imagination.* trans. Della Cooling. London and New York: Methuen.

Bhabha, Homi K. 1984. "Of Mimicry and Man: The Ambivalence of Colonial Discourse." *October.* 28(Spring): 125–134.

——1986. "The Other Question: Difference, Discrimination and the Discourse of Colonialism." In *Literature, Politics, Theory,* eds. Francis Barker, *et al.* London and New York: Methuen.

Carey, James W. 1975. "A Cultural Approach to Communication." *Communication.* 2: 1–22.

Clifford, James. 1988. *The Predicament of Culture: Twentieth-Century Ethnography, Literature, and Art.* Cambridge: Harvard University Press.

Derrida, Jacques. 1976. *Of Grammatology.* trans. Gayatri Chakravorty Spivak. Baltimore: Johns Hopkins University Press.

Foucault, Michel. 1979. *Discipline and Punish: The Birth of the Prison.* trans. Alan Sheridan. New York: Vintage Books.

———1980. *Power/Knowledge: Selected Interviews and Other Writings, 1972–1977.* ed. Colin Gordon. New York: Pantheon Books.

Ganguly, Keya. 1988. "The 'Other' Woman in *A Passage to India:* Film as Colonialist Discourse." *Women and Language.* 11(2): 11–14.

Gramsci, Antonio. 1971. *Selections from the Prison Notebooks.* eds. and trans. Quintin Hoare and Geoffrey Nowell Smith. New York: International Publishers.

Grossberg, Lawrence. 1988. "Wandering Audiences, Nomadic Critics." *Cultural Studies.* 2(3): 377–391.

Hall, Stuart. 1990. "Cultural Studies and its Theoretical Legacies." Paper presented at the University of Illinois, Urbana-Champaign (April).

Haraway, Donna. 1985. "A Manifesto for Cyborgs: Science, Technology and Socialist Feminism in the 1980s." *Socialist Review.* 80: 65–107.

———1988. "Situated Knowledges: The Science Question in Feminism and the Privilege of Partial Perspective." *Feminist Studies.* 14(3): 575–599.

Hartsock, Nancy. 1987. "Rethinking Modernism: Minority vs. Majority Theories." *Cultural Critique.* 7(Fall/Winter): 187–206.

hooks, bell. 1981. *Ain't I a Woman? Black Women and Feminism.* Boston: South End Press.

JanMohamed, Abdul and David Lloyd, eds. 1987. "The Nature and Context of Minority Discourse." *Cultural Critique.* 6/7(Spring, Fall/Winter): 5–12 and 5–17.

Johnson, Richard. 1979. "Three Problematics: Elements of a Theory of Working-Class Culture." In *Working Class Culture,* ed. John Clark, *et al.* London: Hutchinson.

Lorde, Audre. 1981. "The Master's Tools Will Never Dismantle the Master's House." In *This Bridge Called My Back: Writings by Radical Women of Color,* eds. Cherrie Moraga and Gloria Anzaldua. Watertown MA: Persephone Press.

Lugones, Maria C. and Elizabeth V. Spelman. 1983. "Have We Got a Theory For You! Feminist Theory, Cultural Imperialism and the Demand for 'The Woman's Voice.' " *Women's Studies International Forum.* 6(6): 573–581.

Mani, Lata. 1987. "The Construction of Women as Tradition in Early Nineteenth-Century Bengal." *Cultural Critique.* 7: 119–156.

Marx, Karl. [1852] 1962. "The Eighteenth-Brumaire of Louis Bonaparte." In *Selected Works,* eds. Karl Marx and Friedrich Engels. Moscow (reprinted). edited by Robert C. Tucker.

McRobbie, Angela. 1982. "The Politics of Feminist Research: Between Talk, Text and Action." *Feminist Review*. 12: 46–57.

Modleski, Tania. 1989. "Some Functions of Feminist Criticism, or The Scandal of the Mute Body." *October*. 49: 3–24.

Mohanty, S.P. 1989. "Us and Them: On the Philosophical Bases of Political Criticism." *Yale Journal of Criticism*. 2(2): 1–31.

Mohanty, Chandra Talpade. 1984. "Under Western Eyes: Feminist Scholarship and Colonial Discourses." *Feminist Review*. 30: 61–88.

Moore, Henrietta. 1988. *Feminism and Anthropology*. Minneapolis: University of Minnesota Press.

Moraga, Cherrie and Gloria Anzaldua, eds. 1981. *This Bridge Called My Back: Writings by Radical Women of Color*. Watertown: Persephone Press.

Mulvey, Laura. 1975. "Visual Pleasure and Narrative Cinema." *Screen*. 16(3): 6–18.

Parmar, Pratibha. 1983. "Asian Women in Resistance." In *The Empire Strikes Back*, eds. Stuart Hall, *et al.* London: Hutchinson.

Patai, Daphne. 1990. "U.S. Academics and Third World Women: Is Ethical Research Possible?" In *Women's Words: Oral History and Feminist Methodology*, eds. Sherna Gluck and Daphne Patai. New York: Routledge.

Radway, Janice. 1984. *Reading the Romance: Women, Patriarchy, and Popular Literature*. Chapel Hill: Univ. of North Carolina Press.

Rooney, Ellen. 1989. *Seductive Reasoning: Pluralism as the Problematic of Contemporary Literary Theory*. Ithaca: Cornell University Press.

Said, Edward W. 1979. *Orientalism*. London: Vintage Books.

———1983. "Opponents, Audiences, Constituencies and Community." In *The Anti-Aesthetic: Essays on Postmodern Culture*, ed. Hal Foster. Port Townsend WA: Bay Press.

Smith, Paul. 1988. *Discerning the Subject*. Minneapolis: University of Minnesota Press.

Spivak, Gayatri Chakravorty. 1985. "Strategies of Vigilance: An Interview with Gayatri Chakravorty Spivak" (with Angela McRobbie). *Block*. 10: 5–9.

———1986. "Imperialism and Sexual Difference." *Oxford Literary Review*. 8(1–2): 225–240.

———1988. "Can the Subaltern Speak?" In *Marxism and the Interpretation of Culture*, eds. Cary Nelson and Lawrence Grossberg. Urbana: University of Illinois Press.

———1989. "A Response to 'The Difference Within: Feminism and Critical Theory.'" In *The Difference Within: Feminism and Critical Theory*, eds. Elizabeth Meese and Alice Parker. Amsterdam/Philadelphia: John Benjamin's Publishing Company.

Strathern, Marilyn. 1987. "An Awkward Relationship: The Case of Feminism and Anthropology." *Signs.* 12(2): 276–292.

Trinh, T. Minh-ha. 1989. *Woman, Native, Other: Writing Postcoloniality and Feminism.* Bloomington: University of Indiana Press.

Williamson, Judith, 1986. "The Problems of Being Popular." *New Socialist.* (September), 14–15.

Willis, Paul. 1980. "Notes on Method." In *Culture, Media, Language,* eds. Stuart Hall, *et al.* London: Hutchinson.

Part 2

Beyond the Field's Boundaries

Traditional divisions of inquiry in the field of communication can make issues of gender and race invisible or insignificant. By starting with women's experiences and meanings, new categories and new topics of inquiry are brought into focus. Although women's experiences and meanings are not uncontaminated and acultural, they nonetheless point to contradictions or faults in ideology that make it possible to identify points of women's resistance and possible alternatives. These chapters point to some of the areas of inquiry that should be considered important for the field.

5

Theorizing through the Body

Elspeth Probyn

Perhaps we need a moratorium on saying "the body." When I write "the body," I see nothing in particular. To write "my body" plunges me into lived experience, particularity . . .
(Adrienne Rich 1987, 215).

Of all the concepts and keywords within feminist theory, "the body" is perhaps the most widely used and the most difficult to pin down. As a recurring term, it is often taken as a ground, as a basis from which to start, rather than overtly theorized as a concept. However, it is certainly through feminism that the body has, over the years, entered into critical theory. Once despised as being too close, too unscientific, and too feminine, the concept of the body has been slowly accepted by mainstream social scientists. Indeed, the body has been accorded its own sociology, although its status is questioned (Berthelot 1986). One line of thought states that the body offers a veracity not offered by other concepts. According to Arthur Frank, "the enduring belief that the body can provide us with a grounded truth suggests why interest in it should flourish within cultural modernity" (1990, 132). However, within feminism the accent is increasingly on the multiple "truths" that the body and bodies disclose. Important differences exist between what I feel at the level of my body and what she might. As a scientific entity, the body, our bodies, is continually being written upon and inscribed with other's knowledges. From the hospital room to the witness box, from breast-feeding mothers to unhappy surrogates, from the pleasures of fashion to being raped on the streets or beaten at home—these are all bodies inscribed by legal, medical and scientific knowledges; they are also lived in pain, fear, and sometimes pleasure. The question is what to do with them, with ourselves, and how to recognize these bodily facts in our theorizing. We need to turn the body towards other questions; to articulate what Jane Gallop calls "the necessarily double and . . . urgent questions of feminism: 'not merely who am I? But who is the other woman?' " (1988, 177). While I cannot possibly cover all the feminist uses of the body, in this chapter I will raise some of the key ways in which the body has been, and can be, used, by considering it as a theoretical construct, and by beginning to think through what it means to do theory starting from the lived. Thus, we will see both the limitations of the body as well as its *positivity*—the different claims to knowledges produced in theoretical uses of the body. I will then suggest ways in which the body as a concept may be of use within feminist cultural analysis and how we can put ourselves and our experiences of our bodies to work within theory.[1]

The Appeal of the Body

The body is a very evident starting point in feminist theory and practice. Quite simply, we all have one, and, as women, have been variously made to feel them in culturally specified ways. The body is often seen as "point zero"; as Adrienne Rich writes: "Begin ... not with a continent or a country or a house, but with the geography closest in—the body" (1987, 212). Mariana Valverde reminds us that, "Long before any conscious thoughts of sex cross our minds, we all have a sense of our physical, bodily identity. Even as children we develop a sense of how we feel as a human body and how we appear to others" (1985, 29). Valverde raises here the articulation of ourselves and others that happens at the point of the body. We certainly experience our own bodies, yet to what extent is that experience shaped by other bodies, and other images of the female body? Living within the dominant Western culture, women and men are used to seeing women's bodies separated from themselves. Indeed, we are accustomed to seeing bits of women's bodies—a leg on this billboard, a headless torso on another, a pair of lips blindly looking out from the magazine page. The political activity of reclaiming these fragments has been crucial within feminism. As the title of the early Boston Women's Health Collective handbook demonstrates, women need to own *Our Bodies, Ourselves* (1976).

In *Female Desires: How They Are Sought, Bought and Packaged*, Rosalind Coward argues that "the dice are loaded against women liking themselves in this society" (1985, 46). As any female reader of women's fashion magazines knows all too well, women are bombarded with advice on how to change themselves. Of course, the idea of change implies that there is a standard, or even an ideal, which we can strive to attain. Over the years, this "norm" has itself been changed by socio-cultural factors, one of which is feminism itself. Thus, models now are required to look healthy, muscled and not too thin. The fad diets of the seventies are now replaced by "sensible" eating advice and a panoply of workouts. In her study of exercise videos, Margaret Morse argues that now: "exercise can be added to the applications of makeup and clothing and to the body-molding regimes of corseting, diet, and surgical intervention (including plastic surgery and liposuction) as means of achieving femininity" (1987–88, 24).

Not surprisingly, this shift in the public shape of femininity has not lessened the conflicting admonitions addressed to women. A recent cover of *Glamour* combines the following headlines: "Do you think about sex too much?"; "legs! short skirt confidence"; "quick and sexy beauty dares"; "best fall looks"; and, "college shocker: 1 in 7 is raped" (September, 1990). Even here, in a sort of post-feminist mode which celebrates sex and fashion, certain contradictions can be seen. The most pervasive of these is that old conundrum: women are invited, or told, to form their bodies in order to attract (men's) attention—to *dare* to be sexy—although an all too frequent accompanying reality is the brutal fact of rape. This stark reality also faces women who dress to attract other women, or simply to feel good in themselves. As the issue of *Glamour* shows in its juxtaposition of beauty hints ("the seduction of bare skin for daytime dare") and its report on college rape on the next page, the articulation of fashion and violence is dauntingly problematic. On the one hand, even after the years of feminist arguments, socio-juridico discourses still insist that women (and especially women who are neither white nor middle-class) invite rape because of their appearance. On the other hand, if we argue (as did an older feminist line) that women should not dress-up or use makeup, we then play into a vision of society where women, through fear of the consequences, must wear a certain uniform. Moreover, a logic which states that women are interested in style only to grab a man, seems to me to smack of a certain misogyny. As Inge Blackman and Kathryn Perry argue in their article on lesbian fashion, the feminist line of the 1960s and 1970s that "celebrated the 'real' woman beneath her makeup and aimed to set her free from the confines of tight skirts and high heels" (1990, 67) no longer holds. "Lipstick" lesbians or post-post punk women are out to show that you can be feminist and also with it.

In a more mainstream vein, trendy fashion magazines, like *Elle*, are increasingly giving the sort of "politicized" advice formally only found in feminist publications as they flaunt the latest gear. Being able to play with fashion without being accused of "false consciousness" or of betraying the cause, is potentially positive. For one thing, we want to encourage what Rosi Braidotti calls "discursive generations" of feminists, and recognize that "each generation must reckon with its own problematics" (1989, 91). And one of these problematics for me as well as for younger women I know is how to combine the fun of fashion with the struggle to stop the increasing violence against women. As Blackman and Perry ask, "How do we assess that fluidity (of styles and identities) politically?" (1990, 77). We need to question how far playing with style can go before it becomes yet another way of conforming to the dominant ideology of women as objects. We need to ask how we can use our bodies, dressed up or down, to politically act against rape and violence. We need to remember that dangerous contradictions abound and that they are played out in vicious ways upon bodies, on the streets, in clubs, and especially at home. As Coward says of the enduring dominant discourse on women, we still need to recognize "the strictness of this cultural ideal, we need to understand the meanings and values attached to this shape. We also need to understand the mechanisms that engage women in a discourse so problematic for us; and we need to know how women actually perceive themselves" (1985, 40).

In contrast to the murky issue of fashion, one of the seemingly most straightforward examples of women conforming to the strict ideal of Western beauty can be seen in the image of the anorexic. Anorexia nervosa is, of course, a serious illness; in fact, it is one of the few psychiatric disorders that can result in death. However, the anorexic is often taken as a metaphor of our times. She is rendered as a handy illustration of whatever is going wrong at the moment. In *The Body and Society,* Bryan Turner argues that "if hysteria in the pre-modern period was an illness of scarcity . . . anorexia in the twentieth century is an illness of abundance" (1984, 83). In his rather too easy analogy, Turner misses some important points. In modern medical history, anorexia was first "discovered" or named in the 1870s by an English physician, Gull, and simultaneously by a French one, Dr. Laseque. The latter called it "anorexie hysterique" connecting it quite clearly with what Michel Foucault calls the "hysterization" of the female body (1980; 1973). Put quite simply, hysteria comes from the old French word "hystera," the womb. Thus, this term came to be used metaphorically to describe any "female" ailment. This mysterious womb could be blamed for all sorts of things, then allowing for concrete remedies and/or punishments. This movement from the unknown (the womb as unknowable for nineteenth-century male doctors) to the named, can be seen as the translation of "the human body into a finite set of signs called 'symptoms' " which then allows for "a set of prescriptions that impinge once more upon the 'real' human body" (Paula Treichler 1987, 70). In contrast to Turner's sweeping generalizations, the feminist critic immediately wants to ask why societal discourses come to be written almost exclusively on female bodies or on those considered "other," notably the bodies of gay men and men of color.

Anorexia is doubly intriguing: we can literally see societal dictates about thinness and achievement written upon the anorexic's skeletal body at the same time that anorexics lucidly tell us that they are in control. Thus, it is not surprising that in trying to understand the ways in which women engage in the discourse of the body beautiful, many feminists have analyzed the case of anorexia. However, the prevailing explanations of anorexia are divided: on the one hand, the anorexic is seen as conforming strictly to the representations of ideal bodies, and on the other, she epitomizes a struggle against this ideology. One of the early researchers in anorexia, Hilda Bruch, states that she:

> is inclined to relate anorexia to the enormous emphasis that Fashion places on slimness . . . magazines and movies carry the same message, but the most persistent is television, drumming it in, day in day out, that one can be loved and respected only when slender (1978, viii).

Here the anorexic is depicted as a sort of screen or surface that both reflects and absorbs media messages. On the other hand, Susie Orbach, the author of the classic *Fat is a Feminist Issue* (1979), argues in her more recent book, *Hunger Strike: The Anorectic's Struggle as a Metaphor for Our Age,* that anorexia can be seen as a strategy that opposes the dictates of patriarchy. Here the anorexic emerges as less passive than in Bruch's account. As Orbach states: "The individual woman's problem—for which anorexia has been the solution—is that despite a socialization process designed to suppress her needs, she has continued to feel her own needs and desires intensely" (1986, 19). As Valverde more candidly puts it: "after I had got rid of each and every one of my fat cells, I began to get off on not eating, to enjoy starvation as an end in itself" (1985, 33). In my own experience, I developed anorexia along with an obsession with physical exercise; starving along with cross-country running provided an intense and almost deadly form of competition with myself—a runner's "high" with an edge.

While both Bruch's and Orbach's takes on anorexia are important, they also indicate some of the limitations of the body as a heuristic device. In other words, in using the anorexic's body to posit certain ways in which society may be said to be working, other assumptions tend to creep in. Thus, underlying the argument that represents the anorexic as succumbing to media representations, we hear an old dictate about the passivity of women in culture. Put another way, why is it that women are portrayed as "addicted" to soap operas while no one questions the amount of time and energy that men invest in watching sports on television? While Orbach rightfully raises the ways in which anorexia is also a potentially empowering (if limited) strategy for women, she doesn't fully explore the fact that the majority of anorexics are white and middle-class. These uses of the anorexic body tend to belie a very static understanding of the body. In some ways, they are caught up in the popular and mainstream depictions of anorexia as a modern phenomenon. In other words, the image of the anorexic is taken as directly expressive of a general truth of the moment. However, as I have argued elsewhere (Probyn, 1987), white anorexic women can be found at various points in history. Moreover, if, as Angela Carter argues, "flesh comes to us out of history; so does the repression and taboo that governs our experience of flesh" (in Coward 1985, 248), we need to ask why the historical gendered experiences of women of color generally have not led them to use anorexia as a means of voicing their discontent against the differing ways in which they are positioned in patriarchal society. If we must use the female body as a heuristic, then we must insist upon the differences (of race, sexuality, age, etc.) of these bodies.

Differentiating Bodies

Indeed, one of the major problems in using the body as a privileged, central term within feminism is that, if unchecked, this use can slide into a form of essentialism. In other words, it can all too easily be seen as a common element that all women equally experience in the same way. That women do share some biological characteristics (but probably fewer than is commonly believed) cannot be used to underpin the ideology of a mythic Everywoman. We need always to ask, therefore, *whose* body, and in relation to what other bodies and structures of power and inequality. Of course, seen in opposition to men's bodies, women's bodies obviously do somewhat resemble each other. This constructed binarism is then naturalized in many ways, not the least of which is in the expression "the opposite sex." As Coward argues: "We live in a culture which offers the body of the opposite sex as the reward at the heart of the incitement to make sexual relations" (1985, 227). Far from seeing this opposition as natural, or inevitable, Coward argues that the radical unconnectedness of male and female bodies reveals "a sort of failure of the will at the heart of heterosexual desire" (1985, 230). Thus, if we step outside of this binary logic, automatic connections based on biological or anatomical resemblance are harder to maintain. If we move away from the ideology of men's and women's bodies being different, yet made for each other, we can begin to deconstruct "woman" as a unitary category. Quite simply, the multiplicity of women's carnal and corporeal pleasures should instruct us to the fact that the fixity of "woman" is essentially boring and heterosexist.

The problem is that the idea of a unifying body (we are all women) was and continues to be a seductive platform within certain feminisms. Virginia Woolf's statement, "as a woman I have no country, my country is the whole world" became an effective slogan because it appealed to women at a very fundamental level. It heralded an articulation of womanhood, a solidarity of issues that could be politically put forward and addressed. The premise of that unity was, to a large extent, grounded in the oppression of women's bodies, as well as their potential biological capacity to give birth and in their historical bodily function as nurturers. Thus, the female body served a double role: it was the site of women's supposedly shared oppression and served to catalyze anger; and it was a cause for celebration—the uniqueness of half of the population.[2] The body here is replaced by anatomy; as Meaghan Morris has argued of this type of discourse, the logic here is "based on a biological determinism; the difference between males and females is clear, absolute, and initially anatomical . . ." (1988, 47). In part because of its simplicity and in part because of its attention to real resentments or pleasures, this discourse of unity through the femaleness of our bodies can be very rhetorically satisfying. Mary Daly, for instance, inspires and draws women together against a common enemy. As Elizabeth Spelman states: "According to Daly, then, it is through our shared sexual identity that we are oppressed together; it is through our shared sexual identity that we shall be liberated together" (1990, 124). However, as Spelman argues, the centrality of a shared sexual oppression in Daly's discourse is extremely problematic: "this view not only ignores the role women play in racism and classism, but it seems to deny the positive aspects of racial identities." This is, then, "racism pure and simple" (Spelman 1990, 124). Thus while the figure of the body representing women's commonality has a strong rhetorical appeal and participating in an imagined community of Woman may even feel good, we can't forget that this Body casts shadows over women who for concrete geopolitical and cultural reasons cannot or do not want to join into its chorus.

There is, however, slow movement away from a North American feminism based in a supposed "essence" of (white) Woman. The more recent writings of Adrienne Rich have helped to propel this move. In turning her gaze upon herself and her body, she showed that it was possible to be specific about where you came from without being color-blind to the very different experiences of others. In working "towards a politics of location," she starts with her birth in the white section of a hospital: "I was located by color and sex just as surely as a black child was located by color and sex—though the implications of white identity were mystified by the presumption that white people are the center of the universe" (1987, 215). Spelman sees in Rich's specificity of her embodiment in the world a movement towards recognizing the quite different embodiments of women of color. Spelman's important argument also raises the ways in which many feminisms have been afraid to really come to grips with actual bodies. As she says, "somatophobia," "disdain for the body historically has been symptomatic of sexist and racist (as well as classist) attitudes" (1990, 127). In some situations, feminist trepidations about the intimacies of the body come close to homophobia as straight women are seemingly unable to imagine (like Queen Victoria) what women can do pleasurably with other women's bodies. In order to avoid an essentialism of a pure and disembodied feminism, we have to be able to think about the body on several levels, all at once.

This project requires that feminists work to articulate several analytical levels: the experiences of bodies, the potential overdetermination of those experiences, and the ways in which gendering forms our bodies as well as the ways in which bodies are expressed in configurations of sexual preference, ethnicity, race, and age. We also need to think about the conventions and codes of representations and their work in constructing subjectivities. Researching the body may involve several methodologies: semiotic analysis in order to grasp the construction of the body as a sign and trace its meanings; it may require ethnographies and interviewing women about how they feel about their bodies; it can even include theorizing our autobiographies in order to present and contrast experiences.

While Rich's interventions are crucial, we can further extend them with an exploration of the multiple facets of the differentiated body. In thinking through the relation of difference and the body and the gendered experience of the body, I want to now draw on work done by Michele Barrett and Teresa de Lauretis. As Barrett argues in "The Concept of Difference," the many uses of "difference" have become quite confusing, a sort of shorthand for different theories within different feminist debates. As she stresses, "there are not merely *differences* between these various ways in which the concept has been deployed; there are disagreements and outright contradictions" (1987, 39). She identifies three categories of difference, which while they often overlap, do provide us with a theoretical map. The first category, "Difference I: difference as experiential diversity," (p. 30) difference is basically a pragmatic understanding of the difference between men and women and tends to place them within separate socio-cultural spheres, with an emphasis on intrinsic feminine qualities. Within the category "Difference II: difference as positional meaning" (p. 33) difference is based upon the theories of the linguist Ferdinand de Saussure and the French philosopher Jacques Derrida. In this category of difference there is no outside "truth." Rather, meanings are produced in the continuous shift between the signifier (or what is denoted) and the signified (or what is connoted). Here any fixed category of femininity or masculinity is hard to maintain because these categories themselves only have meaning in the interplay of shifting signifiers and signifieds. Difference here also deconstructs any stable idea of a universal subject, the White Man on high who has been regulating History, Progress, and Society. "Difference III: sexual difference" (p. 36) is largely based on the works of the French psychoanalyst, Jacques Lacan, and the French philosopher, Louis Althusser. However, they have been, in turn, reread and theorized by several psychoanalytic feminists (including Kristeva 1986; Mitchell 1974; Rose 1986; Clément 1983). While any attempt to sum up this use of difference (or the other two) is bound to cause trouble and misunderstandings, I think that Jacqueline Rose sums up both the strength and the limitations of sexual difference as a concept: "If psychoanalysis can give an account of how women experience the path to femininity, it also insists, through the concept of the unconscious, that femininity is neither simply achieved nor is it ever complete" (1986, 7; cited in Barrett 1987, 38).

From Barrett's article we can begin to see the various ways in which the concepts of difference can play off the body in theoretical ways. However, against Barrett's contention that differences contradict each other, I want to consider how they might show up different ways in which we use our bodies. A recent film by the American comedian Sandra Bernhard, *Without You I'm Nothing,* is, to my mind, a wonderful example of the difference of differences in play upon the body. In a series of skits (taken from her Broadway show of the same name) and performed in a black Los Angeles club, Bernhard quite literally changes her body as she monologues about being Jewish in a WASP world, sings and appropriates songs from the sixties and seventies, all the while identifying her wish to be black through her desire for a beautiful black woman. Indeed, the film is held together with the longing shots of the black woman—the woman that she wants (to be). The final scene has Bernhard naked except for a G-string and gold tasseled "pasties" on her nipples. She bumps and grinds for herself, for the lone black woman who looks bored, and of course, for us. In this film, then, there is an "experiential difference" at work. This is perhaps the most obvious level at which Bernhard uses her body. Here she biographically recounts how her body felt in relation to the white, straight ideal (and rule) of the sixties. In her reconstruction of the nuclear family she plays off the supposedly clear-cut divisions of mother-father, sister-brother. At the same time that Bernhard seems to long after this blond moment of a supposed cultural truth about femininity, she

91

undercuts this ideology with her body, dressed in parody of the WASP paragon. In its very movements, her changing body shows that difference is always positional. Love songs that are supposedly directed at women by men become in Bernhard's rendition, lesbian and feminist statements. At the level of "sexual difference," Bernhard's show becomes a living testimony to the fact that femininity is indeed a complex and never-finished path. Even the "truth" of Bernhard's nearly naked body is itself encoded within a shifting play of ever-deferred possible meanings. We are and are not voyeurs, it is and is not for the elusive black woman that she dances, she is and is not in power/out of control. Against Helen Reddy's seventies' battlecry "I am Woman, Hear me Roar," Bernhard looks into the mirror, and into the camera, and within the myriad of possible body identities that are all quite deeply but strangely feminist, she tells us how beautiful she is. This is, then, to use the body "across the grain," to upset preconceived notions. In using her body, Bernhard also speaks her body loudly; it becomes an instrument that tells multiple truths and it deeply goes against "the enforced muteness of the feminine body" which as Beverley Brown and Parveen Adams correctly argue, "is the sign both of ignorance and of the inability to intervene politically" (1979, 42).

Putting Our Bodies to Work

While Bernhard's film works as a stunning example of differences, there are also less spectacular ways in which we can put the experiences of our bodies to work within feminist theory and practice. While Parveen Adams has argued that "the woman has no more direct access to her body than the man" (1986, 33), it is inarguable that within our culture women are made to feel their gender in more persistent ways than men are accustomed to. In a *Room of One's Own*, Virginia Woolf recalls a moment when she is walking across the lawns at Oxford. Someone yells at her for doing this, and she writes that at that moment "instinct rather than reason came to my help; he was a Beadle; I was a woman" (cited in de Lauretis 1984, 158). Without being crudely essentialist, one can say that in specific cultural ways, women are made to feel their genders at the level of the body; the culturally learned instinct that tells us we are being looked at, or that our bodies are in the wrong place. Teresa de Lauretis takes this quotation from Woolf to develop an analysis of gendered experience. She asks: "What is instinct but a kind of knowledge internalized from daily, secular repetition of actions, impressions, and meanings" (de Lauretis 1984, 158).

My point is that there are ways of putting these bodily instincts and experiences to work in understanding how we are physically positioned as well as how other women's bodies may be differently placed and felt. In a more recent article, de Lauretis argues for what she calls "technologies of gender" (1987). These social technologies or operations produce certain gendered bodies, the experience of which is both individual and common to women. For instance, the onset of menarche is something that physically happens to women. However, the ways in which the meanings of menstruation are represented can vary greatly; in these representations and in how we represent ourselves (such as "on the rag" and "having the curse") the experience of menstruation becomes part of the process of gendering, both individual and common, felt and represented, different and alike. As de Lauretis states, "the construction of gender is the product and process of both representation and self-representation" (1987, 6).

The task, then, for the feminist critic is to figure, to re-represent, the work of these gendered processes as they touch us at a bodily level. For instance, one of the more graphic episodes of the television talkshow *Oprah Winfrey* gave us the experiential body of a young black woman who had been recently raped. Now, as any viewer of the show knows, *Oprah Winfrey* is ruled by bodies. Indeed, over the last few years we have seen Oprah's body change, and she proudly tells us how much weight she's lost and how her boyfriend feels about it (and her). Oprah has also told of being abused as a child, and relates on a bodily level to her guests and audience members. On this occasion, the show opened with a video simulation of the rape in the Chicago subway system. On every level, the fact of the rape happening *here* is insisted upon. Although that "here" was in fact Chicago where the show is taped, the proximity of the rape becomes a central point. As we watch a very sympathetic (and even, empathetic) Oprah, the rape is recreated in our homes, bringing with it the nearness of its potentiality, the fact that we could have been there, and that there could be here. In the insistence that it has happened "here," this representation reaches into the configurations of our homes, touching our bodies. As I watched, alone in my home in the afternoon, I felt the physical space around me changing. Suddenly, the kitchen where I remembered that the door was open felt a long and frightening way away. This representation insisted upon my gender and my body; as Braidotti puts it, "it pertains . . . to the facticity of my being, it is like *that:* 'I' am sexed" (1989, 101). There is here, however, the possibility of moving from that individual bodily shock of gender to a recognition of other women, to anger at the fact that "they do these things to women." As Oprah gently questioned the woman who had been raped, one was brought into a circle of women (the audience) who seemed to be held together in solidarity. Their bodies leaned forward, as if to help, or hold, or listen better. At home, we saw the studio framed through the triangular movement of the cameras: to the woman, to Oprah, to the audience. Now, of course, this solidarity was fleeting and who knows if it was even real. However, what we can insist upon is the ways in which this representation touches us at the level of our bodies. Even if it is momentary, the experience of this representation enters into our own self-representations—it ever so slightly changes our knowledges, and may even call us forth into action. Again, this may not happen; as a woman watching I may be just irritated at the juxtaposition of rape and the banalities of daytime television advertisements, or I may be sickened by the opportunism of using a woman who has been raped to boost the ratings. However, what is certain is that at the moment of the rape's recreation no woman can feel quite right in her body, quite *bien dans sa peau,* quite well in one's skin.

In remembering this incident, I want to briefly outline two urgent areas of further inquiry. The first concerns the use of the body to continue in the ongoing deconstruction of racism and homophobia within feminism itself. This raises difficult but crucial questions. For instance, the struggle for abortion rights is widely and, in my view, rightly a key issue for feminists. However, we need to articulate that struggle through the different meanings that it may have for women. As Valerie Amos and Pratibha Parmar have argued:

> In asking for abortions on demand, white women are failing to recognize what contraception and abortion *mean* to black women. It may mean being sterilized without your consent, it means black women being used as guinea pigs in experiments for new drugs, it means contraceptives like depo provera which have numerous side effects being used on black women, but not on white women (1981, 147).

Now I do not think that either of the authors are recommending that we not fight for abortion rights. Indeed, in the United States as in Britain and Canada, to name but a few close instances, women's "rights" are being increasingly eroded, and the struggles for our right to control our own bodies must continue. What Amos and Parmar do emphasize is that we can demand universal access to abortion without couching our arguments in universal terms. We must recognize that the meanings of bodies are intimately tied in with other meanings. As Judith Williamson argues, "the body, which is in material terms continuous with that universe, is the point at which structures of meaning become both particularly necessary and particularly easily broken" (1989, 79).

One obvious site where women have yet to fully think through their bodies is in the struggle against ideological constructions of AIDS. As B.

Ruby Rich bluntly puts it: "To speak of sexuality and the body, and not also speak of AIDS, would be, well, obscene" (cited in Carter 1989, 59). And feminists, including myself, have been obscenely slow in reacting to the governmental ravages of people living and working with AIDS. Cindy Patton forcefully argues that "at a time when so many people's lives are being ruined not just by getting AIDS but by the cultural backlash of the epidemic, to refuse to participate in a cultural event which is so politically charged, to decide that it doesn't apply to you, is very strange and wrong" (1990, 124). Of course, straight and lesbian feminists working together to combat the ideological warfare aimed at HIV positive bodies will not immediately eradicate homophobia. Indeed, simply put, in general, heterosexual women have a higher risk of actually getting AIDS than lesbians and therefore should have a self-interest in AIDS activism. However, in the increasing violence of homophobia that defines the cultural construction of AIDS, it is lesbians who are getting hurt. Quite simply, it is about time that feminists of all genders really got serious about acting against homophobia, be it manifested in the silences in our theories or in the brutality on the streets. It is time to put our bodies to work together to make evident the links between homophobia, racism, the cultural construction of AIDS, the attacks on abortion rights, the increase in wife-battering and violence in the home. Too often a binary notion of gender and sexuality works to divide issues into camps—this affects me but not that. If we truly work through our bodies and learn from their sudden and perhaps unexpected desires, we can recognize that a logic of denial, of "this but not that," cannot hold. In other words, the multiple truths of the body force us beyond a theory lodged in duality; they beckon us to move on and to construct a theory of "wild" feminism. Using our bodies as analytic spring-boards we can begin to theorize in an *anaclitic* mode, a mode of thinking that insists that the articulations be made between "this and this". This is then to move beyond the concept of commonality through the one Body and to act in the doubleness of the question of "who am I and who is she?," in the particularities of my body and hers.

Conclusion

In conclusion the words of Rich return: to write my body, to plunge into experience and particularity. From there surely we theorize and reincorporate our bodies into analyses of the social formations in which we live, in which we are embodied. In raising the usefulness of our bodies I want to be clear that I do not wish to reproduce an endless self-reflexive circle, theory as navel-gazing. Rather, the point of these bodies is to instill modesty, but not prudery, into theoretical work. Here then are two good reasons why feminists should put the body, their bodies to work within theory. First, in acknowledging our own particularities, we are forced to approach those of others with care and always remember that our stories, and our bodies, can displace others, that as we speak we may be perpetrating the conditions that silence the subaltern (Spivak 1988), that the question of my body can also displace hers. Second, in putting our gendered bodies to work within our thinking, we make nonsense of several dichotomies that have endlessly plagued Western thought. In other words, let us ride roughshod over any fixed division of: mind/body, reason/ emotion, subject/object, and the rigidness of defined sexualities. As Jane Gallop has said, "Thinking that truly passes through the body only occurs in brief intervals" (1988, 8). While we may not always be able to think through the body, we can use those moments to deepen and inform our theories.

In putting our bodies, experiences, genders and desires to work within theory and practice, we begin to speak loudly, we begin to care about others' bodies as well as our own individual selves. Patton has argued that "the similarity between race and sexuality is that they are two cultural notions which seem to be represented in the body, rather than necessarily conceptualized at the level of language" (1990, 130). The project before us is a theory of the body, and the incorporation of the sound of our bodies within our theories.

Notes

1. This chapter is offered as an incomplete journey in and through "the body." For other takes on some of the ideas presented here see Probyn 1991a and 1991b.

2. In the last several years "French Feminism" or *le Féminisme de la différance* has emerged as an important site within North American feminism in part because it offers another language with which to celebrate the body. However, as there are many accounts of "French Feminism," I refer the reader to them rather than offer a truncated version of a very complex set of debates. Meaghan Morris (1988) provides a much needed discussion of the relation between Mary Daly's work and that of Luce Irigaray. Elizabeth Grosz's *Sexual Subversions: Three French Feminists* (1989) carefully positions the projects of Julia Kristeva and Irigaray and the often neglected (in North America) Michèle Le Doeuff. See also: Elaine Marks and Isabel Courtivron 1980; Jane Gallop 1986; Toril Moi 1985; Alice Jardine 1985; Gayatri Chakravorty Spivak 1981.

References

Adams, Parveen. 1986. "Versions of the Body." *m/f.* Nos. 11/12: 27–34.

Amos, Valerie and Pratibha Parmar. 1981. "Resistances and Responses: The Experiences of Black Girls in Britain." In *Feminism for Girls: An Adventure Story.* eds. Angela McRobbie and Trisha McCabe. London: Routledge & Kegan Paul.

Barrett, Michèle. 1987. "The Concept of Difference." *Feminist Review.* No. 26: 29–42.

Berthelot, J.M. 1986. "Sociological Discourse and the Body." *Theory, Culture & Society.* 3(3): 155–164.

Blackman, Inge and Kathryn Perry. 1990. "Skirting the Issue: Lesbian Fashion for the 1990s." *Feminist Review.* Vol. 34: 67–78.

Boston Women's Health Collective. 1976. *Our Bodies, Ourselves.* New York: Simon & Schuster.

Braidotti, Rosi. 1989. "The Politics of Ontological Difference." In *Between Feminism and Psychoanalysis.* ed. Teresa Brennan. London and New York: Routledge.

Brown, Beverley and Parveen Adams. 1979. "The Feminine Body and Feminist Politics." *m/f.* No. 3: 35–50.

Bruch, Hilde. 1978. *The Golden Cage: the Enigma of Anorexia Nervosa.* Cambridge: Harvard University Press.

Carter, Erica. 1989. "AIDS and Critical Practice." In *Taking Liberties: AIDS and Cultural Politics.* eds. Erica Carter and Simon Watney. London: Serpent's Tail.

Clément, Catherine. 1983. *The Lives and Legends of Jacques Lacan.* Trans. Arthur Goldhammer. New York: Columbia University Press.

Coward, Rosalind. 1985. *Female Desires: How They are Sought, Bought, and Packaged.* New York: Grove Press.

de Lauretis, Teresa. 1987. *Technologies of Gender.* Bloomington: Indiana University Press.

———1984. *Alice Doesn't: Feminism, Semiotics, Cinema.* Bloomington: Indiana University Press.

Foucault, Michel. 1980. *The History of Sexuality Volume I: An Introduction.* Trans. Robert Hurley. New York: Vintage Books.

———1973. *The Birth of the Clinic: An Archaeology of Medical Perception.* Trans. A.M. Sheridan Smith. New York: Vintage Books.

Frank, Arthur W. 1990. "Bringing Bodies Back in: A Decade Review." *Theory, Culture & Society.* Vol. 7: 131–162.

Gallop, Jane. 1988. *Thinking through the Body.* New York: Columbia University Press.

———1986. *Reading Lacan.* Ithaca: Cornell University Press.

Grosz, Elizabeth. 1989. *Sexual Subversions: Three French Feminists.* Sydney and Boston: Allen & Unwin.

Jardine, Alice. 1985. *Gynesis: Configurations of Woman and Modernity.* Ithaca, N.Y.: Cornell University Press.

Kristeva, Julia. 1986. *The Kristeva Reader,* ed. Toril Moi. London: Basil Blackwell.

Marks, Elaine and Isabel de Courtivron. 1980. eds. *The New French Feminisms.* Amherst: University of Massachusetts Press.

Mitchell, Juliette. 1974. *Psychoanalysis and Feminism.* London: Allen Lane.

Moi, Toril. 1985. *Sexual/Textual Politics.* London: Methuen.

Morris, Meaghan. 1988. "A-mazing Grace: Notes on Mary Daly's Poetics." In her *The Pirate's Fiancee: Feminism, Reading, Postmodernism.* London: Verso.

Morse, Margaret. 1987/8. "Artemis Aging: Exercise and the Female Body on Video." *Discourse.* X.1: 20–54.

Orbach, Susie. 1986. *Hunger Strike: The Anorectic's Struggle as a Metaphor for Our Age.* New York: W.W. Norton & Company.

———1979. *Fat is a Feminist Issue.* London: Hamlyn.

Patton, Cindy. 1990. "Mapping: Lesbianism, AIDS and Sexuality: An Interview with Cindy Patton by Sue O'Sullivan." *Feminist Review.* Vol. 34: 120–133.

———1989. "The AIDS Industry: Construction of 'Victims', 'Volunteers' and 'Experts.'" In *Taking Liberties: AIDS and Cultural Politics.* eds. Erica Carter and Simon Watney. London: Serpent's Tail.

Probyn, Elspeth. 1991a. "Gendered Bodies and Everyday Selves." *Social Discourse/Discours social.* Vol. 3, Nos. 3 and 4: 179–188.

Probyn, Elspeth. 1991b. "This Body Which Is Not One: Speaking an Embodied Self." *Hypatia.* Vol. 6. No. 3: 111–124.

———1987. "The Anorexic Body." In *Body Invaders: Panic Sex in America.* eds. Arthur and Marilouise Kroker. Toronto: Oxford University Press.

Rich, Adrienne. 1987. "Notes toward a Politics of Location." In her *Blood, Bread and Poetry.* London: Virago Press (New York: W.W. Norton & Company, 1985).

Rose, Jacqueline. 1986. *Sexuality in the Field of Vision.* London: Verso.

Spelman, Elizabeth V. 1990. *The Inessential Woman: Problems of Exclusion in Feminist Thought.* London: The Women's Press (Boston: Beacon Books, 1988).

Spivak, Gayatri Chakravorty. 1989. *In Other Worlds.* London and New York: Routledge.

———1988. "Can the Subaltern Speak?" In *Marxism and the Interpretation of Culture.* eds. Cary Nelson and Lawrence Grossberg. Urbana: University of Illinois Press.

Szekeley, Eva. 1988. *Never Too Thin.* Toronto: The Women's Press.

Treichler, Paula. 1987. "Escaping the Sentence: Diagnosis and Discourse in 'The Yellow Wallpaper.'" In *Feminist Issues in Literary Scholarship.* ed. Shari Benstock. Bloomington: Indiana University Press.

Turner, Bryan S. 1984. *The Body and Society.* Oxford: Basil Blackwell.

Valverde, Mariana. 1985. *Sex, Power and Pleasure.* Toronto: The Women's Press.

Williamson, Judith. 1989. "Every Virus Tells a Story: The Meanings of HIV and AIDS." In *Taking Liberties: AIDS and Cultural Policy.* eds. Erica Carter and Simon Watney. London: Serpent's Tail.

6

Harassment and Everyday Life

Cheris Kramarae

"Men that I haven't seen since I was a little girl will say, 'Ohhh, you're a woman now.' My definition of sexual harassment is the way members of one sex behave toward members of the other which belittles, dominates and places restrictions on the movements of the other.... reinforcement of the dominance of one person over another."

(Black woman in her early 20s)

"I used to think of sexual harassment as physical harassment or words referring to a person's body. Now that I've worked in more public places, such as the airport in Chicago, I have heard sexual harassment in many forms. Guys, even my boyfriend's friends, have said things to me jokingly, but it is intimidating. I think that is the biggest part of what I consider sexual harassment, intimidating words and actions."

(White woman in her early 20s)

"My male boss sometimes takes me out to dinner saying "I'll teach you the job," but always ends up giving compliments about my looks. Verbal sexual harassment forces women to be sex objects or stereotyped women. By giving women a fear of losing a job or friendship, it forces them to be sexy, polite, obedient, dumb, cute, weak, and smiling. Sexual harassment prevents women from being smart, active, assertive, independent and professional human beings."

(Asian woman, mid-20s)

This essay is about everyday *verbal* sexual or gender harassment, the behavior that, along with the touching, patting, pinching, leaning over, and cornering, provides the persistent support for related acts of physical sexual terrorism such as rape, and wife-battering. Sexual harassment is not primarily about sex, or physical attraction, or about boys' and men's attempts to be "nice" to girls or women. It is about the expression and enforcement of power and a binary gender hierarchy.[1] Boys *will* be boys, even if they must initiate or support a large repertoire of harassing actions to maintain their difference and dominance.

The length of the list of specific verbal behaviors of males gives an indication of the variety of forms. The list includes intimidating, coercive or offensive sexual jokes, persistent requests for dates, nonreciprocal types of compliments, demeaning references to women present or absent, anonymous or signed notes and letters; calling women crazy, sexual remarks, paternalistic or sarcastic tone of voice, teasing, and suggestive or insulting sounds including whistling and sucking.[2] Boys learn the basic principles early and "play" them out; Barrie Thorne (1993) discusses forms of gender harassment on playgrounds and in classrooms. I focus on adult sexual harassment, but am conscious of the importance of learning the ways children learn gender in part from learning how to harass females. I am also concerned in this essay to point out some of the different forms that sexual harassment takes for white women and women of color. Harassment is used to construct both gender and race, so white women experience somewhat different treatment from white men than, for example, black women experience from black men or white men.

The women I interviewed[3] and the women in the many surveys on sexual harassment often explain that their understanding of the force and meaning of sexual harassment changes as they experience yet new forms. The length of the list of specific verbal behaviors gives an indication of the variety of forms. The figures for the number of cases of sexual harassment are not collected by officials—or even by the people who experience them. One young white woman I asked to talk about harassment said,

> Had you asked me a year ago and I had kept track of the number, I would have a voluminous file. Mostly they just happen and I don't keep track. I wish I had a nickel for every time someone told me to smile; apparently my natural countenance is too serious-looking. Some other remarks stick in my mind. A high school gym teacher (and football coach) often said to me "Why don't you get involved—join the pom-pom girls!" I was already involved in a few activities. I was upset because of his ignorance of my other activities and his choice of suggestion. A pom-pom girl—in high school stereotypically an underachiever in academic subjects. Often I forget the specifics of the remarks, especially the problematic compliments. I think people are more careful in what they say to a boy or a man—even if only because in the back of their minds they think the man can physically hurt them. (White woman in her 20s)

101

For many women, sexual harassment is experienced many times, every-day. It is so common and so integral an aspect of men's interaction with women that, as Gloria Steinem reminds, "A few years ago this was just called *life*" (1983, 149).

Sexual harassment is rampant, but not random. In many studies more than 90% of formal complaints about sexual harassment are made by women about men. In the workplace (that is, places of paid employment), most of the complaints are against "more powerful" persons, and approximately one third are against co-workers. Of course, close analysis of formal complaints is not very telling, because so few people who are harassed make formal complaints. Few women know whether the institutions they work in and around have any official harassment policies. Increasingly the institutions do, often using the terms set forth by the (U.S.) Equal Employment Opportunity Commission, which, in interpreting Title VII of the 1964 Civil Rights Act, defines sexual harassment as un-welcome sexual advances, requests for sexual favors, and other verbal or physical conduct of a sexual nature, which creates an intimidating, hostile, or offensive work environment. Freada Klein, adjunct professor at MIT's school of management, and a management consultant who specializes in sexual harassment cases, points to some studies that have shown that only one percent of employees who are harassed make formal complaints (in Norma R. Fritz 1989, 6). Complaining about it can often just bring on more.

Complaints are highest in companies where men are 75 percent or more of the workforce, and lowest in companies where women are more than 75 percent of the workforce (Fritz 1989). Women working in nontradi-tional fields may be especially vulnerable to sexual harassment because they are where they "don't belong" (Hughes and Sandler 1986, 3). While sexual harassment is basic to our education as we learn about what is respected, expected and required of women and men in every discipline (Spender 1982a, 37), it is behavior that is seldom analyzed as a problem in the schools; it is often learned even more forcefully on the job.

Business and other institutions now are expressing concern about sexual harassment and professional journals carry many articles about the extent and expense of the problem. This is a new concern by management, initiated not from managers' concerns and policies but from much feminist action, including the invention of the term sexual harassment to define the wide range of behaviors expressing unwanted imposition of sexual requirements or generalized sexist attitudes in relationships of unequal power. At the time of its coinage and use in legal arguments in the 1970s, sexual harassment was the only U.S. legal term defined by women. (See the quotes from Catharine A. MacKinnon and Lin Farley under "Sexual

Harassment" in Kramarae and Treichler with Russo 1985.) The term has been useful in showing the relationship of the many manly acts that perpetuate a vicious, institutionally supported cycle of sexism. *Sexism* is itself a word recently coined and distributed by feminists to describe the institutionalized and systematic expressions—including discrimatory hiring practices and public policies—that women are inferior, stereotyping often intertwined with racism. We will need a more extensive vocabulary to spell out what is going on with the interaction of sexism and racism. Following are two illustrations of sexual harassment, similar in expressed sexist attitudes, but different in the way racism is acknowledged. The first is from a medical student:

> One of the most painful reminders of my insecure status occurred during my junior clerkship in internal medicine. Wearing a lab coat and carrying a stethoscope, I walked into a patient's room at the Veterans' Administration Hospital. The patient, an elderly white man, had been admitted ... [I] introduced myself as a student doctor. I proceeded to ask him questions about his medical history. Later, the white male intern came out of the patient's room. "You know what that guy asked me," he laughingly announced. "Why didn't that girl clean up while she was in here?" My being mistaken for a maid became a joke on the ward team, all of whom, other than myself, were white and male.
>
> The next morning on rounds, the attending physician said, "Let's go see Vanessa fluff up some pillows." I did not find the episode humorous. I was angry. I was shaken. Despite my difficulties [as a black, working class woman trying to work in a white, middle-class male dominated profession], I had begun to define myself as an aspiring physician and expected others to see me as one. (Gamble 1990, 59)

The other is from a nurse in her mid-30s:

> I try to have good relationships with patients, wanting them to treat me as someone who knows a lot about their health and well being. Then when I go on rounds with this doctor he continually says patronizing things to the patients such as, "I always bring Carol along. She's so beautiful that we all feel better around her." He told one man that I had freckles all over my body.

The second "incident" above does not mention the race of the participants, an absence which in much writing and talking in the U.S. is code for *white*. White feminists now give the obligatory acknowledgement about multiple oppressions. Many of us, however, have difficulty recognizing our own control over terminology and labelling, because of the very structures of racism. As Yolanda Moses points out, in many cases of harassment "it is difficult to identify whether or how much the attitudes and behaviors are based on racism or sexism. It is clear, however, that racial and sexual stereotypes work together to reinforce negative images of black women" (1989, 5). She points out that programs in Women's Studies and Black Studies departments are usually administered by white women and black men—not black women. Such organizational structures preserve some of the existing hierarchy of power, with fundamental implications for our understandings and behavior. For example, sexual harassment fused with racial harassment has multiple origins, coming from many white women as well as from white and black men. And white women and black women in comparable situations are likely to receive different types of harassing remarks from white men and black men, who work from differing sexual and racial stereotypes. For example, it may be that in some situations paying more attention to, and saying more sexually harassing statements to, white women may be a part of white men's expression of both sexism and racism.[4] In other cases, women of color are especially targeted as recipients of jokes and other remarks about their sexuality, and about affirmative action. Because racism and sexual harassment are officially condemned, people of color deal with many implicit expressions of racism and sexism. Philomena Essed (1985) in her studies of the interpretation processes used by black women in their understanding of everyday racism gives examples of the ways black women often experience sexual harassment and racism in the same interaction. She writes that at times racism and sexism reinforce each other. In one of her examples a woman has been told by a doorman at the disco that she and her girlfriend may enter "our place" but she can't bring black men with her. Because she has already paid she decides to stay and dance with her friend:

> She and I started to dance together, but suddenly a white man put his hands on my buttock. I was absolutely furious. I called him names and said: "How dare you presume that you can grab any black woman that crosses your path!" (90)

The woman experiences mutually reinforcing sexism and racism. At other times, Essed notes, racism and sexism can be each other's mirror image. She gives an example offered by a black woman in a group of students required to write a joint paper: "The white girls would only ask each other to participate in their group, and I would remain alone.... they thought they have more to say than I did. My suggestions were evaluated longer before they were accepted for the paper." If "boys" were substituted for "white girls" we would describe it as a case of sexual harassment. In both racism and sexism, passive acts, such as ignoring, overlooking, and withholding support are frequent forms of implicit discrimination (Essed 91).

White men, in "me-tooism" statements, point out that men also experience sexual harassment, and, of course, some men do experience it. But much less frequently and usually much less severely than white women and women of color. (And evidently with fewer deleterious psychological and physical effects [Strauss 1990].) Nationally, approximately 95 percent of all reports involve men harassing females (Truax 1989). Sexual harassment is not just about specific individual instances of touching or expressions with sexist overtones. It is about women's and men's places in our society, and the multiple, often subtle ways, we are told about our places. As the cover of *Thought & Action* (Spring 1989) states as preface to a symposium on sexual harassment, "Few men will verbalize their belief that women are subordinate, but many still operate on that basis." That resulting "operation" has implications for all of women's lives. Similarly, few white women and men will state that people of color are inferior, but many of us, who are quite ready to express our abhorrence of police beatings of blacks, for example, still participate in establishing the entire racist climate which supports the beatings, that is, in establishing hostile conditions for people of color.

Women discover that sexual harassment has many forms and perpetrators; all need close inspection. Seventy percent of the sexual harassment cases filed with the Equal Employment Opportunity Commission are based on "hostile environment" problems (Versespej 1988) in places of employment, but most women report them as also occurring with great frequency in the home, at the county fair, and on the streets—reporting them, however, only when encouraged or when they think there is a chance that there might be some changes possible since many people claim that the actions described here are harmless. As with other feminist critiques of men's repression and hostility, much of the explanations involve telling stories, until an adequate, shared vocabulary is available—itself a major problem for women in a culture where the establishment of language rules and usages is considered a male prerogative. As many of the women I've interviewed have said, long stories are often needed, since the meaning of one remark is often dependent upon a history of events. Here, I'm unable to include the long stories. The shorter stories, however, add up to a saga about how many men try to keep many women in their place. In this short essay, I describe only a few types of verbal harassment. I include only brief mention of the commands for emotion control and jokes, because they have received more attention elsewhere; I give more attention to problematic terms of address, compliments, and street harassment. As the illustrations make clear, the harassment does not happen only to the young and "attractive," although many of the harassing remarks and sounds imply that women who are not young and attractive are less worthy of men's attention.

Commands for Emotion Control: *"Hey, How About A Smile?"*

Approximately half of all women working outside their homes have jobs that call for emotional labor (e.g. the soothing provided by flight attendants) (Hochschild 1982). And the other half are encouraged to incorporate that labor into their paid work. Like all good servants we are to indicate at all times that we are happy with our lot.

> Recently, I had an acquaintance say to me after seeing my anger over something, "I thought menopause didn't start until 50." He totally disregarded the validity of my anger, joked with it. (White woman in her 20s)

> The owner of the restaurant would always tell me to smile, which at first didn't bother me, but after a few times, began to annoy me. Granted, I was in the service "profession" so I should look happy and eager to make the customer happy; however, the times he thought I should be smiling were when I was away from the customers' presence. Why did I always have to be smiling? (White woman in her 30s)

> I worked, checking ID's at the door. Many times people (men and a few women) would say "Smile," or "Why aren't you smiling," or "Come on, smile!" (White woman in her 30s)

> Last night I was sitting, just listening to a band. *Two* guys asked me why I wasn't smiling. As if *I* was to be *their* entertainment. (White woman in her early 20s)

> Apparently my natural countenance is too serious-looking. What makes me upset by the "Why don't you smile?" comments is that these people are not really concerned about me. I just have to *look* happy. (Black women in her 20s)

> They will ask, "Why are you being such a bitch?" Or "Is it that time of the month?" I hate these comments men feel they can make. What *is* the purpose? (White woman in her 20s)

Just Joking: "Honey, The Whole Office Is Behind You. Please Keep Moving (Ha, Ha)"

Women are required to hear a lot of "friendly joking." (One clerical worker reported the statement above, from her boss.) These are the questions we need to ask: Is the joking reciprocal? Does the joker use the same "play" around the boss as he does to the secretary? If not, what power elements are operating?

> Most of the women in the [manufacturing] company are secretaries; several have college degrees. The man I work for calls all women, no matter their age, "my little girl." In a meeting I had with him he was explaining a machine called a "clustermat" which was two machines joined together to operate with greater efficiency. One of the women in the group asked how they came up with the name, and he said to me, "Do you know what a cluster is?" I sort of nodded, and he said, "Well it's a gang bang and these two machines are like *fucking!*" (White woman in her 20s)

As many of the women I talked with noted, often the jokes appear designed to disconcert, or, if not designed for that, seem to work the better for the joker if they do.

> I watched the interaction at a fast food counter. He said, "I'll have two of those, two of those ... [listing other items] and a phone number." The woman put his requests in a bag until he asked for her phone number. She was momentarily confused—"A What?" and then acted (perhaps felt) stupid. She'd brought more attention to his request through her "mistake" at misunderstanding his "order." She was serving him. He furthered his request for "service" outside the food order. Somehow the woman had become a pastry. (Report from a young white woman witnessing the encounter.)

In business and industry the "jokes" are often printed. For example, "The Smart Man's Creed, or Why Beer Is Better than Women: After you've had a beer, the bottle is still worth a dime." Workers at Goldman Sachs in Boston circulated this and other sexist literature to their colleagues while denying that this behavior constituted sexual harassment (If this essay dealt also with visual gender harassment I would point out that men at the same firm also attached photographs of bare-breasted women to descriptions of new female employees in copies of the company newsletters, and passed the newsletters around the office [Nichols 1988].) Just a bit of fun, girls. Where's your sense of humor?

That question, "Where's your sense of humor?" (and the related commands such as "lighten up") are often markers of harassment. When girls and women indicate their displeasure at a sexist joke, the rejoinder is often a remark intended to make *them* feel they are at fault—*another* harassment, in addition to what has already occurred—a common "blame-the-victim" response to sexual harassment complaints.

"Compliments": "What A Terrific Little Saleswoman We Have Here."

> My boss always tells me that I look good when I wear a dress. In fact he says, "How FINE you are looking today!" I think he does it to encourage me to wear skirts, which bothers me. And the way he says it also bothers me. (Black woman in her 40s about white boss)

Compliments are defined as expressions of admiration, approval and encouragement (Wolfson 1981), and as expressions of praise and solidarity (Robert Herbert 1990). It is "unquestionable" that compliments are valued; they are as critical to social success as oxygen is to breathing (Knapp et al. 1984). Given the very positive connotations past research assigns compliments, why do so many black and white women know some "compliments" as problems? How could any compliments be described as sexual harassment? Is it just discourtesy on the part of women to complain about men's courtesies?

There is precedent for this kind of feminist analysis. We know that at one time chivalry, supposedly male protection of and kindness to women, was promoted by most institutions in Europe and North America. But some of our foremothers were not fooled and pointed out that far from representing courtesy and protection, as men have pretended, the actions included under chivalry work to secure women in subordinate positions. In the 17th century Mary Astell called chivalry a praise of women's incompetence by those "who under pretence of loving and admiring you, really serve their own base ends" (cited by Spender 1982b, 44).

Compliments serve a number of functions in interaction—for example, to express friendship, to smooth and get forgiveness, to bridge gaps created by offences, to make someone feel good (Holmes 1988). They can also make the addressee feel uncomfortable. Because they are functionally complex speech acts, they can be very useful for subtle harassment.[5] I suggest that many remarks, including many compliments that men in our culture address to women are designed to serve the following base ends: 1) To teach women that we exist primarily as adjuncts to men. 2) To teach us that our primary activities should be in housekeeping, and in the nurturing and ornamental activities women are sometimes encouraged to perform outside the household. 3) To teach us that our activities are trivial in comparison to the activities of men. 4) To coerce and intimidate us by reminding us of our place in society and thus remind us of the possible use of economic sanctions and physical force.

Knowing that women and men don't receive the same complimentary treatment helps us understand the reasons for some of the problems. Women receive more compliments in general, and more compliments about appearance and attire than do men, no matter what their occupation or status (Knapp et al. 1984; Wolfson and Manes 1980). Men are more likely than are women to receive compliments about performance—about how well they've done their job. That is, gender is evidently a more determining factor about the number and types of compliments received than is the gainfulness or type of job.

Men are much more reluctant to tell a man that he looks good. Looking at compliment forms we can see some homophobia in operation. A summary from Robert Herbert's (1990) analysis of the work of J. Manes and Nessa Wolfson (1980) and Janet Holmes (1988) shows striking differences in syntactic patterns of compliments. Women give more first person compliments "I like your haircut"; first person compliments are rare from males, and especially when addressing other males. Second person compliments "Your hair looks good cut that way" are more common from females to males and from males to females than males to other males. Impersonal compliments "Nice haircut" are heard most frequently between male speakers. Of the compliments from females to females, more than three-fourths have a personal focus compared with less than a third of those from males to males. Are the men trying to avoid any hints of same-sex attraction, hints which could mess up the male/female heterosexual hierarchy for them?

We can learn something about the functions of men's compliments by noting not only where they are present but where they are absent—the times women do not get praise for a job well done, for example. Or when they are praised too much for too little. An example: A waitress performing the simple act (in comparison with the difficult work of keeping all the orders in order) of leaning over and wiping off a table is told by a male customer at a nearby table, "I like the way you do that" (white woman in her 30s). Or when they receive "other-than" compliments, which come where one might expect a compliment. An example:

109

As chairman [sic] of a college psychology department, I have served on numerous departmental committees. One year, when I was a member of the budget committee, we were allotted more funding than usual for capital expenditures. Although the department consisted of equal numbers of male and female professors, our four-member committee was made up solely of women.

We conducted a detailed study of department needs and priorities, then presented our findings in a lengthy itemized report during the annual budget meeting.

Imagine our indignation when the first comment was "Wow! The girls went on a shopping spree!" (Letter, *Savy*, Sept. 1984, 82)

We could also learn a lot by considering the compliments that secretaries usually get with the remarks that women in less traditional "women's" jobs get; secretaries can perform their work well and still be considered as remaining in the private (that is, women's) sphere, not threatening to men. Women managers, on the other hand, get more compliments from men that compare them to men or as one of a separate category of workers. I've collected "problematic compliments" from more than fifty women in various occupations. Women "out of sphere" report many compliments such as "You gave that talk like a man!"; "Few women I know could do that"; and "I gave you a good recommendation; I said you were one of the best women we've had working here."

We can learn by considering when the compliments are offered. Women are often startled and distressed by the intrusion of the statements because they often cause a sudden transition in topic from what the woman is discussing. A middle-aged white women whose voice is lower than most women's voices finds that this characteristic is unexpectedly commented on in phone conversations:

I called up the mechanic and asked about my car, which was in the garage being fixed. He said, "Your voice is so interesting—sexy. It excites me." I didn't know what to say so I said, "I don't know what to say. Thank you, I guess." But I wasn't pleased. I didn't want to excite that mechanic; I called about my car.

A secretary reports that she seldom has a quick reply to the company salesmen's compliments/insults because she never knows when and how they will come at her. For example, one day a salesman come into the office with three male clients, and asked the secretary to step out from behind her desk. She did, and he said, "Look. And she can type too." A white woman in her 30s, talking with a white faculty colleague, same age, about a crisis, said, "I've got to get this report done to save my ass." He replied, "There's no ass I'd like more to save." He does this intrusive complimenting to many women faculty, most of whom haven't figured out a way of indicating their disapproval without being considered prudes. This time the woman expressed her disapproval with an emphatic "Bob!" He said, "No, honest." He has switched the topic from the crisis to her body, seeming to assume that she will appreciate or at least accept this comment on her body from a male. When she tries, in a non-threatening way, to indicate her disapproval, he declares that he means what he says, as if somehow that makes the topic switch above reproach. Women don't control the timing, and often feel uneasy about complaining about the intrusive remarks because the speakers seem so certain that the remarks are complimentary enough to justify their being said at that time.

Stranger Compliments: "Hey Pretty, How're You Doing. . . . Hey Cunt Answer Me."

Women in public places are considered "out of place" and many men treat them as objects to jeer and intimidate as are others who are noticeably different—people who are fat, ugly, or are people of color or white people out of "their area." Supposedly, politeness norms state that strangers in public are not to stare or comment on each other's appearance or actions. Women do evaluate men they see and hear in public, of course, but they don't publicly announce the evaluation to them. Yet women in public often receive men's evaluations—compliments or insults—because they are in men's public. (Public places are only for some of the public; they are often hostile environments for girls and women.) Some of the remarks are specific comments on women's appearance ("Great legs") or general comments on their looks ("Look at that 10" or a whistle)—seemingly compliments. Some street remarks disparage a woman's looks or moral character. Carol Gardner (1981) writes:

> Street remarks often accuse women of inferior looks, improper carriage or attire, inappropriate actions, and moral defects. It is not only unattractive, sloppy women who receive these remarks; it is also comely and well-groomed ones. These remarks are delivered by all classes and races of men, singly and in groups; sometimes they are spoken jokingly, sometimes they are spoken with vehemence and even accompanied by punches, tweaks, or blows. . . . (333)

We are taught that men's compliments are the highest compliments we—supposedly socially, intellectually and economically their inferiors—can receive. Consequently, many women have mixed reactions to street remarks. What is clear, however, is that women have been confused and frightened about street remarks for ages, because they are something *done* to women to call attention to women as women, and as women away from the supposed safety of their home place.

The following letter, from the British journal *Womanhood,* December 1898, sounds too familiar today:

> A matter of great importance to all women, and one which I have never known to be publicly discussed, is the grave annoyance to which women—and particularly young girls—are subjected, by being followed and spoken to by men when walking through the streets alone. The men do not necessarily belong to the class of tramps and loafers, but, on the contrary, are often well dressed and seemingly respectable.... Can any of your readers suggest a solution of this difficult problem? It is sad to think that even at the present day a woman cannot go out and return to her home without the fear of being molested. But since the innate chivalry which one pre-supposes in every man has not hitherto sufficed to secure unprotected women from impertinent vexation of the kind described, it seems to me highly necessary to discuss the subject from all sides, and to find if possible both a preventative and a remedy for the evil. (55)

In response another writer argued that a girl or woman can handle such situations by looking straight ahead. "She must not smile, or blush, or appear nervous, however nervous she may feel" (55). This procedure had carried the writer through difficult situations where she "was utterly unprotected, the streets deserted, and if I had been made away with no one would have been any the wiser" (56). As these letters hint, there are unlabeled links to be drawn among men's compliments to women, their street remarks, and physical assaults.

Elizabeth Arveda Kissling and I (1991) found the same perceived (although often unacknowledged) relationships of compliments, verbal hostility, and physical attack in the more than 100 responses of women and men made to an initial computer network question about the comments boys and men make to girls and women on the street. Quite clearly many women hear those comments as connected to other experiences in their lives that threaten their dignity, privacy and safety, and these comments are attempts to remind women of what men say are the proper activities and location of women.

> When being scanned by people and whistled at, I feel that I am dehumanized, transferred to a kind of animal in an auction, or merchandise in a store window which is nakedly displayed and exposed to the interested, potential purchaser. (Young Asian woman studying in the US)

As Carol Gardner (1981) notes, "There is no sure way for a woman to pass down the street and not be commented upon." A student reported to me that she walked down a street in San Francisco, wearing a sweat shirt, green Army pants and hiking boots, and heard a young man ("a boy" she said) call out, "Hey cunt. What ya doing?" On the same street a middle-aged Hispanic woman reported receiving, "Hey momita! How's it goin'?" Any woman can expect to receive unexpected comments when they are out "alone" (which men thinks means without a man) but especially young women, because they are at the stage in their lives when men might consider them beautiful or might reproach them for not being beautiful. Female power or show of independence of any sort often brings forth hostile statements. bell hooks (1981) discusses the ways that black women in particular, no matter their job, talents and professional status, are treated as creatures to whom anything can be said at any time. In Lorraine Hansberry's play *To Be Young, Gifted, and Black,* a young black domestic worker says:

> In these streets out there, any little white boy from Long Island or Westchester sees me and leans out of his car and yells—Hey there, hot chocolate! Say there Jezabel! Hey you—Hundred Dollar Misunderstanding! YOU! Bet you know where there's a good time tonight . . . (quoted in hooks 1981, 58)

Later in the play a black middle-age professional woman says:

> "Hey there, hot chocolate! Say there, Jezabel! YOU . . .! "The white boys in the streets, they look at me and think of sex. They look at me and that's all they think! (quoted in hooks 1981, 59)

bell hooks points out that such remarks are actually examples of a "calculated method of social control" (60). These examples also show us that the private sphere is a conceptual, not always geographical, place. Black women, who have had to clean, cook and care for white families and industries as well as for their own families, have not been *allowed* to stay home. Yet boys and men consider them fair game (and the hunting metaphor is appropriate here) for men's sport of hassling when the women are on public streets, which are considered by many men as their domain;

113

women are encouraged to consider public streets as under men's control. Even the police, who are employed to help maintain justice for all, often caution women that for their own safety they should not be in "public" places when it is dark; harassment of women is so pervasive and so entrenched that the idea of a curfew *for men* is still an outrageous idea for many people.

Naming Difference: "Sweetie, The Whole Office Thinks You Are and Have The Best Little Duster in the Place."

Young black man to young white woman in class who is talking about the "insulting" way people addressed her when she works as a sales clerk:

> What? There's something wrong with calling someone 'Honey' and "Dear"? No really. I want to know! What's wrong with calling someone 'Honey'? I do it all the time. To be friendly."

The ways we address each other are based on status and social relationships. For example, a "honey" is not at the moment a boss or a president or someone accorded respect for her work skills. Terms of endearment voiced in the same situation when "ma'am" might also be used require our attention. As Alette Olin Hill (1986) writes, terms of endearment such as "honey" and "dear" are familiar terms used by close friends, families, and lovers—and also used on women by strangers. They may be used in some cases as synonyms of "lady" but not of "sir" or "gentleman." "Honey" and other sugary terms (such as sugar, sweet) and other food addresses (such as peach, cupcake) are frequently used by men publicly addressing unknown women and girls, but not other men, except as an insult. Terms of address are used frequently by men to remind women in many situations and in many occupations that whatever they think they are, they are really first and foremost female. If the woman has said or done nothing to try to mark their being female as the most salient characteristic in the situation, then the terms are often experienced as sexual harassment.

> Last summer I worked at a car dealership. Most of the salespeople were men. Some of them were nice. Others treated me as a lower life form. Every time they wanted something they would make up nicknames for me or call me honey or sweetheart. I hated this. (White woman in her 20s)

114

> I cannot think of an instance where I thought I was being sexually harassed. I have, however, said things that might fall into this category. My friends and I may refer to a girl as a chick or call her honey. While it may seem like no big deal to us, it may be for her. (White man in his 20s)

There *has* been some change in sexist and racist behavior. Writing about the emergence of a "new" racism, Philomena Essed (1988), Michael Lacy (1990) and Dennis Howitt and J. Owusu-Bempah (1990) are documenting the replacement, in some contexts (such as when a person of color is present) of some of the crudest components of racist verbal harassment with some more subtle techniques of harassment which, nevertheless, go hand-in-glove with the old familiar types of acts (such as paying a person of color significantly less than a white person is paid). Philomena Essed writes of the "increasingly sophisticated and subtle forms of racism, which are hard to assess by means of traditional methods of controlled observation, testing, and proof . . ." (6). We can see similar changes and charges when looking at the current forms of sexual harassment. At the moment, because they are trying to avoid legal cases, more managers are talking about sexual harassment, issuing warnings and guidelines on how to avoid being charged with sexual harassment. However, managers of most institutions, including the U.S. government, have not shown signs of really caring about the lives of women and (especially if they are single) their children. For example, more than 30 percent of workers, most of them women, earn a less-than-adequate wage. Only seven percent of low-wage workers received any form of assistance from government income-support programs (Spalter-Roth, Hartmann and Andrews 1990.) We can't expect sexual harassment to stop until other, linked discriminatory practices are eliminated.

No Conclusive Words

Liz Stanley (1984) argues that

> All women are threatening [to men] because they are women and not men; nonpersons, and not people. They have to have power done to them, otherwise the closed logical system by which men's being is created and confirmed crumbles to nothing. (1984, 76).

In order to understand the way compliments, terms of address, street remarks and other types of verbal sexual harassment work to maintain opposition, we need to consider the way sex differences are ordered in our culture. The gender hierarchy in the U.S. is in two parts and only two parts. That there are (a few) women managers does not contradict these statements. Those women are known to be unusual or out of order. In general, there are subordinate females and dominate males with prescribed behavior for each, a hierarchy that actually ignores "natural" sex differences and the evidence that the signs of "sex differences" are not universal. There are some women who are taller than some men, some groups of men who do not have beards, some cultures where males and females differ in spatial ability and some where they do not. As one biologist writes, it seems that "social environment [which includes, in our culture, sexual harassment] multiplies and magnifies, in many ways, an average kernel of intrinsic predisposition" (Lambert 1987, 141). Social customs and policies (and sexual tyranny) are based on the proposition that there is a natural, universal hierarchical order of sexual dimorphism (two forms) rather than a bimodal distribution with some overlap or a continuum, as Susanne Kessler and Wendy McKenna (1978) have argued. (See the discussion in Lambert 1987 about the pervasive and critical moral judgment in our culture that any perceived biological differences among people justify social inequality.) Sue Wise and Liz Stanley (1987) point out that "men who sexually harass are adept at turning any- and everything that women do into women's objectification and their own superiority." They write that these men look at the world through "sex-coloured glasses" in order to make themselves so much more than mere women (81).

In all cases men suggest that women "ask for it"—that is they ask for men's responses to their appearance or at least can't reasonably object to it. Compliments, street remarks and physical assaults are all often used by men as reminders to women that they are subject to men's observations, criticism, and control. For each, there are elements of the unexpected and of non-reciprocity. Researchers of compliments and street harassment note that they can occur at any time.

The argument that sexual harassment is a part of sexual terrorism (Kissling 1990; Sheffield 1987) does not mean that sexual harassment and sexual terrorism are the same. Rather, it is an argument that sexual harassment is a form of sexual assault and helps justify the themes and methods of such other components of terrorism as rape, wife-assault, incest, and sexual slavery. These are all very pervasive, vastly underreported crimes, and the rate of conviction for those cases brought to court is low (Russell 1982; Stanko 1985). These crimes are all called "sexual" and certainly they are all based on a sex/gender opposition and hierarchy. They all have to do with power and a process of intimidation. Knowing that the offenders of these acts are often boys and men known by the

116

girls and women they intimidate and attack, helps us understand how basic sexual terrorism is to the control of girls and women—who are trained to rely on men's protection for their happiness, and economic and physical well-being. We are pushed, intimidated and harassed into dependence upon men, but are, of course, very unsafe in that dependence.

Because of individual and collective feminist action, many institutions have policies regarding sexual harassment; they have had to in order to avoid lawsuits, court costs, executive time and tarnished images. The same institutions pay relatively little attention to the relationship between verbal harassment and physical violence, that is, little attention to the ways the individual cases of sexual harassment are related to cases of rape, wife-battering, and other forms of sexual terrorism. The attention given by institutional bosses and law enforcers to a few individuals who dare talk about injuries is still *on the individual.* Decisions are made about whether she is telling the truth, about whether she is overreacting, about whether she is cooperating with authorities, about getting her medical attention, and about reestablishing law and order.

The treatment of "victims" itself tell us a lot about the power relations between women and men. Sara Scott and Alison Dickens (1988) writing about rape cases, argue that services for women who have been raped "are now a contested area in which professionals are competing for control—a process which invariably results in the nationalization of feminist understandings" (44). Outrage against the rapist has been replaced by professionals' concern about getting the victim back "to normal"—back to the workplace, the family, heterosexual relations—back into the patriarchal structures that remain basically unchanged. For victims of sexual harassment, we need more than, say, adjustment sessions with therapists. Without a reworking of sexist and racist ideology and action, the individual "cure" won't take.

Everyday sexual harassment abounds; it is a social problem of "pandemic proportion" (Thomann and Wiener 1987). It has little to do with physical attraction, provocative appearance, or sex. It has a lot to do with the ways boys and men maintain a gender hierarchy in everyday interaction with girls and women. Men, even those who are quite sure that they never harass women, need to ask themselves why so many men do and what institutional practices need to be changed so that boys and men no longer produce so much violence against girls and women.

Notes

1. The term "gender harassment" might make clearer the intentions and effects of the actions. However, in this essay I use the more common term "sexual harassment."

2.   In response to complaints of a 26-year-old woman who reported a workman on a city job made kissing noises at her, the City Council in Cambridge, England, ordered workmen to stop harassing women if they want to keep their jobs. In a poll conducted by the city's paper the next day, respondents said the new policy of firing workers who make "amorous advances" is too harsh (*Cambridge Evening News* 9:8; 9:9, 1990).

3.   Unless otherwise indicated, the quotes come from some of the more than 120 women in universities, secretarial pools, and department stores with whom I have discussed sexual harassment, "problematic compliments," and street harassment. Some examples of problematic compliments come from my 1985 paper on "Speech Crimes." While I asked the same general questions of the women, I did not attempt a carefully conducted survey. My intent was to use what situations presented themselves to learn more about women's understanding of sexual harassment. I thank Elizabeth Arveda Kissling for her help with library research and for her own provocative and very useful analyses of street harassment as international terrorism of women.

4.   In their study of responses of letters to British organizations offering voluntary work, Dennis Howitt and J. Owusu-Bempah (1990) found that those letters signed with a "white" name (Croft) received different replies than did those with a "Black" name (Kumari). "Whites" were more likely to be offered suggestions of other organizations to approach for work. "Whites" received more encouraging replies. There was no blatant racism in the replies. The authors of the article refer to the "new racism" which seems to be as effective at maintaining a racist society as were the more direct racist acts. We need to listen for the particulars of any new permutations of both racism and sexism.

5.   There is a close relationship between these problematic compliments and the expressions of "civil racism" which Michael Lacy (1992) describes as subtle, ambiguous, polite language about racial matters that advertently or inadvertently reproduces racial inequalities. It is language, he states, that is difficult to challenge because of its "civility."

References

Essed, Philomena. 1985. "Racism in Everyday Experiences of Black Women." In *Women, Feminist Identity, and Society in the 1980's: Selected Papers.* eds. Myriam Diaz-Diocaretz and Iris M. Zavala. Amsterdam: John Benjamins Publishing, 81–100.

Essed, Philomena. 1988. "Understanding Verbal Accounts of Racism: Politics and Heuristics of Reality Construction." *Text.* 8, 5–40.

Fritz, Norma R. 1989. "Sexual Harassment and the *Working Woman.*" *Personnel.* February, 4–8.

Gamble, Vanessa Northington. 1990. "On Becoming a Physician: A Dream Not Deferred." In *The Black Women's Health Book*. eds. Evelyn C. White. Seattle: Seal Press, 52–64.

Gardner, Carol Brooks. 1981. "Passing By: Street Remarks, Address Rights, and the Urban Female." *Sociological Inquiry*. 50(3–4): 328–356.

Herbert, Robert K. 1990. "Sex-Based Differences in Compliment Behavior." *Language in Society*. 19 (June), 201–224.

Hill, Alette Olin. 1986. *Mother Tongue, Father Time*. Bloomington, Ind.: Indiana University Press.

Holmes, Janet. 1988. "Paying Compliments: A Sex-Preferential Politeness Strategy." *Journal of Pragmatics*. 12(3): 445–465.

hooks, bell. 1981. *Ain't I A Woman*. Boston: South End Press.

Hochschild, Arlie Russell. 1982. *The Managed Heart: Commercialization of Human Feeling*. Berkeley: University of California Press.

Howitt, Dennis, and J. Owusu-Bempah. 1990. "The Pragmatics of Institutional Racism: Beyond Words." *Human Relations*. 43(9): 885–899.

Hughes, Jean O. and Bernice R. Sandler. 1986. "In Case of Sexual Harassment: A Guide for Women Students." A report from the Project on the Status and Education of Women, Association of American Colleges, 1818 R. St. NW, Washington, DC 20009, April.

Kessler, Suzanne and Wendy McKenna. 1978. *Gender: An Ethnomethodological Approach*. New York: Wiley.

Kissling, Elizabeth Arveda. 1991. "Street Harassment: The Language of Sexual Terrorism." *Discourse and Society*. 2(4): 451–460.

Kissling, Elizabeth Arveda, and Cheris Kramarae. 1991. "Stranger Compliments: The Interpretation of Street Remarks." *Women's Studies in Communication*. 14(1): 75–93.

Knapp, Mark L., Robert Hopper, and Robert A. Bell. 1984. "Compliments: A Descriptive Taxonomy." *Journal of Communication*. 34(4): 12–31.

Kramarae, Cheris. 1985. "Speech Crimes Which the Law Cannot Reach or Compliments and Other Insulting Behavior." In Berkeley Women and Language Group, ed. *Proceedings of the First Women and Language Conference*. Berkeley, Calif.: University of California.

Kramarae, Cheris, and Paula Treichler, with Ann Russo. 1985. *A Feminist Dictionary*. New York: Pandora Press/Unwin/Hyman.

Lacy, Michael. 1992. "Toward a Rhetorical Understanding of Civil Racism." Unpublished Dissertation. University of Texas at Austin.

Lambert, Helen H. 1987. "Biology and Equality: A Perspective on Sex Differences." In *Sex and Scientific Inquiry*. eds. Sandra Harding and Jean F. O'Barr. University of Chicago Press: 123–145.

Moses, Yolanda T. 1989. Black Women in Academe: Issues and Strategies. *Project on the Status and Education of Women,* August. (Association of American Colleges, 1818 R St., NW, Washington, DC 20009)

Nichols, Nancy. 1988. "Up Against the Wall Street." *Ms.* November: 66, 68–69.

Russell, Diana. 1982. *Rape in Marriage.* New York: Macmillan.

Scott, Sara, and Alison Dickens. 1988. "Controlling with Kindness." *Trouble and Strife.* 13(Spring): 40–45.

Sheffield, Carole. 1987. "Sexual Terrorism: The Social Control of Women." In *Analyzing Gender: A Handbook of Social Science Research.* eds. Beth B. Hess and Myra Marx Ferree. Beverly Hills: Sage: 171–189.

Spalter-Roth, Roberta, Heidi I. Hartmann, and Linda M. Andrews. 1990. "Who Needs a Family Wage? The Implications of Low-Wage Work for Family Well-Being." Institute for Women's Policy Research report. Washington, D.C.

Spender, Dale. 1982a. *Invisible Women: The Schooling Scandal.* London: Writers and Readers Publishing.

Spender, Dale. 1982b. *Women of Ideas and What Men Have Done to Them.* London: Routledge & Kegan Paul.

Stanko, Elizabeth. 1985. *Intimate Intrusions: Woman's Experience of Male Violence.* London: Routledge & Kegan Paul.

Stanley, Liz. 1984. "Why Men Oppress Women, or How Experiences of Sexism Can Tell Us Interesting and Useful Things About Women's Oppression and Women's Liberation." In *Looking Back: Some Papers from the* BSA Gender & Society Conference. eds. Sue Webb and Clive Pearson. Department of Sociology, University of Manchester.

Steinem, Gloria. 1983. *Outrageous Acts and Everyday Rebellions.* New York: Holt, Rinehart & Winston.

Strauss, Marcy. 1990. "Sexist Speech in the Workplace." *Harvard Civil Rights Civil Liberties Law Review.* 25(1): 1–51.

Thomann, Daniel A., and Richard L. Wiener. 1987. "Physical and Psychological Causality as Determinants of Culpability in Sexual Harassment Cases." *Sex Roles.* 17(9/10): 573–591.

Thorne, Barrie. 1992. *Gender Play: Girls and Boys in School.* New Brunswick, N.J.: Rutgers University Press.

Truax, Anne. 1989. "Sexual Harassment in Higher Education: What We've Learned." *Thought & Action: The* NEA *Higher Education Journal.* 4(1): 25–38.

Verespej, Michael A. 1988. " 'Hostile Environment': It Has Made Sexual Harassment a Mine Field." *Industry Week.* March 21: 21.

Wise, Sue and Liz Stanley. 1987. *Georgie Porgie: Sexual Harassment in Everyday Life.* London: Pandora.

Wolfson, Nessa. 1981. "Compliments in Cross-Cultural Perspective." TESOL Quarterly. 15(2): 117–124.

Wolfson, Ness, and Joan Manes. 1980. "The Compliment as a Social Strategy." *Papers in Linguistics.* 13(3): 391–410.

7

The History and Structure of
Women's Alternative Media

Linda Steiner

For nearly 250 years women have recognized the value of establishing and operating their own communications media, literally making their own meaning and communicating it to one another across space and over time. In part, these alternatives have been prompted by women's continuing inability—or reluctance—to use mainstream or even radical/alternative mass media for their purposes. "Massified" media institutions have historically been hostile to women's attempts to negotiate for themselves alternative visions, definitions, ways of being. At worst, mass media ignore, trivialize, or belittle the philosophies and activities of successive waves of the women's movement; at best they dilute or coopt the major concepts. Susan B. Anthony insisted: as long as magazines and newspapers are controlled by men, women's ideas will never get before the public. But there are other, more affirmative reasons why women establish independent media: to articulate and dramatize their emerging interests, to nourish and defend an identity that imbues their lives with meaning. Not only can they thus mount an effective challenge to dominant structures, ideology, and content, but they also derive considerable intellectual and emotional satisfaction from producing and supporting their own women-controlled, women-oriented media. In and through communication they transform and empower themselves. Here women are not a "second-best" audience.

Understanding even before A.J. Liebling said it that "there's freedom of the press for the guy who owns one," women have published books, magazines, newspapers, journals, pamphlets, and newsletters—of various sizes, frequencies, and duration, and with different purposes, audiences, organizations, and financing structures. No wonder that feminist Robin Morgan (1977) includes printing among the skills necessary for women.

121

Print well served eighteenth and especially nineteenth century women. As rail transportation and postal systems improved, paper and postage costs dropped, literacy spread, and printing technology became easier (with the invention of Linotype and then monotype, as well as with easier and cheaper ways to reproduce photographs), print became increasingly useful to women. Danky's list (1982) of almost 1,500 women's periodicals and newspapers begins with *The Female Spectator,* published and edited in Dublin in 1746, and *The Lady's Magazine, or Polite Companion for the Fair Sex,* published 1759–66 in London. In 1834 Ann Oddbody launched the short-lived *Woman,* declaring, "There is a paper *Man* published, why shall not a paper *Woman* be also seen daily in the City of Gotham" (Ross 1936, 14). Although it began in 1849 as a Seneca Falls (N.Y.) temperance organ, the first women's suffrage paper was Amelia Bloomer's *The Lily.* The Doughan and Sanchez list (1987) of British feminist periodicals begins with *Sempstress,* published at least once in 1855.

As print technology became still more accessible in the twentieth century, additional mechanisms have been adapted, including feminist dictionaries, thesauri, and directories; for example, many organizations offer their own version of the Yellow Pages, listing women-controlled businesses, services, and resources. Wire services, news bureaus, and computer networks likewise build on print. Now women are exploiting the potential of radio and recording, television and cable.

Because scholars and activists have been primarily concerned with women's roles and representations in mainstream mass media, these alternative media remain remarkably understudied. The few studies of women's media thus far only take them as containing historical records of specific women's consciousness. But their impact extends far beyond what might be suggested by circulation or audience size; nor is this impact adequately understood through content analysis. This chapter, therefore, after clarifying the concept of women's media, will first outline the general characteristics of women's media, emphasizing their similarities in terms of their definition of communication, their commitment to being women-run and controlled, their non-profit and anti-commercial orientation, and their rejection of professionalism and industrial authority structures. Then I will review various types of media, beginning with an abbreviated summary of nineteenth century suffrage periodicals, to show early, successful experiments with feminist communication. My goal is to convey, primarily through examples, a sense of the enormous range and diversity of women's media while also highlighting their remarkable commonalities. The heterogeneity—stylistic and political—in the women's movement is clearly marked in its media, which advocate different styles, models, and visions. At the same time, certain themes—notably of identity and community—consistently emerge, revealing that ongoing connection between communication and community, communion, and commitment.

The term "women's media" is ambiguous. Given my broad conception of feminism as dedicated to eliminating the oppression of women as well as categorical oppression by race, class, ethnicity, and sexual preference, I will sometimes refer to the women's media discussed here as feminist. Were it not for the historical specificity of this term and the fact that many relevant examples predated the feminist movement (or do not use this term), this discussion would be titled "feminist media." Certainly one must distinguish "women's media" from mainstream newspapers, magazines, television and radio shows targeted at women for marketing purposes.

My description highlights distinctive *structural features* of women's media. Nevertheless, the definition of "women's media" as used here can be grounded in their alternative *content*. When the Alternative Press Index first appeared in 1970, its subtitle read: "An index to the publications which amplify the cry for social change and social justice." One need only add that women's media cry out particularly for social change and justice for women. They deal with gender issues buried, ignored, or distorted in mainstream media. Women's media have variously expressed the differing concerns, the visions, the needs of the movement to eliminate gender oppression, and express the changing, still-emerging identities of the women in this movement. Women's media are oppositional, alternative, resistant in both product and process.[1]

Structural Characteristics of Women's Media

Women's media mandate serving women as a community through communication, such that "source" and "receiver" remain one and the same. More accurately, the operating and ultimate principle of women's media is to express and celebrate viewpoints of specific groups of women. That "particularity" is not always articulated, however, and women's media often exaggerate their ability to speak for all women. "It is WOMAN that speaks through *The Lily*," Amelia Bloomer promised in her debut editorial (January 1, 1849, p.4). Spelling out the claim, WIN (Women's International Network) News, founded in 1975 and still operating out of its Lexington, Mass. office, calls itself "a world-wide open participatory communication system by, for and about women of all backgrounds, beliefs, nationalities and age groups." While the claims to represent all women are exaggerated, women's media do repudiate the language of business in order to embrace the language of sisterhood.

123

This commitment to women generally entails involving women in most or all aspects of production, sometimes each worker learning each part of the process. *The Woman's Advocate,* begun in 1855 in Philadelphia, was subtitled "Devoted to the elevation of the Female Industrial Classes, and produced exclusively by the joint stock capital, energies, and industry of females." The *Advocate's* editor insisted that women perform all the work and enjoy all the profits (January 27, 1855, p. 2). Many contemporary women's publishers and periodicals operate similarly, thus demystifying labor and proving women's intellectual and technical abilities. Olivia, the oldest and largest women's record label, vows to offer training in technical and other fields in the recording industry and to provide jobs with decent pay in non-oppressive conditions (Tilchen 1984, 301).

Most women's media allow, but limit, men's participation. The most well-known papers of both factions of the woman's suffrage movement, articulating very different models for the "new woman," included men at the helm. *Revolution* was coedited by "strong-minded" Elizabeth Cady Stanton and the rather genteel abolitionist Parker Pillsbury; originally subsidized by George Francis Train, it had several regular male contributors likewise controversial for their politics, if not for their gender. The much longer-lived and more "responsible" *Woman's Journal,* for years the official organ of the major American suffrage organization, was cofounded by Lucy Stone and her husband Henry Blackwell and included men on its board. These days, men may help produce women's media (a Norwegian woman's radio station lets men constitute one-third its volunteer staff [Skard 1989]), but they very rarely edit or publish feminist periodicals. Certainly contemporary women's media require women's control, and usually ownership.

Because the goal is authentic communication, women's media tend not to require professional experience or formal training in mass media. Women approach these media precisely for that opportunity to work intensively, for no or low pay, with a community of similarly-impassioned women on a cause they find important. Often—and this is true of nineteenth century suffragists and twentieth century feminists—women see their involvement in media as continuous with their other social-change activities. They are activists dedicated to bringing forth knowledge to bring about transformation, not neutral observers distributing information commodities. Onlywoman Press's publishing-printing collective asserts, "We are quite committed to making what we do an act of participation within the Women's Movement instead of turning out products like hot dogs" (Cadman, Chester, and Pivot 1981, 35).

Unfortunately, staff members often and sometimes rapidly suffer "burnout"—physically exhausted and emotionally drained. With limited ability to hire trained substitutes, many periodicals die after one year, or one issue. Joreen (Jo Freeman), who spearheaded the first publication of the contemporary feminist movement, regards *Voice of women's liberation movement* as a tremendous success:

> Its purpose was to reach any potential sympathizer in order to let her know that there were others who thought as she did and that she was not isolated or crazy. It also functioned to put women in contact with other like-minded women in the same area and thus stimulated the formation of new groups (1975, 110).

But the "Herculean task" of putting out a paper with unpaid labor (it grew from 3 to 25 pages) proved overwhelming, and *Vwlm* died after sixteen months.

Among the foremost implications of the announced commitment to communication is that women's media are not profit-motivated. They may not intend to lose money and may not oppose financial success; several women's periodicals have broken even for a time. On the other hand, "there is no record to date of a skilful entrepreneur making a fortune on a feminist paper" (Doughan and Sanchez 1987, xiii). Failing to attract enough appropriate advertising revenues or subscriptions, and with news-stand sales rarely significant, they must resort to fund-raising, personal donations, and institutional subsidies. After publishing *Revolution* for two and a half years, Susan Anthony was $10,000 in debt (the $1 she received for selling the paper and its subscription list to Laura Bullard was stolen). The first edition of *Feminist Revolution*—a 1975 book published in news-print format—required many hours of volunteer time as well as $6,000 upfront, of which $5,200 represented donations from 200 individuals (Redstockings 1978, 10).

If they run advertising, women's media usually limit what kind of advertising is acceptable; they carefully judge the quality and use of the good or service potentially advertised, who is offering it, and how the ad itself would be designed and worded. *Spare Rib* and *Outwrite* (now defunct) have been the only large feminist periodicals that have consistently managed to attract profitable advertising without compromising themselves politically. Conversely, dependence on advertising revenue "imposes enormous limitations" on what *Viva,* a feminist-leaning magazine in Kenya with a male editor, can publish (Gallagher 1981, 138).

As another example, the WIN News's coverage of the 1985 UN conference in Nairobi produced $1,310 in revenue and received a grant of $2,420; this covered less than one-quarter of costs. Nonetheless, its organizers believe it succeeded in the minds of both participants and "receivers": "It proved that women can use the most advanced technology to communicate among themselves and to the world" (Kassell and Kaufman 1989, 236–237). Parallel economic conflicts and problems agonize other feminist media. The London-based publishing company Virago, for example, given the expense of print runs under 10,000, raised eyebrows for using Hong Kong (that is, lower-paid) typesetters. Seccombe-Eastland's (1988) study of a bookstore collective illustrates several strategies its members developed to avoid directly confronting the "major contradiction" emerging between its feminist-separatist theory/ideology and its business practices/ needs. Lont's study of Holly Near's Redwood Records shows individual staff members differing on the profit/politics dichotomy, with the company itself only gradually discovering a "middle ground by becoming economically solvent without losing the political value of its message" (1988, 244); a wrenching organizational restructuring in the interests of business and a "more commercial sounding album" was required for Redwood to recover from a $75,000 debt. Cadman, Chester, and Pivot (1981, 88) claim feminists' moral ambivalence about money betrays theoretical confusion, but surely legitimate matters of principle are at stake.

Women's media are typically self-conscious about subscription rates, sensitive that overpricing will limit access for those most needing to hear their messages. To illustrate "the true nature of the female role by reverse example as well as the high price of independence," *Notes from the First Year* cost women $.50, but cost men $1.00 (Freeman 1975, 116). Analogously, *Union Wage,* produced by and for women wage-earners, offered unemployed women discounts. The Canadian *Womanist* solicits advertising—so that it can be distributed free—and *Sinister Wisdom* is free to women inmates.

Women's media are nearly always small, because they address geographically and/or stylistically specific populations. Rejecting the "lowest common denominator" approach, they consciously define their audience very narrowly, making this obvious to audiences not only through content, but also choice of name (from *Revolution* to *off our backs*) and graphic design. One pre-Civil War women's right's editor was bitter about *Una's* low circulation, but insisted, "We would prefer a smaller audience . . . looking for the fresh warm thoughts of our contributors . . . to seeing them crowded in out-of-the-way corners of political papers" (*Una,* February 1855, p. 25). Women's recordings have been labelled "for women only" or "for lesbians only." The Salt Lake City bookstore mentioned earlier (Seccombe-Eastland 1988) excluded men on Friday nights. As with these other features, the sisterhood and solidarity promoted by this exclusivity has its downside. Women's media often alienate potential sympathizers with their highly particularized version of their cause and their audience;

this provides an easy opening for ridicule and accusations of self-ghet-toizing. But it is not a question of elitism. I believe it represents an authentic attempt to communicate to and with those who care.

Egalitarian management and structures present perennial challenges for women's media. Most nineteenth and early twentieth century feminist publications operated with one or two individuals at the top as editor and publisher, often one and the same. Although these women were by no means conventional, the hierarchies were. But second-wave feminists tend to be rigorously self-conscious about the politics of their practices. Bor-rowing from other feminist practices, such as the consciousness-raising group, today's feminists experiment with revolving control, investing au-thority in the community or eliminating authority altogether. *Union Wage,* published in San Francisco 1971–82, patterned its organization on a sim-plified trade union model, one person saying "getting a grip on *Union Wage's* organization was like trying to seize a bowl of jello" (Downing 1984, 99). For a time it tried to hold entirely to the politics of consensus, dismissing voting as a concession to male power structures; eventually it returned to majority rule. *Quest: a feminist quarterly,* on the other hand, has "a system of shifting horizontal leadership," with full-time staff en-joying enlarged responsibilities and authority; staff acknowledge how the practical demands of producing *Quest* conflict with political goals (Bunch 1981, xix–xx). Likewise, the organizational chart of a government-spon-sored feminist filmmaking collective in Canada shows a fairly clear hier-archy, a "dissonant" fact which apparently brings distress to some, but not all, its members (Taylor, 1988).

Several women's recording labels, publishing houses and periodicals are run as collectives, with work and responsibilities dispersed. This way no single editor, programmer, or director can be accused of monopolizing status or authority. Sometimes these media maintain anonymous or egal-itarian structures specifically to thwart mainstream media, which only deal with designated officials and authorities. According to the 1970 statement of purpose of *off our backs,* still collectively-run:

> [W]e are attempting to build . . . non-exploitative ways of relating to one another based on trust and concern rather than political expe-diency. We have serious personal/political intentions in breaking down hierarchical and elitist structures, and for experimenting with leaderless groups and collective decision-making. In dealing with the media these revolutionary principles and practices are destroyed (Ferro, Holcomb, and Saltzman-Webb 1977, 117).

Experiments to create and sustain a feminist workplace often proceed, not surprisingly, at the expense of efficiency. The decision to replace two

127

stubborn male typesetters with a woman delayed two issues of *Lily*—but Bloomer claimed it was a great moral victory. A century later, *off our backs* proudly explained that the paper was late because two editors had given birth the previous week: "Unlike most male-dominated enterprises, we are happy and willing to meet the human needs of our staff" (Armstrong 1981, 230). *It Ain't Me, Babe*'s collective held open meetings in 1970 for local women to chose content for the satiric paper; but these were a "disastrous failure" (Hole and Levine 1971, 272). Later they made each page the responsibility of one member, explaining, "[T]he membership of our collective is tentative and uncertain. . . . If the paper looks motley and ununified it is because each page is the expression of a different woman" (273).

That last quote also suggests why feminists disregard complaints (Winship 1987) about the messy look of their media. A slick smoothed-edge "professional" appearance or sound is irrelevant, perhaps politically undesirable. Kitchen Table Press designs its covers specifically to illustrate that its authors are women of color. Many periodicals maintain a crowded lay-out, with little "white" space; few bother with the expense of glossy color photographs.

Feminists try to practice what Donna Allen, of the Women's Institute for Freedom of the Press, emphasizes about the importance of allowing people to speak and judge for themselves. Downie (1989) points to lessons supplied by the *Allegheny Feminist* (1976–1980), which evolved from a patriarchal model, where a few people control what is printed, to a feminist model extending control to the readership. Later, Downie's *Pittsburgh Feminist Network News* offered institutional "members" the right to fill, unedited, a 3″ by 5″ space each month. Essentially, Downie says, she offered subscribers not only freedom of the press, but responsibility—to define themselves. Ironically, she claims, people want to be edited and are uninterested in developing alternative protocols for news gathering. She concludes somewhat wistfully, "Perhaps as more and more women learn to speak for themselves, and find they have a voice in some feminist periodical, the time will come again to try to build a communications medium, based on trust, a common worldview, and equally shared power" (201).

Celebrating its tenth anniversary in 1988, *Broomstick* reaffirmed its commitment to reclaiming the untapped "woman-power" of women over 40 by publishing the real, personal experiences of subscribers. The editors promised to provide a network of midlife women—not a platform for experts.

Preference for democratic structures leads to renunciation of formats perceived to be authoritarian, although people disagree on what is democratic or elitist. A typical means of promoting readers' involvement is by expanding the space for reader responses and submissions. Ann Arbor's *herself* and *Sojourner: The Women's Forum* run no editorials, claiming they are a mechanism by which editors impose personal opinion and stifle dialogue. *Media Report to Women* gives priority to facts and direct quotation over opinion and paraphrase; it promises not to attack people or pass judgment on their actions or ideas.

Furthermore, while the women's media and the movements for which they speak have seen their share of ambitious women, including some who openly criticize each other, they are notable for their willingness to recirculate each other's information, to publicize, help, and advise each other. Feminist communicators are relatively disinclined to regard each other as competitors, even when they disagree. Rather, they find social and intellectual inspiration in one another. Amelia Bloomer often referred to the "spiritual communion" of women editors (March 1, 1850, p. 23). Women's news services are grounded in sharing; even women publishers affirm the support and advice they derive from each other, if only from knowing that they face identical contradictions (Cadman, Chester, and Pivot 1981, 41).

Ms. is significant as the proverbial exception proving the rule. The magazine, begun in 1972 with a million dollar bankroll, enjoyed support from established commercial media, including Warner Communications and *New York* magazine, and was led by media professionals with considerable mainstream experience, including Gloria Steinem as coeditor. It was printed on glossy paper, with full color and a slick design, all to attract national subscribers (ultimately 500,000) and advertisers. Radical feminists disparaged *Ms.*'s liberal, middle-class, individualistic bias; after resigning as a contributing editor, Ellen Willis attacked Steinem as imposing an unchallenged ideology and using the magazine as propaganda for her political agenda (1978, 170–171). On the other hand, many regarded it as a useful bridge, passing on, albeit in diluted form, feminist ideas to the larger society (Armstrong 1981). And even *Ms.* experimented with communal decision-making, requiring high-status workers like writers to tackle relatively low-status work like typing (*Ms.* 1974). After 17 years and several changes in management, *Ms.* went under. In 1990 it was revived as a bimonthly ad-free cutting-edge "magabook"; despite its willingness to attract fewer subscribers at a higher price, it continues to sell out instantly at bookstores and newsstands.

All this should suggest the grounds on which I distinguish the focus of this chapter from other media targeted at women. That is, this description excludes both slick, professional contemporary women's magazines like *Savvy* and *Working Woman* (although Kessler [1984, 85] characterizes such periodicals as feminist) and service magazines, with their emphases on prevailing middle-class definitions of glamour, fashion, beauty, and domesticity. White women's magazines—the *Redbooks* and the *Glamours*—as well as their Afro-American counterparts like *Essence,* and their counterparts in South America, Asia, Europe, and Africa, vary among themselves and change over time. But they all tend to be controlled by professionals, often male. Indeed, business executives often control the professional communicators, insisting on a professional top-down industrial model. Commercial magazines are calculated to attract the right kind of consumers to attract maximum advertising revenues to produce huge profits. Conversely, these magazines ignore women who do not or cannot buy. Whether women are voiceless or disenfranchised is irrelevant. Finally, these mainstream magazines are not produced with the intention of challenging gender definitions in order to emancipate and empower women. Whether as a result of direct, conscious ideological preferences of their management, pressure from advertisers (or from the presumed necessity of attracting sufficient advertising) or as a result of carefully-researched marketing strategies, they endorse and promote conservative definitions of women prevailing at historically specific times.

Here, I acknowledge potential parallels to Radway's (1984) argument that romance novels offer women readers the opportunity to protest and escape temporarily the limited role prescribed by patriarchal culture, in part by reclaiming and altering these texts in their own interest, in part by taking time out from their duties as wives and mothers. Service magazines of the type just mentioned may function analogously. Winship, defending her own preference for curling up in bed with *Woman's Own,* complains that women's magazines "are the soaps of journalism, sadly maligned and grossly misunderstood" (1987, 7). Readers may defend service magazines—with their heavier non-fiction components of recipes, fashion, domestic advice—as helping them become better women, better lovers, mothers, wives. Perhaps these magazines too are subversive; often when women are reading these magazines they are catching private time for themselves, albeit limited in scope and duration. Equivalent legitimation might be extended to women-targeted talk shows, dramas, and soap operas. But such defense primarily rests on "pleasure" and the emotional satisfaction derived in respite from—not challenges to—oppressive duties and responsibilities. And sheer pleasure is not the basis of my definition of women's media. Indeed, whether because the explicit content and form of the discourse makes readers uncomfortable and angry (for example, by taking up issues such as rape, domestic abuse, discrimination in employment) or because, given financial exigencies or political principles, the design and format are unfamiliar and difficult, consumption of some women's media may be frustrating, even painful.

Nineteenth Century Periodicals

The early American women's rights movement relied on many communication strategies and devices, but essentially it came together as such and sustained itself over time through its periodicals. Women who resisted then dominant definitions of "true womanhood" were geographically isolated. They enjoyed few opportunities to meet in person, despite local and state meetings and conventions. Therefore, suffrage periodicals were crucial in reassuring readers that they were united in a community that gave their lives a sense of significance and purpose, on behalf of a worthy cause that ultimately would triumph.

Using rhetoric later echoed by modern feminists, readers testified that these periodicals transformed both their understanding of themselves as individuals and of women as a group. In reading them, they claimed, they entered a whole new social landscape, found a whole new way to be women. A Rochester subscriber wrote, "Since *The Revolution* has removed the bandages from our eyes . . . we begin to see women as 'trees walking' " (October 29, 1868, p. 260). These earlier periodicals suggested new values, emphasized new standards, and discovered new heroines. Over time, their periodicals taught them various new ways to talk, dress, think, judge, and name themselves. With varying success they argued for the plausibility of granting honor and status to the new woman committed to these new ways. To varying degrees they bolstered the morale of converts (the religious language is intentional) and attracted the uncommitted. These periodicals explained and legitimized the instrumental and expressive purposes of the movement.

Many of the 80 or so suffrage periodicals published in the United States were fairly limited in both duration and distribution, but several achieved national circulation and fame. A few enjoyed a long life, including *The Woman's Journal* (1870–1931), Clara Bewick Colby's *Woman's Tribune* (1883–1909), and *Woman's Standard* (1886–1911). Many were published in the Midwest and Far West, including the *San Francisco Pioneer,* 1869–73; Abigail Scott Duniway's *The New Northwest,* published 1871–87 in Oregon; and *Queen Bee,* published in Denver 1882–95. By 1910, nearly every state had some suffrage organ. Besides the regional dynamic, only a few periodicals were explicitly directed at particular populations, such as *The Farmer's Wife,* 1891–94; and *The Woman's Exponent,* published 1872–1914 for and by Mormon women. Otherwise, the suffrage press presumed to speak for all "new women." But whether they merely ignored African-American and other women or they intentionally put gender concerns above race, these really were middle-class white women's periodicals celebrating middle-class white women's concerns.

Several "new women's" periodicals were not specifically suffragist, including *Woodhull and Claflin's Weekly,* put out 1870–76 by two New York City sisters who advocated free love, dress reform, mystical religion, and Victoria Woodhull for President. Margaret Sanger edited and published *The Woman Rebel* in 1914, until she was indicted by a federal grand jury for using the mails to disseminate information on contraception; her *Birth Control Review* lasted 1917–40. Charlotte Perkins Gilman edited and published the *Forerunner,* 1909–16, carrying her own feminist articles, editorials, poetry, and serialized fiction (including "Herland").

The Contemporary Women's Press

As suggested earlier, second-wave feminists became convinced that mainstream mass media exploited, distorted, belittled, or patronized women and the women's movement. From San Francisco to New York, they staged fairly dramatic "invasions" of newspapers and magazines, especially women's magazines. One women's coalition permanently took over *Rat,* a New York underground paper notorious for its pornography and ridicule of women. Launched in January 1970 with Robin Morgan's "Good-bye to All That," the *Women's Rat* continued for three years before falling prey to internecine warfare (Morgan 1977). Just as nineteenth century reform-minded women were disturbed by their second-class status in the abolition and temperance movements (Seneca Falls women launched *The Lily* because male prohibitionists let them do nothing beyond donating money), so in part the considerable sexism (both in content and practice) of alternative presses of the sixties prompted feminists to establish their own media. But it was precisely because they realized that they could never win their own revolution without their own media that many rights-oriented publications began in 1968, including the still-published organ of the National Organization for Women.

By 1971 over one hundred women's liberation newspapers, magazines, and journals were being published; by 1973, over 130, in nearly every state (Hole and Levine 1971, 271; Mather 1975). An explosion of more specialized journals followed; some advocated moderate politics or radical separatist politics, others concentrated on philosophy, legislative action, or health. These media supported and empowered feminist communities, giving them muscle and energy. Not infrequently, feminist media provided information of vital import to women. For example, *herself* scooped larger media in reporting the health dangers of DES (Armstrong 1981, 231). Many embraced global approaches, lending moral support to women in national liberation movements and in socialist countries. Feminist periodicals emerged in this period around the globe, including Mauritania, Senegal, Ghana, Sri Lanka, Uruguay, Japan, Hong Kong, Holland and South Africa. A feminist samizdat (self-published paper) even appeared once in the Soviet Union (Gallagher 1981, 139–40). About 70 are being published in the United Kingdom (Cadman, Chester and Pivot 1981, 71). The largest woman's movement periodical now is *Emma,* in Germany, with a circulation of 300,000; the oldest is *Hertha,* published in Sweden for 130 years.

Particularization (one might say "separatism") continues today; the more specialized the periodical, the more adherents have the physical and psychological space for experimenting in building the architectures in which they feel most comfortable. Kranich estimates that over 80 of the 1,500 periodicals emerging in the 1968–88 period were by and for women of color. Whether generally alienated by the racism and classism of white feminists or personally rejected by white feminist media (Davenport 1983, 85), and in part affirmatively recognizing the value of their own expressive media, African-American, Asian, Latina, and Native American women have established their own periodicals. These cover a range of issues, including imperialism, classism, prostitution, rape, homelessness, genocide, sterilization abuse. Many were very short-lived, but 20 were in press in 1988, most of these enjoying some official sponsorship (Kranich 1989). Current publications include *Dakota Women of All Red Nations; Literary Express,* published by a Chicago collective of "wimmin of color from all walks of life"; *Malintzin: Chicana Newsletter/Carta Informante Chicana,* published in San Antonio; and *Common Ground-Different Planes,* dealing with reproductive health.

The Ladder was the first major lesbian periodical (1956–72); Potter lists 60 lesbian journals in press in the United States in 1982, some nationally known, some regional, and many representing particular groups, for example, for African-Americans or Asians, professions or interests from "dykecological gardening" to science fiction. Several national and regional lesbian archival projects are significant for their work in preserving these and other materials. Lesbian periodicals are now also published in Australia, Brazil, Britain, Canada, Germany, Italy, Mexico, and the Netherlands. Many literary and "arty" journals continue, such as *Kalliope,* which publishes women's art and photographs as well as fiction and poetry; *Helicon Nine,* which often includes a tear-out recording; and *Hot Wire,* covering women's music. *Lilith* serves Jewish women; *Mom's Apple Pie* is a newsletter for lesbian mothers.

Beyond the purview of this chapter are feminist novels and poetry (such as Marge Piercy's); trade nonfiction (although some had major import, like *Our Bodies, Ourselves*) and scholarly journals such as *Signs;* documentary and feature films by individual women; as well as other visual media, including graffiti, such as feminist messages in public or women-only sites; slide shows; comic strips (Wimmin's Comix), painting and other art media (I have in mind communal events like Judy Chicago's *The Dinner Party*). As relevant and crucial to the movement as they are, I can only mention the significance of their attempts to bridge the gap between academic and popular views of feminism, often not only reaching but also touching quite large audiences. The underground women's comic strips—their creators and their characters—effectively rebel against conventional popular images of women (Mitchell 1981). Again, in their production, process is crucial; women's recording studios like Olivia or Ladyslipper are acutely sensitive to matters of political principle not only regarding content but also decision-making generally.[2] More importantly, they also contribute to the making and remaking of definitions of women, thereby transforming their audiences. One independent black film-maker says, "We hope that with our films we can help create a new world, by speaking in our own voice and defining ourselves" (Larkin 1988, 173). Women again testify to the personally dramatic impact of a Chicana book, an African-American women's art exhibit, or women-identified album. Important to mention here, nevertheless, is Studio D of the National Film Board of Canada. Studio D has gone beyond its 1974 mandate to make films by, for, and about women; it now heralds its explicitly feminist goals (Taylor, 1988).

Feminist publishing houses are relevant here, for they not only "generate" women's work, but also drive it, define it, and encourage it. Donna Allen's Women's Institute for Freedom of the Press, founded in 1972, helps both academics and grassroots activists by publishing an extensive *Directory of Women's Media* and *Media Report to Women,* as well as *The Celebate Woman* (irregularly since 1982) and undertaking other ambitious projects. Feminist and lesbian presses, of which there are now hundreds in a dozen countries, often are the first to articulate new political issues, to support new literary talent, and to showcase authors from outside white, heterosexual, middle-class circles (Loeb et al 1987, xiii). An important representative of this trend is Kitchen Table: Women of Color Press, founded in 1981 to publish Third World women, particularly lesbians; it does not publish white authors. In 1984 the editorial board officially declared, "Our work is both cultural and political, connected to the struggles for freedom of all of our peoples" (B. Smith 1989). Kitchen Table is a revolutionary tool, says one cofounder, "a vehicle for shaping ideology which serves as a foundation for making practical social and political change" (Smith 1989, 207). Mainstream commercial and academic publishers are increasingly willing to accept feminist manuscripts, some establishing specialized feminist imprints (for instance, Routledge & Kegan Paul has Pandora). Nonetheless, just as lesbian singers might prefer to sign with a woman's label, some writers prefer to sign with a feminist or lesbian house, which will appropriately publicize their work with the relevant, if smaller audience, and not require them to dilute their politics. "Fortunately, the influx of mainstream publishers into the feminist marketplace of ideas has not squeezed out women's independent publishing" (Loeb et al. 1987, xii).

Public libraries and conventional sales outlets are unlikely to stock feminist media in the ways they carry *Time* or *Newsweek*.[3] Moreover, standard reviewing media give short shrift to feminist books, although these are reviewed in the feminist periodicals, from the *Women's Review of Books* (Massachusetts) to *Aunt Edna's Reading List* (Hawaii). A variety of alternative distribution networks have emerged as crucial. The biannual International Feminist Book Fairs, first held in Oslo in 1984, are well attended. Feminist bookstores, of which 88 operated in the United States in 1985 (Schulman 1988, 106), often issue newsletters or organize other events—poetry readings or lectures, for example—to provide continuing support for and critique of the movement. Some publishers have mail-order catalogs or clubs, although this may have the unintended and unwanted effect of undermining feminist bookstores. In 1977 a British group began the Women's Liberation Bookbus, to distribute literature in small towns (Cadman 1981, 89). Womyn's Braille Press in Minneapolis provides feminist and lesbian feminist material in large print, braille, and tape cassette. Finally, although Women in Distribution folded in the United States, national alternative networks distribute feminist material in Germany and England.

Broadcasting

The U.S. broadcasting structure demands (and this is historically obdurate and not likely to change) large audiences to generate enormous amounts of advertising revenue to support large-scale investment. Highly bureaucratized and dependent on complex technology, it uses well-trained professionals and technicians. This severely constrains possibilities for a feminist television channel or station; "subjects of struggle" are not likely to be consistently televised "subjects of information," especially in prime-time. There are exceptions. Four feminist television series have been aired in Holland, including "Rok en Rol," a short-lived show interchanging humorous sketches with serious interviews. "Ot en . . . hoe zit het nu met Sien" was proposed in 1975 to the Dutch National Broadcasting Company by a well-known Dutch feminist; it ended in 1982 when its consciousness-raising format lost its appeal (Hermes and van Zoonen 1987). Even in a relatively small country, television programming aims for large, homogeneous audiences; Hermes and Van Zoonen emphasize the virtual impossibility of even satisfying all feminists, who demand that each feminist program present their own perspective as feminists, although these perspectives vary greatly.

Some feminists excavate regular television programming (and other mainstream mass media) to find feminist "references." Gray describes how, while recovering from a mastectomy, she discovered "Woman to Woman," in which diverse women discussed their experiences with problems ranging from breast cancer to strip searches: "The hidden world of women's experience, long concealed from all of us by the silencing norms of patriarchy as well as by the human barriers of geography, social class, race, age-cohort, and privacy was suddenly opened up to me by a simple turn of the TV dial" (1989, 84). Echoing sentiments of suffrage press readers, she adds:

> My isolation was bridged, my self-pity was broken into by the reality of their life-traumas which were different than mine. . . . And never in one support group of women friends could I have found the sharing on the variety of topics which my well-researched TV support group provided (84).

Gray believes Phil Donahue and Oprah Winfrey connect women up differently, but that they too educate and culturally integrate home-bound women, thus reducing their cultural isolation and providing instantaneous consciousness-raising (88–90). She asserts these programs can show women how they are oppressed, can give voice and hearing by other women to the voiceless.

I do not agree with Gray that these network television shows radicalize their audiences. Nevertheless, it is not impossible for television to engage women in a "new schooling"; a Portuguese woman's group regularly produces radio and television programs. Certainly video technology is increasingly accessible, cheaper, and easier to learn. Working on community-based cable-cast videos has provided exhilarating "consciousness-raising" (Gallagher 1981, 123–24).

Given the technology of radio broadcasting and the financial viability of specialized radio stations, one might expect radio to be relatively hospitable to woman's programming. It is not. Early radio restricted itself essentially to "homemaker" programs, beginning with "Mrs. Page's Household Economy," hosted by Ruth Crane in Detroit from 1929–44; her later radio and television shows called "Modern Woman" were equally domestic (Beasley and Silver, 1977). One "women's" radio station (WOMN, in Connecticut) was a male-owned commercial enterprise.

In 1969 WBAI-FM (a listener-sponsored station) introduced feminist radio programming with a combination of taped consciousness-raising sessions and live telephoned responses. One WBAI colleague recalls that women listeners were greatly touched by "CR"; eventually the feminism of its producer dominated the station, "driving out the front door, screaming and kicking, a number of her staunchest male adversaries" (Post 1974, 104). Since then, a couple of stations, primarily "alternative" ones, have scheduled women's programming or have responded to criticism by permitting feminist groups to produce something. Spark (1987) argues that even Pacifica—the radio network most committed to providing a critique of sexism, racism, and classism—does not practice what it preaches and ignores manifestations of these problems within its own organization. (Cadman, Chester, and Pivot [1981] similarly accuse radical publishers and bookstores of underrating women's abilities, sexually harassing women, and structuring themselves along patriarchal lines.) Among the few organized Feminist radio groups in the United States have been Boston Women's Community Radio, Radio Free Feminists in Atlanta, and Suzie Cream Cheese Collective in Chicago. Sophie's Parlor Media Collective has produced a weekly show for a Washington, D.C. FM station for almost 20 years while the San Francisco-based WINGS distributes a half-hour radio show to international subscribers. RadiOracle was created in Oslo in 1982, when Norway first allowed private stations; this women's radio station, depending largely on volunteers, tries to make "the strength, resources, activity, and progress of women visible to the public, cultivating diversity, exuberance, and depth more than impartiality, objectivity, and rapidity" (Skard 1989, 141).

In Australia, a unit formed originally to help women staff participate in radio programming decided to create its own feminist weekly radio show, "Coming Out, Ready or Not." Gallagher appreciates the difficulty of organizing cooperative structures within a hierarchical setting:

> Pursuing its aims of attaining gains for *all* women, the cooperative has tried to create noncompetitive, egalitarian, supportive work conditions: skills, knowledge and experience are shared; policies are discussed cooperatively; programme/production positions are selected by the cooperative and rotated annually; struggles with management

are pursued independently of the union, through direct action and collective bargaining (1981, 134).

Radio Donna, a daily two-hour feminist opt-out, now defunct, from a leftist station in Rome, provides another lesson: in 1979, while taping a broadcast about abortion, members of its housewives' collective were physically attacked by Fascists (Gallagher 1981, 141).

Santa Cruz (1989) emphasizes the macro-level (national and international) influence of alternative news services and information networks such as Isis (which collects and reproduces, in English and Spanish, documentation on specific themes), Agence Femmes Information (France), Frauenpress (Germany), DepthNews (Philippines and Japan) and the International Women's Tribune Centre (for Third World women, based in New York). After three years of operation, in 1980, the women-owned HER SAY had over 100 radio subscribers plus feminist magazine subscribers (Armstrong 1981, 232). Inter Press' Women's Feature Service distributes news stories written by Third World feminists. Santa Cruz herself founded both Unidad de Communicacion Alternativa de la Mujer (the Women's Alternative Media Unit) and FEMPRESS, which compiles information from correspondents in nine countries and sends out a 30-page bulletin to 840 recipients throughout Latin America. She quotes a *Mujer*-FEMPRESS correspondent:

> *Mujer* is weaving the network of Latin American feminism on a continental scale: connecting groups, circulating news, analyzing issues, overcoming distances, languages, race, diverse political climates and cultures.... In this cross-national bulletin, feminist consciousness spreads quickly—information about the women's movement in neighboring countries both legitimates and energizes—and Latin American feminism discovers and forges its own kaleidoscopic identity (1989, 259).

One should not exaggerate the tangible or symbolic successes of these organizations; many serious problems are not solved by information. But it is true: "Sisterhood emerges through the differences, showing common realities" (Santa Cruz 1989, 259).

New Technology

Although considerable and significant difficulties with access, computer literacy and cost remain unresolved, computer networks may be more efficient and cheaper for both women's group/community and individual communication, both within and across professions and geographic areas (rural or urban, and international). Smith and Balka (1988) have great hopes for word processing, mailing-list computer programs, and, especially, computer networks and bulletin boards in feminist work, in uniting and mobilizing women. Balka helped design the Women and Technology Computer Network to allow women to exchange information about technology, paying particular attention to its gendered impact. Smith celebrates the potential benefits of a (less-specialized) feminist computer network that would allow dispersed women to "chat"—to check in with each other, exchange ideas, tell stories, ask for or provide aid—and to create a community. "It's too early to tell how *our* computer networks and bulletin boards may be different than others. I do know that feminist communication in the forms now available tends to stress interaction, redefinition, and cooperation" (91). Because integrating these options into feminist computer communication is important, Smith recommends designing the system with user-generated categories and with non-verbal signals or graphics to indicate personality and emotion. Even without such options, feminist computer networks and bulletin boards could help create, nourish, and maintain both general and more specialized feminist communities.

Many feminist journals can be manually searched through published indexes. But not all standard indexes are available for searching on-line. The alternative feminist press is "almost invisible" in existing printed indexes and on-line sources; nor do all libraries carry on-line specialized bibliographic databases on women, such as Catalyst Resources for Women (Wheeler 1984, 129). Solving this problem requires not only financial investment and political pressure but also further education, given the problem of the relatively low use of on-line computer catalogs by women (Wheeler, 132).

Rush sadly predicts that in the emerging communications revolution involving information technology, women's voices will again not be heard:

> A quick survey of women's roles when other revolutionary technologies were introduced indicates that men have always played the more active role in shaping these technologies and determining their use, while women have generally been the passive recipients of what has been offered or trickled down after the 'real' needs were met (1989, 8).

Granted, women did not invent most communications technologies. Patriarchal, commercial, governmental and military uses of these technologies do not serve women's interests. But women's passivity should not be exaggerated. Not only are women active, resistant interpreters of mainstream offerings, but they have also established identities, communities, and whole worlds through their creative adaptations of media. To succeed in a way consistent with feminist goals and politics has required exploiting (and sometimes subverting) the technologies and experimenting with structures and systems. It remains to be seen how women will design, use, and manage computer technologies or other technologies to come. But women have already demonstrated that media can be "done" differently, can "do" different things. While women's media will not significantly change mainstream media institutions, they do offer a serious critique of dominant media structures and professional and institutional practices. They present a challenge and model for oppositional media. Furthermore, feminism and women's media have given voice to people who otherwise would be left mute. Through their own communications, women will continue to take great satisfaction in remaking and redefining themselves and their worlds.

Notes

1. I believe these characteristics result from feminist politics, not from being created by women per se. Allen (1989, 72), among others, believes women as a sex have a distinctive (i.e., egalitarian, noncompetitive) communication style. Rush calls for a communication system built on women's world views and experiences, reflecting our metaphors of the world, our psychology, politics, economics, and culture" (1989, 18). This perhaps overstates the extent to which women have a single, unique set of world views, experiences, metaphors; an examination of women's media reveals diverse psychologies, politics, and culture. Certainly this is an area for research.

2. Also beyond my purview are women's musical festivals and concerts. But Scoville (1981) discusses the commitment of women performers to honesty and a sense of responsibility and accessibility to audiences, manifested, for example, by offering discounts to poor women.

3. West and Katz (1977) show that some librarians—perhaps themselves radical— understand their responsibilities to alternative and radical audiences.

References

Allen, Donna. 1989. "From Opportunity to Strategy: Women Contribute to the Communications Future." In *Communications at the Crossroads: The Gender Gap Connection*. eds. Ramona R. Rush and Donna Allen. Norwood, N.J.: Ablex Publishing Corp.

Armstrong, David. 1981. *A Trumpet to Arms: Alternative Media in America.* Los Angeles: J.P. Tarcher, Inc.

Beasley, Maurine and Sheila Silver, eds. 1977. "Ruth Crane: Early Days in Broadcasting." In *Women in Media: A Documentary Source Book.* Washington, D.C.: Women's Institute for Freedom of the Press.

Bunch, Charlotte. 1981. "Introduction." In *Building Feminist Theory: Essays from Quest.* eds. Quest staff. New York: Longman Inc.

Cadman, Eileen, Gail Chester and Agnes Pivot. 1981. *Rolling Our Own: Women as Printers, Publishers and Distributors.* London: Minority Press Group.

Danky, James P., ed. 1982. *Women's Periodicals and Newspapers from the 18th Century to 1981: A Union List of the Holdings of Madison, Wisconsin Libraries.* Boston: G. K. Hall & Co.

Davenport, Doris. 1983. "The Pathology of Racism: A Conversation with Third World Wimmin." In *This Bridge Called My Back: Writings by Radical Women of Color,* eds. Cherríe Moraga and Gloria Anzaldua. New York: Kitchen Table Press.

Doughan, David and Denise Sanchez. 1987. *Feminist Periodicals 1855–1984: An Annotated Critical Bibliography of British, Irish, Commonwealth and International Titles.* New York: New York University Press.

Downie, Susanna. 1989. "A Community-Based Medium: The Story of the Pittsburgh Feminist Network News." In *Communications at the Crossroads: The Gender Gap Connection,* eds. Ramona R. Rush and Donna Allen. Norwood, N.J.: Ablex Publishing Corp.

Downing, John. 1984. *Radical Media.* Boston: South End Press.

Freeman, Jo. 1975. *The Politics of Women's Liberation.* New York: Longman.

Ferro, Nancy, Coletta Reid Holcomb, and Marilyn Saltzman-Webb. 1977. "Statement of Purpose" (from *off our backs,* March 1970). In *Women in Media: A Documentary Source Book.* eds. Maurine Beasley and Sheila Silver. Washington, D.C.: Women's Institute for Freedom of the Press.

Gallagher, Margaret. 1981. *Unequal Opportunities: The Case of Women and the Media.* Paris: The UNESCO Press.

Gray, Elizabeth Dodson. 1989. "The Daytime Talk Show as a Women's Network." In *Communications at the Crossroads: The Gender Gap Connection.* eds. Ramona R. Rush and Donna Allen. Norwood, N.J.: Ablex Publishing Corp.

Hermes, Joke and Liesbet van Zoonen. "Fun or Serious Business: Dutch feminist? television programmes, 1975–1987." Paper presented to the Third International Interdisciplinary Congress on Women, Dublin, Ireland, July 1987.

Hole, Judith and Ellen Levine. 1971. *Rebirth of Feminism.* New York: Quadrangle Books.

Kassell, Paula and Susan J. Kaufman. 1989. "Planning an International Communications System for Women." In *Communications at the Crossroads: The*

Gender Gap Connection. eds. Ramona R. Rush and Donna Allen. Norwood, N.J.: Ablex Publishing Corp.

Kessler, Lauren. 1984. *The Dissident Press: Alternative Journalism in American History.* Beverly Hills: Sage Publications.

Kranich, Kimberlie A. 1989. "Celebrating Our Diversity/Women of Color Periodicals: 1968–1988. In *1989 Directory of Women's Media.* ed. Martha Leslie Allen. Washington D.C.: Women's Institute for Freedom of the Press.

Larkin, Alile Sharon. 1988. "Black Women Film-makers Defining Ourselves: Feminism in Our Own Voice." In *Female Spectators: Looking at Film and Television.* ed. E. Deidre Pribam. London: Verso.

Loeb, Catherine, Susan E. Searing, and Esther F. Stineman. 1987. *Women's Studies: A Recommended Core Bibliography 1980–1985.* Littleton, Colo.: Libraries Unlimited.

Lont, Cynthia. 1988. "Redwood Records: Principles and Profit in Women's Music." In *Women Communicating: Studies of Women's Talk.* eds. Barbara Bate and Anita Taylor. Norwood, N.J.: Ablex Publishing Corporation.

Mather, Anne. 1975. "A History of Feminist Periodicals: Part II." *Journalism History,* I, 108–111.

Mitchell, Dolores. 1981. "Humor in California Underground Women's Comix." In *Women's Culture.* ed. Gayle Kimball. Metuchen, New Jersey: The Scarecrow Press, Inc.

Morgan, Robin. 1977. *Going Too Far.* New York: Random House.

Ms. staff. 1974. "How Ms Magazine Got Started." In *The First Ms. Reader.* ed. Francine Klagsbrun. New York: Warner Communications, Co.

Post, Steve. 1974. *Playing in the FM Band.* New York: Viking Press.

Potter, Clare. 1982. "The Lesbian Periodicals Index." In *Lesbian Studies: Present and Future.* ed. Margaret Cruikshank. Old Westbury, N.Y.: The Feminist Press.

Radway, Janice A. 1984. *Reading the Romance: Women, Patriarchy, and Popular Literature.* Chapel Hill: The University of North Carolina Press.

Redstockings. 1978. *Feminist Revolution.* New York: Random House.

Ross, Ishbel. 1936, 1974. *Ladies of the Press.* New York: Harper & Row. Reprint by New York: Arno Press.

Rush, Ramona. 1989. "Communications at the Crossroads." In *Communications at the Crossroads: The Gender Gap Connection.* eds. Ramona R. Rush and Donna Allen. Norwood, N.J.: Ablex Publishing Corp.

Santa Cruz, Adriana. 1989. "Alternative Communication and Latin American Women." In *Communications at the Crossroads: The Gender Gap Connection.* eds. Ramona R. Rush and Donna Allen. Norwood, N.J.: Ablex Publishing Corp.

Schulman, Mark. 1988. *Gender and Typographic Culture.* In *Technology and Women's Voices: Keeping in Touch.* ed. Cheris Kramarae. London: Routledge and Kegan Paul.

Scoville, Ruth. 1981. "Women's Music." In *Women's Culture*. ed. Gayle Kimball. Metuchen, N.J.: The Scarecrow Press, Inc.

Seccombe-Eastland, Lynette. 1988. "Ideology, Contradiction, and Change in a Feminist Bookstore." In *Women Communicating: Studies of Women's Talk*. eds. Barbara Bate and Anita Taylor. Norwood, N.J.: Ablex Publishing Corporation.

Skard, Torild. 1989. "Norway: Two-Edged S(word)s for Women Journalists." In *Communications at the Crossroads: The Gender Gap Connection*. eds. Ramona R. Rush and Donna Allen. Norwood, N.J.: Ablex Publishing Corp.

Smith, Barbara. 1989. "A Press of Our Own: Kitchen Table: Women of Color Press." In *Communications at the Crossroads: The Gender Gap Connection*. eds. Ramona R. Rush and Donna Allen. Norwood, N.J.: Ablex Publishing Corp.

Smith, Judy and Ellen Balka. 1988. "Chatting on a Feminist Computer Network." In *Technology and Women's Voices: Keeping in Touch*. ed. Cheris Kramarae. London: Routledge and Kegan Paul.

Spark, Clare. 1987. "Pacifica Radio and the Politics of Culture." In *American Media and Mass Culture: Left Perspectives*. ed. Donald Lazere. Berkeley: University of California Press.

Taylor, Anita. 1988. "Implementing Feminist Principles in a Bureaucracy: Studio D of the National Film Board of Canada. In *Women Communicating: Studies of Women's Talk*. eds. Barbara Bate and Anita Taylor. Norwood, N.J.: Ablex Publishing Corporation.

Tilchen, Maida. 1984. "Lesbians and Women's Music." In *Women-Identified Women*. eds. Trudy Darty and Sandee Potter. Palo Alto, Calif.: Mayfield Publishing Co.

West, Celeste and Elizabeth Katz, eds. 1972. *Revolting Librarians*. San Francisco: Booklegger Press.

Wheeler, Helen R. 1984. "Mass Media and Communications." In *The Women Annual Number 4: 1983–84*. ed. Sarah M. Pritchard. Boston: G.K. Hall & Co.

Willis, Ellen. 1978. "The Conservatism of Ms." In *Feminist Revolution*. eds. Redstockings. New York: Random House.

Winship, Janice. 1987. *Inside Women's Magazines*. London: Pandora.

8

Pornography's Active Subordination of Women: Radical Feminists Re-Claim Speech Rights

Ann Russo

In the early to mid-1980s, I found myself, a white, lesbian and radical feminist, in the midst of intense and provocative debates over sexuality and pornography in the feminist movement. These debates were very emotionally and politically charged for me because, although I opposed the mass industry of pornography, parts of me were unsure, ambivalent, and confused in trying to formulate my responses to some of the challenges from so-called "pro-sex" and anticensorship feminists. I found myself challenged by some of their analyses, particularly around issues of sexual repression and the complexities involved in understanding the centrality of sexualized power relations to women's experience of sexuality. Given my personal history of both Catholicism, sexual abuse, and violence within and outside the family, I have always implicitly understood that the sexual, emotional, and intellectual responses of women to pornography are complicated and not always well-defined according to strict political categories.

As a result of my own turmoil and confusion, I chose to delineate, compare, and analyze the contemporary pornography debates among feminists for my dissertation, from which this paper is condensed. The dissertation focuses on the feminist debates over the introduction of the civil rights antipornography ordinance into local city and county politics in the United States, which was written by antipornography feminists. It was introduced through city councils in Minneapolis, Minnesota and Indianapolis, Indiana; the county board in Los Angeles County, California; and by popular referendum in Cambridge, Massachusetts and Bellingham, Washington. It won by popular vote in Bellingham, but was immediately challenged on constitutional grounds (for details of the history see Baldwin 1986, 1984; Osanka and Johann 1989). The introduction of the civil rights

144

ordinance and its popularity prompted the creation of a self-identified *feminist* opposition group, the Feminist Anti-Censorship Taskforce, who publicly and legally organized to challenge the law and the tenets of the feminist antipornography movement in general (Chew 1985; Irvine 1985; Irvine and Turley 1985). I compared the two opposing feminist perspectives on pornography, which, in general, can be summarized as follows.

The feminist antipornography perspective focuses on the sexual subordination of women (emphasizing sexual violence and victimization of women) and is specifically associated with the civil rights ordinance written and proposed by Andrea Dworkin and Catharine MacKinnon; in contrast, the anticensorship perspective, sometimes calling itself "pro-sex," focuses on the problem of sexual repression of women (emphasizing concern about women's sexual passivity and the limitations imposed on sexual expression and exploration) and is specifically associated with the Feminist Anti-Censorship Taskforce (FACT), the major group that organized to oppose the ordinance.

The feminist debates over pornography caused intense polarization in the women's movement leading to major shifts in organizations, loss of friendships and affiliations, and feelings of despair and hopelessness. Many feminists see no hope of resolution on these issues and have retreated from the issues of sexuality and violence. I wrote my dissertation in response to this polarization and to my own turmoil and confusion in articulating responses to the challenges of the anticensorship and "pro sex" feminists. I am convinced that my own conflicts and contradictions in addressing pornography are similarly felt by many women who are trying to formulate perspectives on the issues—who are antipornography, who have been harmed by pornography, who believe that pornography is destructive to our strivings for equality and mutual respect—but feel immobilized by the rhetoric which makes antipornography feminists into antisexual prudes who want to censor all sexually explicit material. The feminist antipornography movement and the civil rights ordinance have been seriously misrepresented and maligned in the feminist as well as mainstream press. I wrote this essay, derived from my dissertation, as another attempt to present a more accurate presentation of feminist antipornography theory and politics.

In this essay, I focus on two central aspects of the antipornography feminist perspective and contrast them with the anticensorship and "pro-sex" feminist perspective. The two aspects are 1) the definition of pornography which is derived from women's experience of abuse and victimization, and 2) the interpretation of women's experience which recognizes and gives social legitimacy to women's claims of harm through pornography. In contrast to the anticensorship and "pro-sex" feminists who define pornography as primarily images and representations divorced from social reality, antipornography feminists define pornography as the production, consumption and distribution of pictures or words that involve the active sexual subordination of women. This definition, for instance, allows us to address the harm to women who are coerced into pornography or who are forced to work, live, or be educated in an environment flooded with pornography. Secondly, in contrast to the anticensorship and "pro-sex" feminists who attribute women's criticism of pornography to women's sexual ignorance, antisexual sentiment, or moralistic and repressive perspectives, antipornography feminists make visible and give voice to women's concrete experiences of pornography, and believe women when we say we have been harmed. In the typical debates over pornography women's experiences and lives are usually invisible and socially meaningless. The antipornography perspective embodied in the civil rights ordinance gives the harm to women in the forms of coercion, assault, abuse, forced sex, defamation and subordination social and legal recognition and meaning.

Pornography as Active Subordination

The definition of pornography has been open to question in all of the debates, including among libertarians and moralists. Yet most agree that pornography has to do with representations, images, ideas, and fantasies of sexuality, not processes, actions, and real life experiences of sexuality. While some argue that pornography as representational image may have an external influence on reality, specifically the treatment of women or the social construction of sexual relations, they do not conceptualize pornography as actively involved in the construction of that reality, specifically in women's subordination. The civil rights ordinance proposed by antipornography feminists defines pornography as the active sexual subordination of women in its production, consumption and distribution. Here pornography is conceptualized as an issue of sexual subordination and violence, and defined as processes and actions, rather than solely as images and speech.

The civil rights ordinance (Dworkin and MacKinnon 1988, 36) states:

> Pornography is the graphic sexually explicit subordination of women through pictures and/or words that also includes one or more of the following: (a) women are presented dehumanized as sexual objects, things or commodities; or (b) women are presented as sexual objects who enjoy humiliation or pain; or (c) women are presented as sexual objects experiencing sexual pleasure in rape, incest, or other sexual

assault; or (d) women are presented as sexual objects tied up or cut up or mutilated or bruised or physically hurt; or (e) women are presented in postures or positions of sexual submission, servility, or display; or (f) women's body parts—including but not limited to vaginas, breasts, or buttocks—are exhibited such that women are reduced to those parts; or (g) women are presented being penetrated by objects or animals; or (h) women are presented in scenarios of degradation, humiliation, injury, torture, shown as filthy or inferior, bleeding, bruised or hurt in a context that makes these conditions sexual.

The use of men, children, or transsexuals in the place of women in [the paragraph] above is also pornography.

The definition of pornography in the ordinance is not actionable by itself; the complainant must prove that the material is actively involved in subordination. Dworkin (1986b, 298–299) explains, "It has to be trafficked in, somebody has to be forced into it, it has to be forced on somebody or it has to be used in a specific kind of assault; so that the hypothetical question about whether I think that is subordination or not depends a great deal—has the women been forced into it? I want to know. What is the sociology around it, is it being used on people, are women being forced to watch it and then do it; and those are the kinds of issues, that is what is required to trigger this law." By casting the ordinance as sexual inequality, harm and discrimination, it is taken out of the realm of morality, puritanism, and individual taste.

The key term is "subordination," defined as the "active practice of placing someone in an unequal position or in a position of loss of power" (Dworkin and MacKinnon 1988, 39). Subordination is a "broad, deep, systematic dynamic discernible in any persecution based on race or sex," which involves hierarchy, objectification, submission, and violence, and each of these are central to the functioning of pornography (Dworkin 1986a, 265–267). The definition is not limited to overt physical violence, because in pornography, sexual coercion and force are presented as indistinguishable from sex. Like rape law, if the ordinance hinged on explicit overt violence contingent on evidence of brute physical force, then it would not address many of the crimes against women, including those of pornography.

Pornography is a *practice* of subordination, not simply images and speech about subordination. It is not fundamentally *about* sex, but *is* sex; not *about* subordination, but *is* subordination; not *about* violence, but *is* violence. This is an important distinction because as Dworkin and MacKinnon (1988, 24) argue: "Once pornography is framed as concept rather than practice, more thought than act, more in the head than in the world, its effects also necessarily appear both insubstantial and unsubstantiated, more abstract than real."

This distinction is lost on the anticensorship feminists. First, they conceptualize pornography as solely speech, not practices or actions, and as speech with much broader boundaries than that prescribed in the ordinance. Throughout their arguments, they substitute "sexually explicit speech" for the term pornography, and so erase the definitional distinctions of action and subordination. They rarely address the processes of production, consumption, or distribution. Instead, they refer to images and fantasies disconnected from people and material conditions, thus defining the issue solely as one of interpretation, not discrimination. This allows them to argue that pornographic speech is absolutely distinct from its making or use. The FACT legal brief (Brief Amici Curiae of FACT 1985, 37) states: "Images and fictional text are not the same thing as subordinating conduct. . . . Although ideas have impact, images of discrimination are not the discrimination." Or as Deirdre English (1980, 48) writes:

> The fact remains that no matter how disturbing violent fantasies are, as long as they stay within the world of pornography, they are still only fantasies. The man masturbating in a theater showing a snuff film is still only watching a movie, not actually raping or murdering . . . There is something wrong with attacking people, not because of their actions, but because of their fantasies—or their particular commercial style of having them.

Those who support the arguments of FACT define pornography as "mere" representation belonging to the minds of the individual producer or consumer, as if it did not have to be produced and as if its effects only existed by choice and in the realm of individual privacy and sexual fantasy.

In contrast, the feminists against pornography address pornography as active subordination through the processes involved in its production, consumption and distribution. These processes are discussed from the feminist antipornography point of view below.

The Production of Pornography and the Active Subordination of Women

First and foremost, pornography involves the active subordination of women (or in some cases men) in its production. Yet in the current context, a woman's body, what is done to it, and the language ascribed to her as her speech is legally defined as the publisher's speech, which is then protected as *his* speech, *not* hers; such a formulation denies the human being in the pornography and the activities necessary to produce the representations.

Many women in pornography are actively subordinated in its production. Many are coerced into participating by way of the industry or through their personal relationships. The obstacle to recognizing this harm is that the pornography claims to accurately represent women's true identities, sexualities, and desires. Antipornography feminists point out, however, that many women (usually when they are children or adolescents) are coerced into pornography because of poverty and/or incestuous assault, rape, and battery. While young girls and women do make decisions, and thus "choices," to enter prostitution and/or pornography, the context is not of economic and social opportunity and freedom. As Teish (1980, 116) suggests with respect to black women who are street prostitutes:

> The fact that the number of Black 'working girls' on Prostitution Row is disproportionate to our number in the society bespeaks an economic and cultural crime. Facing the greatest degree of discrimination in education, jobs, and federal aid, some poor Black women have been forced to the streets. Here they sell interracial fantasies to suburban businessmen: Friday Night in the Ghetto. And here they are exploited by the Pimp, the Peddler, and the Police.

Teish speaks to the social reality of many young black women, a reality having little to do with opportunity and self-defined choices, and much to do with economic exploitation and racism.

Many of the women in the industry have been sexually assaulted as children and were brought into prostitution and pornography at an early age. Some young women get into it because they are running away from sexually and physically violent homes and are picked up by pimps or pornographers offering them food, shelter, promises of love, and a home. Some get into it because they are prostituted and forced into pornography by their fathers, uncles, husbands, brothers, or lovers who act as their pimps, the pornography made of them is often used to blackmail them into continuing their life in the industry (see Silbert and Pines 1984). Some others get into it because they are attracted to the promises of glamor, adventure, and excitement offered in media depictions of women in the sex industry and see it as a way out of their current circumstances. And/or some others get into it because they internalize the shame and inferiority associated with the sexual abuse they have experienced and come to believe that their bodies and sexuality are their only means of survival ("Working in the Body Trade" 1981). Antipornography feminists question

the claims of individual choice and happiness in prostitution and pornography given many of the women's histories of sexual abuse, poverty,
drug addiction, and alcoholism (see for instance, Leidholdt 1987).

Moreover, it has been documented that the producers of pornography
actively harass, abuse, rape, assault, and murder the women they use in
the pornography. Dworkin (1989, 70–100) demonstrates in her history of
the Marquis de Sade, for instance, that he sexually exploited and murdered
women, and that these exploits were the substance of his writings. In the
contemporary context, Linda Lovelace [Marchiano] (1980) has spoken out
publicly about the physical and sexual torture she endured as the wife of
Chuck Traynor, some of which was directly involved in the making of
the film *Deep Throat;* and Peter Bogdanovich (1984) has written about
Dorothy Stratten's "career" in pornography, which involved incredible
sexual abuse and eventually murder. Women continue to come forward
and speak out about the sexual abuse, rape, and murder of women in the
industry (see *Pornography and Sexual Violence* 1988).

A major barrier to recognizing that the production of pornography involves active subordination is that many believe that the sexuality presented in the pornography is the authentic sexuality of the women in it
(Dworkin 1981a, 232). The information, stories, and scripts accompanying
the photographs are often written in the first person and the consumer is
led to believe that the sexuality presented is consistent with the woman's
own individual identity and desire. As Dworkin and MacKinnon (1988,
43) point out, unlike other forms of modeling, "The viewers have a sexual
stake in believing that the women in pornography are not models or actors
but truly feel and want what the script calls for . . . the consumer believes
that the woman in the material *belongs* there, that she is fulfilled in her
nature by the acts performed on her." Such beliefs are responsible for the
dismissal and denial of women's claims of harassment, coercion, abuse,
and violence within and outside the context of pornography. MacKinnon
(1984, 181), speaking to the problem of credibility, writes:

> Understand, the documentation of the harm as it is being done is
> taken as evidence that no harm was done. . . . Too the victims are
> often forced to act as though they are enjoying the abuse. One por-
> nographer said to a woman he abducted and was photographing while
> bound: 'Smile or I'll kill you. I can get lots of money for pictures of
> women who smile when they're tied up like you.'

The smile of the woman in the pornography makes the *harm* to the women
presented invisible, and consequently her claim of abuse socially unbe-
lievable.

150

The ordinance recognizes the realities of women's lives and the context for many women's participation in the making of pornography. It makes it possible for a person to seek monetary damages from the pornographers as well as to obtain an injunction to stop the further marketing and distribution of the specific pornography made of her under conditions of coercion, intimidation, or without her knowledge. This gives control back to the human being who has been made into and sold as pornography against her will, and is crucially important because the continual marketing, distribution and consumption of the pornography perpetuates the woman's victimization and abuse. As Linda Lovelace [Marchiano] stated at the hearings in Minneapolis, "Virtually every time someone watches the film they are watching me being raped" (see *Pornography and Sexual Violence* 1988, 29). The ordinance also recognizes the situation of women whose lovers, husbands, or fathers, for instance, have taken pictures of them without their consent and then sold them onto the market, and/or women who are photographed and/or filmed while being raped by a stranger and find that the photographs are being sold on the market as pornography.

Antipornography feminists conceptualize pornography as an active process, not as an artifact or object. The ordinance recognizes the women in the pornography as human beings and gives women control over the continued use of their bodies in pornography in cases where it was produced under conditions of coercion, abuse, and violence, or was made without their knowledge. Defining pornography as action, not speech, recognizes that women are actively involved in the production of pornography. Dworkin (1985, 3) writes,

> When pornography is photographic, it is indisputably action. It gets perceived as speech because the woman in the photograph is effectively rendered an object or commodity by the pornography; the perception of the photograph as speech itself denies the human status of the woman in it. The so-called speech belongs to whomever took or sold the photography—the pornographer—not to the woman used in it, to whom things were done as if she were an object or commodity, and who indeed continues to be sold as an object or commodity. The woman is excluded from recognizably human dialogue by the uses to which she is put.

The anticensorship feminists rarely address the issues raised by antipornography feminists concerning the processes of production, except to rely on the argument that women are exercising free choice to have "careers" in pornography. They minimize the conditions of coercion, abuse, and violence. When challenged with evidence about economic, physical and sexual coercion, they argue that pornography is representation, images, and artifacts, not reality; if a woman has been coerced, the problem is the coercion, not the pornography (Duggan, Hunter, and Vance 1985). They fail to recognize the impact of the consumption and distribution of pornography made of women against their wills on the women themselves and on the consumers of pornography who come to believe women "choose" to be harmed in these specific ways.

"Pro-sex" feminists essentially believe that the sexuality ascribed to the women in the pornography accurately represents their chosen sexual identities and practices. This is evident, for instance, in the inclusion of prostitutes and women in pornography in their listings of sexual minorities, and in their perception of the antipornography critique as a condemnation of the women in the industry, rather than of the producers, pornographers, pimps, and/or johns who are actively involved in the subordination of women.

Use of Pornography in Harassment, Abuse, Battering, and Rape

Pornography also actively subordinates women when it is used to undermine, intimidate, harass, batter, and sexually assault women. The ordinance recognizes the harm to women when pornography is forced on women in the workplace, in education, in the neighborhood, in the home, and/or in the context of therapeutic relationships by doctors, psychiatrists, and/or therapists; and when it serves as a major source, motivation and guide for the men (and women) who are perpetrators of violence against women.

In the context of education and employment, for instance, the forced presence of pornography significantly undermines women's efforts towards gender equality and human respect among peers. It contributes to a hostile and intimidating environment for women, which can result in poor job or academic performance, a high drop-out and turnover rate, and a generalized lack of initiative and confidence among women. For instance, at a speak-out on pornography in New York City, Diane Phillips, one of the first women hired as a longshorewoman, testified on how she "endured relentless harassment, not the least of which was omnipresent pornography in highly visible places." After complaining about the harassment, the men on the job proceeded to flood the job site with even more pornography, until she was eventually transferred (Carole Post 1982, 1; also see *Pornography and Sexual Violence* 1988, 77–79). Women on college campuses have also spoken out about the negative effects that pornography has had on their ability to concentrate, to sleep, to feel safe and comfortable, and ultimately, to succeed.

Pornography is also used in the home in the context of intimate relationships to intimidate, harass and abuse women and children. Women have spoken out about the use of pornography by their husbands, lovers, and boyfriends, and its damage to their feelings of self-worth, confidence, sexual identity, and equality within these relationships (see, for instance, Charles 1985; Mithers 1988; *Pornography and Sexual Violence* 1988, 64–70). Women working in battered women's shelters attest to the intricate relationship between men's sexual and physical battering of women and the use of pornography to intimidate women into performing sexual acts against their will (see *Pornography* 101–106, and 65–66 [gay male context]). In addition, pornography is often used to season young women into prostitution, and to manipulate, justify, intimidate and force children to perform sexually for adult men, including fathers, ministers, brothers, and uncles (see *Pornography* 70–75, 123–125).

In each of these cases, pornography damages women's physical and sexual lives, as well as our emotional and intellectual lives. Women are very much defeated by pornography when it is used against us in our public and private lives. These harms are generally not recognized by the law, and the impact on women remains invisible, because the harms are interpreted as personal problems and therefore trivial and insignificant. Moreover, because pornography is understood as speech, and the issue as one of individual consumption and an individual's privacy, its specific use and abuse with respect to the women affected by this consumption, whether in private or public, is not part of the discussion.

In contrast to feminists against pornography, anticensorship and "pro-sex" feminists align themselves with those who have historically not believed women's claims of sexual intimidation and coercion, particularly in the home and family. With respect to the ordinance's provision that addresses how pornography is forced on women, Duggan, Hunter, and Vance (1985, 148–149) question the term "force," particularly in the home, where the use of pornography is a "personal" choice. Those authors agree that it might be interesting to provide a protection of sorts against domestic harassment, but they state that " 'forcing' is not an easy concept to define . . . It is hard to know what degree of intrusion would amount to forcing images onto a person who shares the same private space." While they accept that the concept of force might be legitimate in workplace harassment where the relationships are characterized by status hierarchy, they question it in domestic life where the relationships are "personal," "consensual," and the hierarchy of male/female is seemingly not as explicit. The "pro-sex" feminists end up protecting private sexual life from any discussion by holding onto underlying presumptions of consent and equality in heterosexual relationships. They also claim that the focus on pornography in intimate and familial relationships is antisexual in motive, rather than against "real" abuse and violence, which they separate from pornography. Duggan, Hunter, and Vance (1985, 150) write: "Focusing on pornography rather than on the relationship and its social context may serve only to channel heterosexual women's recognition of their own intimate oppression toward a movement hailed by the far right as being antiperversion rather than toward a feminist analysis of sexual politics." They also misinterpret the civil right's ordinance force provision to be actionable against the pornography, when in fact the focus, in this case, would be the perpetrator. This misinterpretation allows them to claim that the feminist antipornography perspective displaces the problem of harassment and violence onto images, rather than actions.

Pornography is actively involved in women's subordination when it is used to motivate, justify, guide, and/or enhance sexual assaults and murders. For instance, serial murderers and rapists of women are often avid readers and users of pornography, and the type of pornography consumed usually correlates with the particular methods of sexual torture and murder (see *Pornography* 59–60, 109–110). At the Minneapolis hearings, professionals who work with sex offenders testified to the relationship between pornography and the sexual violence their clients had been involved in, and human service workers and counselors who work with children and adult victims of sexual abuse and rape testified that pornography is often directly involved (*Pornography* 107–108, 111–114). A Native American woman at the Minneapolis hearings told her story of being raped by two white men who made racist remarks and referred to the pornographic video game called "Custer's Revenge" while they were assaulting her. (*Pornography* 34; also see Reilly 1982). Silbert and Pines (1984) also have documented the role of pornography in the rape and assault of street prostitutes in San Francisco.

In contrast to the antipornography feminist argument that pornography is used to actively intimidate, harass, abuse, and assault women, the anticensorship and "pro-sex" feminists, separate pornography—as image and representation—from its consumption and use. They ignore and/or dismiss the testimony of women speaking out about the effects of pornography in their private and social lives, and of professionals who work with victims and perpetrators of sexual violence. They simply claim that the pornography is not connected to the abuse. They seek to damage the credibility of the testimony and analysis by saying that it has antisexual undertones and is linked to a repressive morality, rather than a feminist politics. For this reason, they dismiss the evidence by claiming that the women (and men) are intolerant and sexually repressed. In the FACT legal brief (Amici Curiae of FACT 1985, 34–35) submitted in opposition to the antipornography ordinance, they write that the Minneapolis hearings on pornography "did not, in fairness, reflect a reasoned attempt to understand the factors 'central' in maintaining 'sex as a basis for discrimination.'" In some of the literature, the women who have testified about the harm resulting from pornography are even referred to as "born-again victims" (see, for example, Vance 1986; Elshtain 1982).

Anticensorship feminists also take issue with the academic research that suggests a relationship between the representation of sexual violence and men's reported attitudes and behaviors of aggression. First, they argue that the analysis is too simplistic; Nan Hunter (1986, 52) writes, "The anti-porn conditioning theory relies on a highly simplistic 'you see it, you do it', version of behaviorism. It ignores context as determinative of meaning. It ignores the reality that sexual images are often coded, layered, and ambiguous or contradictory in their meanings." Moreover, in response to the research indicating changes in attitudes, Vance (1985, 40) says:

> We don't know how short-lived these changes in attitude are, or how they affect behavior in a natural setting. There is no demonstrated connection between attitudes and actual propensity to rape.... Can you really believe you simply read pornography and then go out and act upon it?

They further dismiss the research findings by criticizing the methods used and the inferences drawn between the research and "real life." They characterize the data presented by the antipornography movement as "highly selective and grossly distorted" and as being "limited to studies of a narrow class of violent imagery," which they claim is not the majority of pornography on the market (Brief Amici Curiae of FACT 1985, 19–20).

In summary, by dismissing the testimony of survivors of the production and/or use of pornography, and the related testimony of workers and activists in the field as antisexual, they participate in the cultural and societal denial around women's claims of sexual coercion and violence. They seem to collude with the male "sexual liberation" agenda that says women are merely acting out of their sexual repression and morality and thus their interpretation is suspect, or that women are making false accusations about the role of pornography in their abuse.

In contrast, antipornography feminists believe the stories of women who have been victimized and treat the stories as legitimate evidence against pornography. This is partly because we conceptualize the consumption and use of pornography as practices, integrally related to attitudes, behavior, and human relationships, rather than as images and representations consumed by individuals in the context of private fantasy, completely separate from social relations.

Pornography Creates Context Conducive to Sexual Violence

Pornography subordinates women by contributing to a climate in which male sexual domination and assault are condoned and legitimated as normal sexual relations. According to antipornography feminists, gender inequality, the sexuality of sadomasochism, and misogyny are intricately fused in pornography to produce sexual pleasure and arousal for its producers and consumers. The messages of heterosexual pornography are that men naturally need and desire to sexually humiliate, degrade, intimidate, and violate women, and that women naturally accept, love, and desire that violation (MacKinnon 1984). The eroticism of sadomasochism is variegated in pornography by incorporating racial, ethnic, sexual, and other forms of bigotries, which play themselves out in this culture. For instance, pornography nourishes and promotes racism through the sexualization of women and men of color. Like other media, it differentiates women according to race and color. Rarely are women of color portrayed in "mainstream" pornography (meaning heterosexual pornography directed to a white audience); and when they are, the presentation is quite different from that of white women. Leidholdt (1983, 20) reports. "In pornography's most brutal genre, bondage, black women were literally enslaved, blindfolded and gagged, their bodies criss-crossed by ropes or wrapped in chains. Or they were posed in stiletto boots, wielding cat o'nine tails, under the heading, 'Black Bitch.' "

The racism of pornography, however, is not simply an issue of equal representation, nor one of physical appearance. Rather, as Gardner (1980, 113) argues, it is the issue of "how pornography capitalizes on the underlying history and myths surrounding and oppressing people of color in this country which makes it racism. . . ." She points out that black women were raped and black men were castrated as common slave practices. This history is capitalized on in pornography which presents images and stories of southern slave plantations where black men ravish and rape white women, which of course reverses the true power imbalance inherent to a white dominant slave system (see also Leidholdt 1983; Dworkin 1989). This pornography cannot be understood separate from the ever-present myth of the black male rapist, nor from the racist criminal justice system, which one-sidedly and systematically convicts black (and other men of color) for the rape of white women (Davis 1981). Moreover pornography presents women of color as sexually insatiable and always available which also cannot be separated from the reality that white men have raped, tortured, and enslaved black women (and other women of color) during slavery and into the present with impunity (Dworkin 1989; Ross 1982; hooks 1981). The sexualization of gender and racial inequality in pornography for the purposes of entertainment creates a context in which the inequality, degradation, and violence women and men of color face in this society is normalized and legitimated.

Anti-Semitism is also a common staple of pornography; the sexualization of Jew-hatred cannot be disassociated from the historical use of pornography before and during the Nazi war years, which fueled anti-Semitism and eventually contributed to the torture and killing of Jews. This propaganda continues with the proliferation of a genre of pornography which makes entertainment out of the sexual torture and mutilation of what they claim are "wanting" and "desiring" Jewish women in concentration camps (Dworkin 1989; Leidholdt 1983). In these and other cases, the histories of racism, bigotry, torture, and murder are sexualized and made into entertainment, and all women, and particularly racial and ethnic women and men, bear the repercussions through the mass production, consumption and distribution of pornography.

Pornography as a major institution of sexual and racial power, which is actively involved in the subordination of women (and in relevant cases men), makes equality impossible because it sexualizes and legitimates gender and racial inequality and bigotry as entertainment. Dworkin and MacKinnon (1988, 49) maintain that "By making a public spectacle and a public celebration of the worthlessness of women, by valuing women as sluts, by defining women according to our availability for sexual use, pornography makes all women's social worthlessness into a public standard." In addition to the evidence from women's lives, antipornography feminists draw upon social science research studies that show that pornography contributes to creating a culture in which violence against women is understood as acceptable, natural and normal, as well as entertaining and fun.

Pornography links the subordination of women to sexual arousal, such that men (and women) are sexually conditioned to be aroused by power and domination. In order to neutralize the explicit subordination of women in pornography, pornography claims that women desire and enjoy submission and subordination. Dworkin (1980, 239) writes, "In all pornography, the 'belief in victim pleasure' is fundamental and overwhelming. Pornography effectively encourages and promotes rape by encouraging and promoting this belief, this lie, about the pleasure of the victim in being forced and hurt." Moreover, any time that women are presented in pornography as resisting sexual subordination, their resistance is presented as pretense or sexual ignorance. These messages of pornography cannot be separated from the facts that men who rape, convicted and nonconvicted, tend to believe that their victims derive sexual pleasure from the experience; and that the general public assumes women either consent to sexual assault and/or are in some way responsible for it (Baldwin 1984). Basically, pornography desensitizes men (and women) to sexual abuse and violence; in the words of Dworkin (1981b, 205), it "numbs the conscience, makes one increasingly callous to cruelty, to the infliction of pain, to violence against persons, to the humiliation or degradation of persons, to the abuse of women and children." For instance, a 21-year-old woman was gang-raped in a bar in New Bedford, Massachusetts. She was thrown onto a pool table and brutally and repeatedly raped by a group of men while the rest of the customers in the bar watched—taunting the victim and cheering on the assailants. It just so happens that a feature photo essay had appeared in *Hustler* three months before this rape, entitled, "Dirty Pool." In this feature story, a young waitress in a working-class bar is similarly gang-raped, except according to the fictional story, while initially frightened, after she is "held down by the men and penetrated again and again, orally and vaginally, by penises and pool cues," she is described by the pornography as a "willing, eager participant." The Women Against Pornography (New York) argue that while there is no evidence of a direct causal relationship between this pornography and the specific rape in New Bedford:

> There is a relationship between the fact that a well-known, widely read men's magazine openly celebrates the gang-rape of a woman and the fact that a group of ordinary men can watch four of their peers rape and torture a woman for three hours and condone if not celebrate the assault.

It is noteworthy that in the subsequent August 1983 issue of *Hustler,* a "picture postcard" appears which is said to have come from New Bedford. It features a woman laying across a pooltable waving to the audience with the statement, "Greetings from New Bedford, Massachusetts, the Portuguese Gang-Rape Capital of America." Along with completely trivializing the woman's rape, *Hustler* also makes an ethnic slur against the Portuguese community, thus specifying the act as "Portuguese" rather than generically male (meaning white, middle-class).

Antipornography feminists emphasize the connection between the message of pornography—that women want sexual abuse and violation—and the denial on the part of society, both publicly and privately, of the harm to women both in and out of pornography. The police, the courts, the media, and the general public typically do not believe women who struggle to gain recognition, empathy, and justice after experiencing sexual harassment, abuse, and violence. They typically blame the violence on the women; at some level, they believe that the women wanted it, or asked for it, or deserved it. Pornography is a major mechanism which facilitates, condones, and perpetuates these beliefs.

In contrast to the interlinking of the eroticization of inequality in pornography to the realities of sexism, racism, and bigotry, anticensorship feminists argue that pornography, as images and representations, is primarily about sexual fantasy, not reality. In privatizing and individualizing pornography as fantasy, they suggest that the sexualization of power disparities in fantasy is absolutely distinct from "real" power relations. They accept the traditional public/private division, which defines the sexual arena as a separate sphere, and within this arena, they believe that complexity overrides "simple" sexism and misogyny because power dynamics may be central to sexual excitement and arousal. They believe, therefore, that there are a variety of interpretations available for the power dynamics in pornography, and that women may gain a sense of sexual power and control in pornography. Their concern over the interpretation of pornography stems from the fear that judgments about harm and violence in truth have more to do with antisexual dogma, which may in turn, encourage sexual repression in women. In contrast to the antipornography focus on inequality and abuse, therefore, they focus on what they feel are the sexual possibilities for women in pornography which might liberate women from sexual repression (Snitow 1985; Webster 1986). Pornography, they argue, flouts conventional sexual mores, ridicules sexual hypocrisy and underscores the importance of sexual needs; they believe the benefits of pornography from sexual exploration and experimentation are more important than the sexual violence and inequality, which they minimize and deny, in part by always defining pornography as sexually explicit imagery and representation completely separate from social relations.

Antisexual Sentiment or Political Resistance?

By defining pornography as the active sexual subordination of women through its production, consumption, and distribution, antipornography feminists redirect the analysis of pornography from one of images and representation, and thus interpretation, to actions and specific harms, and thus power and gender inequality. Anticensorship feminists never accept this redirection of the discussion; in response to feminist claims of harm, they charge that antisexual sentiment and moralistic interpretation, rather than harm, underlie the feminist antipornography movement. The difference in their approach to women's experience of pornography is clear by how each group approaches women's stories and responses documenting the harmful effects of pornography.

First, the antipornography feminists believe, and subsequently integrate into their analysis, women's (and men's) stories about the harassment and abuse they experienced through the production, consumption and/or distribution of pornography. We accept and believe the information and testimony from social workers and experts that link pornography to specific violence against women. We fundamentally challenge the characterization of these stories and accounts as simply anecdotal and/or the product of "born-again victims." Such characterizations trivialize women, and undermine their courage in speaking out about abuse in intimate contexts. Dworkin (1989, xxvi) eloquently says of the defenders of pornography who dismiss stories as anecdotal:

> [T]hey misuse the word to make it denote a story, probably fictive, that is small, trivial, inconsequential, proof only of some defect in the woman herself . . . What does one do when women's lives are worth so little—worth arrogant, self-satisfied ridicule and nothing else, not even the appearance, however false, of charity or concern . . . The first person stories are human experience, raw and true, not mediated by dogma or ideology *or* social convention; 'human' is the trick word in the sentence. If one values women as human beings, one cannot turn away or refuse to hear so that one can refuse to care without bearing responsibility for the refusal. One cannot turn one's back on the women or on the burden of memory they carry.

The feminist antipornography analysis is based on harm, not morality; on subordination, not antisexual sentiment.

In contrast, anticensorship & "pro-sex" feminists consistently claim that the stories and subsequent analysis are anti-sex, rather than anti-violence. Even in the case of Linda Lovelace [Marchiano], they claim that the abuse was alleged, and that it is problematic to focus on the case because people may react to the information because of the sexual explicitness, rather than the alleged coercion and harm. Because they insist on absolute distinctions between sex and violence, they fail to see the difficulties and, many times, impossibility of separating the two in most cases of *sexual violence.*

In general, these feminists argue that women's aversion to pornography and "deviant" sexual practices emanates from sexual repression and ignorance, rather than from women's experience of the aggression and power-orientation of men's sexuality and violence. The major contextual feature of women's sexual lives, according to them, is *lack* of sexual experience and little contact with pornography. Paula Webster (1984, 393) argues, for instance, that the reason the group Women Against Pornography has attracted so many women is because sex is taboo for women:

> Denying their curiosity like the Oedipal daughter, they insist that they could never do anything like that or want anything like that. They assume that women who like talking dirty, anal sex, voyeurism, or even vibrators are suspect, certainly not feminists. . . . How do we understand the difference between ourselves and the women who send their photos to *Hustler,* or write letters to *Penthouse Forum,* or buy sex toys, split-crotch panties, and dream of being dominated or becoming dominatrixes?

The anticensorship and "pro-sex" feminists consistently assume that the feminists fighting pornography are unfamiliar with or have never been affected by pornography, and that they are not sexually active outside of heterosexual (or lesbian) monogamy. This is evident in their labeling of antipornography feminists "prudish," "uptight" and into "vanilla sex." They believe the focus on sexual violence increases women's fears and shame around sexual exploration and experimentation which emanate from ignorance and fear of difference, rather than from life experience. Vance (1984, 20) writes: "Our relative ignorance about the actual range of sexual behavior and fantasy makes us into latter-day sexual ethnocentrists; the observer is convinced that her own sex life is normal, understandable, and tasteful, while the observed's preferences may be frightening, strange, and disgusting . . ." This antisexual rhetoric, they argue, enhances the Right's antisexual values.

Antipornography feminists disagree; women's response to pornography, sadomasochism, objectification, and voyeurism is not a result of our lack of experience, "prudery," and sexual inhibition. First of all, many, many women activists in the antipornography feminist movement have joined because of our experiences with the production, consumption, and/or distribution of pornography. Second, the movement does not encourage sexual repression by criticizing pornography. We argue instead that pornography is dependent on sexual repression: It serves to both intensify the eroticism of inequality and to privatize the harm women experience from forced sexuality in our personal lives. Repression functions to hide sexual activity, not stop it from happening. The problem with repression is that it controls women's public talk and analysis of the sex that we have been

161

forced to endure. For instance, antipornography feminists suggest that in reality many women are incestually abused and assaulted as children by some family or near-family member despite the incest taboo. The taboo has not been on the sexual activity, but on girl children and women speaking out against the abuse and assaults (Rush 1980). Dworkin points out that pornography can only have an aura of taboo "if one refuses to face what the content of pornography actually is and how the forced acts of sex in it correspond to women's lives." She critiques the male intellectual tradition, which continues to refuse to face the relationships between pornography and women's real lives (Wilson 1982, 24).

The feminists against pornography in unquestioningly believing women's stories of sexual violence, challenge sexual relations as they are currently constructed and practiced. In this sense, the claim that antipornography feminists are "anti-sex" is accurate. We criticize the prevailing sexual ideologies and practices that make it difficult (if not impossible) for people to distinguish between sex and violence, particularly when it comes to women's claims of intimidation, coercion, rape, and assault. In contrast to the "pro-sex" feminists, we are not suspicious of women's criticisms of sex; we do not fear that our interpretation of women's subordination is really veiled puritanism and/or is simply indicative of women's sexual repression, and thus a problem with women. Instead, we argue that because women have been victimized through sexuality, then the solution cannot simply be more sex—unless that sex is different from abuse. The point of the campaign then is to politicize women's response to pornography and male sexual domination, rather than dismiss or trivialize women's responses.

Similarly, the goal of the feminist antipornography movement is not to repress pornography, but to publicize its messages and its sexual and racial exploitation of all women and some men through its production, consumption and distribution. We seek to expose pornography and set its processes up for discussion and debate. The issue is not the amount of sex nor the fact that it is publicly available, but rather the issues are the sexism and racism of pornography, the structure and dynamics of eroticized inequality, and the pervasive amount of sexual abuse and violence in pornography's production, consumption and distribution.

Speech Rights for Women

In response to the feminist critique of pornography as embodied in the civil rights ordinance, anticensorship feminists and other liberal and libertarian groups claim that freedom of speech is being endangered, and that feminists are colluding with the right wing against sexual speech and ultimately sexual freedom. Antipornography feminists have begun to point out, however, the defense of "free speech" never addresses how pornography encroaches upon women's rights to speech. Pornography, in fact, actively silences women, thus minimizing women's chances of exercising our freedom of speech. Pornography silences the women on its pages by accompanying the photos with sexist and misogynistic language and sexuality; it silences the women not in the photos who are sexually assaulted with and because of pornography; it silences women's resistance to forced sex with the labels of prudery and frigidity, and claims that "no" really means "yes"; it silences women by discrediting women's charges of sexual assault and abuse; and it silences all women's claims to human worth and dignity. Dworkin (1986a, 268) writes:

> The women flattened out on the page are deathly still, except for *hurt* *that* *Hurt* *me* is not women's speech. It is the speech imposed on women by pimps to cover the awful condemning silence ... Real silence might signify dissent ... The pimps cannot tolerate literal silence—it is too eloquent as testimony—so they force the words out of the woman's mouth. ... The silence of women not in the picture, outside the pages, hurt but silent, used but silent, is staggering in how deep and wide it goes.

The civil rights ordinance restores speech rights to women who have been silenced by pornography. Dworkin (1989) provides a glimpse of the meaning of such rights for women speaking out against the pornography that hurt them. She writes:

> What the survivors [at the Minneapolis hearings] said was speech; the pornography had been throughout their lives, a means of actively suppressing their speech. They had been turned into pornography in life and made mute; terrorized by it and made mute. Now, the mute spoke; the socially invisible were seen; the women were real; they mattered ... The women came forward because they thought that the new civil rights law recognized what had happened to them, gave them recourse and redress, enhanced their civil dignity and human worth. The law itself gave them *existence:* I am real; they believe me; I count; social policy at last will take my life into account (xxx).

References

Baldwin, Gordon. 1986. "Pornography: The Supreme Court Rejects a Call for New Restrictions." *Wisconsin Women's Law Journal.* 2:75–83.

Baldwin, Margaret. 1984. "The Sexuality of Inequality: The Minneapolis Pornography Ordinance." *Law and Inequality.* 2 (August): 635–670.

Bogdanovich, Peter. 1984. *The Killing of the Unicorn: Dorothy Stratton (1960–1980)*. New York: William Morrow.

Brief Amici Curiae of Feminist Anti-Censorship Taskforce in support of Plaintiffs. 1985. *American Booksellers v. Hudnut*. U.S. Circuit Court of Appeals (7th Circuit). Docket No. 84–3147. 8 April.

Charles, Beth. 1985. "The Pornography Explosion." *Ladies Home Journal*. (October): 104–106, 162–164.

Chew, Sally. 1985. "Just the Facts: Talking with Members of the Feminist Anti-Censorship Taskforce." *New York Native*. 14–27 January: 15–20.

Davis, Angela. 1981. *Women, Race and Class*. New York: Random House.

Duggan, Lisa, Nan Hunter, and Carole Vance. 1985. "False Promises: Feminist Antipornography Legislation in the United States." In *Women Against Censorship*. ed. Varda Burstyn. Toronto: Douglas and McIntyre. 130–151.

Dworkin, Andrea. 1980. "Women Lawyers and Pornography." In *Letters from a War Zone: Writings 1976-1989*. New York: E.P. Dutton, 1989. 235–46.

———. 1981a. "Pornography and Male Supremacy." In *Letters from a War Zone: Writings 1976-1989*. New York: E.P. Dutton, 1989. 226–34.

———. 1981b. "Why Pornography Matters to Feminists." *Letters from a War Zone: Writings 1976-1989*. New York: E.P. Dutton, 1989. 203–05.

———. 1985. Brief Amicus Curiae, *American Booksellers Association v. Hudnut*. U.S. Circuit Court of Appeals (7th Circuit). Docket No. 84–3147. 28 February.

———. 1986a. "Against the Male Flood: Censorship, Pornography and Equality." In *Letters from a War Zone: Writings 1976-1989*. New York: E.P. Dutton, 1989. 253–275.

———. 1986b. "Pornography is a Civil Rights Issue." In *Letters from a War Zone: Writings 1976-1989*. New York: E.P. Dutton, 1989. 276–307.

———. 1989. *Pornography: Men Possessing Women*. New York: E.P. Dutton.

Dworkin, Andrea, and Catharine MacKinnon. 1988. *Pornography and Civil Rights: A New Day for Women's Equality*. Minneapolis, Minnesota: Organizing Against Pornography.

Elshtain, Jean Bethke. 1982. "The Victim Syndrome." *The Progressive*. June: 42–47.

English, Deirdre. 1980. "The Politics of Pornography: Can Feminists Walk the Line?" *Mother Jones*. (April): 20+.

Gardner, Tracey. 1980. "Racism in Pornography and the Women's Movement." In *Take Back the Night*. ed. Laura Lederer. New York: William Morrow. 105–114.

hooks, bell. 1981. *Ain't I a Woman*. Boston: South End Press.

Hunter, Nan. 1986. "Feminists Oppose Anti-Porn Ordinance." *Aegis*. 40:52.

Irvine, Janice. 1985. "Carole Vance Discusses FACT." *Sojourner*. December: 18–19.

Irvine, Janice, and Donna Turley. 1985. "Boston FACT Women Speak Out." *Bay Windows.* 19 September: 4.

Leidholdt, Dorchen. 1983. "Where Porn Meets Fascism." *WIN.* 15 March: 19–24.

Leidholdt, Dorchen. 1987. "In Memoriam: Althea Flynt, 1955–87." *Women Against Pornography Newsreport.* IX.1 (Fall): 8.

Lovelace, Linda, with Mike McGrady. *Ordeal.* New York: Berkley, 1980.

MacKinnon, Catharine. 1984. "Francis Biddle's Sister: Pornography, Civil Rights and Speech." In *Feminism Unmodified.* Cambridge: Harvard University Press, 1987. 163–197.

Mithers, Carol Lynn. 1988. "If Your Lover Uses Porn." *Glamour.* (November): 274.

Osanka, Franklin, and Sara Lee Johann. 1989. *Sourcebook on Pornography.* Lexington, Massachusetts: Lexington Books.

Pornography and Sexual Violence: Evidence of the Links. 1988. Reprint of *Public Hearings to Add Pornography as Discrimination Against Women.* 12–13 December 1983. Minneapolis, Minnesota: Government Operations Committee, City Council. London: Everywoman Press.

Post, Carole. 1982. "Pornography and Our Self Image: Women Speak Out." *Women Against Pornography Newsreport.* (Spring): 4–5.

Reilly, Kristen. 1982. "WAP, NOW, Native American Protest Racist/Sexually Violent Video Game." *Women Against Pornography Newsreport.* (Fall): 1.

Ross, Loretta. 1982. "Rape and Third World Women." *Aegis.* (Summer): 39–48.

Rush, Florence. 1980. *The Best Kept Secret: Sexual Abuse of Children.* New York: McGraw Hill.

Silbert, Mimi H., and Ayala M. Pines. 1984. "Pornography and Sexual Abuse of Women." *Sex Roles.* 10.11/12: 857–868.

Snitow, Ann. 1985. "Retrenchment v. Transformation: The Politics of the Antipornography Movement." In *Women Against Censorship.* ed. Varda Burstyn. Toronto: Douglas and McIntyre. 107–120.

Teish, Luisah. 1980. "A Quiet Subversion." In *Take Back the Night,* ed. Laura Lederer. New York: William Morrow. 115–118.

Vance, Carole. 1986. "The Meese Commission on the Road." *Nation.* 2/9 (August): 1+.

Vance, Carole. 1985. "What Does the Research Say?" *Ms.* (April): 40.

Vance, Carole. 1984. Introduction to *Pleasure and Danger: Exploring Female Sexuality.* ed. Carole Vance. Boston: Routledge & Kegan Paul. 1–28.

Webster, Paula. 1986. "Pornography and Pleasure." In *Caught Looking: Feminism, Moralism and Pornography.* ed. Feminist Anti-Censorship Taskforce (FACT). New York: Caught Looking. 30–35.

Webster, Paula. 1984. "The Forbidden: Eroticism and Taboo." In *Pleasure and Danger.* ed. Carole Vance. London: Routledge and Kegan Paul. 385–398.

Wilson, Elizabeth. 1982. Interview with Andrea Dworkin. *Feminist Review.* 11 (June): 23–29.

"Working in the Body Trade." 1981. *Aegis.* (Autumn): 18+.

9

Women's Revolutionary Place

Angharad N. Valdivia

The situation of women in the Third World[1] has recently aroused the interest of Western feminist scholars. This welcome effort to understand the complex, rich, and varied situations of women around the world promises to enrich women's studies and broaden a previously problematic ethnocentric tendency. Inevitably, this shift has also come to inform studies in mass communications. Once we broaden our horizons, we have to consider the relationship between feminism,[2] the mass media, and Third World revolutionary movements and governments, because, as Mattelart (1986) has noted, women function as a powerful symbol and source of support for both revolutionary and conservative political forces. In particular, women in Latin America have been active participants in social movements. However, their participation needs to be studied case by case, as there are different groups of women with different interests and a resulting variety of gender politics.

While many countries throughout Latin America have attempted, or are in the process of attempting, a revolutionary change, I will focus primarily on my study of revolutionary Nicaragua, its women's organizations, and its mass media, where the opportunity for a feminist case study that would explore the intersection of gender politics, revolution and the press was too great for me to ignore. Specifically, I study the role and influence of women within media organizations as well as the discourse about women and women's issues in the mainstream press. The process and form of women's claims should present us with concrete evidence of the spaces women can and do occupy during a revolutionary situation.

Theoretical Discussions

Since the late 1960s, modern feminists[3] have engaged in a discussion of whether socialism and feminism are compatible. Many of the early feminist writers emerged from male-dominated leftist movements and parties in

167

which they experienced discrimination, dismissal, and ridicule of gender politics (Sargent 1981; Rowbotham 1973). Leftist activists, guided by a Marxian analysis of class, tended to exclude other social divisions such as gender, race, and ethnicity. As a result, feminist scholars disagree on the usefulness of Marxism for the analysis of women's oppression. Einsenstein (1977), for example, acknowledges that Marxism has often excluded women as a class but argues that Marx's "revolutionary ontology" is useful for women's liberation. Hartmann (1981) writes of an unhappy marriage, pun intended, between socialism and feminism but, much like Einsenstein and others (for example Delphy 1988), sees hope in a clearer theoretical "wedding" between these two separate fields. Others (see contributors to Sargent 1981; Barrett 1980) argue that a "wedding" isn't possible or shouldn't be attempted. While that debate has yet to be settled, it has mainly been carried on by Western scholars studying their own societies or those of the Soviet Union, the Eastern European bloc, and China.

Women's rights have formed part of the new political platform of various socialist governments. Studies of those countries, with exceptions (such as Keig [1979] and Di and Hong [1988]), suggest that political changes have not necessarily brought about attitudinal changes. Women are expected to fully participate in the economic sphere while remaining responsible for household duties and the added time-consuming duty of securing goods in scarcity. State sponsorship of gender equality is strong when it coincides with development policies and wanes during periods when gender and state politics differ (Molyneux 1985; Wolf 1985; Wolchick 1989).

Studies from Third World revolutions are beginning to influence socialist-feminist formulations. Many studies note the difficult struggle of Third World women facing neocolonial relations, economic embargoes, and war as well as prevalent sexism within revolutionary ranks (Urdang 1979, 1989; Harris 1985; Molyneux 1985; Benallegue 1983; Delloye 1980; Ferdows 1983). Molyneux (1985), in an extremely insightful consideration of gender politics in the Third World, adds that many feminist issues such as "the nuclear family, relations between men and women and the institution of marriage" are regarded as unproblematic in contemporary socialism (p. 1,024). I would add that private/public sphere divisions are also ignored.

As in other Third World regions, the countries of Latin America differ greatly from each other. With the possible exception of Cuba, there are wide chasms in income distribution in every country. Class, thus, becomes an unavoidable area of study. Latin Americans are conscious of their class standing and the class divisions in their country; this has strong implications for women who identify themselves by class and gender (Nash and Safa 1976; NACLA 1980). Ethnicity and race also take on a different life in the Third World, where ethnicity is as much a cultural as a biological construct (Spivak 1988). Rural people, in most countries, especially women, have high rates of illiteracy, infant mortality, maternal deaths at childbirth, and levels of poverty, as well as very little access to education and health services (CEPAL 1982; Bingham and Gross 1985).

Most Latin American people also have little access to formal politics. However, it must be noted that class may be more of a barrier than gender. Upper- and middle-class women have been more active in traditional politics (NACLA 1980, 24), although working-class women have not been silent. Groups of Latin American women have organized even during extremely repressive times, thus defying the passive and apolitical labels assigned to them (Agosin 1987/88, Cohen 1974, Jacquette 1976; Schmidt 1976/77; Kirkwood 1983; Bonder 1983; *Des Chiliennes* 1982; Randall 1980b and 1981a; Espejo 1980; LAWG 1987; Martinez 1981; Thomson 1986; Alegria 1987; New Americas Press 1989; Araujo 1980; Barrios 1979). Actions such as boycotts (of products and elections), hunger strikes, street protests, grafiti-painting, crop choice,[4] union and guerrilla activism, and clandestine support services for revolutionary movements should all be considered important ways of political participation. In genocidal wars, such as the current war in Guatemala, survival itself can be an act of defiance. In most of these cases, what women do in their everyday activities propels them to form political groups, which often extend to larger issues (New Americas Press 1989; Smith 1987; Kaplan 1982; Chinchilla 1979; Jaquette 1973). While espousing neither a gender nor an ideological platform, these women were nevertheless a powerful symbolic threat to their countries' dictatorships.

Conservative women's movements have also influenced political outcomes in several countries, often with help from and participation in the mainstream media (Mattelart 1986; Thomson 1986). Most notably, the women of Chile played a pivotal role in the overthrow of the Allende government. Mattelart (1986) asserts that the women's "manipulation" by rightist forces was made easier by the Left's dismissal of both gender politics and the role of the media, a process similar to that in Brazil in 1964. While most of the literature on these organizations suggests that right-wing women are manipulated, upper-class women stand to lose many privileges from a revolutionary change. Thus, their reaction to revolutionary movements and policies should not be considered mere manipulation. The participation of lower-class women in conservative movements is a bit more difficult to explain, but we should not immediately assume that these women are operating under false premises either. In a

169

study of urban and rural, lower- and middle-class women, Mattelart and Mattelart (1968) suggested that lower-class urban women are the most affected by middle-class aspirations and by the costs of modernization—factors which may affect their conservative stance.

Despite the calls of feminist scholars for more contextualized research (Gallagher 1980; Steeves 1987), Mattelart's work (1986) stands nearly alone as an example of a study of women and the media during revolutionary times. While the Cuban experience, for example, has inspired scholars to examine feminist issues ranging from the general situation of women to the value of domestic labor, childcare and reproduction policies (Randall 1981b; Stone 1981; Holt-Seeland 1981; Purcell 1973; Nazzari 1983; King 1977; Aguirre 1981; Cole and Reed 1986; Casal 1980; FMC 1980), none of these authors addresses the conjunction of women, power, and the media. Given the theoretical issues, it would be important to find out how women, both conservative and revolutionary, find and express their voices during a revolutionary period. It is unclear if the lack of attention to media issues stems from the scholars or the Cuban government and women's organization's own programs. However, in Nicaragua, cultural and gender issues have been discussed since the years preceding the overthrow of the Somoza dictatorship. Nicaragua thus presents feminist communications scholars with a situation in which the intersection of gender, power, and the mass media issues have been extensively debated. Women in Nicaragua managed to voice their demands in the press throughout the Sandinista period and their making of meaning deserves to be studied.

Nicaragua

My choice of Nicaragua as a site of study was influenced as much by the above theoretical questions as by my personal history and experience. I left my native Chile prior to the Allende presidency, a child of a member of the conservative middle-class, which refused to support or even participate in a socialist experiment. Though too young to understand the implications of my emigration at that time, I have since dwelt on the circumstances that led to my residence and citizenship in the United States. From the perspective of a graduate feminist student in the U.S. academy, the Nicaraguan revolution appeared to provide a setting for exploring the lessons of the Chilean experience in a living laboratory.[5]

Indeed, women's participation in the Nicaraguan insurrectional struggle was decisive. Likewise, their participation in the economy was and continues to be indispensable. Poor Nicaraguan women were active in both the urban and rural economy (WIRE 1982, 24) and headed most of Nicaragua's families (Randall 1981a, 24). At the time of the revolutionary triumph, thirty-percent of the guerrilla forces were women, and in some age cohorts the participation of women surpassed that of men (Randall 1981a; Deighton et. al. 1983). This is not to imply that women did not face discrimination when they joined the guerrillas (Stephens 1988), but that they overcame these obstacles and provided a needed measure of participation.

When the Sandinista forces (FSLN) triumphantly marched into the capital city of Managua on July 19, 1979, the rich terrain of Nicaraguan politics and culture included a number of living and defunct women's organizations. The largest was AMPRONAC, which had begun in 1977 as a middle-class organization to protest the "national problematic"[6] and had grown in both membership and class representation until, in the last days of the insurrection, it supported the FSLN in its revolutionary struggle. While some AMPRONAC women organized protests, brought people from the countryside for testimonials, and cared for the wounded, others clandestinely joined the guerrillas or provided supportive services to the FSLN.

AMPRONAC's creation was not entirely autonomous. Lea Guido, a founding member who became head of the women's organization in 1985, claims that the organization of women was suggested to her by Jaime Wheelock, an FSLN commander and the Minister of Agrarian Reform during the Sandinista years (Randall 1981a, 2). The FSLN had consistently included women's rights in their public proclamations (Stephens 1988; *Latin American Perspectives* 1979) and another member, Gladys Baez, had previously attempted to start a woman's organization (Baez 1980; Randall 1981a). However, once it began to agitate, AMPRONAC followed its own agenda, sympathetic to the FSLN but peripheral to it.

On July 19, 1979, Sandinista forces marched into Managua, the capital city, and assumed control of the government. Among the Sandinista commanders was Dora Maria Tellez, a symbol of women's contribution to and "claims"[7] from the revolutionary government. Nicaraguan women were both active in the public sphere and organized into special interest groups. Meanwhile, the Sandinista government followed a "traditional socialist" path regarding women's policies (Stephens 1988, 4). Legal reforms, political and economic participation, and equal rights and responsibilities within the family were constitutionalized. The government created an office of legal services for women, Oficina legal de la Mujer (OLM), as well as a research center, Oficina de la Mujer (OM), both of which are independent of AMNLAE (AMPRONAC became AMNLAE in September 1979; see p. 179). Women, especially those who had reached high positions in the FSLN, were appointed to head important government posts, including ministries and regional committees, with the government explicitly fol-

171

lowing a path of affirmative action. Granted, a woman occupied the traditionally female position of health minister, but others headed the Sandinista police and Sandinista urban workers (CST), while others presided over the influential regional committees. Rhetorically, women's issues became a favorite topic of speeches (for example, Borges 1982). Other mass organizations, including the agricultural workers (ATC), and CST formed women's groups.

The situation of women became a legitimate area of study (OM 1987a and 1987c). Studies revealed that despite some advances, Nicaraguan women continued to face obstacles in agricultural and industrial production. One major benefit was that, unlike in other agrarian reforms in Latin America, Nicaraguan women were declared legal beneficiaries of land redistribution policies (Deere 1985). However, their integration as equal partners into cooperatives was riddled with ideological and material obstacles (CIERA 1984). The situation was similar in the agro-export industries (INM 1987) and in the textiles and clothing industries (OM 1987b). Though women comprised a major proportion of workers in those economic sectors, they occupied the lowest-paid levels and had little access to training, with the exception of units with female managers.

Undoubtedly, the war of aggression had a negative effect on women's lives as well as on government policies towards women (Montenegro 1987b). To begin with, the Contra war diverted much of the government budget to defense, causing some feminist critics to insist that "the constant need to give priority to the defense of the country and the revolution has forced women's issues into the background" (Stephens 1988, 13). More directly, the strategical shift within counter-revolutionary ranks from attacking army units to terrorizing the civilian population meant that women and their children were exposed to increasing violence. The war also forced women to provide for their families alone, because an increasing number of men were conscripted by the draft. Attacks on rural cooperatives, health centers, and schools had a heavier impact on women, because they had been the major beneficiaries of those social services. Also, reduced production and galloping inflation reduced the incomes of most families, most of which were and are headed by women.

Stephens adds that while the war may have increased civilian opportunities for women (the "Rosie the Riveter" effect), it may have also fueled sexism because "society increasingly comes to praise skills and sacrifices that are associated almost exclusively with men" (1988, 14). In fact, this was the basis of one of the biggest disagreements between AMNLAE and the Sandinista government, when AMNLAE objected to the exclusion of women from combat forces. The issue was uneasily resolved by allowing women to volunteer for the army but not incorporating women in the front lines until three years later.

Nevertheless, AMNLAE attempted to maintain its stance of supporting the government while advocating women's rights. One aspect that suggested that AMNLAE was less autonomous than it would have liked to admit, was the abrupt change of its leaders. AMNLAE's first secretary general was Gloria Carrion, one of APMRONAC's original founders. She was replaced by Glenda Monterrey who was later replaced by Lea Guido. All of these replacements were announced by the government, and there is little evidence that the AMNLAE membership was asked about these transfers or whether they minded them.

AMNLAE did go through program changes throughout the revolutionary period. *Envio* (1987) traced a three-stage history for the women's organization. The first stage, 1979–1982, found AMNLAE focusing its energies on the national reconstruction, because Somoza left the country in a state of total chaos and extreme debt. Women were mobilized to increase production in the formal labor market. Additionally, AMNLAE organized volunteer units to support the literacy and health crusades. For many women this was the beginning of a conscious formulation of their oppression as women despite the focus on national reconstruction (*Envio* 1983). Domestics, merchants, and prostitutes all organized to demand the rights due them, their "reivindicaciones."

During the second stage, 1983–1986, AMNLAE, like the other mass organizations, emphasized defense by mobilizing women to form reserve battalions. The growth of the movement of "Mothers of Heroes and Martyrs" dates back to this period, when the mothers and/or wives of mobilized and/or deceased husbands and sons were added to the mothers of the victims of the Somoza period. These women provided services for the military, and AMNLAE functioned as an intermediary ensuring that both the men and the mothers were provided for. However, women who fell outside of this group felt isolated and AMNLAE began to try to correct this oversight. Nevertheless, this period included a lively debate about abortion and domestic violence, bringing two previously private themes into the public debate (*Envio* 1987, 46). Likewise, AMNLAE grass-roots groups brought up the high incidence of wife-abuse, statistically documented by a study from the OLM, which revealed that most divorces were due to wife-abuse. AMNLAE prepared slide-shows and publications discussing the issue, which in Nicaragua is euphemistically called "sopa de muñeca" (doll's soup).

As a result, AMNLAE entered its third stage in 1987 with the realization that everyday problems were as important to their membership as addressing more structural legal issues. This realization coincided with an

OM document that argued that there had not yet been a "politics which redefined the social role of women, the traditional division of labor, or the ideology which defines different roles for the sexes," all of which were necessary for "the construction of a new society" (Montenegro 1987b, 90). AMNLAE officially changed from an organization to a women's movement, encouraging its members to participate within their areas of activities rather than duplicating efforts and meetings. While that move sought to integrate the women's movement into all other organizations, it also potentially weakened the one organization whose primary goal was to support women. AMNLAE's new role, rather than organizing women, became to "promote the identification of the particular problems of women so that they reach the status of problems of the revolution" (Montenegro 1987b, 92).

One major boost to Nicaraguan women was the much awaited FSLN Proclamation on Women (FSLN 1987). The document reaffirmed the FSLN's stance on women's liberation within the Sandinista liberation, while also acknowledging that women, "especially those from the working classes," faced additional obstacles that placed them in a situation of "greater oppression" (p. 11). Although, the proclamation did not really present any new ideas, it signaled to women that their struggle still occupied a position of priority within the government agenda despite the incredible exigencies of the war. Sofia Montenegro interpreted the proclamation as a sign that the government would "no longer postpone radical or innovative solutions" (1987b, 86). Barahona (1987) interpreted it as a sign that the FSLN had to subordinate, but not postpone, both class and gender struggles, given the situation of imperialist aggression that Nicaragua faced. Entire journal issues were devoted to gender politics (see *Cuadernos de Sociologia* 1987) and a journal, *Documentos Sobre La Mujer*, was created exclusively to discuss gender issues. Though the problems facing the beleaguered nation in 1987 were immense, many women believed that gender issues would continue to be addressed.

Nicaraguan women, especially those from the lower-classes, experienced gains in education and health benefits through a national literacy crusade and more health clinics. Also, legal reforms ranged from changes in divorce laws to the designation of women as beneficiaries of the land reform. Additionally, the incorporation of women into mass organizations and other political bodies meant that they had a voice in their nation's policies.

However, as in other revolutionary situations, right-wing women were also active in Nicaraguan politics. In fact, both the government and the opposition actively sought the support and allegiance of Nicaragua's women. Although the first year of the revolutionary period saw little disagreement over gender issues, by late 1980, right-of-center parties began forming their own women's groups. The Christian Democrats' Partido Social Democratic (PSC), Social Democrats' Partido Liberal (PSD), and Liberal (PL) parties each organized a women's group. These women engaged in more traditional activities such as providing food baskets, Christmas parties, and the like for the poor. On a more political tone, in 1985 the PSC women sent their own delegation to the Nairobi Decade for Women Conference to counter-balance AMNLAE's participation.

In addition, by 1984, a group of women named themselves the "Mothers of Heroes and Martyrs" in a direct affront to the pro-Sandinista organization by the same name. The issue of who was the real Nicaraguan mother remained a hotly contested issue until the last days of the Sandinista government. While the government and AMNLAE were providing support services to families of mobilized soldiers in order to maintain their allegiance, the opposition was recruiting converts by preying on the fears of those who might be drafted. While one group supported the Sandinista effort, the other supported the counterrevolutionary forces. The original group had the support of the government, AMNLAE, and Christian-based communities, while the newer group was supported by opposition parties and the Catholic Church hierarchy.

Although originally she did not officially affiliate with that group, Violeta Barrios de Chamorro became increasingly involved in the activities of the conservative "Mothers of Heroes and Martyrs" group. As the widow of the slain editor of *La Prensa,* the country's conservative newspaper, Doña Violeta would have provided a powerful symbolic figure to any faction she wished to support. Accordingly she had been one of the original members of the provisional junta (JGRN) from 1979–1980. However, her resignation signaled her return to opposition and her eventual candidacy and election for the presidency revealed how strong a symbolic force she was. Doña Violeta ran as a Nicaraguan wife and a mother desiring peace, yet she symbolized the opposition of the upper classes to the Sandinista government. She demonstrated that women can be very successful in conservative movements in Latin America. Her apparent concern for everyday issues must have appealed to the voters.

The Project

From this account of the revolution, it can be seen that Nicaraguan women faced a new government that rhetorically supported gender equity and acknowledged the importance of access to the means of mass communications. Although the analysis of the three daily newspapers could have been easily conducted from within the comfortable halls of the University of Illinois, where I was working on my doctorate, I felt that neither categorizing nor analyzing the material would be possible without visiting Nicaragua. Much of the available research on the Nicaraguan press was motivated by external concerns. For example, the extensive literature on *La Prensa*'s[8] bouts with censorship appeared to be concerned with the First Amendment, a U.S. and not a universal law. Similarly, some of the studies of Nicaraguan women were slightly critical of their supportive stance towards the government. During the summer of 1988, I sought to ground the study in a Nicaraguan framework as much as possible through interviews with Nicaraguan women in the three major newspapers, in a number of women's organizations, in journalism departments in local universities, in the journalists' union (UPN), and in some relevant government agencies. These interviews[9] enabled me to understand the press debates from a local perspective.[10]

Additionally, I conducted a textual analysis of the three main Nicaraguan newspapers, *Barricada, El Nuevo Diario,* and *La Prensa,* during the period 1979–1988. Both the categories and the sample periods of this analysis were greatly influenced by the above interviews—that is, interview partners suggested some of the major feminist issues discussed in the press and some of the most heated moments of the debate. From the sample, I read every issue of *Barricada* and *La Prensa* for the first year of the revolution (July 19, 1979–July 19, 1980) and selected issues from then until July 1988. I was looking specifically for news frame construction. Would the inclusion of gender politics in the Sandinista period, especially of those issues suggested to me by interview partners, change the focus, and if so, how?

Findings

Interviews with the women journalists working for these newspapers suggested that their participation affected content. In other words, the news frame changed through the efforts of these women. However, a number of intersecting variables, not just their presence, enabled these women to influence content. First, most of the women interviewed selected the newspaper they worked for partly because of ideology. In sum, a revolutionary feminist knew better than to apply to *La Prensa* for a job, regardless of the scarcity of trained journalistic personnel following the Sandinista victory. Second, women both in *Barricada* and *La Prensa* pressed a woman-oriented agenda because of the fluid politics and resulting fluid journalism engendered by the revolutionary experience. Third, government rhetoric and policies regarding gender and culture were perceived by these women as opening a space for voicing their activist feminist journalism. This is not to imply that there was no criticism, both from government officials and certain members of the local feminist community. Disagreement was voiced by some interview partners and was included in the press debate, but nevertheless the debate continued. Fourth, other governmental and non-governmental, national and international women's organizations functioned as both a support network, moral and financial, and a source of news for the women within the newspapers.

More specifically, different experiences led particular women to journalism and to work at a particular newspaper. At *Barricada*, most journalists[11] and all heads of departments were female, with the exception of the sports section editor. Nevertheless within that newspaper, the organ of the FSLN with a commitment to providing a perspective of the urban and rural working classes, women had different levels of training and commitment to gender politics. Undoubtedly, Sofia Montenegro's presence encouraged other journalists in *Barricada* and any outside feminist sources to present demands to that newspaper. Montenegro, who headed the influential editorial page, not only supported the revolutionary cause but was additionally, and foremost, an avowed radical feminist, the only woman who would admit to that label during my entire stay in Nicaragua. In fact, Montenegro had been a feminist before she joined the Sandinista ranks. She joined the revolution because she realized that gender politics could not be pursued under the Somoza regime. She was active in Nicaraguan feminist circles and often introduced feminist debates through her editorials.

Other women at *Barricada* followed a different path to their jobs and feminist stances. One had followed a fairly traditional middle-class path through journalism school and moved up through a series of beats. While assigned to the labor beat, however, she noticed the additional hardships that female laborers faced. She was particularly attuned to these issues because she was a working mother in a two-career family. She often found herself encouraging the female laborers to voice their gender demands.

Another *Barricada* journalist followed a revolutionary path of "empirical"[12] training. Rising through the ranks of grassroots Sandinista activists, she eventually joined *Barricada*. Though possessing a feminist outlook that reflected itself in her work, this journalist did not see anything feminist in her position.

On the other hand, *La Prensa* had neither as many female journalists nor heads of departments. With the exception of Violeta de Chamorro who occupied more of an honorary director position, there were only two female journalists, both university trained, on the staff. One of these journalists covered the traditionally feminine human interest beat, while the other was assigned to the economics beat. Nevertheless, both of these women devoted a considerable part of their stories to women and women's issues. When asked about their emphasis on women, they admitted that it was both a result of their personal experience and of Sandinista government policies. However, this latter reason they qualified with a negative logic by adding that Sandinista policies had increased the everyday hardships for women to such an extent that the press could not afford to ignore them. These women strongly denied reacting to the *Barricada* and the Sandinistas efforts to make women's private problems a matter of public debate and policy. In fact, they did not grant any legitimacy to AMNLAE events, preferring to go straight to the "Nicaraguan woman on the street" instead.

Other relevant participants in the press debate provided yet another glimpse into the plurality of views on women and the press. Lilly Soto, the secretary general of the Nicaraguan Union of Journalists (UPN) advocated a strong role for women in society in general and in the press in particular. She was involved in a research project designed to recover women's contributions to the press in Nicaraguan history. However, Soto also criticized certain newspapers that carried a debate that she felt did not reflect the interests of the masses, who were primarily worried about defense and economic growth. Heliette Hellers, AMNLAE's director of media and information issues, proposed that the press needed to go beyond their present coverage of women and women's issues. Hellers criticized the tendency to cover exceptional women and suggested that a newspaper was needed that would present national and international news from a "feminist viewpoint." Hellers also noted that AMNLAE events and press conferences were occasionally attended by *Barricada* and *El Nuevo Diario*, while *La Prensa* actively avoided coverage of the women's organization.

A textual analysis of *Barricada*, *El Nuevo Diario*, and *La Prensa* revealed that women and their issues became part of the daily debate in revolutionary Nicaragua. An expected area of coverage was the women's organization. Following the victory of the FSLN forces, AMPRONAC changed its name and modified its identity. By then many of the original, non-FSLN members had dropped out of the organization (Randall 1981a). Changing from "a force of support, caring and searching for the wounded, and transporting ammunitions ... to organizing *companeras* neighborhood by neighborhood" brought the women's organization closer to the Sandinista revolution (*Barricada* 8/9/79). AMPRONAC began to emphasize the role of the new revolutionary woman in the reconstruction process by telling its members that "today more than ever, women must be organized because only united and organized will their goals be achieved"

(*Barricada* 8/13/79). In late August AMPRONAC temporarily changed its name to the Federation of Sandinista Women (FMS). Whether due to its similarity to the Cuban organization (FMC) or because some women were uneasy with the close and explicit ties to the Sandinistas that the name implied, in late September the organization became AMNLAE, the Association of Nicaraguan Women Luisa Amanda Espinoza, named after the first FSLN woman to die in combat. AMNLAE began a long and complex process of organizing women and working within government priorities. It vaccilated between claiming that "AMNLAE was created and fueled by the FSLN, because women represent an important social force within our revolutionary process" (*Barricada* 9/20/79) and charting out a more independent line. In response to Fidel Castro's admonition that "there is no women's liberation without a revolution," AMNLAE responded that "there is no revolution without women's participation" (*Barricada* 3/2/80). *Barricada* and, to a lesser extent, *El Nuevo Diario*, continued to report on the evolving identity of AMNLAE, often including differing opinions from a variety of members. There was no specific spokesperson that either newspaper relied on for the "official" line nor was there an effort to set the debate into an either/or frame. In contrast, *La Prensa* began to report on non-AMNLAE, conservative women's organizations while simultaneously reducing its coverage of the women's mass organization, so that by 1984 a *La Prensa* reader would have had no way of knowing that AMNLAE even existed.

Throughout the period that I studied, women as individuals and women's issues continued to appear in the news frame of all three newspapers. Women appeared as agricultural and industrial workers, merchants, mothers, soldiers, prostitutes, government officials, mass organization leaders, martyrs, heroes, seamstresses, judges, domestics, and beggars. Not surprisingly, each of the three papers offered different coverage, and each claimed to represent all Nicaraguans. *Barricada* presented many rural and urban female workers issues, often including an AMNLAE members' perspective. Usually, but not always, *Barricada*'s coverage of women's issues supported Sandinista policies. *El Nuevo Diario* provided supportive coverage of both Sandinista policies and women's issues while incorporating some traditional approaches to the coverage of women such as an emphasis on physical attributes and an occasional instance of sensationalist, "women as victim" stories. *El Nuevo Diario's* independent stance sometimes resulted in some fairly critical coverage of certain issues but not of the government itself. *La Prensa* originally, through 1979, supported government policies, but became increasingly critical of the government and all of its policies as soon as Violeta de Chamorro resigned from the provisional junta. *La Prensa*'s traditional bourgeois base of financial support and readership was evident from its focus as well as from its sources.

An early topic that presaged the different approach to women's issues to be taken by *Barricada* and *La Prensa* was the issue of makeup. In an effort to curb its negative balance of trade, the Nicaraguan government resolved to reduce imports of cosmetics. *Barricada* printed an AMNLAE editorial agreeing that given the current situation of the country, cosmetics were a luxury that Nicaraguans could not afford (12/2/79). Additionally, the AMNLAE editorial questioned the ideal of beauty and positioning of women that using cosmetics implied. *La Prensa* included a letter to the editor signed by several women protesting the measure and claiming that makeup was necessary for "women's intrinsic feminine nature" (12/5/79).

Another debate, which generated a great deal of coverage and popular discussion,[13] was over abortion. *Barricada* and *El Nuevo Diario* began carrying a number of editorials and articles about abortion in the summer of 1985. *La Prensa* reluctantly joined them in early 1986, though most of its articles were against abortion. This lively discussion included AMNLAE members, government officials, nurses, doctors, people on the street, patients recovering from street abortions, the clergy, and journalists. The issue was discussed from a variety of perspectives including religion, feminism, law and health, with no consensus, but most participants in the discussion agreed that it was time to publicly discuss a topic affecting many women, regardless of class or political affiliation.

Other heavily debated issues were women in the military, merchant women demands, domestic worker legislation, student elections, and literacy crusade participation. *La Prensa*'s coverage illustrated the inevitable contradictions arising from a liberal/bourgeois institution attempting to survive in a socialist society. On the other hand, *Barricada* demonstrated the basic dilemma between feminism and socialism. Gender issues continued to be addressed despite the worsening economic and political situation. If there was a centrist position to be found, *El Nuevo Diario* provided it. Though supportive of the government and its women's policies, *El Nuevo Diario* also adopted many liberal ideas about both the press and women. Its position on any given issue was unpredictable since it was just as likely to take a traditional Catholic stance as a more radical feminist one.

Conclusion

I have now provided an overview of the ways that some women have participated in Latin American revolutionary politics and the gains that women achieved within revolutionary governments. Generally, I have tried to counter the prevailing belief that Latin American women are both passive and conservative. To begin with, surviving in the difficult conditions in which most Latin American women live requires anything but passivity. Next, although many of their histories are just beginning to be written, recent scholarship suggests that women have actively participated in many revolutionary movements. In both cases, a feminist vision has helped to interpret women's everyday activities as potentially revolutionary (Smith 1987). Finally, the participation of conservative women's groups cannot be dismissed as manipulation because those women are also actively protecting their interests. Here too, women's everyday activities lead them to oppose revolutionary governments and join counterrevolutionary forces.

The experience of Nicaraguan women provides much material for students of the relationship between gender, socialism, and the media. The women of AMNLAE continuously strived to keep their own agenda in addition to helping the government with theirs. Their efforts were rewarded, at least rhetorically, by the 1987 proclamation reaffirming the need for a feminist agenda despite the exigencies of the war (FSLN 1987). That AMPRONAC pre-dated the Sandinista government also helped women during the revolutionary period in Nicaragua. Women's strong participation in the economy, the family, and the military prior to the revolutionary victory enabled them to make demands upon the Sandinista government based on their contribution. Following the revolutionary victory, many Nicaraguan women abandoned the traditional feminine ideal of passive self-abnegation and began to demand improvements in their condition, despite the country's difficult situation.

My interviews and textual analysis of women and of in the press suggest that at some point in the editorial process someone realized that women's support and input was crucial in a situation of contested legitimacy of just about every social institution—in other words, in a revolutionary situation. *Barricada* and *El Nuevo Diario* revealed that women's issues could not be easily resolved nor could they be shelved during a war. The divisions within AMNLAE and the tensions between the organization and the government were not obscured. That *Barricada* appointed Montenegro for the influential editorial page editorship signaled a maturity that no other revolution has demonstrated. That both *Barricada* and *El Nuevo Diario* covered the working classes and their everyday problems brought women to the fore of almost any issue. And *La Prensa*'s reaction—to go to the individual on the street—reinforced this alternative news frame. Women could not be avoided, and they refused to be silenced. That applied to conservative and revolutionary women, both of whom found a media outlet for their demands.

181

Notes

1. I use this term for lack of a better one. I do not mean it to be a perjorative judgment, nor do I pretend that there aren't enormous differences between countries whose main commonality appears to be the general level of poverty of their population.

2. Although I'll use the word *feminist* whenever referring to women's progressive movements in the Third World, I should add that many of these women reject that term. In my many interviews with Nicaraguan women, only one called herself a *feminist*. She added that feminism has become something of a dirty word among Third World women, who see Western feminism as very bourgeois and of little use to them. She also added that much of the received notion of Western feminism has come from the international press, which has much to gain from fostering that image.

3. I use the term *modern* to underscore the fact that women such as Alexandra Kollontai and Rosa Luxemburg began to address these issues at the turn of the twentieth century in Europe.

4. By this I mean that the choice of which crop to plant can be a political statement. Among the alternatives here are the agro-export crops that the government prefers, "drug" crops, or subsistence crops.

5. I borrow the use of this term from Sofia Montenegro who used it to refer to her country.

6. The euphemistic name of the organization pointed to its class roots. AM-PRONAC stood for "Women's Association in Front of the National Problematic." The "national problematic" as stated in AMPRONAC's platform referred to human rights abuses, or the increased incidence of finding one's relatives dead and mutilated in a creek near one's house.

7. The word that Nicaraguans, especially women, use is "reivindicaciones." The concept includes a notion of rights granted in return for the immense contribution of Nicaraguan women during the insurrectionary period. There is no direct translation for this word, but I owe Thomas Guback credit for his suggestion of the word "claims."

8. *La Prensa* is the press organ of the Nicaraguan bourgeoisie. During the Somoza years, *La Prensa* fervently opposed the military dictatorship. During the first stage of the Sandinista period, *La Prensa* grew extremely critical of that government.

9. Not everyone granted interviews. The women at *El Nuevo Diario* denied me interviews by way of postponements and cancellations. The head of the government media office, another woman, never returned my calls. However everyone else, including women at *La Prensa*, was more than willing to meet with me for an open-ended session.

10. By "local" I mean a perspective informed by Nicaraguans. I do not mean to imply that there was a unified perspective nor that my participation was totally

unbiased. In fact, one of my major findings was the amazing variety of perspectives held by participants in this debate and power struggle.

11.   This was the situation in the summer of 1988.

12.   "Empirical" is the term Nicaraguan used for on-the-job training as opposed to journalists who went to journalism school.

13.   Many of the women I interviewed claimed that people in the streets were avidly following the abortion debate.

References

Agosin, Marjorie. 1987/88. *Scraps of Life: Chilean Arpilleras.* Trenton, N.J.: The Red Sea Press.

Aguirre, Benigno. 1981. "Women in the Cuban Bureaucracies" In *Women in the Family and the Economy,* eds. G. Kurian and K Gosh, eds. Westport, Conn · Greenwood Press.

Alegria, Claribel. 1987. *They Won't Take Me Alive: Salvadorean Women in Struggle for National Liberation.* London: The Women's Press.

Araujo, Ana Maria. 1980. *Tupamaras: Des Femmes d'Uruguay.* Paris: Editions des Femmes.

Baez, Gladys. 1980. "Porque de Nosotras Se Espera Todo." *Nicarahuac.* 1(1, July/ August): 45–65.

Barahona, Milagros. 1987. "Que Es la Proclama del FSLN Para Nosotros?" *Cuadernos de Sociologia.* 4–5(May–December): 137–140.

Barrett, Michele. 1980. *Women's Oppression Today: Problems in Marxist Feminist Analysis.* London: Verso Editions and NLB.

Barrios de Chungara, Domitila. 1979. *Let Me Speak.* New York: Monthly Review Press.

Benallegue, Nora. 1983. "Algerian Women in the Struggle for Independence and Reconstruction." *International Social Science Journal.* 35(4): 703–717.

Bingham, Marjorie W. and Susan H. Gross, eds. 1985. *Women in Latin America— from Pre-Columbian Times to the 20th Century.* St. Louis Park, Minn.: Glenhurst Publications.

Bonder, Gloria. 1983. "The Study of Politics from the Standpoint of Women." *International Social Science Journal.* 35(4): 569–583.

Borge, Tomas. 1982. *Women and the Nicaraguan Revolution.* New York: Pathfinder Press.

Casal, Lourdes. 1980. "Women in Cuba." In C. Berkin and C. Lovett, eds. *Women, War, and Revolution.* New York: Homes & Meier Publishers.

CEPAL. 1982. *Cinco Estudios Sobre la Situacion de la Mujer en America Latina.* Santiago de Chile: United Nations Press.

Chinchilla, Norma S. 1979. "Mobilizing Women: Revolution in the Revolution." *Women in Latin America: An Anthology*. Riverside, Calif.: Latin American Perspectives.

Chuchryk, Patricia. 1989. "Suvbersive Mothers: The Women's Opposition to the Military Regime in Chile." In *Women, the State, and Development*. eds. S.E.M. Charlton, J. Everett, and K. Staudt. Albany: State University of New York Press.

CIERA. 1984. *La Mujer en las Cooperativas Agropecuarias en Nicaragua*. Managua: CIERA.

Cohen, Paul M. 1974. "Men and Women and the Latin American Political System: Paths to Political Participation in Paraguay." Paper presented at the annual meeting of the American Political Science Association.

Cole, Johnnetta B. and Gail A. Reed. 1986. "Women in Cuba: Old Problems and New Ideas." *Urban Anthropology and Studies of Cultural Systems and World Economic Development*. 15(Fall/Winter): 321–53.

Cuadernos de Sociologia. 1987. "Mujeres: Aspectos de una Realidad en Transformacion" 4–5(May—December): 58–139.

Deere, Carmen D. 1985. "Rural Women and State Policy: The Latin American Agrarian Reform Experience." *World Development*. 13(9): 1037–1053.

Deighton, Jane, Rossana Horsley, Sarah Stewart, and Cathy Casin. 1983. *Sweet Ramparts: Women in Revolutionary Nicaragua*. London: War on Want and Nicaragua Solidarity Campaign.

Delphy, Christine. 1988. "Patriarchy, Domestic Mode of Production, Gender, and Class" In *Marxism and the Interpretation of Culture*, L. Grossberg and C. Nelson eds. Urbana: University of Illinois Press.

Delloye, Isabelle. 1980. *Des Femmes D'Afghanistan*. Paris: Editions des Femmes.

Des Chiliennes: Des Femmes en Luttes au Chili, at Carmen Gloria Aguayo de Sota. 1982. Paris: Editions des Femmes.

Di, Hou and Li Hong. 1988. "Women in China's Socio-Economic Development." In *Women and Economic Development*. ed. K. Young. New York: Berg/UNESCO Press.

Eisenstein, Zillah. 1977. *Capitalist Patriarchy and the Case for Socialist Feminism*. New York: Monthly Review Press.

El Tayacan. n.d. *Que Pensamos las Mujeres de Nosotras Mismas?* Managua: El Tayacan.

Envio. 1983. "Women in Nicaragua: A Revolution Within a Revolution." 3(25, July): 1c–9c.

Envio. 1987. "Mujeres: Mas Espacio y Mas Voz." 6(78), December.

Espejo, Paz. 1980. *Des Femmes du Nicaragua*. Paris: Editions Des Femmes.

Federacion de Mujeres Cubanas (FMC). 1980. *Mecanismos Nacionales Para la Promocion de la Mujer*. New York: United Nations.

184

Frente Continental de Mujeres Contra La Intervencion. n.d. *Somos Una Sola Fuerza.* Republica Dominicana: Editorial "Buho."

FSLN. 1987. *El* FSLN *y la Mujer.* Managua: Editorial Vanguardia.

Gallagher, Margaret. 1981. *Unequal Opportunities: the Case of Women and the Media.* Paris: UNESCO.

Hartmann, Heidi. 1981. "The Unhappy Marriage of Marxism and Feminism: Towards a More Progressive Union." In *Women and Revolution: A Discussion of the Unhappy Marriage of Marxism and Feminism.* ed. L. Sargent Boston: South End Press.

Harris, Joan. 1985. "Revolution or Evolution?" *Africa Report.* 30(March/April): 30-32.

Holt-Seeland, Inger. 1981. *Women of Cuba.* Westport, Conn.: Lawrence Hill & Co.

Instituto Nicaraguense de la Mujer (INM). 1987. *Mujer y Agroexportacion en Nicaragua.* Managua: Centro de Documentacion del Instituto Nicaraguense de la Mujer.

Jaquette, Jane. 1973. "Women in Revolutionary Movements in Latin America." *Journal of Marriage and the Family.* 35(2): 344-354.

Jacquette, Jane. 1976. "Female Political Participation in Latin America." In *Sex and Class in Latin America.* eds. J. Nash and H.I. Safa. New York: Praeger Publishers.

Kaplan, Temma. 1982. "Female Consciousness and Collective Action: The Case of Barcelona, 1910-1918." In *Feminist Theory, A Critique of Ideology.* eds. N.O. Keohane, M.Z. Rosaldo, and B.C. Gelpi. Chicago: University of Chicago Press.

Keig, Nita. 1979. *Women's Liberation and the Socialist Revolution.* New York: Pathfinder Press.

King, Marjorie. 1977. "Cuba's Attack on Women's Second Shift, 1974-1976." *Latin American Perspectives.* IV(1-2, winter and spring): issues 12 and 13, 106-119.

Kirkwood, Julieta. 1983. "Women and Politics in Chile." *International Social Science Journal.* 35(4): 625-637.

Latin American Perspectives. 1979. "Documents: Why the FSLC Struggles in Unity with the People." VI(1, winter): issue 20, 108-113.

Latin American Working Group (LAWG). 1987. *Central American Women Speak Out for Themselves.* Toronto: LAWG, October.

Martinez, Ana Guadalupe. 1981. *El Salvador: Une Femme du Front de Liberation Temoigne.* Paris: Editions des Femmes.

Mattelart, Armand and Michele Mattelart. 1968. *La Mujer Chilena en una Nueva Sociedad.* Santiago, Chile: Editorial del Pacifico.

Mattelart, Michelle. 1986. *Women, Media, and Crisis: Femininity and Disorder.* London: Comedia.

Molyneux, Maxine. 1985. "Legal Reform and Socialist Revolution in Democratic Yemen: Women and the Family." *International Journal of the Sociology of Law.* 13(May): 147–72.

Montenegro, Sofia. 1987a. "Las Ideas Sobre la Mujer." *Cuadernos de Sociologia* 4–5(May–December): 59–82.

Montenegro, Sofia. 1987b. "La Emancipacion Femenina Entre la Crisis Economica y la Agresion en Nicaragua." *Cristianismo y Sociedad.* XXV/4(94): 85–94.

NACLA. 1980. "Latin American Women: One Myth—Many Realities." XIV(5) September–October.

Nash, June and Helen I. Safa, eds. 1976. *Sex and Class in Latin America.* New York: Praeger Publishers.

Nazzari, Muriel. 1983. "The 'Woman Question' in Cuba: An Analysis of Material Constraints on Its Solution." *Signs.* 9(2): 246–63.

New Americas Press. 1989. *A Dream Compels Us: Salvadorean Women in Struggle.* Boulder, Colo.: South End Press.

Oficina de la Mujer (OM). 1987a. *Informe: Inventario de Proyectos Para la Mujer en Nicaragua.* Managua: Ministerio de la Presidencia.

Oficina de la Mujer (OM). 1987b. *Fuerza Laboral Femenina en la Rama Textil-Vestuario: Segregacion, Salarios y Rotacion.* Managua: Ministerio de la Presidencia.

Oficina de la Mujer (OM). 1987c. *Realidad y Perspectiva: Bibliografia Nacional Anotada Sobre la Mujer en Nicaragua.* Managua: Ministerio de la Presidencia.

Purcell, Susan K. 1973. "Modernizing Women for Modern Society: The Cuban Case." In *Female and Male in Latin America,* A. Pescatello ed. Pittsburgh: University of Pittsburgh Press.

Randall, Margaret. 1980b. "La Mujer en la Insurreccion." *Nicarahuac* 1(1, July/August): 34.

Randall, Margaret. 1981a. *Sandino's Daughters: Testimonies of Nicaraguan Women in Struggle.* Vancouver: New Star Books.

Randall, Margaret. 1981b. *Women in Cuba: Twenty Years Later.* New York: Smyrna Press.

Rowbotham, Sheila. 1973. *Women's Consciousness, Man's World.* Baltimore: Penguin Books.

Sargent, Lydia, ed. 1981. *Women and Revolution: A Discussion of the Unhappy Marriage of Marxism and Feminism.* Boston: South End Press.

Schmidt, Steffen W. 1976–77. "Political Participation and Development: The Role of Women in Latin America." *Journal of International Affairs.* 30(2): 243–260.

Smith, Dorothy. 1987. *The Everyday as Problematic: A Feminist Sociology.* Boston: Northeastern University Press.

Spivak Chakravorty, Gayatri. 1988. "Can the Subaltern Speak." In *Marxism and the Interpretation of Culture*. L. Grossberg and C. Nelson eds. Urbana: University of Illinois Press.

Steeves, H. Leslie. 1987. "Feminist Theories and Media Studies." *Critical Studies in Mass Communications*. 4(2): 95–135.

Stephens, Beth. 1988. "Women in Nicaragua." *Monthly Review*. 40(4): 1–18.

Stone, Elizabeth, ed. 1981. *Women and the Cuban Revolution: Speeches and Documents by Fidel Castro and Vilma Espin*. New York: Pathfinder Press.

Thomson, Marilyn. 1986. *Women of El Salvador: The Price of Freedom*. London: Zed Books Ltd.

Urdang, Stephanie. 1979. *Fighting Two Colonialisms: Women in Guinea-Bissau*. New York: Monthly Review Press.

Urdang, Stephanie. 1989. *And They Still Dance: Women, War and the Struggle for Change in Mozambique*. New York: Monthly Review Press.

WIRE. 1985. *Nicaraguan Women: Unlearning the Alphabet of Submission*. San Francisco: Ragged Edge Press.

Wolchick, Sharon. 1989. "Women and the State in Eastern Europe and the Soviet Union" In *Women, the State and Development*. S.E.M. Charlton, J. Everett, and K. Staudt eds. Albany: State University of New York Press.

Wolf, Margery. 1985. *Revolution Postponed: Women in Contemporary China*. Stanford, Calif.: Stanford University Press.

Part 3

Case Studies in Making Meaning

These chapters focus our attention on more specific examples of how meanings are made on the basis of gender, race, and class. Representing examples of feminist research, the authors have used a range of feminist methodology, including textual analysis, historical investigation of primary sources, in-depth interviews, discourse analysis, and ethnography. Topics range from analysis of difference on "Frank's Place" to the invisibility of African American women journalists to Chinese American and Puerto Rican women's talk about identity to pink collar workers' meanings about a labor strike.

10

Big Differences on the Small Screen: Race, Class, Gender, Feminine Beauty, and the Characters at Frank's Place

Jackie Byars and Chad Dell

There are numerous approaches to feminist textual analyses and ours is firmly embedded within the theoretical milieu loosely known as "cultural studies."[1] Cultural studies scholars define culture as the process through which we circulate and struggle over the meanings of our social experience, social relations, and therefore, our *selves;* we acknowledge television as a central site for struggles over meaning in industrialized societies, a site for struggles over difference. In television studies, however, the analysis of television texts has been marginalized in favor of studies of audiences, technologies, and institutions;[2] still, some cultural studies scholars take on the task of textual analysis, explicating the power relationships that determine meaning, as categories such as gender and race—and their intersections—are discursively constructed and manipulated, and this strain of cultural studies scholarship is one increasingly inhabited by feminists.

A dominant trend in recent feminist scholarship is significantly increased attention to the intersection of race and gender; in television studies, this should translate into an increased emphasis on the analysis of television representations of characters from nondominant cultures and how they work to reinforce or challenge dominant ideologies. In an article on the representation of African American men in mid-1980s situation comedies, Herman Gray called for increased "emphasis on how individual images are produced and what they mean culturally . . . particularly a consideration of how ideologies of race and race relations are created and legitimated through television content and production practices" (Gray 1986). However, as Jane Rhodes has argued, few scholars have examined the television representation of "complex social positions, i.e., minority women" (Rhodes 1989). This analysis of the discourses that intersect in the characters at *Frank's Place* aims to help fill that gap.

Reading Positions

But we cannot proceed without some attention to our reading positions and to the consequent limitations on our readings. Beyond acknowledging the inherent polysemy of cultural texts and the possibilities and actualities of multiple readings of any given text, we must pay attention to the controversy within cultural studies over the analysis of groups and of representations of groups of which the analyst is not a part: Should men write about representations of women? Should whites write about the representations of people of color? One of us is a woman, one of us is a man; both of us are white, and both of us are seriously concerned with the various ways difference is translated into "Otherness" and with the political ramifications of that translation. We are disturbed that many men—fearful of the disapproval of and rejection by women—remain silent on questions of gender inequity, and we are disturbed that, at academic gatherings dominated by white folks, the frequent ritual incantations of the Major Categories—"race, class, and gender"—are almost as frequently followed by a resounding silence on questions of race. Male silence on gender inequity and white silence on racial inequity are serious mistakes, almost as serious as the presumption that we—or anyone—can speak *for* someone else. We can speak only *for* ourselves. But as Leslie Roman so eloquently puts it, while we cannot speak for the members of groups of which we are not a part, we can speak *with* them (Roman 1990). But members of dominant groups cannot even speak *with* [double entendre intended] members of nondominant groups unless we understand their experiences, and understanding does not come from book-learning. In her contribution to this collection, Marsha Houston quotes Maria Lugones' advice to white feminists who want to speak intelligently about the experiences of Hispanas: "Follow us into our world" (Lugones and Spelman 1983, 576). Houston emphasizes that white feminists should follow "not just intellectually—through reading and observation—but physically and emotionally." Feminist research "must be grounded in direct, not vicarious, relationships with women who are different from us. . . . we must allow the experiences of women different from us—our mutual experiences of one another—to reshape our theories and redirect our research" (Houston, this volume, p. 55). Our analysis of the characters at *Frank's Place*—the very questions we ask—is grounded in such relationships and motivated by the desire to contribute to the growing body of feminist scholarship which aims to illuminate and challenge the ways television participates in a hierarchical social formation structured by racism and sexism.

Analysis of the series' characters and how they handle the predicaments in which they find themselves presents a valuable way to examine the many things the series says to its viewers about difference and to illustrate the complex ways the series makes these statements, reinforcing certain ideologies and challenging others. The series' regular characters serve as the main point of articulation of both series and socially constructed notions of difference. As the series manipulates categories of "otherness" in its character construction, we can see the inflections of discourses of race, skin color, ethnicity, class, education, age, abilism, regionalism, and nationalism on the representations of gender;[3] the interplay of social, representational, and ideological codes in the representation of feminine "beauty;" the influence of media intertextuality on interpretation; and the relation of genre and gender.

Frank's Place—*The Series*

At the end of the first episode of the unfortunately short-lived CBS series *Frank's Place,* Miss Marie—the Chez Louisiane's respected elderly "waitress emeritus"—tells a confused Frank Parish, "The son *must* become the father. There's no other way." Uprooted from his calm existence as a professor of Italian Renaissance history at an unnamed Boston college, Frank has been summoned to New Orleans, where he has inherited the Chez (emphasis on the "z"), a restaurant-bar at the center of a middle-class African American neighborhood, from the father he never knew, the father he is expected to become. His rightful "place," he is now informed, is at the helm of the Chez. A 1980s Everyman, Frank struggled through twenty-two episodes to discover the nature of his proper "place" at the Chez, in the community, and in patriarchy. With him, a small—since in network terms, fourteen million viewers is considered "small"—but faithful audience came to know the fascinating and sometimes charming group of characters that populated the Chez as, week after week, the series presented slice after slice of their lives. Fans of the series searched their television schedules weekly to track down *Frank's Place,* as CBS repeatedly moved it around the prime time schedule, paradoxically abusing the series it had helped to nurture into existence and finally cancelling it after a single season (1987–1988). (One of the series' executive producers, Hugh Wilson, commented that when your own mother can't find your show, you know you're in trouble.) However, despite its brief network tenure,

Frank's Place contributed significantly to American culture in the late 1980s. The series' generic innovations, its primarily African American ensemble cast, its masterful and unique televisual style, and its (generally implicit) acknowledgement of intra-racial hierarchies combined to make it one of the most interesting, innovative, and important series seen on prime time network television in the late 1980s. Now, in the early 1990s, the series has returned on cable television—in syndication on BET, the Black Entertainment Network.

One of the series' most delightful contributions to American television programming results from its irreverence toward generic expectations. One of the relatively few series to experiment with the not-quite-a-sitcom half-hour format some critics in the popular press have called the "dramedy"—because it tends to include more dramatic elements than the classic situation comedy—*Frank's Place* resisted definition as a standard sitcom, constructing new conventions of sitcom "realism." (Hugh Wilson said that when the producers and writers were in a quandary as to what direction to take with a particular episode, they would ask themselves what a sitcom would do; then they would choose a significantly different tack.) Most episodes blend comedic and dramatic elements, though some rely heavily on slapstick comedy and others are almost entirely dramatic. Many episodes also deny the comfortable closure of the standard sitcom.

Still, *Frank's Place* draws on the history of the workplace sitcom, and in doing so, draws on the sitcom's association with the feminine. Genres are distinguished both by particular ideological problematics and by distinct constellations of characters. Genres such as the sitcom—centered on problematics located within a stable social order and generally involving the processes of social integration—have been called "feminine" and contrasted with "masculine" genres concerned with the restoration/imposition of order on a community temporarily slipped into the realm of chaos/disequilibrium (Schatz 1981). Still, *Frank's Place* seemed to have been formed from a distinctly masculine perspective, and information concerning the conditions of its production confirms this speculation. (Hugh Wilson commented on the desire to include a—just one—woman on the writing staff and of problems that arose with the one woman who was initially included. After she was fired, no effort was made to replace her with another woman. The production team was overwhelmingly male.) But its regular characters can easily be described as a "workplace family," and the series focused on the integration of its protagonist, Frank Parish (played by Tim Reid), into the social order of the Chez and the community of which it was a part.

In contrast to the individualistic, capable male protagonists in "masculine" genres (such as traditional detective series or action adventure series, where the hero restores social order), Frank Parish is a vulnerable, fallible character—often the source of rather than the solution to problems, and his developing romance with the attractive mortician Hannah Griffin (played by Daphne Maxwell Reid), which dominated two episodes and frequently appeared as an important subplot in several others, places the series even more firmly among the "feminine" genres concerned with the creation and maintenance of family units. Still, while the series' point of view is generally Frank's, and viewers' perceptions of the other characters are most frequently—though not always—influenced by his perspective, the series' sitcom heritage also permits it to modify the traditional individualism of the male protagonist by drawing on yet another element of the workplace sitcom, the ensemble cast, which disperses representations of masculinity and femininity across numerous characters, allowing the presentation of numerous constructions of African American femininity and masculinity.

Frank's Place: The Characters

In fact, *Frank's Place*'s most important contribution to American television programming in particular and to American culture in general is in its construction of new ways of representing African Americans. African Americans figure as major characters in only a very few television series, most prominently in situation comedies such as *The Cosby Show* and *227*. Herman Gray has pointed out that these sitcoms depict successful middle-class African Americans who are distanced from the realities of a racist society; their "racial and cultural experiences are, for the most part, insignificant." These sitcoms aim to appeal to "the utopian desires in blacks and whites for racial oneness and equality while displacing the persistent reality of racism and racial equality or the kinds of social struggles and cooperation required to eliminate them." *Frank's Place* is an exception; in it "racial identity matters" (Gray 1989, 383). Henry Louis Gates, Jr., concurred, claiming that *Frank's Place* has come closer than any other television series to representing the "truly different world" of African Americans in the United States, presenting "the fullest range of black character types" yet seen in American television programming (Gates 1989). Nine of the eleven regular characters are African American, unusual in and of itself on prime time network television, and even the two white characters (both male) are "othered" in distinct ways; the lawyer Cy "Bubba" Weisberger is Jewish, and the assistant chef Shorty is Cajun (sometimes his dialogue even requires subtitles). The series delineates a complex interplay among discourses of race, class, and gender, implicitly

195

and explicitly calling attention to the manipulation of difference through the construction of its characters as sites for ideological struggle and as points of access for its viewers, making available a multiplicity of potential meanings to a highly diverse audience. Like all series designed to appeal to a broad and varied audience, *Frank's Place* was polysemic, combining ideologically progressive messages with messages far more conservative; such messages are embodied in the series' characters.

Among the series' regular characters, much more diversity is exhibited in its seven male characters than in its four female characters, and they generally occupy more powerful positions than do the female characters; the male characters also functioned much more overtly as sites for ideological struggle over difference. The series' constructions of masculinity and race are especially important in light of the history of African American male imagery in the United States, where racial and sexual hierarchies have functioned to reinforce each other. Most stereotypes of African Americans have their roots in the era of slavery (Davis 1971), when as Hazel Carby explains, "Black manhood could not be achieved or maintained because of the inability of the slave to protect the black woman in the same manner that convention dictated the inviolability of the body of the white woman" (Carby 1989, 35). The historical images of the shuffling Uncle Tom, the animalistic savage (seen as a sexual threat to white women), and the child-like happy Sambo, all functioned to exclude African American men from the category of "true men" while simultaneously soothing the consciences of white slaveowners (Takaki 1979).

Much recent African American male imagery—particularly in the mass media—has been characterized by an assimilationist tendency (nonthreatening to whites); the image of "new black male" promulgated in mid-1980s television situation comedies *(Webster, Different Strokes, Benson)* made race invisible, inviting and confirming the view of the United States as an open multiracial social order while erasing racial identity and ignoring the reality that the United States remains an institutionally racist society (Gray 1986, Larkin 1988). But in the series *Frank's Place,* struggle over race and gender are evident, and its most developed character, Frank Parish, is, of course, a prime locale for struggle over both race and gender. With this character, the series simultaneously confronts African American male stereotypes and participates in the construction of the "new man."

African American stereotypes are juxtaposed and played against one another in this character. The Uncle Tom is nowhere to be seen, but Frank's superstitious nature and lack of effectiveness as a competitor tend to reinforce the stereotype of the ignorant, ineffectual Sambo, while his education and initiative challenge this very stereotype. And the stereotype of the African American as a "creature under the domination of his pas-

sions, especially his sexuality" (Takaki, 1979, 114) is invoked when Frank—
a tall, good-looking, single restaurateur—attracts the notice of many female characters. But although Frank is positioned as a sexually passionate
man (particularly in two episodes in which he is cheered on to prove his
sexual prowess by the male segment of the regular cast), his passions are
directed only toward African American female characters; the "threat" of
interracial sexual relations never arises (and the "threat" of homosexuality
only arises through jokes). In addition, the character functions—like many
white male characters—to challenge essentialist, macho notions of "masculinity" by displaying such "feminine" qualities as non-aggressive behavior and sensitivity, which have only recently become acceptable in males
(fictional and non-fictional). In short, the character functions as a site for
the interplay of characteristics traditionally defined as "masculine" and
"feminine," the character offers a new way to envision a new masculinity." Seen as a site for the hegemonic struggle between residual, dominant, and emergent ideologies of race and gender, this character displays
struggles over the meanings of "masculinity"; while Frank may *replace* his
father, he can never *become* him.[4]

In the premier episode (September 14, 1987), Miss Marie has a "spin"
put on Frank by a voodoo practitioner in order to keep him from selling
the restaurant and leaving New Orleans, but Frank returns to Boston,
where voodoo apparently works quite well. In the second episode, a series
of otherwise inexplicable catastrophes destroys every aspect of his life in
Boston (September 21, 1987); the plumbing in Frank's apartment inex-
plicably goes berserk, the laundry loses his clothes, the building housing
his office burns down, any phone he attempts to use mysteriously ceases
functioning, and his girlfriend leaves him for a (female) golf pro. Finally
Frank returns and commits himself to the Chez and New Orleans, even
selling his prized collection of antique Italian statuary to pay his father's
gambling debts (November 30, 1987). He settles into learning how to run
a restaurant and slowly begins to function in the Chez and its community,
eventually taking on—with distinct modifications—his father's reputation
as a patriarchal pillar of the community, but his efforts to adjust are not
without failures. In an early episode (September 28, 1987), Frank buys a
sprinkler system for the kitchen and then purchases lobsters (for an extremely good price), unaware of the fact that lobsters require an expensive
salt-water tank. The sprinklers go off in the middle of preparations for a
catering job that Frank has reluctantly accepted. The formidable Bertha
Griffin-Lamour (a character reminiscent of the stereotypical powerful African American matriarch, except that she's confined to a wheelchair),
owner of *the* local funeral home, bullies him into catering a party celebrating the engagement of her daughter Hannah, with whom Frank is

falling in love, to Dr. Lamar Boysenberry (the first black All-American quarterback, at LSU, currently on the faculty of Tulane's medical school). Frank cuts his still significant losses by including lobster on the menu and is rewarded by the discovery that Dr. Boysenberry has a high, feminine voice that embarrasses Hannah; in the episode's final scene, Frank's pleasure at this discovery implies that some combinations of masculinity and femininity are, in fact, not appropriate.

The Chez's head cook, Big Arthur, and his assistant, Shorty, share a more traditional and immediately visual indicator of "masculinity"; both characters are very powerfully built. This physical construction of the masculine body is, in Big Arthur, enhanced by his height (emphasized through low-angle shots). Big Arthur is the Chez's "enforcer," and his physical prowess enables him to defend his honor when his reputation is threatened by a rival chef—from an upscale restaurant—who steals his recipes and publishes them as his own (December 7, 1987). In a boxing match (stylized, in the manner of *Rocky, Raging Bull,* and numerous other fight films), Big Arthur bests and receives a public apology from his (white) rival. Big Arthur's cooking is (within the realm of the series) legendary, but still, secure in his accomplishments, he refuses to call himself a "chef," emphasizing his allegiance to the working class by insisting that he is a "cook." His assistant Shorty, on the other hand, aims to transcend his working class position, defining himself as "assistant chef." Both Shorty and Big Arthur are powerfully defined as "other" in relation to Frank by both class and appearance. Darker and physically more powerful than Frank, Big Arthur presents a visual "other," while the European American Shorty presents both a visual and—with his thick Cajun accent—an aural "other." Struggle over "masculinity" does not occur *within* the characters of Shorty and Big Arthur, because of their physical characteristics and their overriding "masculine" devotion to their vocation, but they represent a traditionally masculine pole among the characters in the series, allowing us to see the struggle over masculinity *among* the characters.

The character Cy "Bubba" Weisberger inhabits the other pole, functioning as a parallel to and sounding board for Frank; like Frank, Bubba is a site for the interplay between characteristics traditionally defined as "masculine" and "feminine" and the ongoing ideological struggle over what it is to be gendered as "appropriately male." They are strikingly similar characters, sharing age (thirtysomething), class (middle), and education. They are or have been professionals (Bubba is a lawyer, and Frank, now a restaurateur, had been a college professor); both are members of an ethnic minority; and as Frank now does, Bubba works independently, not wishing to be affiliated with a large law firm. Long ago resigned to his "place" (though that place leads the audience and the other characters to underestimate him) Bubba is a quiet man—slim, blond, and balding. Structurally external to the restaurant's economic structure, he is nevertheless part of its social structure. He serves as the restaurant's attorney and proclaims himself—along with the entrepreneurial, philandering Reverend Tyrone Deal—a "fixture" at the Chez. Bubba often joins the Reverend Deal and Cool Charles (a young man "adopted" by Frank's late father, who does odd jobs around the Chez) to function as a chorus that comments (orally and/or visually) on Frank's fortunes and misfortunes.

Discourses of ethnicity and regionalism intersect humorously when Frank first realizes and is puzzled by the fact that Weisberger's nickname is "Bubba." William Safire reports that the term *bubba*—a pet name for "brother"—is common among African Americans as well as European Americans in the South. However, the use of the term "bubba" most familiar to those outside the region is synonymous to "redneck" or "good ol' boy" and "refers to [white] Southern conservatives" (Safire 1990, 24). Austin, Texas, radio personality Cactus Pryor described this stereotypical "Bubba" in an interview published in a *National Geographic* article: "Bubba is a good ol' boy . . . [he] likes the NRA and Bubba dips snuff and Bubba likes Ollie North and Bubba likes to fish and hunt and eat barbecue and talk about women . . . Bubbas are hard not to like because they're friendly. They hate Yankees. Bubba wears cowboy clothes" (Moize 1990, 63). Southerners perpetuate the myth, the stereotype, and outsiders often believe it.[5]

Frank, raised in the northeast and naive about the way of the Deep South, obviously thinks that "Bubba" can only refer to uneducated, gentile good-old-boy hicks, not to well-educated and articulate Jewish lawyers. In the South, a child nicknamed "Bubba" will often be called by the name his entire life, whether he fits the stereotype or not. And Bubba Weisberger is not the stereotypical "Bubba." Neither is he a stereotypical lawyer, and his economic status is not commensurate with that of the stereotypical lawyer. Indeed, at one point, he bemoans the fact that he is having trouble getting his clients to pay him. If they would pay, he would be wealthy; he would have "*hundreds* of dollars." But wealth is not Bubba's aim; he is content with his lot and surprises others when he quite capably defends his threatened community in an episode entitled "The Bridge" and provides evidence of the existence of an emergent ideology of masculinity. (This episode, originally broadcast October 5, 1987, written and directed by Hugh Wilson, won an Emmy Award for writing.)

Bubba defends the Chez against a lawsuit brought by the most feared attorney in New Orleans, a character who also challenges stereotyping; she is a large, intimidating white woman who tells Bubba and Frank that she is close to the plaintiff's family and intends to take every cent she can get for them. Bubba investigates the case against the Chez. An elderly man, apparently served too many drinks at the Chez, has been killed as he drove off a bridge, but Bubba discovers that he was dying of cancer. When Bubba suggests to the man's African American doctor that the man may have committed suicide, the episode demonstrates that racial stereotyping is not solely the province of whites; the doctor simply responds, "That's a white man's crime."

Bubba then goes into "the projects" to talk with the widow. Braving first the young African American men who glare at him and then her angry son, Bubba gains access to the widow; quietly and persistently, but compassionately, he talks with her about the Chez, where Miss Marie has served her and her husband graciously even though they could afford only a meager tip, where Frank's father held meetings about civil rights when nobody else would dare. He informs her that the Chez does not have insurance to cover her claim and will surely close if she pursues it, and finally she admits that her husband's death was a suicide and agrees to drop her claims against the Chez. Reinforcing stereotypes of "the projects," Frank and Big Arthur—with his baseball bat—"rescue" Bubba, demanding that he never return unescorted. His perception and persistence gains the respect of the opposing attorney, who assures him that the widow will not suffer financially and then offers Bubba a job. He declines; the status and material rewards associated with law firms—and with (generally masculine) success in the business world—hold little appeal for Bubba, who has demonstrated that masculinity can encompass bravery and sensitivity, persistence and compassion, success through consideration, and quiet resourcefulness.

Frank, at least initially, seems attracted to financial success and its trappings. In the first episode he is impressed by the Chez's active lunch business, when in fact it is only marginally profitable. In another episode, Frank reads books on restaurant management and hires a consultant to help him increase business profits (February 3, 1988). His efforts end in disaster, because neither he nor his expert understand the dynamics of the neighborhood and its place in the city. To increase "night business," he opens a new take-out window, next to the bar, but it is frequented by local women who are surprised and dismayed to discover their unsuspecting husbands carousing at the Chez. Because he is told that white folks won't come to the neighborhood at night, he advertises for tourists and institutes a valet parking service; slip-ups result in a stolen car. And he hires musicians, expecting—and advertising—a jazz band, which a sleazy agent replaces at the last minute with a band of white hillbillies. An excruciating final scene finds Frank retreating to his apartment (upstairs from the Chez) as the hillbilly band serenades an audience comprising a family of flamboyantly tacky (and obliviously racist) white tourists and the expectant—then appalled—sophisticated African American locals with a racist rendition of "Pick a Bale 'o' Cotton." The episode dramatically illustrates that, at *Frank's Place*, race matters.

So does skin color, although even in this remarkable series, inequities based on differences in race and skin-color most often remain implicit, with lighter-skinned African Americans shown to be implicitly privileged, reinforcing practices common in social "reality." The series explicitly calls attention to the importance of skin color only rarely, most dramatically in an episode in which Frank is invited to visit—with the possibility of joining—two different men's clubs in New Orleans, clubs distinguished not only by class and money but by skin color (October 12, 1987). This episode also implicitly comments on age and African American history as it develops the character of Tiger, the Chez's bartender. Tiger, the oldest male character, is respected for his age and experience. An historian, a font of information, Tiger provides historical and informational insight, the aspect of his character highlighted in this episode.

The importance of difference in skin-color, implicit within the confines of the Chez, becomes explicit when Frank ventures into the larger community of New Orleans, and Tiger's role as historian is clarified. After Frank meets and is invited to a local men's club by a fellow Brown University alumnus, Tiger—assured that Frank is interested in "lodge work"—invites Frank to a meeting of his club, The Drivers. Men's clubs, Tiger informs Frank (and, as a result, the viewers), are quite popular in New Orleans (reinforcing the notion that Southerners—even African Americans—are traditionally patriarchal). Frank accompanies Tiger to a meeting of The Drivers, an organization composed of working-class, generally darker-skinned African American men. Tiger tells Frank of the club's history; formed by cable car drivers, the club serves as the locale for male socializing and as the conduit for their participation in the larger community's celebration of Mardi Gras. During the meeting, it becomes obvious that Frank's father, Ennis, had been well-known to the club's members, who make Frank welcome, constantly refilling his glass. Frank and The Drivers have a rollicking good time, after which Frank wakes with a hangover; Tiger, as folk-healer, provides a remedy. Then Frank accompanies his new acquaintance—his fellow "Brown man" (occasional class- and region-specific references to their status as "Brown men" puzzle the working-class members of The Drivers)—to his club, The Capital C Club, an organization of upper-middle-class, light-skinned black men; there Frank encounters sophistication, monied privilege, and snobbery toward the portion of the community represented by The Drivers.

Before the visits, Tiger prevented Anna Mae from telling Frank about the real nature of The Capital C Club. But after the visits, she informs him that he is "colored," an adjective Frank hasn't heard in years; he is too dark-skinned to pass the "paper bag test" (if your skin is darker than a brown paper bag, you're too dark for the club). Tiger tells Frank that in New Orleans, color used to be a major determinant of difference. Anna Mae asserts, "Still is." Frank, lighter-skinned than Anna Mae or Big Arthur, is still too dark to pass the "paper bag test." Finally, he realizes how he has been manipulated; he has been used as a guinea pig by the more progressive young members who want to challenge the inequities inherent in this Capital C Club policy. Frank has all the other appropriate credentials for membership (education, social status, economic status), but his skin color, relatively light among the African Americans at the Chez, was dark enough to position him as "colored" or creole with a little "c"—not a Capital "C"—in the larger New Orleans community. Disturbed, Frank confronts his fellow "Brown man," saying that all his life he's been the only black in a series of schools and organizations and that he has no intention of "being the only black in a black man's club."

In the last scene, he accepts the offer of membership from Tiger's club, The Drivers, settling into his "place" (his father's place?) in the neighborhood and flipping a look of resignation toward the camera—and, of course, the audience—in the episode's final freeze frame.

As an (educated, middle-class) outsider learning about the community, Frank functions to recuperate the black Other for a largely white audience, but sometimes—as in this episode—he also functions in the series to call into question retrogressive recuperation; this is not true of the female characters. In them, the series' most conservative practices became evident. While the series occasionally called attention to inequity based on skin-color and class, this was particularly rare in the series' treatment of female characters, where these inequities remained implicit; feminine attractiveness was consistently related to light skin color, straight hair, thinness, relative youthfulness, and middle-class status.

A number of discourses intersect in each of the four female characters (all African American). They are all economically independent working women, but they represent specific class differences. Hannah and Bertha are solidly middle-class; their appearance and education are indicators of their affluence. Miss Marie and Anna Mae, on the other hand, are working-class. Unlike Hannah and Bertha, Miss Marie and Anna Mae are rarely costumed out of uniform, or perhaps equally to the point, Hannah's and Bertha's expensive and stylish appearance *is* the occupational uniform of the middle class. Class distinction and its almost inevitable corollary—education—can also be inferred from the characters' language usage and

202

accents. Anna Mae finished only high school, and her language usage reflects her education. Bertha speaks in a slow, deliberate, cultivated manner, and Hannah's voice is practically devoid of accent. Anna Mae and Miss Marie, in contrast, bring to their voices an accent more specific to the South, an accent specificity often associated in televisual narratives with a working-class background.

All four of the female characters possess some degree of power. Miss Marie and Bertha are considered matriarchs in the community and exercise considerable amounts of influence, although both women are represented as physically handicapped. Miss Marie often requires a cane when walking, and her power comes from the respect she is accorded for her age, wisdom, and connections to practitioners of voodoo. A pillar of the community and one of its foremost businesspeople, Bertha is confined to a wheelchair, the strength of her iron will often displayed through terrorizing her chauffeur. Hannah is well respected in the community, deriving some of her power from her association with her mother. Anna Mae is the least powerful (and darkest skinned) of the four but has some (limited) power because of her position as the Chez's head waitress. None of the characters could be considered "powerless," though in a medium in which women are frequently represented as deriving much of their power from their association with men, it is significant that none of these four characters are specifically attached to men, and only Hannah is seen to have any potential for such an attachment. Television, a medium dominated by white men, has tended to confine black female roles to white models of "good wives" and to black matriarchal stereotypes (Rhodes 1989); *Frank's Place* fails to provide an exception. Both Miss Marie and Mrs. Griffin-Lamour perpetuate the stereotype of the black matriarch (with much of Mrs. Griffin-Lamour's authority the result of an inheritance from her late—and second—husband, the mortuarian Mr. Lamour), and Anna Mae's very limited power is confined even more by the series' refusal to consider her a serious candidate for romance. By representing Hannah as the most likely candidate for marital attachment, the series positions her—like good, white, television wives—primarily in relation to potential spouses: the result of her ability to evoke erotic desire.

Age eliminates Miss Marie and Mrs. Griffin-Lamour as objects of erotic desire for the other characters, and this is made explicit when Frank is shocked by mistaking the interest of two visiting African musicians in Anna Mae for an interest in Miss Marie. While some series in the 1980s ventured to depict romance among older adults, *Frank's Place* left the area untouched; this leaves Anna Mae and Hannah. A comparison is instructive. While the differences in Hannah's and Anna Mae's occupations, educations, and family situations magnify the distinctions between them, powerfully indicating class difference, *appearance* is the most immediate indicator of the separation between the two characters, and skin color was one of the most evident differences; difference is distinctly marked in the representation of these female bodies. Hannah represents conventional notions of African American "beauty" and "femininity" as initially constructed by European Americans (Carby 1989) and then incorporated into African American culture. Hannah is light-skinned and has long straightened hair, gleaming white teeth, manicured nails, and a thin but curvacious figure; she is always impeccably groomed and fashionably dressed. Anna Mae represents Hannah's "plainer" counterpart. Both the same age and both single, they are visually distinguished by appearance. Anna Mae is darker-skinned than Hannah, with more natural hair and more classically African American features. The working-class Anna Mae generally avoids noticeable make-up and is most often costumed in peasant-style work clothes. The physical appearance of the character Hannah is often enhanced by soft lighting, "sexy" costuming, flattering camera work, and Daphne Maxwell Reid's performance.

Regular viewers of the series may have found the textual evidence of their developing romance enhanced by extra-textual evidence gleaned from newspaper and television talk-show interviews promoting the series, which revealed that the actors that play Frank (Tim Reid) and Hannah (Daphne Maxwell Reid) are, in "real life," married. The series' representational practices reinforce their developing romance; as Hannah becomes the focus of Frank's romantic life, the actress often performs in a manner that accentuates her sexual attractiveness and her availability to Frank. In the second episode (September 21, 1987), after Frank returns to New Orleans from Boston, he dreams that the Chez is a hot night spot populated by glamorous people. In the dream sequence, the emphasis on Hannah as the "beautiful" erotic object becomes explicit. The camera privileges Frank's point of view as he enters the bar and looks across the room. He spots Hannah, dressed in a revealing outfit, and she signals Frank with her eyes. In slow motion, they make their way toward each other across the crowded bar, gently pushing aside all those in their path, until they meet and touch as the music reaches the peak of a crescendo and Frank awakens to a decidedly grittier reality. Frank's "fantasy Hannah" exaggerates the representational conventions generally used to indicate the character's beauty and attractiveness.

In comparison, the representational codes of the series position Anna Mae in opposition, as not very attractive. Behind the scenes, the producers and the actress who played Anna Mae struggled over the meaning of the character, and occasionally this struggle seems evident in the series. While the producers had hired a relatively large woman (larger than Daphne

Maxwell Reid) to play Anna Mae, the actress lost weight and began working out in order to cultivate a more conventionally attractive body (read: thin and firm). However, the representational practices of the series consistently operated to undermine this impression. The exceptions emphasized the rule: in two episodes Anna Mae wears more make-up than usual, first to impress Frank (October 19, 1987) and then to impress a group of filmmakers shooting a scene at the Chez (February 22, 1988). In both episodes, she is ridiculed for her efforts. In yet another episode, a troupe of African musicians and dancers visiting the United States give a private dress rehearsal performance for the workers of the Chez and their friends, and Anna Mae dressed up to attend the rehearsal (March 7, 1988). Only in this episode is she presented as a credible object of erotic desire, and in this case it was Africans—not African Americans—who saw her as attractive, inflecting a gendered notion of skin-color and attractiveness with a discourse of nationalism.

The differences that define the characters Hannah and Anna Mae are rarely articulated and are most explicitly drawn out in an early episode, when Hannah decides to break her engagement to Dr. Lamar Boysenberry; Anna Mae is distraught (October 26, 1987). When Hannah comes to the Chez to talk with Anna Mae, we learn that they were close childhood friends until Hannah—and the other bridesmaids—went to college, leaving Anna Mae behind, a single mother. Anna Mae expresses how much she appreciates having been asked to be a part of her wedding party, Hannah's way of remembering a common childhood and her overt overlooking of the differences that have placed them in very distinct positions. This wedding was Anna Mae's big opportunity to be, however temporarily, an equal again. Hannah is puzzled when Anna Mae tells her how surprised she was to be asked to be a bridesmaid. As Anna Mae says, "Well, you know . . ." The clarity of class boundaries are often seen more distinctly from the bottom up. "All those other bridesmaids of yours," Anna Mae says, "Lucinda Partridge and Mary Sue Delahoosie. Pretty high cotton for me to be in. You know, with me, I'm just proud not to be on welfare. That's my big claim to fame." Clearly, class differences dominate this episode. But the episode is about more than class; it is equally important to note how the *social codes* of "reality" (appearance, dress, makeup, etc.) are encoded through *representational codes* (the technical codes of casting, costuming, camera work, and lighting and the conventional representational codes of character, dialogue, and narrative) and, finally, organized into coherence and social acceptability by *ideological codes* of race, class, and gender. In this case, skin color and hair style become significant.

The temporal proximity of the first broadcasts of *Frank's Place* to the distribution of Spike Lee's film *School Daze* makes clear the importance of intertextuality in the process of producing readings. Portions of the film's content and portions of the series *Frank's Place* deal with an identical issue, though the film confronts the intersection of femininity, beauty, skin color, and hairstyle far more explicitly (and progressively) than does the television series. Lee's film, set in a historically African American college, pits groups of female characters against each other. The light-skinned, straight-haired "Wannabes" (want-to-be-white) and the darker-skinned, kinky-haired "Jigaboos" confront each other in a stylized production number that culminates in their facing the camera together and singing about "good" (straight) and "bad" (kinky) hair. As the relation of skin-color to constructions of feminine "beauty," long an issue in African American communities, has entered the larger realm of popular culture (dominated by European Americans), it has become impossible for us to read *Frank's Place* without attending to the intersections of these particular discourses.

Considering the attention the series pays to skin color in the episode in which Frank visits the two men's clubs, it is ironic that—in its casting practices—the series implicitly engages in the very activity it explicitly condemns. In one episode (October 19, 1987), this becomes impossible to ignore, as the implicit relationship of light skin color with feminine beauty comes very close to the surface. Frank hires and then lusts after a woman the male characters unilaterally consider "beautiful." Ruby is very light-skinned and she wears costumes that accentuate her figure. The male characters practically drool over Ruby and joke about Frank's "chances" with her. The secondary plot contrasts Ruby with Miriam Margaret—the dark-skinned, bespectacled daughter of a prominent preacher—in pursuit of Frank. In sequential scenes, Frank rebuffs Miriam Margaret's advances and then turns to make advances toward Ruby, who rebuffs him. While it is distinctly possible to read the episode as parodic, the contrast in the physical appearance of the two female characters and the proximity of the two scenes calls attention to the contrasting physical appearances of the two female characters. Miriam Margaret's lack of conventional "beauty" is expressed in *social codes* such as lack of makeup, is enhanced by the *representational codes* of full lighting and unflattering camera work and costuming—glasses, frumpy polyester clothes—and is organized to associate the negroid both with the "ugly" and with animalist aggression, reinforcing the "naturalness" of racist *ideological codes*. Ruby's beauty is emphasized as the *social codes* indicating the socially constructed notion of feminine beauty—straight hair, light skin, and skillfully applied makeup—are enhanced by *technical codes* (flattering costuming, soft lighting, and soft focus), which softened Ruby's appearance and were organized into a coherent whole through the association of race and gender that associates "whiteness" with feminine beauty—an *ideological code* that continues to reinforce dominant, and racist, ideas and practices.

Frank's Place makes many progressive statements, particularly in its representation of a wide range of African American characters, but its limits are as important as its contributions to American culture. Although the series does present a fairly wide range of representations of African American men, it offers a much narrower range of representations of African American women. Although the producers of the series were clearly concerned with the social ramifications of the representation of racial difference, offering viewers with similar concerns a space in television discourse, they remained relatively oblivious to the ways in which gender and class inflect race, effectively ignoring the portion of the viewing public concerned with this particular intersection. Even as this exceptional series makes explicit and at times problematizes currently placed markers that divide, categorize, privilege, and "other" members of our society—such as current constructions of gender, race, skin color, ethnicity, class, education, age, abilism, regionalism, and nationalism—and while its brave attempt to do so may have ultimately insured the series' demise on prime-time network television, the series, regrettably, rarely moved beyond this level of discussion towards attempts at intervening in these constructions. And, for feminist critics, intervention in the struggle over gendered meanings *is* the point.

Notes

1. The original and much longer version of this essay was written for a day-long seminar on television and interpretation organized by Jimmie Reeves and Richard Campbell for the 1988 meeting of the Speech Communication Association in New Orleans (attended by co-author J. Byars); each of the papers written for the seminar concerned *Frank's Place* and exemplified a different approach to television criticism. One of the two executive producers of the series, Hugh Wilson, attended and was the focus of much of the seminar (Tim Reid, who played Frank Parish, was the other executive director). Information about the conditions of production included in this essay was obtained during that session.

The series premiered on CBS on September 14, 1987, and ran through March 22, 1988 (22 episodes). Created by Hugh Wilson, it starred Tim Reid, Robert Harper, Daphne Maxwell Reid, Francesca P. Roberts, Frances E. Williams, Virginia Capers, Tony Burton, Charles Lampkin, Lincoln Kilpatrick, William Thomas, Jr., and Don Yesso.

2. Raymond Williams made this point in a published interview (Heath and Skirrow, 1986).

3. The ways in which the discourses of sexuality and religion inflect the representation of gender in *Frank's Place* are also fascinating; because of space limitations, discussions of these complex areas have been eliminated.

4. Drawing on the work of Nancy Chodorow (1980) and Carol Gilligan (1982), coauthor J. Byars (1988) has argued that the series *Spenser for Hire* also provides evidence of such changes in the meanings of "masculinity"; it is not a traditional detective series in that its protagonist manifests both masculine and feminine characteristics and operates similarly to the character Frank Parish in the process of reconstructing masculinity. And Janice Radway (1984) draws on Chodorow's work in her analyses of male characters in romance novels and their appeal to female readers, observing that these characters also embody a peculiar mix of masculine and feminine characteristics, offering the nurturing we all desire. But not all feminist theorists consider the expansion of masculinity to include nurturing a positive step for women; rather, they see it as an expansion of male power. See, for instance, Janice G. Raymond's (1986) critique of Chodorow.

5. The most interesting recent work on stereotyping is T.E. Perkins' "Rethinking Stereotyping" (1979).

References

Byars, Jackie. 1988. "Gazes/Voices/Power: Expanding Psychoanalysis for Film and Television Theory." In *Female Spectators: Looking at Film and Television.* ed. E. Deidre Pribram. London: Verso Press.

Carby, Hazel. 1989. *Reconstructing Womanhood: The Emergence of the Afro-American Woman Novelist.* New York: Oxford University Press.

Chodorow, Nancy. 1980. *The Reproduction of Mothering.* Berkeley: The University of California Press.

Davis, Angela. 1971. "Reflections on the Black Woman's Role in the Community of Slaves." *Black Scholar.* 3 (December), 3–15.

Gates, Henry Louis, Jr. 1989. "TV's Black World Turns—But Stays Unreal." *The New York Times,* Sunday, November 12. 1H and 4H.

Gilligan, Carol. 1982. *In a Different Voice.* Cambridge: Harvard University Press.

Gray, Herman. 1986. "Television and the new black man: black male images in prime-time situation comedy." *Media, Culture, and Society.* Vol. 8, 223–42.

Gray, Herman. 1989. "Television, Black Americans, and the American Dream." *Critical Studies in Mass Communication.* 6(4): 376–386.

Heath, Stephen, and Gillian Skirrow. 1986. "An Interview with Raymond Williams." In Tania Modleski, ed., *Studies in Entertainment: Critical Approaches to Mass Culture.* Bloomington: Indiana University Press.

Lugones, Maria and Elizabeth Spelman. 1983. "Have we got a theory for you! Feminist Theory, Cultural Imperialism and the Demand for 'The Woman's Voice." *Women's Studies International Forum.* 6 (6): 573–581.

Larkin, Alile Sharon. 1988. "Black Women Film-makers Defining Ourselves: Feminism in Our Own Voice." In *Female Spectators: Looking at Film and Television,* ed. E. Deidre Pribram. London: Verso Press.

Moize, Elizabeth A. 1990. "Austin: Deep in the Heart of Texans." *National Geographic.* 177 (6, June 1990); 50–72.

Perkins, T.E. 1979. "Rethinking Stereotypes." In Michele Barrett, et al., *Ideology and Cultural Production.* London: Croom Helm.

Radway, Janice. 1984. *Reading the Romance.* Chapel Hill: University of North Carolina Press.

Raymond, Janice G. 1986. *A Passion for Friends.* Boston: Beacon Press.

Rhodes, Jane. 1989. "Black Women and Realist Television Drama." Paper presented to the Feminist Scholarship Interest Group at the 39th Annual Conference, International Communication Association, San Francisco.

Roman, Leslie. 1990. "Narrating Otherness and Difference: Why We Need a Theory of Socially Contested Realism." Paper presented at the Conference on Cultural Studies in Britain and America, University of Texas at Austin.

Safire, William. "Bubba, Can You Paradigm?" *New York Times Magazine,* October 21, 1990, 23–24.

Schatz, Thomas. 1981. *Hollywood Genres: Formulas, Filmmaking and the Studio System.* New York: Random House.

Takaki, Ronald T. *Iron Cages.* New York: Alfred A. Knopf, 1979.

11

Mary Ann Shadd Cary and the Legacy of African-American Women Journalists

Jane Rhodes

In 1890, journalist Gertrude B. Mossell called for the black press to "secure the assistance of some wise, helpful, intelligent and enthusiastic women." Mossell, a prominent writer, activist and intellectual, wrote proudly of the ability of the black press to educate, instill racial pride, and promote commercial enterprises. But she complained that African American women were kept on the periphery of the world of black journalism: "They are admitted to the Press association [sic] and are in sympathy with the male editors; but few have become independent workers in this noble field of effort, being yet satellites, revolving round the sun of masculine journalism" (Penn 1891, 490).

Mossell's comments underscored the status of African American women journalists in the nineteenth century: They made significant contributions to the press and society, and at the same time were rendered invisible by a largely white, and exclusively male profession.

This obscuring of African American women's experience has meant that today's scholars and journalists know little about their contributions to the profession, and to American culture and politics. As writers and editors, these women communicated to the rest of the nation their distinct interpretations of the meaning of race, gender and class both before and after the Civil War. A logical place to begin studying the work of these African American women is through the story of Mary Ann Shadd Cary, who published her own newspaper in Canada in the 1850s.

Although Shadd Cary was a pioneer in African American journalism, little has been written about her contributions to the field. Ironically, more attention has been paid to Shadd Cary's role as a political figure in studies of African American abolitionism and nationalism during the period. Thus, to examine the histories of African American women journalists we must rely on the literature in a variety of disciplines, including women's history, black history, political science, and literary criticism, as well as on primary sources. When we move outside the narrow confines of journalism history, there is a rich array of material on these women waiting to be explored.

The Problem with Journalism History

Historical scholarship in this field has consistently presented a view of the press and the practice of journalism as being the sole province of white males. The most popular textbooks on the subject present a historical sweep from Benjamin Franklin to Woodward and Bernstein, in which women and persons of color are either absent or marginalized.

This criticism of journalism history is nothing new; more than 15 years ago James Carey labeled the field "an embarrassment" for its narrow focus, isolation from the rest of the historical profession, and its lack of a cultural perspective (Carey 1975). Historical studies of the press have focussed almost entirely on influential white men and powerful news organizations, and at least one feminist scholar has argued that women's experiences have not been integrated into the values and perspectives underlying this inquiry (Covert 1981). When the focus has turned to racial and ethnic minorities, these groups have been compartmentalized in or isolated from the discipline rather than integrated into the field.

Recent writing, especially in journalism textbooks, has tended to replicate these patterns rather than produce a more holistic and inclusive interpretation of the press. For example, one recent text traces the philosophical roots of American journalism with no mention of women and persons of color; another book presents news as an abstract concept that is classless, genderless and without racial and ethnic identity (Atschull 1990; Stevens 1988). A recent study of the nineteenth century press acknowledges the influence of alternative media begun by African Americans, Native Americans, women and abolitionists, yet does not discuss individual journalists or publications from these groups (Dicken-Garcia 1989). Thus, today's students and teachers must rely on a handful of new books that independently explore such subjects as women in journalism and the black press, the result being that material on African American women journalists often falls through the cracks.

Black Women's Studies

This trend—losing African American women in the scholarship—is particularly ironic given the explosion of interest in African American women's history and literature. The last 15 years have seen an evolution of black feminist literary criticism, the growth of Women's Studies and African American Studies as academic disciplines, and the commercial success of numerous contemporary black women authors. In fact, one scholar has suggested that "Afro-American women have written themselves into the national consciousness" (Wall 1989, 1). At the same time, literary figures such as Zora Neale Hurston, Lorraine Hansberry, and Harriet Jacobs have been resurrected, analyzed, and given their rightful place in the academy of letters.

The study of African American women requires attention to race, gender and class as social constructions. Scholars of African American women argue that singularly racial or gender-based analyses neglect the complexity of black women's experiences. One scholar described this experience as a dialectic of black women's "historical role as a laborer in a society where ideals of femininity emphasized domesticity" (Dill 1979, 553). More recently, a historian used the theme of black women's dual burden of racial and sexual oppression as a means for developing a more sophisticated understanding of a distinct black women's culture (Higgenbotham 1989).

This focus on race, class and gender has produced a multidimensional picture of African American women in the nineteenth century. They were active leaders of slave resistance movements, central figures in slave families and plantation households, entrepreneurs, abolitionist leaders, educators, and founders of benevolent organizations. The extent to which African American women were able to participate in these activities depended on whether or not they were freeborn, their class and level of education, and the region in which they lived. Most black women struggled to squeeze out meager lives at the bottom of the nation's economic stratum.

Despite the difficulties that most nineteenth century black women faced, recent scholarship has found among them poets and fiction writers who were widely read during the Victorian era by both black and white audiences. Yet, little attention has been paid to African American women as nonfiction writers and journalists. I suspect this gap represents the problematic way in which journalism and the press is viewed by some historians and literary analysts; as a vocation or occupation that does not make a lasting cultural contribution. Writing and editing for the press is deemed to be a utilitarian process for achieving some end such as mobilizing audiences against slavery or lynching. While newspapers and magazines are examined as historical documents, there's little interest in the story behind those publications or the people who produced them. It is hoped that this analysis will begin to correct this inequity.

Mary Ann Shadd Cary

The Antebellum Years

Histories of the press have usually pointed to Ida Wells-Barnett, who began her career in the late 1880s, as the first African American woman journalist. However, African American women were writing, editing, and publishing for a variety of periodicals decades before the Civil War. African American women likely turned to journalism as early as 1827 when the first black newspaper, *Freedom's Journal*, was founded in New York City. However, research on this paper has not extended beyond anecdotes and biographies of its founders, Samuel Cornish and John Russworm. Thus, it is not known who and how many African American women contributed to this early journalistic effort.

We do know that African American women contributed to many of the white-owned abolitionist newspapers of the period, as well as later black-owned publications. In the 1830s small numbers of free, educated black women in New York and Philadelphia formed literary societies in an effort to find support and a collegial environment for their writing, as well as a forum for their antislavery activities. These women became a pool of talented writers for publications such as the *Liberator*, William Lloyd Garrison's influential abolitionist newspaper, the *Colored American*, the nation's second black newspaper, and Frederick Douglass' *North Star*. For example, abolitionist-writer Sarah Mapps Douglass and other members of the Female Literary Association of Philadelphia, founded in 1831, became regular contributors to the women's columns in the *Liberator* (Sterling 1984, 112). Maria Stewart, the first American woman to give a public lecture in 1832, was also a writer who published her essays in the *Liberator* (Sterling 1984, 154).

By the 1850s, African American women writers were presenting their work in diverse forms. Francis Ellen Watkins Harper became one of the best-known literary figures of the nineteenth century when she began publishing her poetry and short stories in the 1850s and her novel *Iola Leroy* in 1892. During the antebellum period she wrote articles and essays for abolitionist newspapers including the *Liberator* and the *National Anti-Slavery Standard*. She articulated abolitionist and feminist themes and called for an emphasis on education, temperance and moral uplift in the black community (see Washington 1987; Sterling 1984; and Giddings 1984). Harper, Stewart, Douglass and other African American women writers of the period were also closely associated with several magazines that showcased black intellectual and creative expression, including the *Repository of Religion and Literature and of Science and Art,* a journal of the African Methodist Episcopal Church begun in 1858, and the *Anglo-African Magazine* founded in 1859 (Bullock 1981).

213

Research Focus: Mary Ann Shadd Cary

Several historians, including Gerda Lerner, have labeled Mary Ann Shadd Cary as the first black woman newspaper publisher and editor in North America. However, as the above discussion indicates, this is a somewhat dubious assumption since other African American women were journalists in this period. My research indicates that Shadd Cary was a unique historical figure in several ways: As a journalist she played a leadership role in the black communities of Canada West (now Ontario Province) and in the black abolitionist movement; as a feminist she integrated the themes of women's suffrage and social reform into her writing; and she was a leading proponent of a black nationalist ideology that advocated the emigration of African Americans to Canada.

Shadd Cary was born Mary Ann Camberton Shadd in 1823 in Wilmington, Delaware to a family of free blacks. Her father, Abraham Shadd, was an active abolitionist and the family's home was said to be a station on the underground railroad. Shadd was educated in Quaker schools and began a teaching career at the age of 16. She moved to Windsor, Canada in 1851 to open a school that would serve the community of escaped slaves who fled to Canada following passage of the Fugitive Slave Act of 1850. Shadd Cary became an ardent supporter of black emigration to Canada, and in 1852 published a tract on the subject, which placed her in the forefront of this growing black nationalist movement. The following year Shadd Cary joined forces with Samuel Ringgold Ward, a prominent black abolitionist minister and editor, to found the *Provincial Freeman*. Ward's name initially appeared on the masthead as publisher and editor to lend the paper credibility, but shortly thereafter he left Canada, and the *Provincial Freeman* was under Shadd Cary's control and influence. In 1856 the *Provincial Freeman* became the official newspaper of the black emigration movement, and Shadd Cary was closely associated with famed black nationalist Martin R. Delaney. In that same year she married Toronto businessman Thomas Cary, who assisted with fundraising and publishing activities for the newspaper.

In her four-year tenure as editor and publisher of the *Provincial Freeman* Shadd Cary used her hard-hitting, analytical writing style to criticize the failures of the white-controlled abolitionist movement in the states, and to argue for the superiority of the Canadian abolitionist's agenda. She also carried on a lively debate with Frederick Douglass, who opposed black emigration schemes and suggested that Shadd Cary's efforts would go to better use in the United States. In an 1854 editorial titled "The Humbug of Reform" she argued that white antislavery advocates exploited the cause for their own political gain:

It is a difficult matter for an American to take a liberal view on subjects involving the interests of colored Americans, disconnected from the selfishness of individual gain, personal or pecuniary. The position assumed by the majority who oppose Negro Slavery, is, that it works positive evil to the white classes, and, for our own profit, it should be abolished; the inherent wickedness of the system is lost to sight, but "our" interests as white freemen, may not be subserved by its continuance." (*Provincial Freeman* May 27, 1854).

Shadd Cary's newspaper served a dual function as a platform for her political ideology, and as a means of discourse and information for the black community in Canada West. She urged her black neighbors to adhere to the values of the social reform movements of the era including temperance, education, and industry. She also used the *Provincial Freeman* to counter racist commentary issued by the local white community. In the following editorial she lambasted the racial stereotypes of a local paper, the Chatham *Western Planet*.

"The Planet gets worse, and worse! Something more than bare assertion of regard for colored people must take place to make the community believe it. We all heard, a few days ago, of the Editors of anti-slavery tendencies, and yet, whenever it can put a word in edge-wise, which will bear injustly upon colored men it does so ... Who patronize the saloons, taverns &c,, in this place? Indians and colored men only? No! We believe in passing a strictly prohibitory law that will not only prevent Indians and colored men from getting drunk, but will stop white men from drinking as well and not only the "inferior" classes about Chatham, but a drunken Editor occasionally." (*Provincial Freeman* July 26, 1856).

In 1857 Shadd Cary passed control of the newspaper to her brother Isaac Shadd so that she could focus on her political activities and her family. Shadd Cary continued to write for the paper, which lasted until 1859, as well as writing letters and editorials regularly for abolitionist papers including the *Liberator* and the *Weekly Anglo-African*. She also edited Osborne P. Anderson's memoir, *A Voice from Harper's Ferry*, published in 1861 (Ripley 1986). By studying the work of Shadd Cary, and other African American women journalists, we begin to broaden our definitions of black women's political and social roles during this period, and we gain an appreciation for their impact on American life and culture.

Jane Rhodes

After the Civil War

By the outbreak of the Civil War, there had been approximately 40 newspapers and 11 magazines published and edited by African Americans. But the exigencies of war prompted a hiatus from these journalistic activities. Some black abolitionists channeled their energy into recruiting black soldiers and aiding the Union Army effort. Mary Ann Shadd Cary was the only woman commissioned as an official recruiting agent, finding black men to fill regiments in Connecticut, Indiana, and Massachusetts.

At the end of the war only about two dozen black newspapers and magazines were still being published, but the improved opportunities for African Americans brought growth to black journalism. Literally days after the war ended, black publications began cropping up in the South and the West. As the nation entered Reconstruction, the black press began a renaissance, with an estimated 1,200 new publications established between 1865 and the turn of the century. African American women played an active role in these developments. They started their own publications, wrote and edited women's columns, and contributed to white newspapers. I. Garland Penn, the author of a 1891 survey of the black press, devoted a chapter to "Our Women in Journalism" in *The Afro-American Press and Its Editors.*

The North's urban centers of the 1880s and 1890s were the setting for an active network of dozens of black newspapers and magazines that relied on the talents of women journalists. Gertrude Mossell, whose comments are cited in the beginning of this article, began her career in Philadelphia when her first article appeared in the *Christian Recorder* while she was a high school student. She edited the women's columns for *The Philadelphia Echo* and *The New York Freeman,* and contributed to white newspapers including *The Philadelphia Press* and *The Times.* She became a correspondent for the highly respected journal *The Indianapolis Freeman,* founded in 1888 as the "colored Harper's Weekly," which paid tribute to her in its pages: "Mrs. Mossell is one of the most gifted as well as versatile women writers in the country, and rightly does the race honor and appreciate her genius" (Penn 1891, 407). In the late 1800s, racial segregation was the rule in journalism, just as it was in most of American society. Thus, it is important to note the extent to which at least a handful of African American women were able to break the color barrier.

Bostonian Lilliam A. Lewis revived the ailing black newspaper *The Boston Advocate* with her creation of a "They Say" column of gossip, commentary, and criticism, which she wrote under the pen name Bert Islew. She also became the private secretary of a well-known white woman columnist for *The Boston Herald,* an association that provided Lewis the chance to write for the newspaper's society pages. In Chicago, Georgia Mabel DeBaptiste was a regular correspondent for newspapers, including *The Baptist Herald, the African Mission Herald,* and the magazine *Our Women and Children.* Meta E. Pelham left teaching to become a full-time reporter for the *Detroit Plaindealer,* a black newspaper founded in 1883, which attributed its success and longevity in part to her influence: "To Miss Meta Pelham is due the credit of this aid, who has always taken an active interest in the paper, and often contributed to its columns. For the past two years she has become one of its essentials in the office, and she devotes her whole time to the work" (Penn 1891, 420).

African American women were making similar inroads in the Southern states. One study suggests that the rapid growth of Southern black newspapers in the 1880s and 1890s set the stage for black women to participate as journalists (Wade Gayles 1981). An analysis of the lives of 14 such women found they were among the first generation of educated blacks in the south, were involved in the establishment of women's clubs and organizations, and were frequently associated with publications of the black church. Their enterprise as writers and editors, however, rarely paid the bills; thus, most of these women earned a living as teachers (Wade-Gayles 1981).

Living in the South also forced these journalists to seek markets for their writing far from home; either the well-established black journals in urban centers or the handful of Northern white newspapers that published African American writer's work. For example, Victoria Earle Matthews, based in Georgia, was a prolific writer for black newspapers across the country including *The National Leader,* the *Detroit Plaindealer,* the *Southern Christian Recorder,* the *Boston Advocate* and the *New York Age.* She also contributed to mass circulation dailies including the *New York Times,* the *New York Herald,* the *New York Mail and Express* and the *Phonographic World.* In Kentucky, Mary V. Cook wrote for *The American Baptist* under the pen name Grace Ermine and was editor of the education section of *Our Women and Children.* Josephine Turpine Washington, born into Virginia's black middle-class elite, started her writing career with an article in the *Virginia Star* in 1877, and went on to contribute to many of the nation's black journals, including the *New York Freeman, Christian Recorder,* and the *A.M.E. Church Review* (Wade-Gayles, 1981; Giddings, 1984).

African American women who played prominent roles in literature and politics also worked as journalists. Poet and novelist Frances E. W. Harper, discussed earlier as an important antebellum writer, continued her prolific career until the end of the century. I. Garland Penn referred to Harper as a "time-honored contributor to the Afro-American press" and said "she has been the journalistic mother, so to speak, of many brilliant young women who have entered upon her line of work so recently" (1891, 421, 422). Writer and educator Anna Julia Cooper, author of the landmark book on race relations and women's rights *A Voice from the South, by a Black Woman of the South,* edited the woman's section of the *Southland,* a monthly magazine published in 1890–91. Cooper's goal was to broaden the focus of the women's sphere in journalism from domestic to intellectual and political concerns, and she stressed the need for black women to obtain higher education (Bullock 1981, 102, 103). Cooper also contributed to several newspapers and *McGirt's Magazine.*

Probably the best known of these women was Ida Wells-Barnett. She began her journalism career in 1889 when she was invited to become editor and partner of *Free Speech and Headlight,* a small weekly in her hometown of Memphis, Tennessee. Wells had developed a reputation as an articulate activist for black rights in Memphis, and wrote scathing editorials on lynching and discrimination. In 1892 a white mob attacked, sacked and burned the *Free Speech* offices while Wells was out of town, and she was warned not to return to the south. She remained in the East and joined the prominent black editor, T. Thomas Fortune, at the *New York Age,* where she wrote a dramatic series of articles on lynching that mobilized black and white opposition across the nation. Her pamphlets "Southern Horrors," published in 1892 and "A Red Record" published in 1895 were the most detailed and precisely researched records of lynching in existence. She traveled across the country on lecture tours, contributed to numerous publications including the *Chicago Tribune,* and was one of the founders of the National Association for the Advancement of Colored People (NAACP). She was also active in the founding of the National Association of Colored Women, the women's club movement, and the Urban League (Franklin and Meier, 1982).

The post-reconstruction period also introduced the first periodicals targeted at a female audience, and featuring the work of African American women. The earliest of these efforts may be a monthly literary journal, *The Joy,* founded in 1887 by A. E. Johnson, a woman poet from Baltimore. Johnson is said to have launched the magazine as a place for women to publish their stories, poetry and essays. *The Joy* lasted until 1889–90 and received complimentary reviews from both black and white contemporaries (Penn 1891, 423–5).

Our Women and Children was founded in 1888 by William J. Simmons with the purpose of informing and educating women, and providing a forum for young writers. Kentucky-born Lucy Wilmot Smith edited the magazine's woman's section after editing the children's column of *The American Baptist* and contributing to papers including *The Baptist Jour-*

nal, The Journalist, and the *Boston Advocate.* Her columns called for women's suffrage and education, and she won respect from her press colleagues, one of whom said "She frequently writes for the press, and wields a trenchant pen" (Penn 1891, 380). Other contributors to *Our Women and Children* included Mary V. Cook, the education editor; Ida Wells-Barnett, who edited the home department; and Ione E. Wood, the temperance editor who also taught in Simmon's Louisville, Kentucky school (Bullock 1981, 167–68).

Ringwood's Afro-American Journal of Fashion was established in 1891 in Cleveland by Julia Ringwood Costin, who employed eight well-known women writers as section editors. One of these was Mary Church Terrell, an educator, anti-lynching activist, and organizer of black women's clubs at the turn of the century (Bullock 1981, 168). *Ringwood's* was part of a national trend in publishing, which sought to capitalize on "women's interests" in domestic life, including *Ladies' Home Journal,* founded in 1883.

Perhaps the best known of the black women's publications of this period was the *Woman's Era,* founded in Boston in 1894 by Josephine St. Pierre Ruffin. The magazine has been closely linked to the black women's club movement at the turn of the century and it became the official journal of the National Federation of Afro-American Women when the organization was founded in 1896. The publication touted a prestigious array of talented black women as its editors and contributors, including Victoria Earle Matthews, Mary Church Terrell, Gertrude Mossell, and Fannie Barrier Williams (Bullock 1981, 169–70; Sterling 1984). Ruffin combined her involvement in the women's club movement with an active career as a journalist for a black weekly newspaper and her membership in the New England Women's Press Association. Her goal for the journal was to represent the interests of women's clubs across the country and to motivate black women to become active in service and reform movements in their communities. In the magazine's opening editorial she said:

> The stumbling block in the way of even the most cultured colored woman is the narrowness of her environment. But let the fact be emphasized that in the work for the betterment of the world the claims for recognition of this class cannot be overlooked, it is a large and growing factor in the intellectual as well as industrial life of the country; and the strength of the chain of woman's advancement will be determined by the strength of this weak link" (*Woman's Era* I, March 24, 1894).

The *Woman's Era* was published until 1897.

By the end of the nineteenth century, African American women were writing, editing, and publishing their own journals at an ever-increasing pace. Journalist and novelist Pauline Hopkins played a major role in bringing African American journalism into the twentieth century. The *Colored American Magazine* was founded in Boston in 1900 by two young men who planned an intellectual journal with a blend of literature, social, and political commentary. Pauline Hopkins was initially hired to edit the magazine's women's section but she quickly became the magazine's chief writer and was named literary editor in 1903 (Bullock 1981, 106–8). Hopkin's fiction has been the subject of recent interest by literary scholars. Four of her novels—"Contending Forces," "Hagar's Daughter," "Winona: A tale of Negro Life in the South and Southwest," and "Of One Blood. Or, the Hidden Self"—were serialized in the *Colored American* and at least one scholar has suggested that Hopkins sought to create a black literary renaissance through the magazine more than twenty years before the one in Harlem emerged (Carby 1988; Carby 1987). Hopkins also wrote columns, articles, and essays for the magazine and is credited with having a strong influence on the journal's editorial style and quality. Hopkins and her colleagues hoped to cultivate a black magazine audience that would benefit from the *Colored American's* sophisticated writing and radical politics, but this dream died when the conservative Booker T. Washington provided financial support to the ailing magazine and moved its offices to New York City with a new staff (Carby 1987; Bullock 1981). The magazine finally folded in 1909 and Hopkins died in 1930 in relative obscurity.

Questions of Race and Gender

It is insufficient to base the study of African American women journalists on the kinds of brief sketches outlined in the previous pages. Each journalist deserves to have her work and her life carefully analyzed. For example, we need to know what were the prevailing themes and issues for these journalists, and how they expressed them. We must examine how these writers conformed to or deviated from journalistic norms of the period; and what role, if any, did their race and gender have on the style and content of their writing? How did these women view their roles as journalists? Was it one of the few professions, along with teaching, available to educated black women? Was journalism the only means of political expression for a group denied suffrage and political office? Was journalism a means to gain exposure and launch a literary career, such as Pauline Hopkin's experience suggests?

Another key question is the role gender played for these women as they attempted to function in the male-dominated world of journalism. As Gertrude Mossell argued 100 years ago, women journalists were often respected by their male peers, but were denied power and visibility. One scholar has suggested that Pauline Hopkins was not publicly recognized for her editorial influence on the *Colored American* because of resentment from her male colleagues (Carby 1988, xxxi). Fifty years earlier Mary Ann Shadd Cary faced similar opposition from her male readers, who complained openly about her role as editor. The appearance of Samuel Ringgold Ward's name on the *Provincial Freeman's* masthead was a typical nod to social conventions, which insisted on male authority and male leadership. For at least the first year of publication, Cary signed her editorials with the initials M.A.S. so as not to attract attention to her gender. But in the small black communities of Canada West everyone knew the editor was a woman, and Cary was the subject of angry letters, editorials, and public complaints about her role at the newspaper.

Many other women journalists simply plied their trade without recognition, or used pen names, such as Lillian Lewis' "Bert Islew." This also highlights the possibility that there were other women writing for periodicals of the period who remain unknown. African American women journalists were clearly constrained by a Victorian social structure, which sought to control women's activities and influences. At the same time, their privileged class position and level of education gave them mobility and modes of public expression outside the reach of most women in this period.

One scholar suggests that free blacks in antebellum America sought to replicate the gender conventions of white society, and called for black women to fulfill the "true womanhood" ideals of a gentler, domesticated role (Horton 1986). The same scholar points to Mary Ann Shadd Cary as unusual among black women of this period because she was able to combine an active career with her roles as wife and mother (Horton 1986). Another historian suggests that given their oppressed status, African American women made great strides in obtaining education and status throughout the nineteenth century. But this progress was tempered by sexism in the black community, which became increasingly visible by the end of the nineteenth century (Perkins 1983).

The answers to these and other crucial questions must be informed by an understanding of the African American experience. Gender relations differed among whites and blacks of the period, and varied in the African American community because of economic status, region, and other factors. Thus, terms like sexism must be employed carefully. Evaluations of class distinctions were also determined by race. For example, Mary Ann

Shadd Cary was literate, well-traveled, and had access to political figures—middle-class in white terms—yet she often faced destitution in her efforts to keep her newspaper operating and feed her family.

In studying African American women journalists we must also consider the networks and bonds they formed. Many of these women knew each other through family, schools, churches, club membership, and professional ties, and they often aided each other's efforts to have their work published. Some carried on lively intellectual debates that highlighted black women's unique circumstances. In her *Voice from the South*, Anna Julia Cooper took issue with Gertrude Mossell's published view that African American men had aided women's progress (Sterling 1984, 435).

Finally, we must examine the interplay between African American women journalists and the social movements in which they were involved. Almost universally these women were not engaged in writing simply for the joy of the process; they wrote to express their views about slavery, temperance, feminism, racial uplift, lynching, and other crucial issues. They wrote and published newspapers and magazines to educate the black community and promote moral principals. They functioned as journalists to spur their readers on to activism and social change. And these women took on these often thankless tasks to create a window on the black community that would be open to the outside world, thus seeking to free African Americans from the isolation imposed on them by the segregated white press.

Most important, perhaps, is the recognition that African American women journalists tell us a great deal about how race, class and gender intersected in their lives, and in the life of the nation. Unlike their white male counterparts, these women were not mere observers of the cultural and political dynamics that shaped this country in the nineteenth century—they were directly and negatively effected by the policies of slavery and reconstruction, and by the lack of women's suffrage and political power. They were the products of a racist national ideology that denied African Americans citizenship and self-determination at the same time that they were shaped by Victorian notions of a woman's place in society. The fact that these women were able to carve out careers as writers and journalists should be viewed not only as a remarkable feat, but as a central contribution to African American women's survival. The task remains to appropriately place them in the canons of journalism history. Only then will we begin to understand the complex processes by which all women made meaning in nineteenth century America.

References

Altschull, J. Herbert. 1990. *From Milton to McLuhan: The Ideas Behind American Journalism.* White Plains, N.Y.: Longman.

Bryan, Carter R. 1969. "Negro Journalism in America Before Emancipation." *Journalism Monographs.* no. 12. (Sept. 1969) Association for Education in Journalism and Mass Communication.

Bullock, Penelope L. 1981. *The Afro-American Periodical Press 1838–1909.* Baton Rouge, La.: Louisiana State University Press.

Carby, Hazel. 1987. *Reconstructing Womanhood.* New York: Oxford University Press.

———. 1988. "Introduction" to *The Magazine Novels of Pauline Hopkins.* New York: Oxford University Press.

Carey, James. 1975. "The Problem of Journalism History." *Journalism History.* 1(Spring). 3–5, 27.

Covert, Catherine L. 1981. "Journalism History and Women's Experience: A Problem in Conceptual Change." *Journalism History.* 8: 1, 2–5.

Davis, Marianna W. ed. 1982. *Contributions Of Black Women to America.* Vol. 1. New York: Kenday Press.

Dicken-Garcia, Hazel. 1989. *Journalistic Standards in Nineteenth-Century America.* Madison, Wis.: University of Wisconsin Press.

Dill, Bonnie Thornton. 1979. "The Dialectics of Black Womanhood." *Signs: The Journal of Women in Culture and Society.* 4: 31, 543–555.

Franklin, John Hope and August Meier, eds. 1982. *Black Leaders of the Twentieth Century.* Urbana, Ill.: University of Illinois Press.

Giddings, Paula. 1984. *When and Where I Enter.* New York: William Morrow and Co.

Higginbotham, Evelyn Brooks. 1989. "Beyond The Sound of Silence: Afro-American Women in History." *Gender and History.* 1: 1, 50–67.

Horton, James Oliver, 1986. "Freedom's Yoke: Gender Conventions Among Antebellum Free Blacks." *Feminist Studies.* 12: 1, 51–75.

Kessler, Lauren. 1984. *The Dissident Press.* Beverly Hills: Sage.

Lerner, Gerda ed. 1973. *Black Women in White America.* New York: Vintage Books.

Penn, I. Garland. 1891. *The Afro-American Press and its Editors.* Springfield, Mass.: Willey and Co.

Perkins, Linda M. 1983. "The Impact of the 'Cult of True Womanhood' on the Education of Black Women." *Journal of Social Issues.* 39: 3, 17–28.

Ripley, C. Peter. 1986. *The Black Abolitionist Papers vol. II: Canada, 1830–1865.* Chapel Hill: University of North Carolina Press.

Stephens, Mitchell. 1988. *A History of News.* New York: Penguin Books.

Sterling, Dorothy, ed. 1984. *We Are Your Sisters: Black Women in the Nineteenth Century.* New York: W.W. Norton and Co.

———. 1985. *Black Foremothers: Three Lives.* Old Westbury, N.Y.: The Feminist Press.

Wade-Gayles, Gloria. 1981. "Black Women Journalists in the South, 1880–1905." *Callaloo.* 4: 1–3, 138–151.

Wall, Cheryl, ed. 1989. *Changing Our Own Words: Essays on Criticism, Theory and Writing by Black Women.* New Brunswick, N.J.: Rutgers University Press.

Washington, Mary Helen. 1987. *Invented Lives: Narratives of Black Women, 1860–1960.* Garden City, N.Y.: Anchor Press.

White, Deborah Gray. 1987. "Mining the Forgotten: Manuscript Sources for Black Women's History." *The Journal of American History.* vol. 74: 237–242.

Wolseley, Roland E. 1978. *The Black Press U.S.A.* Ames, Iowa: Iowa State University Press.

12

The Construction of Chinese American Women's Identity

Victoria Chen

And all the time I was having to turn myself American-feminine, or no dates. There is a Chinese word for the female I—which is "slave." Break the women with their own tongues!
—Maxine Hong Kingston *The Woman Warrior*

In her celebrated autobiographical fiction, Maxine Hong Kingston (1977) described her experiences as a Chinese American growing up in a family that demeaned girls. In addition to having to make sense of her mother's inculcation on how to be a good Chinese girl, Maxine also needed to struggle in her adjustment to mainstream American white culture. Like many Chinese American women, Kingston's bicultural identity is constructed through an array of stories with which she grew up, some contradictory and others ambiguous. Her mother, Brave Orchid, told Kingston that she would "grow up a wife and slave, but she taught me the song of the warrior woman, Fa Mu Lan. I would have to grow up a warrior woman" (Kingston 1977, 24). The subversive myth of the Chinese warrior woman provided Kingston a coherent theme in her writing and empowered her to enact her bicultural identity as a prominent ethnic and feminist writer.

Like any minority group, Asian American women throughout the past century and half have been portrayed by the media in various ways that belie their own voices, and these stereotypical images have profound impact of how they see themselves in a predominantly white society. Briefly, the images of Asian American women have evolved from the subservient prostitutes and cloistered heathens associated with the early immigrants, to the submissive and exotic "other" women in the first part of the century, to the more recent "model minority" and ethnic writers who fearlessly confront the status quo of Asian American women (Yung 1986).

Although Chinese immigrants have been in this country since the middle of 19th century, the first two anthologies of Asian American women came out only in 1989. The titles of both, *The Forbidden Stitch: An Asian American Women's Anthology* (Lim and Tsutakawa 1989) and *Making Waves: An Anthology of Writings by and about Asian American Women* (Asian Women United 1989) suggest the long struggle that these women have engaged in for their private voices to be acknowledged and heard in public. Along with other work, these two anthologies specifically probe a central dilemma of Asian American females, and indeed of all minority cultures. What is bicultural gender identity? What does it mean? How does an American-born Chinese daughter strive for a coherent life script between her family and the larger society?

I have become increasingly interested in these issues over the past ten years. The sharpening awareness of the discordant ways of life between myself and my parents provided a fundamental curiosity, which has extended to my academic research. Before moving to Canada, I was educated in a Chinese school for six years and then switched to an American school for six years in Taiwan.

I often find myself struggling between two sets of cultural realities, each with its own beauty and coherence, as well as contradictions and limitations. Over the years, I have concluded that "incommensurability" is perhaps the best word to describe the cultural differences between Chinese and the dominant Eurocentric American traditions. Not only do these two realms of discourse have a limited basis for comparison, they also lack a shared vocabulary to even address the differences between these two cultures. Worn out by my continuous but futile effort to persuade my Chinese parents that a woman's pursuit of her intellectual interests is a legitimate and desirable personal choice, I have decided to enhance the quality of my struggle by listening to other Asian American women's voices and learning from their accounts.

Within the field of communication, very little work has been done specifically on Asian American women's identity. Mainstream intercultural communication research is often conducted with a paper-and-pencil measurement approach, which fails to provide an understanding of the complexity and richness of any individual's life story and communication patterns. This paper attempts to illuminate the theme of bicultural gender identity by reviewing available literature in Asian American studies and presenting a study of one American-born Chinese woman, whom I will call Alice Hong. My analysis of Alice Hong's own story is intended to illustrate how a woman constructs her bicultural identity being a Chinese daughter in American society.

Bicultural Gender Identity

> Written American history has traditionally either denied the existence or distorted the experience of women of color. As a result, Chinese American women, despite the fact that they have been in the United States since 1834, have remained an invisible or misunderstood entity.—Judy Yung *Chinese Women of America: A Pictorial History*

The construction of one's cultural identity is a social process. An individual cannot fully claim his or her identity as wished because who one is or what one does is a *coconstruction* between the person and the society; identity has to be publicly acknowledged. When discussing the role of literature in defining Asian American realities, Kim (1987, 88) argued that "claiming America for Asian Americans" means "inventing a new identity, defining ourselves according to the truth instead of a racial fantasy, so that we can be reconciled with one another in order to celebrate our marginality." Kim spoke of the inadequacy of stereotypes and fantasies of Asian American women that abound, because media portrayal of ethnic groups is a powerful means to create something "real" for the white American society. The images of Chinese American women have no doubt changed—and yet, some myths are tenacious—since the 1830's, when the first group of Chinese women arrived in America. Because of cultural biases and language barriers, early Chinese pioneering women were by and large represented through a distorted historical record. Photographs depicted them as helpless and fragile women with bound feet and dressed in exotic Chinese clothing. Images of these nameless women as slave girls and prostitutes were rife, and yet these people took no part in telling the American society who they really were. As Yung (1986, 4) asked, "Who were these women? If they could speak for themselves, what would they say about their lives in America?"

Although roles of Chinese women in America in the first half of this century had somewhat "improved" compared with their earlier sisters, who had painfully paved the road for the subsequent generation, they were still limited to the exotic and sexy China Doll, or the diabolic Dragon Lady, as depicted in the popular 1940's comic "Terry and the Pirates." Even today, clumsy racial fantasies about Asians continue to flourish in the West. As Kim (1987, 89) pointed out, "Familiar representations of Asians—always unalterably alien" include "helpless heathens, comical servants . . . and, only in the case of women, exotic sex objects imbued with an innate understanding of how to please, serve, and titillate." Many women had to struggle with discrimination and cultural conflicts both at

227

home and outside. Even after emigrating to America, many Chinese families still reinforced the feudalist and patriarchal values in traditional China by deemphasizing the role of women. While the majority of the earlier Chinese American women were not literate enough or had no opportunity to record their own stories in writing, most of the subsequent generations of American-born Chinese daughters for a long time were not encouraged to articulate their experiences. Even worse, they were taught to believe that their experiences were not legitimate or significant in any way.

Few women had the courage of Jade Snow Wong. In 1945 Wong published her autobiography *Fifth Chinese Daughter,* in which she captured the repression and emotional turmoil that she experienced with her family as a San Francisco-born Chinese daughter. Although taught to be obedient and respectful at home as well as deferring to her father and brothers, Jade Snow bravely confronted the opposition from her parents in issues such as dating and going to college.

For the last few decades, Chinese American women have increasingly participated in fighting for a public place for their own stories. They have become more aware of their civil rights and taken pride in their ethnic identity. Writing about their bicultural experiences is encouraged, and more recognition is given to a different set of criteria for evaluating their life and work. However, the struggle for a new voice and a different identity can be a long and painful process. Kingston's writings—and more recently Amy Tan's (1989) *The Joy Luck Club*—describe the intensely emotional journey that Chinese American women undergo and the prices that they have to pay in order to empower themselves within the constraints of family and social systems.

Against the stereotypical demure and exotic images, young Asian American writers do not see the need to present themselves and the Asian worlds in the best possible light, because the dual cultural enmeshment indeed suggests that it is an intrinsically imperfect world. Asian American daughters, "while embracing the American present, inform us of the painful familial and psychological divisions that Asian ethnicity can give rise to in a deeply homogenizing society" (Lim and Tsutakawa 1989, 12).

In *The Woman Warrior,* Kingston told of her struggle to sort out the conflicting stories told by her mother. Exulting in the myths of glorified swordswomen, she also felt threatened by tales of female children sold off as slaves by poor parents. She remembered growing up hearing sayings such as "girls are maggots in the rice," "it's more profitable to raise geese than daughters," "feeding girls is feeding cowbirds," and "when you raise girls, you are raising children for strangers." When she told her mother "I got straight A's, Mama," her mother replied, "Let me tell you a true story about a girl who saved her village" (Kingston, 1977, 54). Kingston's mother told her that she could not eat straight A's. Being an educated girl did not save Kingston from the threat of being sold as a slave; "my American life has been such a disappointment" (Kingston, 54). The low status of girls in the traditional Chinese culture had been transplanted to America.

Carma Hinton's documentary entitled "Small Happiness" showed life in "Long Bow," a small, rural village in Northern China, in the mid 1980's. In the opening scene, an old man explained, "To give birth to a boy is considered a great happiness; to give birth to a girl is a small happiness. Well, you can't say it's no happiness, but there is a difference between big and small happiness." The contented grandfather then pointed to a boy and said, "This is my grandson; he is a great happiness." Pointing to the girl standing next to the boy, he said, "This is my granddaughter, and she is a small happiness." A main reason for this blatant preference of sons over daughters in the traditional Chinese families, especially in the countryside, is that sons can contribute to farming and remain in the household to perpetuate the family lineage as well as to take care of the aged parents. Daughters, on the other hand, will be married off to another's household; as the old saying goes, "You raise daughters for the other's family." The unequal status of a son's and daughter's marriage can further be understood in the etymological structure of the Chinese language. The Chinese character for "marrying off" a daughter consists of a woman and a family, meaning "finding a family for a woman." However, the character for a man to "marry" consists of a woman and the word for "gain," meaning "to gain a woman into one's family." As Hinton mentioned in "Small Happiness," Chinese sons play the important filial role of opening the door for the future generation (perpetuating the family lineage) by bringing home a wife. A Chinese daughter, on the other hand, needs to fulfill her filial duties by obeying her father at home, her husband when married off, and her son when the husband is deceased.

The Chinese classic, Book of Songs, celebrated the birth of a son (cited in Yung 1986, 10):

> So he bears a son,
> And puts him to sleep upon a bed,
> Clothes him in robes,
> Gives him a jade sceptre to play with.
> The child's howling is very lusty;
> In red greaves shall he flare,
> Be lord and king of house and home.

But when a daughter was born:

> Then he bears a daughter,
> And puts her upon the ground,
> Clothes her in swaddling clothes,
> Gives her a loom-whorl to play with.
> For her no decorations, no emblems;
> Her only care, the wine and food,
> And how to give no trouble to father and mother.

Hinton pointed out in "Small Happiness" that in the countryside of China, being "childless" for a woman means that she has not given birth to a son. Given the elevated status of sons in a Chinese family, it is no doubt that giving birth to a boy is one way to elevate the daughter-in-law's own status in her husband's family. Protecting and spoiling the son thus become "natural" and "necessary" for many Chinese parents, because the son bears the status and the hope for the entire family and is expected to take care of the parents when they grow old.

The low status of Chinese girls leads to the submergence of their voices. Kingston (1977) recounted her cruel torture of a silent Chinese girl in school to get the girl to talk. Perhaps projecting her own fear and resentment on the other girl who reminded Kingston of herself in school, Kingston (1977, 193) said, "I did not speak and felt bad each time that I did not speak ... The other Chinese girls did not talk either, so I knew the silence had to do with being a Chinese girl."

Kingston's experiences are not unfamiliar to other Chinese American women. Standing astride two worlds, each with its beauty and pain, Asian American daughters face both familial and societal difficulties in constructing a coherent sense of identity. DEAR DIANE: Letters from Our Daughters (Wong 1983) is a collection of letters from Asian American daughters who wrote to Dear Diane about their personal problems. Signed with names such as "Caught between Contradictions," "Silent Daughter," "Divided," "Lost between the Cracks," and "Made in the U.S.A.," these young women addressed a variety of issues in which they feel "pulled" between what they saw as parental expectations and social norms. One daughter who signed "Double Standard Victim" wrote:

> DEAR DIANE: I'm 17 and have two brothers, one 19, the other 15. My parents let the two of them do whatever they want. They can stay out after school and go out in the evenings. They can even have girlfriends. With me, it's totally the opposite. Whenever I go out

230

(which isn't too often), I get the third degree . . . This double standard stinks. It's so unfair. What do you think? (Wong 1983, 9)

Another who signed "No Old Maid" wrote:

DEAR DIANE: I am 24 years old, and I plan to go to graduate school. My parents, though, insist that I get married and start having a family instead. In fact, they are already picking out young men for me to meet. They don't want me to end up an old maid, like my auntie. I'm not interested in getting married in the near future . . . almost everyone in the community greets me by asking when am I going to settle down and get married. Is there a good way to get other people to let me live my own life? (Wong 1983, 41)

As much as these Asian American women see (or even blame) themselves for being Americanized, at the same time they also represent the "other" to the white American society. In other words, from the parents' point of view, these daughters are never Chinese enough, and from the American perspective, it is difficult to relate to them simply as "American" women, born and reared in this society. Kim (1987, 87) cited some letters in the "Dear Abby" column that reflect a gulf between Asian Americans and the descendants of European immigrants: "Two Irish Americans wrote that they could not understand why an American of 'Oriental' descent would complain about being asked 'what are you' within five minutes of being introduced to a 'Caucasian.' " Asian American readers responded by pointing out that the same question may sound innocent when asked of a Caucasian; however, "when it is asked of an Asian, it takes on a different tone . . . When I say, 'I'm from . . . Portland, Oregon!' they are invariably surprised . . . because they find it hard to believe that an Asian-looking person is actually . . . American . . . Being white is not a prerequisite for being . . . American." (Kim 1977, 87).

Chang (1989, 176), in her short story, noted the remorse and guilt of not being Chinese enough and the paradoxical chagrin at always being "residually Chinese": "The only time I feel Chinese is when I'm embarrassed I'm not more Chinese—which is a totally Chinese reflex I'd give anything to be rid of!" Kingston, in an interview, said, "It's strange that I talked-story in Chinese but wrote in English." Being simultaneously enmeshed in two cultures, Kingston sees herself as embodying a synthesis of contradictions, not Chinese in some ways, American in others, but a whole person; a new kind of being who integrates diverse cultural experiences.

Similarly, Chan (1984) argued that Asian Americans possess neither a genuine Asian perspective nor a wholly American one, and Kim (1987) pointed out that the most telling feature in the production of Asian American fiction and poetry was their distinct American-ness. Through various forms of writing by Asian Americans, we see that bicultural identity is simultaneously expressed and constructed through this ambivalence and ambiguity that characterize the tension of living in the interface of two cultural worlds. Recent writings of Asian American women share a strong voice to claim "We are not exotic . . . This is our life. It makes sense to us. It is for you, the other, to understand us" (Lim and Tsutakawa 1989, 12).

Striding between two cultures, ambiguity is central to Asian American women's experience. However, it is not always easy (if possible at all) to present neatly a coherent picture of bicultural identity to people who prefer unity and clarity in the life story of others. One white male critic of Kingston's *The Woman Warrior* complained that "it's hard to tell where her fantasies end and reality begins" (cited in Kim 1987, 93). Therefore, the troubling aspect of Kingston's book for this reader was the "confusions" in "her depiction of some Chinese women as aggressive and verbal and others as docile, as if there can only be one type of Chinese woman" (Kim 1987, 93). Asian American women can derive strength and "double vision" from living with ambiguity and paradoxes. Kim (1987, 111) concluded that instead of remaining foreign or being subordinated by the dominant ideology, Asian American writers express "the desire to remain as 'others' by defining our own 'otherness'."

To illustrate how women struggle with these themes in their individual lives, I now present the narrative of Alice Hong, an American-born Chinese woman. Alice was contacted through the Asian American Students Association at a university in New England. I interviewed her in a private setting for two hours and later transcribed our conversation. I will present here only portions of the interview which I consider as relevant to the construction of bicultural identity. This work is one of the seven case studies that I conducted in a larger project studying the intergenerational conflict and bicultural identity in Chinese American families based on the daughter's account.

Alice Hong: One Woman's Story

I was born in Brookline, Massachusetts, in 1964. My dad was born in New York and my mom is from China. Dad graduated from high school, and my mom had two years of college from Hong Kong. We speak Toishan at home. Mom had a stroke fifteen years ago and she is left-brain paralyzed. She used to speak some English; now she understands but does not speak. My dad used to work in the restaurant six years ago and quit because of illness. I can speak Toishan fluently, but with dad I speak mostly English, with mom Toishan. I have one older brother, Dave, and one younger brother, Bob.

My dad is very traditional, and that's weird, because he was born in New York. You know how the boy is really important in Chinese tradition, and that's how he was brought up. But my mom is exactly the opposite, everybody is equal, and actually, I was treated more as a favorite too because I was the only girl. But you THINK that it would be the other way around, that my dad would not go by the Chinese tradition; but he is the only boy in his family with four sisters, and his mother treated him like he was the king; you know, he's the KING.

My grandparents aren't alive any more, but they hated me, and they would treat me so bad and my mother would be like . . . When my brother Bob was born, my grandmother called everyday and talked to my mom. But when I was born, she didn't even call. My mom doesn't treat us like that at all, but my father's favorite is Bob. He just favors the boys more . . . He would tell me and his sisters, . . that everything he did was alright, even if it was against the sisters, but his mom would favor him, everything . . .

When I grew up, I noticed that Bob was treated differently, emotionally; he was paid more attention. When he asked for money, he would get it, and when I asked for a quarter, I wouldn't get it . . . when we were younger, things like that. Also, when Bob got mad and yelled back at my father, my father would say "Just let him cool off." But if it were me, or even my older brother, he would yell back at us and said "I'm your father, who do you think you're talking to . . . "

Bob watched over us, like my dad would yell at me, he'll yell back at my dad to protect me. We're very close. If he asked for a quarter, he got it, and if I didn't, he'd give me his and he'd go back to my dad to ask for another one . . . He knows that he can get another one, my father would just give him anything.

If I argued with dad about something, if I was right, Bob would help me out, and my dad would listen to what he said, but not me. So he would help us out . . . So he's not spoiled in that sense. My father knows that he favors Bob, he says that he doesn't, but how can you say you don't . . . We're not little anymore . . . Even now Bob would get away with a lot of things, and Bob is a lot closer with my father . . . I guess when he was younger, he was SO good, he didn't cry, he didn't complain . . .

My father thinks that my mother is always on my and my older brother's side. So even though she is equal toward Bob too, she has to help us out. Usually not in the middle of the fight, but afterward, she'd say to my father, "You shouldn't treat Bob differently." She's a quiet person, but when she does yell, she has good reasons. Dad isn't like that; he used to be a bad-tempered person.

My family is very different from a lot of Chinese families. If we said we didn't feel like going to school, my parents would say, "Ok, that's all right," so we would think "That's weird" and we would go; we want to go, we never cut school. So we went even though we didn't know we didn't have to go, because my parents didn't force us to go to school. Like in grade school, in the morning, just a joke, "Mom, I don't feel like going," and she'd said "Ok," but we'd all forget about it and we'd go. Even my dad would say, "Well, if you don't feel good, stay at home." So they would never pressure us about school.

All of us did want to go to college; they encouraged us but never pushed us like other Chinese parents. I think they expected for us to go to college, just that we did, and we didn't go against it, we don't know what they would have done if we didn't. Things that my mom would get really mad at, like come home late for a girl; my mom gets worried, but my dad wouldn't say it, he'd just say "what time did you come home . . .;" he wouldn't yell . . . If we get bad grades on our report card, they wouldn't yell at us, but said "why?" They encouraged us to study, what's important, but never pressured us about school, never ever. No pressure about career. My brother always knew that he wanted something chemistry, engineering . . . I could be anything; my mom would give me suggestions.

My older brother Dave, who is 28-years-old, is working and lives at home. Yeah, my parents definitely like to keep us at home. We were gonna move into a new house, but Dave said that if we were gonna move, he'll stay at the old house because it's so close to work, and my mom said, "Forget it, we're not moving." But if he had to stay in the old house, it would have been ok; but for me, for a girl, I could never do that. Just that I'm a Chinese girl and I shouldn't be moving out.

I live in a dorm, but that's school though, anything to do with school is all right. If you go away for school, it's ok; if I had a job far away, I COULD move out . . . but they would prefer me not to . . . I think it's because . . . I know for the girl, why you have to stay home, because you're a girl; and it's not safe for you to live on your own, so they can watch you. But for the guys, I think it's just that they're attached to them. If Dave really wanted to move out, he could; they couldn't stop him, but my parents would prefer him to stay . . . But I know that I have to stay home; I can't move to a different place away from my parents in Boston, but if I move away from Boston, it would be all right.

In the beginning of high school, I used to go out with my brother so I could stay out as late as I wanted. When in junior and senior years, I started hanging out with my own friends; I wouldn't have a curfew, but I would have to tell them when I was coming home. In high school I used to have to ask them to go out but not anymore, now it's just "I'm going out." My dad thinks that mom treats all of us too lax, and he complained about that: "You don't discipline them enough." If something major, he'll yell; he yelled all the time; but usually, if we want to get permission, we ask our mom, rarely, he would go against what she said, unless there was a good reason.

Depends what he's saying . . . He grew up thinking he was right all the time; whatever he says, he is gonna think he's right. So he's brought up that way, now he thinks everything he thinks is right, so it's really hard to argue against him. So if we talk back to him, he would think that it's lack of discipline on my mom's side, because she taught us to talk back; like "Why is my daughter talking back, because she's spoiled by her mother . . ." That's how he would think.

But if he is right about something, I won't yell back at him; but if he is wrong, I tend to yell back. But it doesn't do any good, he'll still think that he's right, and he'll just yell louder. And my mom would try to tell us just not to say anything, just let him yell. He IS the father, so if he's yelling, just let him yell.

No, he doesn't really try to understand our reasons; it's the way he grew up; he's SO stubborn and SO right all the time, that's how he feels. He thinks he's right ALL the time no matter what it is. But he does negotiate more with mom, but a lot of things he's still real strong about, but he talks more with my mom. Plus now we see him once in a while, but mom has to live with him, so she has time to talk to him.

Before my mother had the stroke, she really spoiled us; she did everything for us. As a kid, we never had to clean up, we never had to . . . and after the stroke, it's how we became better kids I think, plus closer as a family. I don't know how she would have raised us if she didn't have the stroke. I think she would have kept on spoiling us . . . It's hard because we have to relate to her, to take care of her; so it's different.

My dad lights incense for Chinese holidays, and they know when the Chinese holidays are. But us three kids have become Christians, and my mother is sort of evolving into Christian too, but my dad is STUCK on Buddhism. We grew up as Buddhist too, but as we grew older, we started to go to church and we decided on our own what we wanted. The boys used to have to do the incense. Since we're Christians now, they won't do it anymore. Dad used to get mad at the beginning, and now it's ok, now he respects just the way we think. Now my father does the incense alone. And we're still there for Chinese New Year and other important

Chinese festivals. He understands what we believe; he doesn't agree with it totally but . . .

Things that I find difficult to accept, just like the Chinese way of thinking . . . They judge people by the way they look; my mom can say, "She has a sharp jaw bone and she's not a nice person. Or his eyes are too close together, or his ears are too small, you can't date him." I didn't understand that but I just accepted it . . . You know, the bigger the ears, the longer the life you have; so if you bring a guy home with small ears . . . yeah, she believes in those things, and she'll judge him right after he leaves . . . "I don't want you to hang out with him, you can be friends with him . . ."

I have both Chinese and Caucasian friends. Before high school there were lots of Asian kids, but after high school they disappeared, so I hung out with lots of Caucasians in high school. And it was ok, and now it's more Chinese people. If I brought Caucasian friends home, they'd be nice, but not as nice as if they were Chinese, because then you could talk to them; my mom could talk to them. If it were Caucasian, she'll just say hi and smile, and couldn't say anymore . . . My dad could, but she couldn't. So how can she like them if she doesn't know anything about them? I don't think Dave would marry a Caucasian, and Bob has a Chinese girl-friend now.

My morals and values are Chinese I think. I think school is very important, and just the way Chinese are brought up to respect other people, and manners are really important. It's so hard to distinguish the American part in me . . . There's no situation when I feel that I'm not Chinese . . . In school I used to see other Chinese people and how they were, and I wished I wasn't . . . I tried to blend in with the Caucasians more. Chinese people are so prejudiced, and I don't like that . . . They're prejudiced against blacks, whites, people from other villages from China, the Japanese; they're against everybody, and I don't like that part.

I never feel that I'm not Asian; it's part of me. In our family gathering, almost everyone of my cousins was born here, and on my dad's side, all my aunts grew up here . . . They all speak English, so I don't feel alienated at all. Yeah, especially here in college, there're so few Chinese people, I'm conscious of me being Chinese all the time. When I hang out with the Chinese, that's ok. When hanging out with Caucasian, I feel Chinese all the time, but not so much when with Asians, because I feel the Caucasians won't come up to talk to me because I'm Asian . . . When I go to a party and if I'm the only Asian, I feel that there's a lot of prejudice, but that could just be me, I'm making myself say that I'm different than everybody else.

I feel more comfortable with Asians but I wouldn't rather, just like I wouldn't not go to a Caucasian party just because I don't feel uncomfortable, it's not fair to me . . . I feel Chinese all the time, regardless with which group, I'm more Chinese with Chinese people, you know how important it is being Chinese with the Asian group . . .

After mom had the stroke, she demands a lot because she can't do a lot of things on her own, so she demands a lot of our time, and I was eight years old. All the other kids were playing, and I had to stay home and help my mom. Dave didn't help but just [did] his homework; he didn't feel like he had to help. Just the girl is closer to the mother . . . and Bob would help too. He's such a neat kid, that's why my parents like him . . . Yeah, I would do everything, vacuuming, cooking, it was hard.

Bob's not that smart, he doesn't get good grades like everybody else in school. They don't get mad at him because of that, they just know that he can't . . . and they worry about it a lot . . . Oh Yeah, they do get mad at him because he's a little irresponsible, like he wouldn't finish the job, like this summer he was painting the house, he would paint half of it and leave the mess and go on doing something else. My dad usually doesn't get mad at him, just like little things, like if you can't take the time out to drive him for shopping . . .

If the youngest one in my family was a daughter? Hmm . . . well, if she's a good little girl . . . my dad might favor her just like Bob, but the son is a plus for him. I know he favors the sons, because he said, "When I pass the house down, I'm giving it to the sons only." And my mom said, "No, you split it." And my dad said, "No, it's not supposed to be like that." But my brothers said, "It's not gonna be like that, once we get it, it's gonna go three ways." Everything that my dad gives them, it's gonna go three ways, but it's gonna be in my brothers' names. I'm close to both brothers, and both of them are closest to me, but they're not that close together; I'm close to both of them. We don't really get jealous of Bob, because we knew that we could use him, to get what we wanted. Dave didn't get jealous because he knew that all he had to do was to ask Bob for something that we couldn't get, and we'd get it . . . Because Bob didn't want to see us hurt; he's really protective for us.

If Bob weren't like that, we would fight with him more, and there would be more tension between him and us. Plus we're older than him, we call it "the little brother's syndrome." Even though now he's bigger than me, if I said something to him, he really had to listen to me because I'm older. He does that to both us. He talked back and complained, but in the end . . . and he listens to my parents in a similar way. He's just like a typical little brother.

I think filial piety is important. I feel like I want to take care of my parents. I don't want them to be alone; I never ever want them to be like that. No, they don't say that, especially for me because I'm a girl, they don't say that I have to live with them. They'd rather not live with one of us, but right near us. They said that they don't want to live in the same house with my brothers, because it creates tension with their wife, but they do want to live close to us.

Saving face is really important to them ... like if the girl gets pregnant ... their reputation. For me it doesn't matter what other people think, so long as my values, I know what I believe and it's good ... like if I dropped out of school, to them, it would look bad to them, so social recognition is more important for them.

Yeah, they especially think marriage is important for the boys; yes, they give pressure on the boys all the time. Just that I have a boyfriend and Bob has a girlfriend, and Dave is the oldest ... So my mom always asked me, "Do you know if he is going out?" but she tried not to ask him. He'd say "Mom, leave me alone." So she'd ask me, and once in a while, she'd say, "Dave, why don't you hang out with so and so?" Ya, she does give him a lot of those; she worries about that a lot.

Analysis

Although Chinese practices of female infanticide or selling girls into slavery do not exist in the contemporary American society, many Chinese American women are subject to a persistent form of unfair treatment and gender bias simply due to their status as a daughter. The importance of sons in Chinese families hardly needs exaggeration. The virtue of filial piety carries different implications for sons and daughters. Traditionally, it is the sons, never daughters, who carry on the lineage and maintain the ancestral tombs. In Alice's family, we see that the two brothers played an important role in religious worship, whereas Alice is not expected to perform the incense ceremony, which commemorates the perpetuation of the family lineage. Instead, she takes on the domestic chores necessary to maintain the household. Although all the children are expected to obey and defer to the parents, especially to the father, it is clear that both sons escape some of the filial duties such as taking care of the physically disabled mother. In fact, Alice has been the major person who holds the family together through daily meals and chores for several years.

Although Alice is getting a college degree just like her brothers, her father still places lower value and significance on her education. Alice's good academic performance does not earn her more respect or favor from her father. Similarly, another woman whom I interviewed, Sandy Wong, stated that although she is the favorite in her family due to her outstanding academic performance, "it would be better for my parents if my brother gets straight A's, or if I were a boy . . . He would probably be the favorite then . . . A boy is definitely a plus." Sandy's parents "kept on trying for a boy and finally got one after three daughters." Her brother, understandably, has much pressure to be successful and has to cope with the high expectations of a son from his parents. Another Chinese American woman, Nancy Wu, stressed throughout the interview that her going away for college is considered "abandoning the family" from her parents and grandparents' viewpoint. She attributed some of her family problem to the fact that her father, who has two daughters, had much less respect from her grandparents than her uncle who has two sons, because according to her grandparents, "two sons are better than two daughters."

These accounts of Chinese American women's experiences suggest that being a successful student in American school does not seem to enhance the daughters' status in their own family. Although the parents may enjoy their daughter's academic performance because it reflects well on them, the daughter's educational accomplishment can never carry the same significance and implication as the son's. While Alice emphasized that she never received any pressure from her parents about school or career, Bob in a separate interview indicated that he felt that one of the few things that he could not negotiate with his father was to quit school. His father, who would buy anything for him, insisted, "Get your college degree before we talk about anything else." Although the lack of pressure to succeed from her parents may be interpreted as a form of freedom given to Alice by the parents, it could well be that the father had higher expectations for his son's academic accomplishment and therefore pushed harder for his success. The focus of Alice's socialization, on the other hand, was more on her sense of filial responsibilities to the family than on her academic performance or individual success. Similarly, Kingston's mother, although bragging about her own accomplishment as a doctor in China, told Kingston that she cannot eat straight A's and should learn to do domestic chores in order to find a husband, or to be a typist like American girls do.

To fulfill her filial duties, Alice is expected to be compliant and to do the cooking and other house chores in the absence of a physically able mother. On the other hand, although she wants to, Alice is not expected to take care of her parents when they get old because traditionally that is the son's filial responsibility. Although growing up in American society, Alice has a deep sense of filial piety and understands what it takes to be a good Chinese daughter (for example, to be obedient, non-argumentative, and domesticated). In *The Woman Warrior,* the heroine Fa Mu Lan impersonated a man in order to take her aging father's place in the army. Despite numerous victories as a brave general, Fa Mu Lan did not earn her distinctive place in Chinese history by having this quality of valiancy; rather, it was her demonstration of filial piety that serves as the moral of the story.

Not every Chinese American woman has the opportunity to appropriate the myth of the warrior woman. Unlike Kingston, who openly challenged some of her mother's inculcations and the traditional Chinese practices, Alice seems to take a generally passive approach in dealing with her familial conflict—as she said, "I don't understand it (the father's reason), but I don't say anything against him." And if she really believed that she was right about something, her mother told her that she should still not say anything because he is the father. As a result of Alice having to stay silent, Bob had to speak on her behalf to negotiate with the father. Similarly, several other Chinese American women indicated that in their family, "children never talk back to father." Sylvia Gao has three sisters in her family and said, "We're never very good at rebelling against my parents . . . We could never voice our anger at our father. If we are mad, we don't say anything." It is not surprising to see that within this kind of familial structure, the daughter's subordinate role and low status are being perpetuated through various forms of interaction. Alice's voice would never carry the same weight as Bob's, if it gets to be heard at all.

Often in a Chinese family, the brothers play the protective role for the sisters. In one instance when Alice went out with a non-Chinese, according to Bob, the parents instructed both Dave and Bob to "keep an eye on this guy, and make sure everything is all right." One woman, Janet Foo, said that her older brother was given the responsibility to take care of her when she was young. And when she was away in college, "he's kind of a third parent in some ways more than he is a brother . . . He would call me up and check up on me every week like my parents; he can be very protective." Sometimes Janet's brother would advocate certain issues for her in front of the parents because her parents believed that "if my brother thinks it's all right, it must be all right for me to do it." While this form of protectiveness can be a sign of affection between the siblings, the kind of subordinate and dependent relationship into which the daughter is socialized is undoubtedly reconstructed through different roles and kinds of activities in the family.

Compared with the way Alice is treated by the father, Bob said, "Oh, I can definitely get away with a lot of stuff." His father rarely said anything negative about what he did, and if in disagreement with his father, "you listen to him and try to reason with him." And for Alice, of course, the hierarchical father-daughter relationship does not provide any possibility for reasoning and arguing for her point. Understandably, Bob feels closest to his father as he said, "When I have a *real* problem, I would go to my dad first since he's pretty liberal-minded about a lot of things . . . He gives me freedom to do what I want to do." Although feeling injustice for his sister, Bob rarely challenged the way his father treated and silenced Alice. To show his care for Alice, however, Bob would negotiate with the father on her behalf when necessary.

Even some of the advice given by DEAR DIANE to the Asian American daughters does not contribute to challenge the status quo. For example, a woman who complained about the constant fighting between her and her mother is advised "Because she's got more experiences, because she's your mom . . . Unless you truly feel she's wrong, try to abide by her wishes" (Wong 1983, 61). This theme of helping Asian American women deal with their conflict by telling them to defer to authority perpetuates the submissive and obedient role of women that is deeply ingrained in the Chinese kinship system. To empower these young women who feel trapped between the two cultural realities, it is necessary, however difficult it may be, to teach them to take a critical perspective in the process of striving for coherence and coordination. Stifling their own opinions to accommodate the tradition or treating them as insignificant merely reconstructs the dominant-subordinate relationship in the family.

It is not difficult to see that from Alice's viewpoint, her father is certainly more traditional than her mother because of his idea of favoring sons over daughters. However, from Bob's perspective, his mother is more traditional because she disciplines him and places more restriction on his freedom than his father does. What seems intriguing to me is that at the end of the interview with Alice, she told me, "Well, Bob would probably tell you that my dad is very traditional because all the things that he did to me." However, Bob evaluated his father's open-mindedness by their father-son relationship instead of taking Alice's experiences and position in the family into account, as she thought that he would. One way to make sense of the closeness between Alice and her mother is that perhaps the mother did not see the need to favor sons in American society, since the family does not rely on Dave and Bob for financial support. Also, unlike traditional China, when daughters were married off to another family at a very early age, Alice has been the major caretaker of her own family, especially her mother, and would probably continue this role even after she is married.

Although the way Alice described how she was treated as a girl in the family seemed to give the impression that these are simply "facts of life," it was not difficult for me to sense her disappointment, regret, helplessness, sadness, or even suppressed resentment in our interview. Perhaps she learned that the way to maintain a harmonious familial relationship in America was to accept the traditional role of a filial Chinese daughter.

While she experienced unfairness with her authoritarian father, Alice's close relationships with her mother and her brothers seemed to make up for what she missed from her father. Alice's narrative suggests that her bicultural identity can be characterized by the tension between two life scripts that she experiences: one celebrates her individual American accomplishment outside of her family (good grades, past president of the Asian American Students Association on her campus); the other emphasizes the importance of a filial Chinese daughter who manages to keep the family together by fulfilling her mother's former roles and silencing herself. Her discourse also suggests an American logic and Chinese content in her bicultural identity. The "American" freedom allowed Alice to pursue her academic interest and to adopt Christianity as her religion. While emphasizing that she had some freedom to do what she wanted to do— an American logic—what she did was to enact her role of a filial Chinese daughter in American society. In her own way, Alice constructed a coherent, although not easily lived, bicultural identity which does not force her to choose to be either Chinese or American. The acceptance of her dual cultural heritage with pride may be one way for Alice to deal with the gender bias in her family with strength and beauty.

Demeaning girls in Chinese tradition can take on various forms. What Alice Hong, as a Chinese daughter growing up in American society, had to cope with included unequal treatment and withdrawal of affection from her father, as well as unpraised (unrewarded) academic performance and extra domestic tasks. Given the diversity of Asian (or any ethnic) American families and the gradually changing images and status of Asian American women, it is not surprising that three other American-born Chinese women that I had interviewed indicated somewhat different experiences from Alice. For them, they were not "mistreated" by their parents simply because of their daughter's status, and their academic performance was highly emphasized by their parents, as one of them put it, "because that would look good on them." However, some of their accounts suggest that gender differences do play a role in their socialization. One woman said, "I think I'm the favorite in the family now because I'm the only one that has graduated from college so far, and I'm getting a real good job offer . . . but I think my brother would have been the favorite if he did better in school . . . A boy is definitely a plus." Another woman said that her parents were proud of her being in graduate school, "but they worried about me being able to find a husband after I get my degree." Her older brother, however, was not subject to the same kind of parental pressure about finding a spouse as she was.

Asian American women are not the only group of women who experience unequal status in social relationships and activities. If we take Kim's

(1987, 111) argument seriously, that Asian Americans should invent a new identity for themselves and that "our claim on America, then, is part of our resistance to domination," then the power of creating this new identity to make a claim on America comes from the reluctance to surrender to media stereotypes and to follow cultural traditions uncritically.

This paper raises questions such as "Can a Chinese American woman be a filial daughter while pursuing feminist ideas in this society?" and "How should a Chinese American woman empower herself without disrupting the familial relationship?" If biculturality and ambiguity indeed are the essential features of Asian American women's identity, Kingston (1977, 35) may have something refreshing and valuable to offer us: "I learn to make my mind large, as the universe is large, so that there is room for paradoxes."

References

Asian Women United of California, eds. 1989. *Making Waves: An Anthology of Writings by and about Asian American Women*. Boston: Beacon Press.

Chan, Anthony B. 1984. "Born Again Asian: The Making of a New Literature." *Journal of Ethnic Studies*. 11 57–73.

Chang, Diana. 1989. The Oriental Contingent. In Shirley Geok-Lin Lim and Mayumi Tsutakawa eds. *The Forbidden Stitch: An Asian American Women's Anthology:* 171–177. Corvallis, Or: Calyx Books.

Kim, Elaine H. 1987. Defining Asian American realities through literature. *Cultural Critique*, 6, Spring, 87–111.

Kingston, Maxine Hong 1977. *The woman warrior: Memoirs of a girlhood among ghosts*. New York: Vintage Books.

Lim, Shirley Geok-Lin and Tsutakawa, Mayumi. eds. 1989. *The forbidden stitch: An Asian American women's anthology*. Corvallis, Oreg.: Calyx Books.

Tan, Amy 1989. *The Joy Luck Club*. New York: G.P. Putnam's Sons.

Wong, Diane Yen-Mei. 1983. DEAR DIANE: Letters From Our Daughters. Oakland, Calif.: Asian Women United of California.

Wong, Jade Snow. 1989. *Fifth Chinese Daughter* (rev. ed., original 1945). Seattle: University of Washington Press.

Yung, Judy. 1986. *Chinese Women of America: A Pictorial History*. Seattle: University of Washington Press.

13

Women's Narratives in a New York Puerto Rican Community

Lourdes Torres

In her study, *The American Story* (1985), Livia Polanyi analyzes a series of stories told in everyday conversation among friends. Through an examination of these stories Polanyi claims that one can deduct "An American world view" (1985, 1). Her purpose is to uncover the linguistic and social constraints that condition the telling of American stories. She argues that the study of stories gives us insight into what the members of a particular group take to be normal, acceptable, and understandable. This paper is motivated by a similar interest in oral narratives in the Puerto Rican community, particularly women's stories, which offer insight into how women's discourse about themselves and their communities exemplifies the contradictions of their lives as Puerto Ricans and as women.

For this paper, I used the few studies on U.S. Puerto Rican discourse; Bennett and Pedraza (1988), Alvarez (1988, 1989), and Ruskin and Varenne (1983). Through a study of discourse strategies and linguistic features these studies suggest methods for interpreting community narratives and other kinds of discourse. Comparing American and Puerto Rican discourse, Ruskin and Varenne (1983), for example, found differences in the organizational features of narratives from the two ethnic groups.

The framework for this study, however, is more closely aligned with the important work by Teun van Dijk on the reproduction of racism in discourse, particularly *Communicating Racism* (1987) and *Prejudice in Discourse* (1984). Van Dijk argues that it is important to study the casual, informal talk about minorities by majority group members, because this discourse is one of the main vehicles for the reproduction of racism. He analyzes how majority-group members speak about minority groups in interviews conducted by other majority-group members. Through the study of individual texts, van Dijk explores the social nature of racism.

Van Dijk's analysis considers the various levels of discourse beginning with aspects of the global organization of talk such as topic and narrative structure. Local discourse features are also studied, for example, semantic moves, which function to connect discourse propositions through the use of strategies such as generalization, example, apparent concessions, repetition, contrast, mitigation, and displacement. Speech acts and conversational phenomena, style and rhetoric are studied as well. The work seeks to make explicit the conscious and unconscious workings of racism to enable us to work toward eliminating it. My own work on women's narratives focuses on minority-group discourse in an effort to understand how internalized oppression operates.

Analysis of Narratives

The narratives and other discourse analyzed for the present study were produced in conversations with New York Puerto Rican women of various ages and generations. The study of women's narratives is a relatively new development in a number of fields (Bate and Taylor 1988; Coates and Cameron 1988; Rosan and Kalčik 1985; Wodak 1980; and Kalčik 1975). Many of those studies posit a gender difference in the telling of narratives or participation in story-telling.

As I have written elsewhere, however, (Torres in press) what may be crucial is not gender but what gender means; gender differences are related to power differences. As Nichols (1983) demonstrates, what may be more important then sex for determining differences in language is the place of a person in the various social networks she or he participates in. Lakoff's groundbreaking book, *Language and Women's place* (1975), posited such characteristics as the use of tags, hedges, polite forms, rising intonation at the end of statements, and empty adjectives as particular to women's speech. Studies by Nichols (1983), O'Barr (1984), and others, however, also find these characteristics in the speech of less powerful persons, male or female, in interactions with persons with more status or power in a particular setting (such as doctor-patient, lawyer-client situations). As O'Barr and Atkins (1980) state, "so-called 'women's language' is in part a language of powerlessness, a condition that can apply to men as well as women in American society." (p. 94). What these studies make clear is that the discussion of differences must always be in context and should analyze the social, economic and political relations in each situation studied.

A typical study from the work on women's narratives should clarify this point. Susan Kalčik in the article ". . . Like Ann's Gynecologist or the Time I was Almost Raped" (1975) studies the structure of personal narratives as they appear in women's rap groups (as these discussion groups have been called). She claims that a particular strategy used by the women is the "kernel story."

According to the author, "kernel stories lack a specific length, structure, climax, or point, although a woman familiar with a genre or subject may predict fairly accurately where a particular story may go. The story developed from the kernel can take on a different size and shape depending on the context in which it is told" (Kalčik 1985, 7). The author describes such stories as fluid and capable of having different points depending on the emphasis the author wishes to stress; because of this characteristic they are termed "emergent structures." They emerge in a particular configuration depending on the specific context and the desire of the narrator. Some become so familiar that a particular reference to the story is all that need be mentioned for the informed listeners to know what story is being alluded to. From her analysis, Kalcik suggests that such fluid, fragmented stories are particular to women's life experience, where they encounter countless interruptions and where their speech is not valued, therefore, they learn to speak briefly and "apologetically." Another character of kernel stories is they are collaboratively developed; this suggests to the author that women recognize their powerlessness and therefore realize they need to work with others.

Unfortunately, Kalčik does not report on similar work on men's rap sessions, where men and women participate, or rap sessions where persons of different races and ethnicities participate, so it is difficult to conclude without further study that the characteristics she points out are particular to women or, rather, can be considered traits of less powerful speakers in general. Contextualizing such work by race and class would certainly render a more telling analysis. Nonetheless, it is certainly positive that more researchers are beginning to study women's discourse seriously after it has long been ignored.

This paper analyzes 30 hours of interviews I conducted with 30 women from Brentwood, a working class suburb of New York City with a significant Latino population. Women from three generational groups were interviewed. First generation speakers were born in Puerto Rico and came to New York in their teenage years. They range in age from 40 to 70. Group 2 speakers either were born in New York or came to New York as young children. They range in age from 30 to 60. Group 3 is composed of persons born in Brentwood who were in their teens when the interviews took place. Participants were selected through a friend-of-a-friend network; in other words, women whom I interviewed put me in touch with friends and family members who were then contacted. Being Puerto Rican, I had easy access to the community. All interviews were conducted in

246

Spanish and dealt with Latino life in the U.S. I elicited information on language, identity, and gender issues. Hints of racism and discrimination are examined as are linguistic and rhetorical strategies used to convey identity. Discourse reveals the values, goals and identity that have been internalized; it reveals the ways group solidarity is expressed and other groups are differentiated.

One issue that particularly interested me was the structuring of internalized oppression in the discourse of the community. Gordon Allport (1958), in his classic study of prejudice, analyzes the effects of prejudice on its victims. Among other traits caused by victimization, Allport names self-hatred motivated by identification with the dominant, oppressing group. Allport finds that often the oppressed come to feel shame or despise themselves for possessing the characteristics that make them hated, such as skin color and foreign accent. He connects this feeling to the ideology in Western societies of individualism, where each person is responsible for his or her fate, so that if he or she is hated it must be their fault. Similarly, Gloria Yamoto (1990) argues that internalized racism occurs because certain racial and ethnic groups are continually being discriminated against and beaten down. This constant, day-to-day assault leads affected groups to believe that the abuse they receive is deserved, to accept abuse as just the way things are, or to believe that it does not occur. As we will see, however, in spite of the pervasiveness and power of dominant group discourse, members of minority groups do struggle against the internalization of prejudices and stereotyping.

Language integrally related to identity has long been a source of both affirmation and discrimination to Latino/a populations in the United States. While language rights issues have usually served to unify diverse Latino/a groups throughout their historical political struggles (for example, around bilingual education and equal access in voting), the use of Spanish as a symbol of a specifically Latino/a identity in the United States has also been contested by Latino/as themselves (Torres, 1990). Language is so important because next to race it is the factor that most clearly establishes difference between Latinos and the dominant group (Flores and Yudice 1990). Those who would argue that assimilation is the route Latino/as should take in order to secure a better standard of living are sometimes in opposition to others who argue for maintaining cultural distinctions.

The issue of Spanish and English use was clearly central in the lives of the women I interviewed. I present here an interesting narrative by A., a group 2 participant, who was a monolingual Spanish speaker when she started attending school, on the subject of language, reproduced in full and analyzed to examine the internalization of dominant group discourse.

The interview was conducted in Spanish, but comments in italics were spoken in English. (The Spanish text is given in the appendix.)

Text A

I: When you started school, you spoke only English?

1) I spoke only Spanish
2) and I'm going to tell you something
3) I had this kid who sat next to me
4) who was named Kevin McReynolds
5) I think it was
6) and the kid was a friend of mine all of my life
7) until he found out I was Latina
8) and then one day he came to school
9) and he sat down next to me
10) *"you dirty spic"*
11) but because I didn't understand much English
12) I thought I had to spit—*spit*
13) and I got ready to and (makes spitting noise)
14) he said, *"uh she spit at me"*
15) right, *that goes to show you*
16) *but you know,* that, it made an impression on my life
17) because it made me ashamed
18) because I realized that I hadn't understood
19) and after that I forced myself to learn English
20) but Kevin showed me when he said, *"you dirty spic"*
21) (humm) . . . he had red hair
22) and had a lot of freckles
23) I said, "but look at that how stupid I am
24) he hadn't said anything to me about spitting"
25) but what shame
26) and the shame made me angry enough to learn English

This narrative shows a structure typical of spoken narratives as defined by Labov (1972).[1] There is an orientation section from lines 2–9, followed

248

by complicating actions interspersed with internal and external evaluations. In lines 21 and 22 there is another orientation sequence followed by more evaluation in lines 23–25 and finally an evaluation/resolution in line 26. Cohesion is established primarily through the use of simple connectives— such as "y" (and) and "pero" (but), although the narrative also contains some more complex constructions, for instance complex sentences joined by temporal conjunctions (line 7).

Labov (1972) and Polanyi (1985) maintain that most narratives contain an evaluation of some sort, which makes clear the point of the story and justifies why the narrator embarked on the telling of the story in the first place. Labov has found that lower-class speakers prefer internal evaluation while middle-class speakers prefer external evaluation.[2] This speaker uses both. Up to line 14 the speaker relies on internal evaluation to describe the events, for example, the degree of the insult described is heightened by the use of intensifiers in line 6, "all of my life"; also, paralinguistic features such as the spitting noise rendered in line 13 and the expression of surprise offered in line 14 offer internal evaluation. Lines 16 through 18 offer an external evaluation; the listener learns the point of the narrative, or why the speaker finds it significant to tell. A. explains through her story that the experience shamed her into learning English—so she learned English. The discourse marker "you know" in line 16 also serves to draw to the attention of the listener that important information, in fact the point of the story, is coming. Lines 20 through 26 serve to reiterate the point by offering a longer version of the same evaluation and a repetition of the insult. This section is interrupted by another orientation (lines 21– 22) as the narrator remembers physical aspects of the boy in her story. She then concludes with more evaluation and a resolution.

One striking aspect of this narrative, which suggests internalized racism, is the identification of the problem and the blame meted out by the speaker. It seems that the speaker has accepted the premise of the argument by some Americans, for example proponents of the English Only Movement, that in order to learn English Latino/as just need to be more motivated. The context of the discussion should be kept in mind. This narrative was produced when the speaker was asked about her educational experiences. The narrator entered into a discussion where she explained her views against bilingual education. This narrative was offered as an explanation as to how A. had learned English and a justification of her position against bilingual education. She didn't need bilingual education; the great shame she experienced as a result of not knowing English motivated her to learn the language.

While the boy's racism is described, A. does not negatively evaluate it. She offers a negative self-evaluation, clearly expressed in line 23. The speaker reported feeling shame and humiliation, and in retelling the story these were again the feelings she expressed. Her feelings toward the boy are not negative; she offers neutral, descriptive adjectives, as in lines 21 and 22, to describe him. What comes across in the narrative is her feeling of inadequacy and how this negative experience forced her to change her behavior quickly. After stating in line 19 that she forced herself to learn English, this is followed in line 20 by a concession, introduced by the discourse coordinator "pero" (but), that Kevin showed her or taught her when he called her a spic. In lines 24–26 the discourse marker "pero" again serves to undercut or excuse the boy's behavior, since, after all, the outcome was that the narrator learned English. She learned that to avoid humiliation and shame she had to quickly learn the language of the dominant group. This in essence is the "moral" of the narrative. Bilingual education is not necessary, children will pick up English quickly with the "right" motivation.

The theme of language and the mixed feelings that it generates was often found in the stories and explanations of all women interviewed. The narratives reveal some insecurity about language, and the internalization of negative assessments that takes place, as well as the lack of criticism toward the context of discrimination. These characteristics do not only surface in narratives related to language issues. B., a 37-year-old Puerto Rican woman offered the following explanation during a narrative on the immigration of her family to the city.

Text B

1) I do know that when I moved to New York

2) my mother was the first Hispanic family in that, in that area

3) and that place was beautiful

4) and then ten years later it was destroyed

5) and I remember that

6) *so* it could be-

7) *you see it L. What can I tell you?*, ha ha ha

8) Look, when I moved there

9) I was five years old and the place was beautiful

10) it was east, it was umm Fulton Street of the South Bronx

11) My mother, my mother who raised me was the first family that moved there

12) and the place was beautiful

13) and fifteen years later that place is, that place doesn't exist.

L: And how do you explain that?

14) well I don't know

15) but I would see the Americans leaving and the Hispanics arriving

16) ... so as, as a young girl what am I going to say?

17) What can I say?

18) and in spite of that

19) I do know that all of my life I am going to work with Hispanic children.

This short narrative exemplifies the contradictory attitudes and feelings community members have toward their group, and specifically the internalization of dominant group stereotypes. On the one hand B. feels that the neighborhood she lived in deteriorated when Latinos moved in; on the other hand she has dedicated her life to helping Latino children. She seems at some level to have internalized the racist American ideology about minority people being dirty and careless; yet she is concerned, as are all speakers, with self-presentation[3] as a Latina, as well as what I, a fellow Puerto Rican, might think. Thus, she does not state information directly but expresses her views rather indirectly through a series of semantic and rhetorical moves (van Dijk 1984, 1987), including contrast, understatements, the use of rhetorical questions, repetition, mitigation, and displacement.

B. never comes out and states that she feels Latino/as destroyed the neighborhood but leads the listener to this conclusion through a series of moves. First she sets up a contrast in lines 3 and 4 for the listener to draw her own conclusions. Line 6 begins with discourse marker "so" in English, which as Schiffrin (1987) notes, can indicate that a conclusion from the preceding units will follow. However, the speaker hesitates and never completes the thought. In line 7 she switches to English, addresses the interviewer with a rhetorical question, and laughs. These three features indicate that she recognizes that her assessment might be problematic for me, an interviewer from the ingroup. Next she proceeds to substantiate her argument, again indirectly. What she resorts to, in fact, is a repetition of the original contrast, now offered with more details. When encouraged by the interviewer to state directly her assessment she relies on the move of ignorance or denial (as defined by van Dyke 1985) in line 4 "bueno yo no se" (well I don't know) and then in 15 again indirectly states the situation without evaluating it. In 16 the discourse marker "so" again suggests that a conclusion will follow, which is warranted by the offered information or by general knowledge of the situation. But rather than a direct conclusion, B. relies on the strategy of displacement to state the conclusion—she as an adult does not makes the point, instead she attributes her understanding of the situation to the perspective of herself as a little girl. In 17 she appeals to me as the interlocutor with another rhetorical question that again avoids directly responding to the issue. While never stated directly, the speaker's point comes across clearly. Indirectly acknowledging that she has offered a negative assessment of her community, she mitigates the harshness of the statement in lines 18 and 19 by stating that in spite of this situation her life's work will always be directed toward the care of Latino children.

That B. should have accepted this stereotype of Latinos should not be all that surprising if we consider the words of Franz Fanon (1967, 152), "There is a constellation of postulates, a series of propositions that slowly and subtly—with the help of books, newspapers, schools and their texts, ads, film, radio—work their way into one's mind and shape one's view of the world of the group to which one belongs." Consequently, racial and ethnic groups living in the same area as the dominant group, exposed to the same ideology, to varying degrees may come to accept some aspects of the dominant group viewpoint even when it casts minority group members in a negative light. Clearly, however, as is evident in B.'s hesitation and discomfort at the discussion, she has not simply adopted the dominant group line but seems to be quite ambivalent about her conclusions.

The presentation of identity in the narratives then is never clear-cut and unambiguous. An analysis of content, discourse features, and strategies reveals how speakers attempt to integrate ingroup and outgroup perceptions, as well as other contradictions. For example, the narratives, while they reveal the belief in traditional values that have usually been associated with Puerto Rican women (for example, Alvarez 1988), such as respect for the authority of males (specifically fathers and husbands), these narratives also contradict the stereotype of the passive Latina woman presented in much of the dominant group discourse on Latinas (see also Valdivia's chapter in this volume). The contradiction is at work in Text C, produced by C., a nineteen-year-old woman born and raised in the community, who works as a teacher in a Head Start Program. The narrative occurred during a discussion on what C. taught the children. Among other things she stated that she spoke to them about how to protect themselves from sexual abuse. She stated that because it had happened to her she felt children should be warned to denounce abusive adults.

Text C

1) I was 15
2) *so* I already had my mind, you understand

3) and at that time I was involved in drugs and all of that

4) *so* I had dealt with a lot of people that were older, you know

5) *so* never—I never—the people I hung out with tried to *take advantage of me* never

6) *cause* I also had my mind, understand

7) but with my uncle

8) when my father left

9) I always tried to find someone to—*to replace,* understand

10) *so* my uncle was *right next door*

11) *so* I felt good, you know, *comfortable,* with him

12) *so I wouldn't mind, you know*

13) but when he tried to get fresh with me that hurt me so much

14) because I trusted in him

15) you know I never thought he was gonna do something like that

16) so I went

17) I flew

18) and I told my mother, quickly

19) *and I really* I . . . I made him feel really bad you know

20) when that happened I spoke with him *right in my mother's face*

21) and I told him,

22) I can't believe you did such a thing

23) tried to do such a thing like that

24) I trusted in you

25) What kind of man are you

26) what if my father does something like that to your daughter

27) how are you gonna feel

28) that's not right

29) What, can't you go out and get some pussy huh?

30) *I'm serious*

31) *I broke*

32) *I went crazy* and was crying and everything

33) that—a mess

34) but because of that I talk about that with the kids.

C. not only confronts her uncle, the abuser in this case, but strives to prevent other children from being abused. The narrative itself has the usual structure of narratives of personal experience. The narrative has a long orientation section from lines 1 to 12, followed by an evaluation section from 13 to 15. The complicating actions from lines 16 to 21 are followed by more evaluation and a section from 22–29, where the speaker reproduced an entire monologue she directed to the abuser. This is followed by another evaluation section, 30–33, a coda and resolution 33–34.

Here, as in most of the stories, we have a syntactically simple narrative. While in the Group 2 narratives, as in the first text we examined, there tends to be more complex syntax; for instance, there were a number of complex sentences, and some independent and subordinate clauses. Here, as in the majority of group 3 texts, cohesion is established primarily through the use of the simple discourse markers (connectives) such as "y" (and), "pero" (but), and, "so." It is interesting that of nine coordinating conjunctions used in the text six are rendered in English (so). These are found primarily in the orientation section and first round of evaluation.

The speaker also often uses the various versions of the discourse marker y'know (you know, entiende, tú sabe) in one of the functions suggested by Schiffrin (1987), in order "to enlist the hearer not just as an information recipient but as a particular kind of participant" to the storytelling. While in her narratives Schiffrin found this particular marker to occur most frequently in the evaluation section of the stories, where the speaker uses it to ensure that the listener understands the point of the story, in my sample they were found throughout the narratives of the second and third generation. In C's story the enlisting marker abounds, especially in the orientation section where it appears seven times; perhaps because of the emotional and very personal nature of the story the speaker wanted to make sure that I understood the setting of the story and to ensure my involvement.

As in most group 3 narratives there is much code-alternation between Spanish and English at the word, phrase or sentence level, which serves a range of functions. In the narratives of the group 2 participants as we would expect, the use of the code-switching is less frequent since Spanish is in many cases the narrator's main language and the one in which they feel more comfortable. In the first narrative, we saw, for example, that code-switching serves two main purposes. First, in lines 10 and 20 it is used to reproduce a quote that was rendered in English. In line 12 it is used to exemplify the narrator's mistake in understanding "spic" as spit, first to reproduce a quote and then to initiate an evaluation. Finally, code-switching occurs in lines 15 and 16 to begin an extended evaluation of the incident.

In group 3 narratives, code-switching is a strategy more frequently invoked, perhaps because the interviews were carried out in Spanish, in most cases not the principal language of the participants. Code-switching serves the functions described for the first narrative in addition to others. For example, in C's narrative, in lines 30–32, the switch to English serves to add force to the most intensive evaluation of the narrative; in line 20 it also serves to intensify the evaluation being made. In some cases, hesitations and pauses in the narrative before a switch suggest that the switch occurs because of a lexical gap as in 6, 9, and 11. As stated before, of the 16 coordinating conjunctions, "so," which occurs seven times and is the most commonly used conjunction, is rendered in English six times. In other narratives, including first-generation discourse, this particular discourse marker is also frequently rendered in English.

While the narrator explains the incident in a very direct and forthright manner it is interesting to observe indirect language used to express the attempted molestation, which is never named directly. Instead, the narrator uses euphemisms as in line 5) "take advantage of," line 13 "tratar de ponerse fresco" (try to get fresh), 15, 23 and 26, "hacer una cosa así" (do something like that). Yet later in the narrative, when referring to the harasser, she loses all timidity and states rather directly in line 29, that she asked him, "¿Qué tú no puedes ir por allá a encontrar crica?" (What, can't you go out and get some pussy, huh?) All indirectness is lost, and the issue becomes one of embarrassing the uncle as an inadequate man because he can't get sex out on the street, but rather he has tried to get sex from a young family member. She can be more direct here, perhaps because he, rather than she, is now the focus of attention, and also because she is venting her anger.

The narrative is heavily evaluated both internally (3 and in the direct quote from lines 22 to 29) and especially externally (2, 6, 13–15, 19, 30–34). In this narration, particularly in the evaluations, we see elements of what Ruskin and Varenne (1983) described as typical of Puerto Rican discourse on conflict. Criticism of the uncle, in this case, is framed not as the violation of individual rights but rather, as a betrayal of his role as a family member.

This narrative affirms traditional values about family roles and about male behavior. Although the man is criticized for violating his role as uncle, it is understood according to line 29 that her married uncle has the right to sex; the problem is that he was looking for access within the family rather than elsewhere. However, the narrative also offers a strong repudiation of the passive roles usually assigned to women: C. fights back, verbally and directly confronts her uncle, and is determined to teach children how to protect themselves from abuse. This seeming dichotomy is present in many of the narratives in my sample.

Conclusion

This essay utilizes linguistic and interpretive approaches to examine the reproduction of outgroup stereotypes, internalized oppression, and social relations in the discourse of Puerto Rican women living in the United States. My project examines how speakers reveal their social ideology and perception of self through topic choice, development of positions, and use of linguistic strategies. Through narrative strategies such as the use of rhetorical and semantic moves, code-switching, repetition, and indirect speech we have seen how community members both manifest and resist internalized dominant group discourse in their speech. In the texts we have examined we can see three "stories" or schemas that pervade the narratives I analyzed. The stories represent dominant group (anglo/male) stereotypes but, as is clearly evident, also prevade "minority" group attitudes. To summarize, the schemas we saw are the following: Text A: If you are really motivated you will learn English quickly without the aid of bilingual education; Text B: Minority group persons are destructive and careless; once they start moving in, the neighborhood deteriorates; and Text C: All men including married men must have access to sex but they must not attempt to find this access with inappropriate family women, because this is a violation of their trusted positions within the family. However, as we have seen these schemas are not unproblematically accepted and produced in the discourse of the speaker; both at the level of content and through the use of linguistic and discourse strategies the contradictory positions Latina women experience are verbalized.

Notes

1. The structure of the story is modelled on William Labov's 1971 study of narratives. To be considered a narrative a story need only contain a temporal conjunction joining two clauses. A fully developed narrative consists of an abstract, an orientation, complicating actions, resolution, evaluation and a coda.

2. Strategies used to evaluate a story may be internal to the main story line of the narrative or external. Evaluative markers may occur at all levels: phonological, lexical, syntactic and discourse (i.e. repetitions, reported speech, flashback, clustering around the peak of story, etc.). External devices (deitic) include generalization from specific to general case, elaboration in text on information previously presented and reported speech.

3. Self presentation (van Dijk 1987) refers to the strategies people use to present a positive image of themselves while at the same time avoiding negative evaluations from interaction partners.

Appendix

(Text A)

I: ¿Cuándo Usted empezó la escuela, solamente hablaba inglés?

1) Yo hablaba mah que español
2) y te voy a decir a ti una cosa
3) tenía un muchachito que se sentaba al lado mío
4) que se llamaba Kevin McReynolds
5) creo que era
6) y ese muchachito era amigo mío toda la vida
7) hasta que supo que yo era Latina
8) entonceh ese día vino a la escuela
9) y se sentó al lado de mi
10) "*you dirty spic*"
11) pero como yo no entendía mucho inglés
12) yo creía que tenía que ehcupir—*spit*
13) y saqué mi galgao y (makes spitting noise) ja ja
14) dijo, "*uh she spit at me*"
15) verdad *that goes to show you*
16) *but you know* que causó una impresión en mi vida
17) porque me dio bochorno
18) porque me di cuenta que no le había entendido
19) que después de eso yo me forcé a aprender inglés
20) pero Kevin me ensenó cuando me dijo, "*you dirty spic*"
21) (humm) . . . el tenía el pelo colorao
22) y tenía muchas pequitas
23) yo decía "pero mira que bruta yo
24) si no me ha dicho nada de escupir"
25) pero pa'que bochorno
26) y el bochorno me dió coraje suficiente para aprender inglés

(Text B)

1) yo sí sé que cuando yo me mudé a Nueva York
2) mi mamá era la primera familia hispana en ese en ese sitio

3) y ese sitio era bello

4) y después a los diez años estaba destruido

5) y yo me acuerdo de eso

6) *so* puede ser . . .

7) *you see it Lourdes. What can I tell you?*, ja ja ja

8) mira cuando yo me mudé allá yo tenía cinco años

9) el sitio era de los más bellos

10) era East, cra, este, Fulton Street of South Bronx

11) y ella fue la primera familia que se mudó

12) y ese sitio era bello

13) y en quince años después ese sitio esta ese sitio ya no existe

L ¿y como te explicas tú eso?

14) bueno yo no sé

15) pero yo veía los americanos yéndose y los hispanos viniendo

16) . . . *so* como, como niña joven que yo voy a decir?

17) ¿Qué puedo decir?

18) sin embargo

19) yo sí sé que toda mi vida yo voy a trabajar con niños hispanos

(Text C)

I: ¿y cuándo te pasó a ti se lo dijiste a alguien?, ¿de qué edad?

1) Yo tenía quince años

2) *so* ya yo tenía mi mente entiende

3) y en ese tiempo yo estaba endroga y to eso

4) *so* yo había bregao con mucha gente que eran major, tú sabe

5) *so* nunca eh- yo nunca—lah personah que yo jangeaba trataron de—*take advantage of me* nunca

6) *cause* yo siempre ha tenido la mente, entiende

7) pero con mi tío

8) cuando mi papá se fue

9) yo siempre ha tratado de buscar alguien para—*to replace*, entiende

10) *so* mi tío estaba *right next door*

11) *so* me sentía bien, tú sabe, -*comfortable,* con él

259

12) *so I wouldn't mind. you know*

13) pero cuando él se trató de poner frehco conmigo

14) eso me dolió tanto

15) polque yo trohté en él

16) tú sabe yo no pensaba que el iba a hacer una cosa así

17) y yo fui

18) y volé

19) y se lo dije a mi mai, rapidito

20) *and I really* yo yo lo hice sentir bien mal

21) cuando eso pasó yo hablé con él *right in my mother's face*

22) y yo le dije,

23) "yo no puedo creer que tú me hiciste una-trate de hacerme una cosa así

24) yo trohtaba en ti

25) que clase de hombre tú eres

26) si mi papa, le hace algo así a tu hija

27) como te vas a sentir tú?

28) eso no está bien

29) ¿que tú no puedes ir por allí a encontrar crica hum?"

30) *I'm serious*

31) *I broke*

32) *I went crazy* y estaba llorando y to

33) eso - un rebolú

34) pero por eso yo hablo de eso con los niños.

References

Allport, Gordon W. 1958. *The Nature of Prejudice.* New York: Anchor Books.

Alvarez, Celia. 1988. "An Interpretive Analysis of Narration in Social Interaction. In Language Policy Task Force.

———1989. "Code-switching in Narrative Performance: A Puerto Rican Speech Community in New York." In *English across Cultures, Cultures across English* eds. Ofelia Garcia and Ricardo Otheguy. Berlin: Mouton de Gruyten.

Bate, Barbara and Anita Taylor. eds. 1988. *Women Communicating: Studies in Women's Talk.* Norwood, N. J.: Ablex.

Bennet, Adrian and Pedro Pedraza. 1988. "Theory and Practice in the Study of Discourse Practices, Cultural Formulations, Consciousness, and Social Change." In Language Policy Task Force.

———1989. "Code-switching in Narrative Performance: A Puerto Rican Speech Community in New York." In *English across Cultures, Cultures across English* eds. Ofelia Garcia and Ricardo Otheguy. Berlin: Mouton de Gruyten.

Coates, Jennifer. 1988. "Gossip Revisited: Language in All-Female Groups." In *Women in Their Speech Communities.* eds. Jennifer Coates and Deborah Cameron. London: Longman Group.

Fannon, Frantz. 1967. *Black Skin White Masks.* New York: Grove Press.

Flores, Juan and George Yudice. 1990. "Living Borders/Buscando America." *Social Text.* 24: 57–84.

Jordan, Rosan A. and Susan Kalčik. eds. 1985. *Women's Folklore, Women's Culture.* Philadelphia: University of Pennsylvania Press.

Jordan, Rosan A. 1985. "The Vaginal Serpent and Other Themes from Mexican-American Women's Lore." In Jordan and Kalčik, eds.

Kalčik, Susan. 1975. " '. . . Like Ann's Gynecologist or the Time I Was Almost Raped'." *Journal of American Folklore.* 88(347): 3–11.

Kramarae, Cheris. 1981. *Women and Men Speaking: Frameworks for Analysis.* Rowley, Mass.: Newbury.

Labov, William. 1972. *Language in the Inner City: Studies in the Black English Vernacular.* Philadelphia: University of Pennsylvania Press.

Labov, William and Joshua Walezky. 1967. "Narrative Analysis: Oral Versions of Personal Experience." In *Essays on the Verbal and Visual Arts.* ed. June Helm. Seattle: University of Washington Press.

Lakoff, Robin. 1975. *Language and Woman's Place.* New York: Harper & Row.

Language Policy Task Force. 1988. *Speech and Ways of Speaking in a Bilingual Puerto Rican Community.* New York: Centro de Estudios Puertorriqueños.

Maltz, Daniel N. and Ruth A. Borker. 1982. "A Cultural Approach to Male-Female Miscommunication." In *Language and Social Identity.* ed. John J. Gumperz. Cambridge: Cambridge University Press.

Nichols, Patricia. 1983. "Linguistic Options and Choices for Women in the Rural South." In *Language, Gender, and Society.* eds. Barrie Thorne, Cheris Kramarae, and Nancy Henley. Rowley, Mass.: Newbury.

O'Barr, William. 1984. "Asking the Right Questions about Language and Power." In *Language and Power.* eds. Cheris Kramarae, Murial Schulz, and William O'Barr. Beverly Hills: Sage.

O'Barr, William M. and Bowman K. Atkins. 1980. " 'Woman's Language' or 'Powerless Language'?" In *Woman and Language in Literature and Society.* eds. Sally McConnell-Ginet, Ruth Borker, and Nelly Furman. New York: Praeger Publishers.

Polanyi, Livia. 1985. *Telling the American Story: A Structural Analysis of Conversational Storytelling.* Norwood, N.J.: Ablex.

Ruskin, Francine and Herve Varenne. 1983. "The Production of Ethnic Discourse: American and Puerto Rican Patterns." In *The Sociogenesis of Language and Human Conduct.* ed. John Bain. New York: Plenum.

Schiffrin, Deborah. 1987. *Discourse Markers.* Cambridge: Cambridge University Press.

Torres, Lourdes. 1990. "Spanish in the United States: The Struggle for Legitimacy." In *Spanish in the United States: Sociolinguistic Issues.* ed. John Bergen. Georgetown, Md.: Georgetown University Press.

———. 1991. "The Construction of the Self in U.S. Latina Autobiography." In *Third World Women and the Politics of Feminism.,* eds. Chandra Mohanty, Ann Russo and Lourdes Torres. Bloomington: Indiana University Press.

———. In Press. "Women and Language." In *The Knowledge Explosion.* eds. Cheris Kramarae and Dale Spender. New York: Pergamon Press.

van Dijk, Teun. 1984. *Prejudice and Discourse. An Analysis of Ethnic Prejudice in Cognition and Conversation.* Amsterdam: Benjamins.

———. 1987. *Communicating Racism.* Newbury Park, Calif. Sage Publications.

Wodak, Ruth. 1981. "Women Relate, Men Report: Sex Differences in Language Behavior in a Therapeutic Group." *Journal of Pragmatics.* 5: 261–285.

Yamato, Gloria. 1990. "Something about the Subject Makes it Hard to Name." In *Making Faces, Making Souls, Haciendo Caras.* ed. Gloria Anzaldúa. San Francisco: Aunt Lute Foundation Books.

14

Telling Stories about Reality: Women's Responses to a Workplace Organizing Campaign

Nina Gregg

When nearly 1,800 clerical and technical[1] (C&T) workers went on strike against Yale University in September 1984, mainstream mass media treated the event as a subject for expert analysis. News accounts offered the opinions of attorneys, managers, economists, public policy makers, and labor leaders on the significance of this unprecedented action by mostly female white-collar workers. With few exceptions, the voices of women workers at Yale were largely absent in the news. While the actions of participants in the events at Yale were newsworthy, these women did not often appear as news sources or authoritative "knowers." In the parlance of feminist theory, most news coverage of the events at Yale represented the intended beneficiaries of the organizing campaign as objects, not agents. The story of these women's concerns and realities fell outside the dominant institutional newsframe. From the perspectives of feminist theory and practice, however, the concerns and realities of the women at Yale were what mattered most.

This chapter discusses women's responses to the organization of Local 34 of the Federation of University Employees and its significance in their lives.[2] The women's accounts of their experiences are examples of women making meaning: making sense of the ongoing realities of their lives, of the possibilities represented by the organizing campaign, the university, and the 10-week long strike. (See Amott and Matthaei 1984; Cupo et al. 1984; Gilpin et al. n.d.; and Ladd-Taylor 1985.) The discussion explores the relationship between women's subjective experience and their responses to the union, focusing particularly on the negotiation of multiple subjectivities of gender, race, and class: How have particular experiences of gender, race, and class contributed to these women's identities? What can we learn from their accounts of their experiences and responses to the union that advances our understanding of how women generate the meaning of their lives?

Positions and Possibilities

The theoretical concept of subjectivity is central to answering these questions. Feminists inquiring into the realities of women's lives have emphasized the fluidity and multiple elements of socially constructed experience that contribute to identity. (See Fransella and Frost 1977; Hollway 1984; and Weedon 1987.) Recent feminist research acknowledges the complexity of women's identities, including the contribution of gender, race, and class experiences and those of more recent categories of analysis such as sexuality and life cycle. (See Bourque and Divine 1985; Bulkin, Pratt, and Smith 1984; Joseph and Lewis 1981; and Swerdlow and Lessinger 1983.) Some of this research documents the variety of ways in which women actively work to assert autonomy and identity, even in situations where such opportunities may appear limited. (See Bookman and Morgen 1988; Finch 1983; Hall 1986; Janiewski 1985; Purcell 1979; Ridd and Callaway 1987; Sacks 1988; Shapiro-Perl 1984; and Westwood 1984, 1985.) The means of assertion—spoken language, behavior and thought— reflect gender and race, class, culture, ethnicity, sexuality, age, and ideology. Teresa De Lauretis refers to these means as the "particular discursive configurations" within which self and identity are understood, including whatever concepts, ideas, and forms of communication may be known and available to express and legitimate one's self (1986, 8).

The conditions De Lauretis claims determine one's understanding of self and identity are evident in each woman's account of her experiences at Yale. Here "discursive configurations" appear not simply as languages or language use, but in the act of positioning one's self within possible social relations of class, gender, race, history, and culture. In De Lauretis' terms, these are acts of "inhabiting" discursive subjectivities or subject positions. (See O'Sullivan et al. 1983, 73-74; and Kramarae and Treichler 1985, 125.)

For feminist communication theory and research, the meanings made in women's responses to the organizing at Yale are particularly significant. By identifying and asserting subject positions in their relationship to the union, the university, and the world at large, these women are creating the meaning of their life experiences. Understanding this meaning-generating activity is crucial for theorizing about women's subjectivity and for organizing women.

264

The history of white-collar organizing at Yale University and the chronology of the Local 34 campaign are important elements of the stories women told of their experiences during the organizing of Local 34. Over a period of more than twenty-five years five groups, including four different unions, attempted to organize clerical and technical workers at Yale (Gilpin et al. n.d., 16–17; McKivigan and Gilpin 1985). Three years of organizing by C&Ts, paid organizers from the Hotel Employees and Restaurant Employees (HERE) union, and blue-collar Yale workers who were members of HERE Local 35[3] culminated in a certification election on May 18, 1983. Although the election was delayed several months by the university's challenges to the composition of the bargaining unit and a contested site for the National Labor Relations Board hearing, the final tally gave Local 34 of the Federation of University Employees (FUE) a 39-vote margin of victory (Gilpin et al. n.d., 29–31). FUE, affiliated with HERE, became the bargaining agent for more than two thousand Yale employees.

Twenty months passed between the May 1983 election and contract ratification in January 1985. The first contract negotiating session took place on October 11, 1983, five months after the certification election. Talks broke down at the seventy-third negotiating session on September 25, 1984, and the next morning Local 34 went on strike over the university's failure to negotiate a contract.

For nearly two years, between the certification of Local 34 as the representative of the bargaining unit and the ratification of a contract, Yale employees and New Haven residents were targets of two opposing strategies: the university's efforts to wear down union members and foster opposition to the union, and the union's extensive communication networks, which informed bargaining unit members of every administration move and turned routine communication into an organizing tool. The existence of the union made the articulation of identity necessary for everyone addressed by the organizing drive and subsequent strike. The variety of responses to the organization of Local 34, and these women's accounts of their responses, affirm a diversity of identity and work done to (re)produce the social relations and subject positions that make diverse identities possible and sustainable. Excerpts from interviews illustrate a relationship between identity, reality, and perceptions of possibility; we hear people creating (and recreating) reality and themselves through the stories they tell. (See Alcoff 1988; Bell 1988; Fisher and Groce 1990; and Personal Narratives Group 1989.)

The realities these women know are experiential as well as abstract (ideological). When the union proposed that Yale did not respect its workers and that they could take steps to obtain respect, it suggested to these women that their assumed place in a given reality was not only inaccurate but also could be improved. It then became possible for women working at Yale to understand their subjective experience in a different way. With that possibility came the necessity of evaluating competing representations of reality, reconciling contradictions and negotiating between identity and experience through personal knowledge.

Each of us experiences a variety of potential subject positions in different places and at different times. Although some positions, such as gender, are experienced in common, each woman I interviewed understood and experienced each "habitation" or position differently. The women's accounts demonstrate their awareness of these differences. For example, some women assumed (about others) that a family history of union involvement would make an individual receptive to Local 34—"because you had that kind of background" (Laura Morrison)—an assumption not supported in the interviews. (See also Costello 1987, 299.) This statement legitimates Morrison's identity by asserting her own subjectivity: She is positioning herself in contrast to other women whose subjectivities, and whose responses to the union, she acknowledges to be legitimately different from her own. Such acknowledgment signals Morrison's consciousness of different experiences, and to some extent acceptance of different "subject positions" and different perceptions of reality.

The negotiation of experience with possibility is evident in Pam Norden's evaluation of the union's relevance to her reality. Norden, a white clerical worker who was not yet forty, projected into the future, locating the meaning of the union through the kind of life she could imagine for herself: "I could conceivably work for the next thirty-five years, I could live alone in marginal neighborhoods, I could approach entertaining myself on weekends as though it were buying a car, and I could retire into deepest poverty. What kind of a life is this?" she asked. Through the process of negotiating possibilities women create a social world in which they can believe and live. Through this process women also create the meaning of that social world and the meaning of their places in it.

Margaret Connolly, a white clerical worker and anti-union activist nearing retirement, believed a union representing clerical and technical workers at Yale would be incompatible with her identity as an autonomous, independent woman. She explained: "Mostly I feel a) they [unions] are taking away freedom of choice and b) stop you from being individualistic. . . . the union was one of the most devastating things that happened to me."

In contrast, Susanna Folsom, a white clerical worker in her early forties, believed a union would make possible the realization of a desired identity:

I was thrilled [when I heard about the union organizing]. Usually people's politics are quite separate from anything terribly real in their

266

own life, and I had been sort of an armchair political person. . . . Even if I was fighting for civil rights or a particular candidate or something, that didn't affect my life in a real way, in as real a way as this. It gave me a chance to express something I'd been wanting to express all my life.

Gender, race, and class came into play in each woman's evaluation of her options as parts of individual experience and as issues raised by organizers, the university, and everyday life. By looking directly at these features of women's lives, we can begin to understand how they experienced each "habitation" or subject position and how each may have contributed to a particular response to the union.

Gender

Despite a widespread public characterization of the events at Yale as a "women's" struggle,[4] few of the women I interviewed described the union and organizing campaign as gender-focused. Nonetheless, acknowledging the dynamics of gender subjectivity contributes to understanding women's responses to the union.

The union's documentation of the compression of women employees into lower labor grades and the unpredictability of promotions and raises confirmed, for those opposed to the union as well as union supporters, gender-based wage discrimination at Yale. (See Federation of University Employees 1984.) The union also documented the difficulty many Yale clerical and technical employees and retirees were having supporting themselves and providing for their families; indeed, the relationship between gender, economic status, and cultural expectations was a factor in several women's responses to the union. One of the reasons Julia McKinney, a white technical worker near thirty, became involved in the union was on behalf of a co-worker near retirement age. Recognizing the relationship between gender, lifetime earnings, and pension benefits, McKinney identified with her co-worker's situation as one she might eventually occupy herself.

In contrast, Jane Bevins and Laura Morrison thought membership in the union would intensify the gender/class relationship. Although both women acknowledged gender-based wage discrimination and the union's success in drawing attention to pay inequities, each asserted her own experience as an example of what sufficiently motivated women could accomplish independently. Bevins and Morrison, both of whom were single mothers near forty, consequently rejected the union's characterization of all bargaining unit members as alike.

A central factor in both women's responses to the union was their status as newly divorced parents. Bevins, a white technical worker, felt she was unable to strike, since her family's survival depended upon her income: "Being divorced with two children to support, I had to work. I needed the paycheck, no question about that. Whether or not I agreed with what the union was doing, I felt I had no choice in the matter."

Morrison also evaluated the union by considering its place in her world. "While I believe in many things the union is promoting, especially for women in clerical and support-staff positions . . . I have to balance all that . . . with my role as a mother and how I do best as an employee. It's a very individual thing," she explained. Like Bevins, Morrison found the union's insistence on solidarity incompatible with her needs:

> I was unemployed, living with a husband who had opened his own business . . . without any real discussion with me and no income coming into the family. We lost everything but the house. . . . And the savings were going down and down and down. And that's when I became very individual, apart from my marriage, because our survival depended on me. . . . If I had gone out on strike I would have lost the one thing I had left for my kids' future, which was a house. And I wasn't willing to take that risk on their future.

Bevins' previous experience in a union-organized workplace contributed to her resistance to Local 34. "My experience had been union operations locked you into slots," she explained. "You couldn't get more pay by being a better worker, you couldn't control your pay raises."[5] At Yale, Bevins said, "I was able to negotiate, what I would get for salary, what I would do. I thought I would make out better as an individual than with a group." Bevins also sensed that to be effective, support for the union meant visibility, which in turn carried a risk "that jeopardized how your employer or supervisor looks at you," a risk she felt she was unable to take. Both women's fundamental commitment to their families' survival came into direct conflict with the solidarity unions count on for their bargaining power in a strike.

Morrison and Bevins also perceived a conflict between competing representations of reality. On one hand, they experienced the material realities of single parenting and their accomplishments as capable and competent parents and workers; for example, Morrison received five pay raises and two promotions in three years at Yale. On the other hand, the union and their co-workers spoke of the reality of inadequate wages and benefits, unfair promotion procedures, and individually powerless workers. While the union's case for better wages and working conditions included the assertion that clerical and technical workers were able and competent (and therefore deserved better treatment), a more salient message for some was that individual workers could not obtain decent treatment on their own. Morrison and Bevins found no confirmation of their self-images, successful autonomous experiences and realities as single parents and heads of households in this element of the union's case. Morrison underscored the importance of the union's failure to recognize several women's achievements by saying, "I don't want to be a clone of a clone of a clone." Organizers' declaration of collective identity seemed to require relinquishing not only the autonomy and flexibility that their family structures demanded, but also confidence in their abilities as individuals and the knowledge of personal accomplishment. The union's representation of reality cast Morrison and Bevins as powerless and—even more important—wrong in their knowledge of their own lives. By rejecting the union's representation of reality, Morrison and Bevins asserted the validity of the meanings they made of their experiences.

Despite the gendered condition of single parenthood and their acknowledgment of sex discrimination in employment, both Morrison and Bevins resisted identifying themselves by gender. Morrison explained, "I don't think I've ever thought of being a woman. I think of people as human beings. I don't really sort them into the male-female categories, even though we [may] play traditional roles." Like Morrison, Bevins preferred not to make gender distinctions. When I asked what being a woman meant to her, she replied:

> My first response: mother, but much more. That's not my sole feeling of what being a woman is. I like not to think of male and female differences, but more of individuals and what they can contribute. Instead of "she's a woman doing this," "she's a person doing this." I don't know whether my actions follow, but I tend not to think about that so much.

In contrast with both Morrison's and Bevins' negative assessments of the union, Susanna Folsom's struggle to be financially secure contributed to the union's appeal. Where Morrison equated pressure from organizers to make a commitment to group solidarity with a loss of individual identity (becoming a "clone"), for Folsom the economic pressures of daily life threatened her survival and her ability to provide a decent home for her child. Where Morrison viewed her position as the result of personal circumstances and individual effort, Folsom saw her subject positions as consequences, in part, of structural forces. Unlike Bevins, who felt she would make out better negotiating the terms of her employment on her own, Folsom believed "we had to organize to take on something as big as Yale." Describing her experiences upon reentering the workforce, Folsom expressed her belief that Yale was "one of many institutions taking advantage of women":

> I naively thought that the job world would welcome women who had been raising kids. . . . Now [in her early forties] I'm in my first secretarial job I've ever had, when it should be a time of my life when I'm getting somewhere. In the last couple of years it's been very painful to have had a good professional start. Instead, I suddenly found myself being used as a secretary. Jobs I applied for demanded my professional background, my editing and writing skills, and yet I was slotted in the low clerical levels and paid accordingly.

Gender subjectivity informed Folsom's evaluation of the union and her sense that the organized power of the union could be used to aid individual women. She had been divorced for a number of years before Local 34 was established at Yale, and described the years after her marriage by gender experience:

> I've been out on my own [after a fifteen-year marriage] ten years. . . . I was shocked by early experiences and attitudes of men, landlords, and the way a single woman is viewed. . . . I was amazed at the different ways you're treated if you're married to a professional male or you're an artist, single, female, living alone. Night and day. . . . I've been shocked at the different treatment, the lot of women who are not protected in some way. . . . I know what it is like to be exposed . . . you're automatically one down if you don't have something protecting you: career, money, marriage, family. I really don't have any of those things. I had all of them ten years ago, and the contrast has been very, very extreme in my life.

In Folsom's view, the union suggested a way in which culturally constructed gender dynamics could be altered, and promised a different reality—one in which Folsom might find a more secure place as a single parent and artist.

While the subjectivity of gender is evident in the experiences of Laura Morrison, Jane Bevins, and Susanna Folsom, the meanings each made of the organizing of Local 34 are specific to her subject positions. Using personal experience as a basis for knowledge about the world, one's place in it, and the possibilities for the future, each woman made sense of the union in a way that accommodated who she was and who she wanted to be.

Race

Although the union documented wage discrimination against people of color, race issues were not originally a distinct focus of the organizing campaign.[6] Nor was racial equality part of the meaning the mass media attributed to the conflict at Yale, as was gender equality. However, for several black women, reconciling the representations of reality made by the university and the union with their life experiences attested to their identities as black women rather than to gender alone. For example, one woman remarked that she "always saw these two issues as integrated: women, minorities, are always marginalized, people who are manipulated and used to set a certain standard, usually a low standard for pay for entry" (May George).

Women of color expressed much more readily than white women the significance of race for their life experiences and their responses to the union. Most white women interviewed did not include race when describing themselves, nor did they identify race as a factor in the material conditions of their lives or in their experiences of and responses to the events at Yale.[7] Nonetheless, it would be a mistake to infer from a lack of mention that race does not figure in these women's identities and their generation of meaning. The identities of white women are constructed within material and subjective experiences in a cultural and temporal location where to be white means an experience of material reality and a place in the dominant ideology different from those of black women *and* black men. Rather, the omission is evidence of these women's unconsciousness, or a less immediate awareness, about the relationship between race, subjective experience, and possibilities (see hooks 1988 and Stanback 1988). The absence of talk about race by these white women is also a reminder of the more general absence of race consciousness among members of the dominant race in a racist society. As bell hooks notes, "In a racially imperialist society such as ours, it is the dominant race that reserves for itself the luxury of dismissing racial identity while the oppressed race is made daily aware of their racial identity" (1981, 138).

The black women I interviewed scrutinized the representations of reality made by the university and the union from a race-conscious perspective. This is a perspective white women did not appear to, and perhaps cannot, share. hooks describes this perspective as a way of seeing "from margin to center" (1984, ix), which aptly characterizes the responses of several black women to the union. Like Susanna Folsom, Arlene Hamilton, a thirty-year-old black clerical worker, also associated gender experience with her support of the union. Hamilton credited Local 34 with enlightening women about the exploitive conditions of their work. "I didn't need the union to tell me I'm worth more, but some people do," she said. "So the union helped some women rise up. Some women are really in a fog!" For Hamilton, however, the union was foremost a means of protection for people of color. Her arrival in New Haven from the Midwest several years earlier coincided with her first exposure to racism. A new awareness of racism and the difficulty she experienced supporting herself came together in her response to Local 34. The prospect of union representation meant protection as a worker and as a black person:

> I've been black all my life. I don't know what it's like to be anything else. It makes me—anybody—special, always noticed. In my job, whatever happens, they notice me first. Since coming to New Haven, being black is harder. It's the first time I experienced racism. I never noticed, no one talked about it. I couldn't understand it, still don't understand a lot of things about racism. . . . I hope eventually people will band together. In New Haven, blacks are treated bad, especially at Yale. There's no support. It's important to support each other. Our union supports us.

Hamilton was involved with Local 34's Affirmative Action Committee. She regarded this group of six women as a vehicle for generating community support for minority concerns and increasing minority hiring at Yale.[8] It was this image of the union Hamilton thought important to present to other people of color:

> I do tell other black folks at Yale and outside [the university]. I think the union is the best thing for somebody who doesn't have protection. . . . I encourage black people to do it because without a union, we don't have any help anyway. At least with a union, if you want more education, better working conditions, you have somebody to support you. Because we really can't do it alone. I've learned that— you can't do it by yourself. You need the support of co-workers, union representation.

May George's involvement with Local 34 also emphasized minority concerns. George, a black clerical worker, was a Yale undergraduate when Local 34 began organizing. After graduation, she became a university employee and increased her involvement with union activities. George described resistance she encountered within the union to making minority concerns a priority:

> There have been very definite problems working with the union—our membership is predominantly white—on this issue, and also because

the visible indicator in our bargaining unit is gender. Gender has sort of overridden race in this whole organizing effort and efforts to secure the goals that we set out for ourselves. I remember a while back wondering if in fact lip service was being given to the issue of race discrimination, because it's a very serious challenge, something that was documented and could be documented again, because we still have some gains to make. But it was something that a clear strategy hadn't been developed on, and something that a clear strategy still needs to be developed on.

George's experiences as a student at Yale foreshadowed those she had later as a Yale C&T. George enrolled at Yale with the intention of majoring in engineering, but changed her mind. Her reasons illustrate how race, gender, and class experience intersected in her choice:

> I decided not to do engineering, for not only academic but attitudinal reasons. The stress and competition in the university; there weren't supportive communities for minority women who were interested in the natural sciences. I felt I was good at literary studies, and wanted to go into it despite not being able to make any money [in that field] and despite my family's protests.

For May George, the union was both a means of personal, individual protection and an organization that could contribute to the movement for social responsibility beyond the university. She grew up in the South and witnessed the impact of the civil rights movement there; for George, the union was an example of the possibility of social change and the power of organized resistance.

May George's margin-to-center perspective drew on her subject positions as both black and female. The intersection of race, gender, and class in the possibilities she perceived for her own life made George sensitive to how minority and gender issues were separated in Local 34's organizing and bargaining strategies. George pointed out how a labor-intensive job description project, in which members of Local 34 interviewed each of the 2,700 workers in the bargaining unit, was designed to document gender, but not race, discrimination. The data accumulated were useful in the argument for a new, more equitable pay system, which reflected the comparable responsibility and comparable worth of widely different jobs, but not for a strategy to address the resolution of minority concerns, such as altering the concentration of minority employees in certain departments and the lowest labor grades.

Race was key to Linda Wilson's first thoughts about Local 34. Because of the exclusionary history of unions, Wilson, a 36-year-old black clerical worker, was initially very opposed to Local 34. The association of "working-class" with white organized labor was problematic for her. "The reputations of unions, they're historically racist," she explained. "My uncle and father were not union people, so [my opposition] was initially coming from what they told me. . . . My father belonged, but he still was not a union person, not gung-ho. My youngest uncle . . . supports unions but he knows that there's a lot of work to be done within unions." Eventually Wilson's own work life at Yale mediated her family's experience with racism and organized labor. When Wilson finally signed a union membership card, she was, like Arlene Hamilton, joining the union as a means of self-protection. "The woman I worked for was very nice to me but very fickle," Wilson explained. "She did something to me, and I saw the type of person she was. . . . I thought about the treatment I was getting, or might, could get, if you had no network or no support system you could go to, or channels you could go through and grieve the process."

Wilson sought protection in union membership as a black woman. She described how consciousness of the intersection of race and gender in her life was fairly recent:

> Lately, I think about it [being a woman] all the time. Like "I know this is happening because I'm a woman." In a store, you ask to see the manager and people talk to you as though you're handicapped. They powderpuff you. A man commands respect. As a woman, I have to get hysterical or come across as cocky. . . . Being a woman is something you grow into. You know what I mean? You're born female, but you grow into being a woman. Being black, I've always been. So it's only now I can look at things and say, this is a women's issue, and it be not black or white. I can look at other things and say, this is a black women's issue. And it's scary—because things can happen because you're a woman, others—a woman and a black woman. And it's scary, it's like double jeopardy. 'Cause when you find out how horrible [being] a woman is, well, multiply that by two when you say a black woman.

Even after Wilson joined Local 34, she maintained a distance from union activities. A perspective from margin to center was apparent in her questioning of the union's decision-making process. Familiar with being excluded because of her race, Wilson was sensitive to what appeared to be a concentration of power in the union leadership:

> At a meeting not too long ago . . . I became aware that certain people come across as leaders. . . . If the majority hush and let one group have their way, that's a big fear of mine. If you have a group of people

that are willing for you to hush and say "we'll run the show," and you're willing to be complacent and just sit back . . . That's dangerous and I don't think any one group should have that kind of power.

When Wilson expressed her concern to union leaders that they were excluding rank and file input and limiting dialogue on a particular issue, she was told the issue had been resolved. Given her initial misgivings about union racism and subsequent experience with what appeared to be a concentration of power, she saw little more in Local 34 beyond personal protection.

The responses of Arlene Hamilton, May George, and Linda Wilson to Local 34 were affirmations of the possibility and desirability of an alternative workplace reality, as represented by the union. When considering what the union might mean for their lives, these three women were also considering whether this organization would or could speak to the interests of people of color. Though the conclusions they arrived at varied, their expectations of what the union could make possible were expectations reflecting the continuing condition of female minority experience, within and without the union—the condition of existence Linda Wilson described as "double jeopardy." The knowledge and experience of a reality in which race (as well as gender) matters grounded the meaning of the events at Yale for these three black women and their responses to the union.

Class

Despite the historic association of the concept of class with labor organizing, class identity was not easily discussed in these interviews. Certainly this does not mean women experience class any less thoroughly than they experience being black, white, or female. Rather, for these women, the relationship of class to identity and the role of class in meaning-making are less apparent and less easily spoken of than are the relationships between gender and race and identity.

One does not inhabit one's class in the same way that one inhabits a physical corpus that is black, white or female, even though class may have material consequences that parallel those of race and gender. As long as class status—which most of the women I interviewed understood as a lifestyle reflecting income and educational level attained, not as a relationship to the labor economy or the means of production—appears changeable (and as long as gender and race are not), an articulation of identity may be less imbued with class than with gender and race.

Material conditions clearly figured in women's thinking about the union. Even before we discussed the concept of class, most women talked about money as a consideration in their daily lives. They mentioned the (in)adequacy of their incomes, concerns about retirement benefits, and the desirability of merit pay. However, few women identified themselves by their material well-being; that is, *who* these women are is not determined by money, even though *what* they may be able to do is often conditioned by available financial resources. For married women, a spouse's occupation or income contributed, as did the woman's earnings, to her life-style or standard of living, but this was distinct from an articulated class identity.

When the topic of class placement came up in the interviews, nearly every woman hesitated about which class to place herself in, and a few women did not place themselves in a class at all. Margaret Connolly, the anti-union activist mentioned earlier, was an exception:

> I'm a working-class woman. I am working, that's what I'm doing.
> What is middle-class? . . . I suppose people who are middle-class are
> people who've got time to think. Because when you're working [class]
> you don't have time to think. . . . it's having time of your own, that's
> what makes the difference.

Connolly's remarks regarding class stand out in part because of her absolute conviction and lack of hesitation. She had moved to the United States from a Western industrial nation in which more of the work force is represented by labor unions. "When I came . . . in '57 . . . I felt I'd have a better life here. Unions were very visible [in my native country]," she explained. Connolly also mentioned, with reference to class, that as one of five children, her earnings had been essential to maintaining her family.

Katherine Hecht, a retired white technical worker and union supporter, was the only other person to identify herself as working-class with the same assurance as Connolly. Hecht was employed from the time she left school (after finishing eighth grade), working first in a rubber plant, then in a munitions factory. She took a second job when her husband became ill, supported three children after his death, remarried and went to work at Yale, where she remained until her retirement. To my question whether she thought of herself as belonging to any particular class, Hecht replied: "I went to work when my father [a bricklayer] wasn't working. You just go on from there. . . . I think when I was young, I'm going to work. Just knew that was it. I was always working-class. When I was young, I started to work. I've been working ever since."

Explicit in Hecht's recalling the circumstances surrounding going to work in her early teens is the certainty that working would be her future; she "just knew that was it." Her support for the union was equally certain:

My family are all union people. My husband, when he was alive, says, "you get a union, join it." The union tries to help people. Not for myself—who did I have to think of, when it was myself [husband died and children grown]? . . . It made me feel good to know I could go out and picket. Fighting for what we wanted! Since I retired, three granddaughters and a grandson are working at Yale. They won't forget the [family] name!

Hecht's and Connolly's explanations of class placement are exceptional in these interviews in their assertion of the relationship between the necessity of working, the kind of work one does, and class identity. Also, Connolly and Hecht had always known themselves to be working-class. When other women identified themselves as working-class, theirs was a new understanding of their place in the world, arrived at through involvement with the union.

Julia McKinney came to New Haven with her then-husband, a Yale graduate student. She had a graduate degree in science and expected to find a job that would enable her to support them both. At the time Local 34 began organizing, McKinney was dissatisfied with her pay and the favoritism her supervisor exercised over raises and promotions. "I was very depressed about my salary," she said. "I think that was the first major thing. When I first joined, to me the union represented a way out of the low salary I was in."

Through her involvement with the union, McKinney came to see class as more than income-based. Even after seeking and receiving a promotion that placed her outside the bargaining unit, McKinney expressed solidarity with the working-class. "If I were somewhere and there was a custodial person, a janitor or a maid and a lower-level management person, I would feel more kinship with the maid or the janitor than I would with the manager," she explained.

For Linda Wilson, placing herself in the working class was as much a response to the experience of working at Yale as it was a response to the organization of Local 34. Wilson initially had been opposed to the union, and at first said she didn't think of herself as a member of any class. Then she qualified her answer: "More and more things happened. I've been reading about it [class]. Now I do, I think of myself as working-class. If you never thought about it, working here at Yale certainly brings it out." The subjectivity of personal experience made class, along with gender and race, identifiable for Wilson.

Several women's identification with labor took shape along with a new sense of their place relative to the social construction of gender and class. Pam Norden was one union supporter who stressed how exposure to and participation in the union organizing campaign enabled her to think about class, and herself, in new ways. The union's claim that Yale clerical and technical employees were underpaid and unappreciated by the university administration coincided with Norden's work experience. "I had been working here for about 3 months when I turned 30," she explained. "Everyone sits down and, like New Year's, you think about your life and what's going on and what will go on. And there I was pulling in $7,500 a year before taxes, and I thought . . . What kind of a life is this? . . . and I didn't see it getting any better."

Norden's consciousness of the intersection of class and gender in graduate school, where she "learned what being a second class citizen was," carried over to her later experiences as a Yale clerical worker:

> When I first started working I decided right away, I hated the notion of being a secretary, which was what I was called. I was totally embarrassed by it. It sounds like pure snobbery, to come from [being enrolled in a graduate program, then to] fall off the class ladder, and I thought—by God, if they're going to mistake me for anyone they might as well mistake me for a grad student. And so I learned that if I dressed too well people would just assume I was a secretary and start walking into my office any old time and asking me if I knew where the bathroom was. But if I looked like a graduate student they might have thought I was really working. And not a personal servant, which is the way Yale students tend to approach clerical workers.

Contributing to Norden's receptiveness to Local 34 was her growing consciousness that the system was failing to deliver for her, that her experiences were not so different from those of other Yale employees, and that no one was necessarily guaranteed any special favors. Her story suggests the negotiation of several subject positions: "I could say, 'hell, I'm a scholar, what have I got to do with a bunch of secretaries?' . . . [then] you start noticing there are people being paid much better than you—not overpaid but paid much better for jobs that involve fewer skills."

Norden's sensitivity to the intersection of gender and class reappears in a description of how she changed through her association with the union. Referring to watching *With Babies and Banners,* a documentary film about the Women's Emergency Brigade and the General Motors sit-down strike in Flint, Michigan in 1937, Norden said, "I remember thinking—these women, they're real heroines of labor. And months later I thought, I'm a real heroine of labor too. I feel kind of honored. I never thought I'd be a heroine of labor."

Julia McKinney shared Norden's identification with labor; she found confirmation of her experiences with the intersection of gender and class dynamics in the union's representation of reality. Over time, the way McKinney saw the world changed, and a new consciousness of class dynamics and class power developed into a broader concern for the needs of other workers, replacing the personal motivation (dissatisfaction with her salary) for her original involvement with Local 34.

McKinney's and Norden's identification with labor signified consciousness of themselves as subjects for whom gender and class could be constraining forces and for whom gender and class identity offered negotiable possibilities.[9] With this consciousness, the ability to negotiate the options depended upon cooperation, not isolation.

Although Julia McKinney, Pam Norden and other white women came to new understandings of class power and their positions within class and gender dynamics, few acknowledged any relationship between their class experiences and their race. As was the case with the intersection of race and gender discussed earlier, consciousness of the intersection of class with race was more acute for black women. Both Linda Wilson and May George associated class issues with minority issues. George referred to the continuing civil rights movement in parallel with an ongoing class struggle:

> Seeing the way a sort of compromise is met between the powers that be and the people on the receiving end of that power. Realizing that the system bucks at some point. And that [with] mass organization and action you can challenge, you can—if not change the thing overall—at least derive some concessions.... I guess not having a limited historical view of history taking place in years or months, but that there is a continuous process that moves beyond us ... larger than all of us put together ... the struggle did not begin, did not end with Local 34 organizing and winning a contract.

Under the circumstances at Yale, competing representations of reality raised serious status and identity questions. The social and cultural norm for most Yale clerical and technical workers was to identify themselves as different from the blue-collar, union-represented workers on the Yale campus. These were mostly male maintenance and food service workers who were represented by Local 35 of the Hotel Employees and Restaurant Employees Union.[10]

The presumed status of C&Ts relative to other university employees had never been in the public eye until the possibility of union representation was raised. Now, college-educated women[11] with white-collar jobs were being invited to locate themselves against or within a reality embracing blue-collar workers (many of whom they knew) as equals in status, intelligence, and social possibility. For white-collar women to ally themselves with this group was a controversial and potentially threatening proposal that met with predictable resistance, since such an alliance had serious consequences for claims of privilege and beliefs of personal potential.

For example, Pam Norden described overcoming feelings of being different from or better than blue-collar workers, reconstructing her sense of herself and her future by class. She revised her assumptions about "men's unions":

> I had a prejudice broken at a rally I went to. . . . They had someone
> from the machinists' union speaking there. A woman from the machinists' union, which sort of surprised me, and she's somebody's
> grandmother. And saying "we want to stop the arms race." And I
> thought—wait a minute, machinists in Connecticut want to stop the
> arms race? . . . And I thought: Gee, I thought these guys were all into
> Rambo. . . . I guess I grouped those men's unions together as being
> somewhere else out there.

Negotiating the competing realities represented by the union and the university compelled each woman to affirm her position in a world of real (even if denied or unacknowledged) differences in social standing and power. Just as Norden and McKinney affirmed their newly perceived subject positions by allying themselves with blue-collar workers, women opposed to the union affirmed their status by differentiating themselves from union members (and, in some cases, allying themselves with the university). Sometimes this differentiation was also by appropriate gender behavior. (See also, Hall 1986.) By characterizing union supporters' behavior as "offensive" or "unacceptable" on the job or on the picket line, women opposed to the union maintained their own status as reasonable and worthy members of a rational society. (On difference, see Benhabib 1987; Eisenstein and Jardine 1980; Hartsock 1983; and Houston, in this volume.)

Criticism of the behavior of union supporters by women who did not join and of the behavior of union opponents by union members was noticeably different from references to conflicts over values and principles. In the latter case, most people accepted differences of opinion; acknowledgment of different realities and ways of thinking was a form of tolerance, adhering to a democratic principle of "freedom of expression." In the case of behavior, however, where status is more clearly at stake, women on either side were much less forgiving; status-threatening behavior did not qualify as a form of expression that merited protection.

Rita Kushner secured her subject position by focusing on differences between herself and women who supported the union. Kushner, a white clerical worker in her mid-forties, began working at Yale in order to help pay for her children's college educations.[12] She had worked her own way through college, and described her family background as working-class. Several relatives had been union members, but she felt strongly that an organization "isn't always the answer for a group of people." In this case, the group involved was one to which Kushner did not want to belong: She labelled most of the Local 34 supporters in her worksite "people with difficulties." In particular, she mentioned "people with a chip on their shoulder, almost a paranoia about authority of any kind." She volunteered that she did not know the details of their individual lives, but wondered "why they haven't found recognition without the banners and the buttons?" When Kushner added, "I feel I'd lose my sense of self if I approached my problems that way [the way union members do]," she expressed the degree to which she perceived a difference between herself and union supporters, and the significance of that difference for her identity.

Laura Morrison's comments on the aggressiveness of union organizers and strikers demonstrated her sense that union members' approaches to their lives differed from her own:

> They behaved very badly, as far as I'm concerned, during the strike. I talked to people over here who wanted to come to work who couldn't. People who were verbally abused, people who were physically abused. There's no place for that, absolutely no place. The flip way in which they picketed, it didn't say 'serious' to me at all. People did go on strike but did not picket, had money, and it was a big vacation. And they were no different before or after, and I [asked]— "Why did you join? Why bother?" Because it was easier for you to join than take a stand, was my conclusion.

By setting themselves apart from their union-supporting co-workers, women opposed to the union also rejected any suggestion that their claims of middle-class status were misguided. Union supporters, whose consciousness of the power relations of class dynamics informed an oppositional world view, could no longer assume that the privileges, possibilities, and acceptance connoted by middle-class status were theirs. But as long as women opposed to the union rejected that world view, they could still believe in the promise middle-class status conferred upon those who professed allegiance to, and behaved in conformity with, standards of acceptable middle-class conduct.

Nina Gregg

Conclusion

The sense women made of the events at Yale corresponded to the sense they made of their places in the world, using difference to affirm those positions and sustain a world view that kept identity and its status and possibilities intact. The meanings generated were self-creating and sustaining for both union members and union opponents. Women opposed to the union managed to keep their subject positions secure; women who supported the union made new places for themselves in new world views.

In telling their stories about the events at Yale, these women were recapturing an earlier moment, a past act of reconciling contradictions of ideology and reality. Telling stories is simultaneously a recounting of the past and a present act of putting one's self in a position that makes life meaningful and tolerable. This narrative of the self resembles what Janet Gunn calls the autobiographical perspective:

> What is made present [in autobiography] is not merely a past that is past. What is presenced is a reality, always new, to which the past has contributed but which stands, as it were, in front of the autobiographer.... And just as placement must be understood as *placing,* an ongoing rather than a settled process, the autobiographical effort at possessing one's life must be understood as a movement toward possibility as much as a turning around to the already achieved (1982, 17–18).

Locating one's self within the events at Yale, and identifying one's self by gender, race, or class—however different such "placings" may be—share this past and future perspective on "where do I belong?" Philosopher Linda Alcoff argues that "the position women find themselves in can be actively utilized . . . [as] a place from where meaning is constructed, rather than simply the place where a meaning can be *discerned*" (1988, 434). Thus placing one's self and one's identity into the present with its promise for the future is an assertion of "what is and will be possible for me"; women evaluating the union made sense of it from the subject positions in which they found themselves at that moment.

The women whose identities stressed individuality and independence were unlikely to support the union, since accepting the concept of collective representation meant recognizing that as individuals, their future possibilities were limited. Claiming to be a member of a middle class—as most union opposers did—was equivalent to professing a belief in the American dream and its promise of all things to all (deserving) people. For these women, the placing of the autobiographical self in opposition to the union (and what it represented) preserved those promised possibilities. Few of these women identified their circumstances as structurally determined, nor did they perceive limitations (other than surmountable personal ones) to their potential realization of individuality. Consequently, they did not consider how the union might mitigate the effects of gender, race, and class, nor did they necessarily believe that it should. Many of these women organized together, as had the members of Local 34, using what they perceived to be the best means to protect their personal objectives and their right to act independently.

Common among union supporters was the belief that changing the conditions of Yale employment was beyond any one individual's control. For union supporters, neither the university's picture of reality nor the promise of the American dream meshed with experience. These women made sense of the events at Yale more through experience than ideology, identifying with a collective body of workers opposed to another, sometimes unnamed, class or group of people with more power than any one of them possessed individually. In contrast with their counterparts who opposed the union, union supporters came to believe that one escapes the boundaries of gender, class, and race neither single-handedly nor by denying the constraints each bears, but by organizing with others to transform the possibilities and by making new meanings.

Despite these differences, distinctions between pro- and anti-union women, between women of color and white women, between working-class and middle-class women, are bridged in light of each woman's attempt to affirm her realities and future possibilities. Returning to the questions I began with, experiences of gender, race, and class contributed to, but did not define, these women's identities. The meaning of each woman's life, and the meaning of the union, were negotiated in the contexts of material and ideological realities and everyday experience. If we wish to understand how women generate the meaning of their lives, listening to their stories provides a beginning.

Notes

1. The designation "clerical and technical" or "C&T" refers to all Yale employees in the bargaining unit represented by Local 34 of the Federation of University Employees. C&Ts at Yale perform a wide variety of jobs, including clerical, editorial, accounting, laboratory, and library work.

2. This chapter is drawn from Gregg (1991), a study of women's subjectivity and the generation of meaning. Included in the larger study are 46 interviews with female and male employees of Yale University, several of which are excerpted

here. The majority of women interviewed were white, as are the majority of members of the bargaining unit represented by Local 34. To protect confidentiality, all names of interviewees are pseudonyms. All quotations are verbatim from interview audiotapes, with editorial clarifications in brackets and any editorial emphases noted.

3. HERE represented about 1,000 maintenance and food service workers on the Yale campus. These workers had organized as part of the United Mine Workers (UMW) District 50 in the 1930s and affiliated with HERE in the late 1950s (McKivigan and Gilpin 1985).

4. These newspaper headlines offer representative examples: "Union's Success at Yale: New Focus on White-Collar Women," *New York Times,* April 10, 1984; "Women's battle for pay equity is fought," Xenia, Ohio *Daily Gazette,* Sept. 6, 1984; "Yale's 'gutsy ladies' seeking man-sized changes," *Philadelphia Inquirer,* Nov. 20, 1984; "Women of Yale," *The Nation,* Dec. 1, 1984; "Women's Work at Yale Wins Respect," *Hartford Courant,* Jan. 27, 1985.

5. Jane Bevins was one of several Yale employees who saw a union contract as a loss of individual control over working conditions and wages. Apparently the union either did not attempt or was unable to convince these women that without a contract they had no consistent or reliable means of control over anything regarding their employment at Yale, except holding Yale to federal regulations on wage and hour standards for full-time employees.

6. This omission contributed to the formation of the Black Caucus, composed of Yale students who worked to bring minority issues onto Local 34's organizing and bargaining agenda. As of this writing, the Black Caucus no longer exists (Tuhus 1988, 11). Negotiations for the second contract and the resulting contract language addressed affirmative action issues more directly than had the first contract. According to one press account, Local 34's second contract (January 1988–January 1992) contains an agreement "to reclassify jobs to redress economic discrimination against women and minorities." This agreement followed the release in the fall of 1987 of "an independent union-funded study . . . [that] documented that Yale pays Black women as much as $1,980 less per year than white men doing comparable work" (Tuhus 1988, 10). The second contract also provided for a community training and hiring program aimed at Latinos and blacks. See also Tynan (1988).

7. For one discussion of the historical nature of the category of race, see Omi and Winant (1986). Palmer notes that race and class were "unexperienced elements in white feminists' oppression" in the 1920s (1983, 154) and suggests that middle-class white feminists' ignorance of race and class issues during the feminist "revival" of the 1960s was rooted in this history (1988, 452).

8. The Affirmative Action Committee was formed after the Black Caucus pressured the leaders of Local 34 to address minority concerns more systematically. According to Fred Meager, a clerical worker and active union member, who is black, hesitation on the part of the Black Student Alliance to support Local 34 was the impetus for developing the Black Caucus. Several women approached

Meager and asked for his help in getting support from the Black Student Alliance and minority faculty members. When minority students and faculty expressed their concern that no black people appeared to be involved with the union, the union leadership was challenged at a meeting (arranged by Meager and others) to "mention this [contract] is going to deal with the problems of blacks or Hispanics or whatever," and not to make of minority concerns "an appendage, off on the side someplace," but to integrate them into the focus of organizing. The Black Caucus grew out of this meeting.

9.   Questions asked in the interviews may have suggested particular formulations of the issues. Due to space limitations, I am unable to discuss here how the research project and interviews upon which this chapter is based are themselves meaning-generating practices. Chapter Four of Gregg (1991) addresses these issues. For feminist perspectives on the politics of research and method see Cannon et al. (1988), Carter and Spitzack (1990), Cirksena and Cuklanz (this volume), DeVault (1986), Finch (1984), Harding (1987), Lather (1988), Paget (1983), Rakow (1986), and Stanley (1990).

10.   Local 35, which provided significant financial resources for Local 34's organizing drive, had a history of strikes against Yale. See Janick (1987).

11.   More than three-fourths of the women I interviewed had attended or completed college. I have been unable to determine whether this is representative of the bargaining unit overall.

12.   Kushner's husband was also a Yale employee, in the managerial/professional (M&P) classification, which was not represented by a union.

References

Alcoff, Linda. 1988. "Cultural Feminism versus Post-structuralism: The Identity Crisis in Feminist Theory." *Signs.* 13(3): 405–436.

Amott, Teresa and Julie Matthaei. 1984. "Comparable Worth, Incomparable Pay. The Issue at Yale." *Radical America.* 18(5): 21–28.

Bell, Susan E. 1988. "Becoming a Political Woman: The Reconstruction of Experience Through Stories." In *Gender and Discourse: The Power of Talk.* eds. Alexandra Dundas Todd and Sue Fisher. Norwood, N.J.: Ablex. 97–123.

Benhabib, Seyla. 1987. "The Generalized and the Concrete Other." In *Feminism as Critique.* eds. Seyla Benhabib and Drucilla Cornell. Minneapolis: University of Minnesota Press. 77–95.

Bookman, Ann, and Sandra Morgen, eds. 1988. *Women and the Politics of Empowerment.* Philadelphia: Temple University Press.

Bourque, Susan C. and Donna Robinson Divine, eds. 1985. *Women Living Change.* Philadelphia: Temple University Press.

285

Bulkin, Elly, Minnie Bruce Pratt, and Barbara Smith. 1984. *Yours in Struggle: Three Feminist Perspectives on Anti-Semitism and Racism.* Brooklyn, N.Y.: Long Haul Press.

Cannon, Lynn Weber, Elizabeth Higginbotham, and Marianne L. A. Leung. 1988. "Race and Class Bias in Qualitative Research." *Gender & Society.* 2(4): 449–462.

Carter, Kathryn, and Carole Spitzack, eds. 1990. *Doing Research on Women's Communication. Perspectives on Theory and Method.* Norwood, N.J.: Ablex.

Costello, Cynthia. 1987. "Working Women's Consciousness: Traditional or Oppositional?" In *"To Toil the Livelong Day." America's Women at Work, 1780–1980.* eds. Carol Groneman and Mary Beth Norton. Ithaca, N.Y.: Cornell University Press. 284–302.

Cupo, Aldo, Molly Ladd-Taylor, Beverly Lett, and David Montgomery. 1984. "Beep, Beep, Yale's Cheap. Looking at the Yale Strike." *Radical America.* 18(5): 7–19.

De Lauretis, Teresa. 1986. *Feminist Studies/Critical Studies.* Bloomington: Indiana University Press.

DeVault, Marjorie L. 1986. "Talking and Listening from Women's Standpoint: Feminist Strategies for Analyzing Interview Data." Presented at the annual meeting of The Society for the Study of Symbolic Interaction, New York.

Eisenstein, Hester and Alice Jardine, eds. 1980. *The Future of Difference.* Boston: G.K. Hall and Co.

Federation of University Employees, Local 34. 1984. "A Report to the Community from the Members of Local 34, Federation of University Employees, AFL-CIO." New Haven, Conn.: Local 34, September.

Finch, Janet. 1983. "Dividing the Rough and the Respectable: Working-class Women and Pre-school Playgroups." In *The Public and the Private.* eds. Eva Gamarnikow, David Morgan, June Purvis, and Daphne Taylorson. London: Heinemann. 106–118.

———. 1984. " 'It's Great to Have Someone to Talk To': The Ethics and Politics of Interviewing Women." In *Social Researching. Politics, Problems, Practice.* eds. Colin Bell and Helen Roberts. London: Routledge & Kegan Paul. 70–87.

Fisher, Sue and Stephen Groce. 1990. "Accounting Practices in Medical Interviews." *Language and Society.* 19(2): 225–250.

Fransella, Fay and Kay Frost. 1977. *On Being a Woman.* London: Tavistock.

Gilpin, Toni, Gary Isaac, Dan Letwin, and Jack McKivigan. n.d. *On Strike for Respect: The Clerical and Technical Workers' Strike at Yale University. 1984–1985.* Ms. in author's possession. Published by Charles H. Kerr, Chicago, 1988.

Gregg, Nina. 1991. "Women Telling Stories About Reality: Subjectivity, the Generation of Meaning, and the Organizing of a Union at Yale." Ph.D. Dissertation, McGill University.

Gunn, Janet. 1982. *Autobiography: Towards a Poetics of Experience*. Philadelphia: University of Pennsylvania Press.

Hall, Jacquelyn Dowd. 1986. "Disorderly Women: Gender and Labor Militancy in the Appalachian South." *Journal of American History*. 73(2): 354–382.

Harding, Sandra. ed. 1987. *Feminism and Methodology. Social Science Issues*. Bloomington: Indiana University Press.

Hartsock, Nancy. 1983. "Difference and Domination in the Women's Movement: The Dialectics of Theory and Practice." In *Class, Race, and Sex: The Dynamics of Control*. eds. Amy Swerdlow and Hanna Lessinger. Boston: G. K. Hall. 157–172.

Hollway, Wendy. 1984. "Gender difference and the production of subjectivity." In *Changing the Subject: Psychology, Social Regulation, and Subjectivity*. By Julian Henriques, Wendy Hollway, Cathy Urwin, Couze Venn, and Valerie Walkerdine. London: Methuen. 227–263.

hooks, bell. [Gloria Watkins] 1981. *Ain't I A Woman. Black Women and Feminism*. Boston: South End Press.

———. 1984. *Feminist Theory. From Margin to Center*. Boston: South End Press.

———. 1988. "Sisters of the Yam: Overcoming White Supremacy." *Zeta*. 1(1): 24–27.

Janick, Herbert. 1987. "Yale Blues: Unionization at Yale University, 1931–1985." *Labor History*. 28(Summer): 349–370.

Janiewski, Dolores E. 1985. *Sisterhood Denied: Race, Gender and Class in a New South Community*. Philadelphia: Temple University Press.

Joseph, Gloria L. and Jill Lewis. 1981. *Common Differences: Conflicts in Black and White Feminist Perspectives*. Garden City, N.Y.: Anchor/Doubleday.

Kramarae, Cheris and Paula Treichler. 1985. *A Feminist Dictionary*. Boston: Pandora Press.

Ladd-Taylor, Molly. 1985. "Women Workers and the Yale Strike." *Feminist Studies*. 11(3): 465–490.

Lather, Patti. 1988. "Feminist Perspectives on Empowering Research Methodologies." *Women's Studies International Forum*. 11(6): 569–581.

McKivigan, Jack and Tony Gilpin. March 12, 1985. Audiotaped interview with John Wilhelm at Local 34 office. Access courtesy Jack McKivigan.

Omi, Michael and Howard Winant. 1986. *Racial Formation in the United States from the 1960s to the 1980s*. New York: Methuen.

O'Sullivan, Tim, John Hartley, Danny Saunders, and John Fiske. 1983. *Key Concepts in Communication*. New York: Methuen.

Paget, Marianne A. 1983. "Experience and Knowledge." *Human Studies*. 6: 67–90.

Palmer, Phyllis Marnick. 1983. "White Women/Black Women: The Dualism of Female Identity and Experience in the United States." *Feminist Studies.* 9(1): 151–170.

———. 1988. "Freed from the Bonds of Womanhood." Review of *The Grounding of Modern Feminism,* by Nancy F. Cott. *Reviews in American History.* 16(3): 448–453.

Personal Narratives Group. 1989. *Interpreting Women's Lives. Feminist Theory and Personal Narratives.* Bloomington: Indiana University Press.

Purcell, Kate. 1979. "Militancy and Acquiescence Amongst Women Workers." In *Fit Work for Women.* ed. Sandra Burman. New York: St. Martin's Press. 112–133.

Rakow, Lana F. 1986. "Rethinking Gender Research in Communication." *Journal of Communication.* 36(4): 11–26.

Ridd, Rosemary and Helen Callaway, eds. 1987. *Women and Political Conflict. Portraits of Struggle in Times of Crisis.* New York: New York University Press.

Sacks, Karen Brodkin. 1988. *Caring by the Hour. Women, Work, and Organizing at Duke Medical Center.* Urbana: University of Illinois Press.

Shapiro-Perl, Nina. 1984. "Resistance Strategies: The Routine Struggle for Bread and Roses." In *My Troubles Are Going to Have Trouble with Me.* eds. Karen B. Sacks and Dorothy Remy. New Brunswick, N.J.: Rutgers University Press. 193–208.

Stanback, Marsha Houston. 1988. "What Makes Scholarship About Black Women and Communication Feminist Scholarship?" *Women's Studies in Communication.* 11(1): 28–31.

Stanley, Liz, ed. 1990. *Feminist Praxis. Research, Theory and Epistemology in Feminist Sociology.* New York: Routledge.

Swerdlow, Amy and Hanna Lessinger, eds. 1983. *Class, Race and Sex: The Dynamics of Control.* Boston: G. K. Hall and Co.

Tuhus, Melinda. 1988. "Organizing Never Stops at Yale." *Guardian.* 23 March: 10–11.

Tynan, Roxana. 1988. "Yale University Unions Make Big Gains in Affirmative Action in New Contracts." *Labor Notes.* 110: 16.

Weedon, Chris. 1987. *Feminist Practice and Poststructuralist Theory.* London: Basil Blackwell.

Westwood, Sallie. 1984, 1985. *All Day, Every Day. Factory and Family in the Making of Women's Lives.* Urbana: University of Illinois Press.

Index

289

Index

Index

Index

Index

Index

Index

Index

Index

About the Contributors

Jackie Byars, an Assistant Professor in the Department of Communication at Wayne State University, publishes on feminist film and television theory and criticism, particularly focusing on the representation of difference. Her book on feminist film theory and film melodramas of the fifties, *All That Hollywood Allows: Re-reading 1950s Melodramas* (1991) is part of the University of North Carolina Press series "Gender and American Culture" and is co-published by Routledge.

Victoria Chen is an Assistant Professor in Communication at Denison University. She is working on an edited book, *Our Voices: Essays in Culture, Ethnicity, and Communication,* with Marsha Houston and Alberto Gonzalez.

Kathryn Cirksena has a Ph.D. in Communication from Stanford University. She was a 1991–92 Fulbright Lecturer in Journalism and Mass Communication at the University of TimiSoara, Romania. Her interests are in feminist theory, research methods, and political communication.

Lisa Cuklanz has completed a Ph.D. in Communication Studies from the University of Iowa. Her dissertation focuses on highly publicized rape trials in the U.S. She and Kathryn Cirksena are currently working on a book based on the framework and ideas in their chapter in this volume.

Chad Dell is a doctoral student in the Department of Communication Arts at the University of Wisconsin-Madison. His primary area of research concerns reading strategies employed by audiences in their negotiation of television texts.

Keya Ganguly was a post-doctoral fellow for 1990–91 at the Pembroke Center for Teaching and Research on Women, Brown University, and joined the Program in Literacy and Cultural Theory at Carnegie Mellon University in 1991. Her research examines the construction of post-colonial identity and the negotiation of immigrant experience. She has published articles on ethnographic theory, colonial discourse, and popular culture.

Nina Gregg teaches communication and feminist theory at the University of Pittsburgh. She received a Ph.D. in Communication from McGill University and was Co-Chair (1990–92) of the feminist Scholarship Interest Group of the International Communication Association. Her research concerns subjectivity and the politics of location in women's generation of meaning. She is currently working on a study of women's responses to changes in their employment status.

Marsha Houston is Associate Professor of Communication and Women's Studies at Tulane University, and is Chair (1991–92) of the Feminist and Women Studies Division of the Speech Communication Association. Her research focuses on ethnicity, class, gender and communication in interpersonal and cross-cultural contexts. She is currently at work on a book on African American middle-class women's culture and communication style.

Cheris Kramarae, Professor of Speech Communication and Sociology, teaches courses on women and technology, and language in social context at the University of Illinois at Urbana-Champaign. She is the author, editor, or coeditor of nine books on women and language including *Language, Gender and Society* (with Barrie Thorne and Nancy Henley); *A Feminist Dictionary* (with Paula Treichler and Ann Russo); *The Revolution in Words* (with Lana Rakow); *Radical Women's Voices of the 1850s* (with Ann Russo); and *Technology and Women's Voices.*

Elspeth Probyn is an assistant professor and teaches sociology of culture at the Université de Montréal, Québec. Her articles on the body, postmodernism and feminist communication theories have appeared in *Hypatia, Cultural Studies, Canadian Journal of Social and Political Theory,* and *Sociologie et Sociétés,* as well as in anthologies, including *Feminism/Postmodernism* (Routledge), and *Body Invaders* (Oxford). She is the author of *Sexing the Self: Gendered Positions in Cultural Studies* (Routledge in press), and she is currently working on the mass media discourses of new traditionalism, post-feminism, and choice.

Lana F. Rakow, former chair of the Communication Department and now Associate Vice Chancellor for Undergraduate Studies at the University of Wisconsin-Parkside, is a feminist scholar with a commitment to holding the field of communication accountable to issues of gender and race. She has edited *The Revolution in Words: Writing Women 1868–1871* (with Cheris Kramarae) and is the author of *Gender on the Line: Women, the Telephone, and Community Life,* in addition to articles and book chapters on the connections between feminist theory and methodology and various areas of communication study.

Jane Rhodes is an assistant professor in the School of Journalism at Indiana University. She is completing her dissertation on Mary Ann Shadd Cary at the University of North Carolina-Chapel Hill. Her research encompasses the study of race and gender in the history and development of the mass media.

Ann Russo teaches "Violence Against Women in Contemporary U.S. Society" at the Massachusetts Institute of Technology and is an associate editor of *The Women's Review of Books.* She is coeditor of *Third World Women and the Politics of Feminism* and *The Radical Women's Press of the 1850s.* She is currently completing a manuscript on the feminist pornography debates.

Linda Steiner teaches in the Department of Journalism and Mass Media at Rutgers University. She has published extensively on women journalists and on nineteenth and twentieth century women's media, especially the women's suffrage press. She is coauthor of *And Baby Makes Two: Motherhood without Marriage.* Her current research interests are in feminist theorizing and journalism ethics, and in the intersections of feminist, literary, and media theories.

Lourdes Torres is an assistant professor of Hispanic Linguistics at the University of Kentucky. She is coeditor of *Third World Women and the Politics of Feminism,* and has published articles on Spanish in the United States, women and language issues, and US Latino/a literature. She is presently working on a book on narratives of the New York Puerto Rican community.

Angharad N. Valdivia received her Ph.D. in communications from the University of Illinois. She has published about women and the mass media in Latin America as well as about the Nicaraguan press. She is an assistant professor at the Pennsylvania State University, currently working on publications by women's centers in Chile.